Mass Customization for Personalized Communication Environments:
Integrating Human Factors

Constantinos Mourlas
National & Kapodistrian University of Athens, Greece

Panagiotis Germanakos
National & Kapodistrian University of Athens, Greece

T0321758

INFORMATION SCIENCE REFERENCE

Hershey · New York

Director of Editorial Content:	Kristin Klinger
Senior Managing Editor:	Jamie Snavely
Assistant Managing Editor:	Michael Brehm
Publishing Assistant:	Sean Woznicki
Typesetter:	Jamie Snavely, Michael Brehm
Cover Design:	Lisa Tosheff
Printed at:	Yurchak Printing Inc.

Published in the United States of America by
Information Science Reference (an imprint of IGI Global)
701 E. Chocolate Avenue
Hershey PA 17033
Tel: 717-533-8845
Fax: 717-533-8661
E-mail: cust@igi-global.com
Web site: http://www.igi-global.com/reference

Library of Congress Cataloging-in-Publication Data

Mass customization for personalized communication environments : integrating human factors / Constantinos Mourlas and Panagiotis Germanakos, editors.
　　　p. cm.
　Includes bibliographical references and index.
　Summary: "This book focuses on the customization of services and communication environments to advance user satisfaction--Provided by publisher.
　ISBN 978-1-60566-260-2 (hardcover) -- ISBN 978-1-60566-261-9 (ebook) 1. Consumer satisfaction. 2. Communication in marketing. I. Mourlas, Constantinos. II. Germanakos, Panagiotis.
　HF5415.335.M37 2010
　658.4'5--dc22
　　　　　　　　　　　　2009015376

British Cataloguing in Publication Data
A Cataloguing in Publication record for this book is available from the British Library.

All work contributed to this book is new, previously-unpublished material. The views expressed in this book are those of the authors, but not necessarily of the publisher.

Soundar R.T. Kumara, *The Pennsylvania State University, USA*
Thomas Mirlacher, *ICT&S Center Salzburg, Austria*
Timo Saari, *Temple University, USA*
Timothy W. Simpson, *The Pennsylvania State University, USA*

Table of Contents

Section 1
Mass Customization in Products and Services

Section 4
Case Studies and Evaluations of Mass Customization

Detailed Table of Contents

Section 1
Mass Customization in Products and Services

Florian U. Siems, RWTH Aachen University, Germany
Dominik Walcher, Salzburg University of Applied Sciences, Austria

In this chapter it is argued that service stores most often offer standardized services, which may not hit the customers' demands. As a new possibility to customize service offerings the life event cycle is introduced, which builds on traditional lifecycle concepts but refines them by a stronger individual perspective. In the first part of the chapter, a short introduction in service management, kinds of services and the relevance of a long term customer relationship for service stores is given. Then the idea of life cycles is shown in general, before in the main part the life event cycle is explained. It is shown that all marketing instruments could be used to enhance individualization of services and to respect the implications of the life event cycle. The paper ends with limitations and future trends.

Ruth Mugge, Delft University of Technology, The Netherlands
Jan P.L. Schoormans, Delft University of Technology, The Netherlands

A better understanding of consumer responses to mass customization can help companies to more successfully introduce mass customization strategies in new products. Only if consumers believe that the value of the mass-customized product significantly exceeds that of an off-the-shelf product, consumers are willing to mass customize a product. This chapter discusses the specific conditions that affect the relative value of a mass-customized product. Characteristics of the consumer who is performing the customization task, the product category that is mass customized, and the specific mass customization process can affect the perceived benefits and drawbacks of mass customization. Based on this understanding, several strategies are presented on how companies could implement mass customization in order to optimize consumer responses and thus offer consumers the greatest value.

Chapter 3

Emmanuel T. Kodzi Jr., Strathmore Business School, Kenya
Rado Gazo, Purdue University, USA

This study explores the relationship between the capabilities of a manufacturing system and the participation of end-users in order determination. Using a simulated customer-direct mode for the customization of selected wood products, it is examined the manufacturing of system attributes that enhance direct interaction with customers. It is further discussed the strategic implications of the choice of customization-mode on fundamental resource requirements, and set out practical recommendations for deploying mass customization as a competitive strategy. End-user participation in configuring customized products requires that beyond desirable attributes such as agility in manufacturing systems, compelling service capability be developed to enhance customer experience.

Chapter 4

Seung Ki Moon, Texas A&M University, USA
Timothy W. Simpson, The Pennsylvania State University, USA
Soundar R.T. Kumara, The Pennsylvania State University, USA

Electronic markets and web-based content have improved traditional product development processes by increasing the participation of customers and applying various recommender systems to satisfy individual customer needs. This chapter introduces a multi-agent system to support customized product family design by recommending customers' preferences in dynamic electronic market environments. In the proposed system, a market-based learning mechanism is applied to determine the customers' preferences for recommending appropriate products to customers in the product family. It demonstrates the implementation of the proposed recommender system using a multi-agent framework. Through experiments, it illustrates that the proposed recommender system can determine the preference values of products for customized recommendation and market segment design in various electronic market environments.

Chapter 5

Ricardo Jardim-Goncalves, Universidade Nova de Lisboa, Portugal
António Grilo, Universidade Nova de Lisboa, Portugal
Adolfo Steiger-Garcao, Universidade Nova de Lisboa, Portugal

This chapter proposes a standard-based framework to assist industrial organizations to develop interoperability in mass customization Information Systems. After identifying the major challenges for business and information systems in mass customization, the authors propose an innovative standard-based conceptual architecture for a combined model-driven and services-oriented platform. The chapter concludes by describing a global methodology for integration of models and applications, to enhance an enterprise's interoperability in the support of mass customization practices, keeping the same organization's technical and operational environment, but improving its methods of work and the usability of the installed technology through harmonization and integration of the enterprise models in use by customers, manufacturers, and suppliers. Its platform aims to stimulate the adoption of mass customization concepts and improve those practices through proper integration and harmonization of information system models, knowledge, and data.

Configurable products are an important way to achieve mass customization. A configurable product is designed once, and this design is used repetitively in the sales-delivery process to produce specifications of product individuals meeting customer requirements. Configurators are information systems that support the specification of product individuals and the creation and management of configuration knowledge, therefore being prime examples of information systems supporting mass customization. However, one could argue that, there is no systematic review of literature on how mass customization with configurable products and use of configurators affect companies. This chapter provides such a review. It focuses on benefits that can be gained and challenges which companies may face. A supplier can move to mass customization and configuration from mass production or from full customization. It also reviews benefits and challenges from the customer perspective. Finally, it identifies future research directions and open challenges and problems.

Section 2
Mass Customization Meets Personalization:
The Case of Adaptive and Intelligent User Interfaces

Mass customization should be more than just configuring a specific component (hardware or software), but should be seen as the co-design of an entire system, including services, experiences and human satisfaction at the individual as well as at the community level. The main objective of this chapter is to introduce a framework, smartTag, for the dynamic reconstruction of Web content based on human factors. Human factors and users' characteristics play the most important role during the entire design and implementation of the framework which has the inherent ability to interact with its environment and the user and transparently adapt its behaviour using intelligent techniques, reaching high levels of usability, user satisfaction, effectiveness and quality of service presentation. The initial results of the evaluation have proven that the proposed framework do not degrade the efficiency (in terms of speed and accuracy) during the Web content adaptation process as well as increases users' satisfaction and efficiency of information processing (both in terms of accuracy and task completion time), while users navigating in the personalized condition rather than the original one.

Chapter 8

The popularisation of mass customization and the need for integration of the user needs into the design, production and marketing phases has called for more innovative methods to be introduced into this area. At present the continuous growth of the world wide web and its rapid integration into peoples every-day lives and the popularisation of new technologies such as ubiquitous computing making possible the computing everywhere paradigm, offers a more desirable alternative for vendors in reaching their customers using more innovative techniques in an attempt to provide each customer with a one-to-one design, manufacturing and marketing service. The integration of ubiquitous computing technologies with machine learning and data mining techniques, which has been popular in personalization techniques, will serve to bring about innovative changes in this area. This chapter presents the state of the art techniques to enable the combination of the abovementioned technologies which will serve to provide innovative techniques applications and user interfaces for mass customization systems.

Chapter 9

Personalized services and products are only successful when the usage context is taken into consideration. For interactive TV services, where usage is typically taking place in a living room, the question on how to develop an interaction technique to enable personalization is central. Based on an extensive literature review a set of requirements for personalized iTV services was developed. Following these requirements, a case study from interactive TV, called vocomedia, shows the development of an interaction concept for interactive TV supporting personalization by using a fingerprint recognition.

Section 3
Innovative Applications and Services with Customized
Adaptive Behaviour

Chapter 10

Roger J. Jiao, Georgia Institute of Technology, USA
Qianli Xu, Nanyang Technological University, Singapore

The fulfillment of affective customers needs may award the producer extra premium in gaining a competitive edge. This entails a number of technical challenges to be addressed, such as, the elicitation, evaluation, and fulfillment of affective needs, as well as the evaluation of capability of producers to launch the planned products. To tackle these issues, this research proposes an affective human factor design framework to facilitate decision-making in designing product ecosystems. An analytical model is proposed to support affective design analysis. A case study of designing living room ecosystem is reported with dual considerations of customers' perceptions and producer's capacities. It is demonstrated that the affective human factors design framework can effectively manage the elicitation, analysis, and fulfillment of affective customer needs.

Chapter 11

Timo Saari, Temple University, USA; Helsinki Institute for Information Technology, Finland;
Helsinki School of Economics, Finland
Marko Turpeinen, The Royal Institute for Technology, Sweden; Helsinki Institute for Information
Technology, Finland
Niklas Ravaja, Helsinki School of Economics, Finland

Psychological Customization systems can customize the experiences of users of various information technology-based products and services. In this context customization entails the intelligent automatic or semi-automatic adaptation of information per user profile, which may systematically manipulate transient psychological states of the user such as emotion or cognition. The chapter presents the psychological and technological fundamentals of Psychological Customization and discusses an example of an application area in emotionally adapted games.

Section 4
Case Studies and Evaluations of Mass Customization

Chapter 12

Kasper Edwards, Technical University of Denmark, Denmark

Product configuration systems (PCS) are a technology well suited for mass customization and support the task of configuring the product to the individual customer's needs. PCS are at the same time complex software systems that may be tailored to solve a variety of problems for a firm, e.g. supporting the quotation process or validating the structure of a product. This chapter reports findings from a study of 12 Danish firms, which at the time of the study have implemented or are in the process of implementing product configuration systems. The analysis reveals that expected and realized benefits are consistent: More specifically, the realized benefits are all higher than the expected benefits. The expected benefits highlight the motivation, and this has implications for human factors as they point in the direction of significant changes to come in the adopting organization. It is observed that product configuration projects are treated as simple technical projects although they should be regarded as organizational change projects.

Chapter 13

Regina Bernhaupt, ruwido, User Experience Research, Austria

Usability and user experience are two important factors in the development of mass-customizable personalized products. A broad range of evaluation methods is available to improve products during an user-centered development process. This chapter gives an overview on these methods and how to apply them to achieve easy-to-use, efficient and effective personalized products that are additionally fun to use. A case study on the development of a new interaction technique for interactive TV helps to understand how to set up a mix of evaluation methods to cope with some of the limitations of current usability and user experience evaluation methods. The chapter concludes with some guidelines of how to change organizations to focus on usability and user experience.

Chapter 14

Pratyush Bharati, University of Massachusetts, USA
Abhijit Chaudhury, Bryant College, USA

Product customization is an important facility that e-commerce offers to its users. On the Web, choiceboard systems have become quite prevalent as the means by which users are able to customize their products. These systems allow customers to configure products and services by choosing from a menu of attributes, components, delivery options, and prices. In the context of a choiceboard environment, this research examines the impact of system and information quality and information presentation on interface satisfaction and decision satisfaction. Further, it examines the impact of the latter two satisfaction factors on overall user satisfaction and intention to use. The research reveals that improved system quality, vis-à-vis choiceboards, leads to better information and decision satisfaction on the part of the users. This in turn leads to higher overall satisfaction and intention to use. The research uses an experiment for data collection and examines these relationships using the structural equation modeling (SEM) approach.

Preface

Since 1994, the Internet has emerged as a fundamental information and communication medium that has generated extensive enthusiasm. It has been adopted by the mass market more quickly than any other technology over the past century and is currently providing an electronic connection between progressive businesses and millions of customers and potential customers whose age, education, occupation, interest, and income demographics are excellent for sales.

Organizations are increasingly offering personalized eService relationships as a way of connecting with customers over a number of platforms and of differentiating their services from those of competitors. Relevant channel and distribution strategies are critical for future advancement of eServices to achieve accessible, customer-focused and responsive services. Following the growing user demands and requirements as well as the rapid development of the technological advancements and infrastructure capabilities the development of eServices should not only focus on making the service available on the Internet, but also examine the different delivery platforms. A multi-channel (WAP, MMS, SMS, Web, Satellite etc.) and a multi-device (PC, mobile phones, PDA, tablet PC, Satellite handset etc.) access mix will improve the access of the services offered, since will be available anytime, anywhere and anyhow through a single point of access entry increasing consequently the business eServices sustainability.

New communication platforms beyond PC-based Internet access are now becoming available allowing the companies to meet these challenges by reengineering their front and back office and business processes, implementing new ways of interaction through a variety of channels (i.e. interactive digital television and third generation (3G) mobile systems driven by common standards open up possibilities for multiple platforms access to services), and restructuring services that accommodate their customers' needs. eBusiness aims to deliver better quality of eServices increasing mass customization and productivity with focused services to be provided by various channels, at a lower cost and time and in a personalized style.

Mass Customization and Personalization are widely appreciated as viable and promising strategies, which aim to provide product and services that best serve individuals' personal needs with near mass production efficiency. Personalization is adapting or sequencing solutions to fit individual differences, expectations, and needs. In contrast, mass customization is adapting to fit common characteristics identified for groups of users. Mass customization is actually the first step in building an individual customers relationship. It may not always be practical to support one user at a time or to build in total personalization capabilities specific to one user. It may be preferable to start with a mass customized solution that identifies a few common critical success attributes that are key for improved performance. However, based on recent technological advances it is possible to implement online services and communication environments accessed via Internet or Web technologies which may be personalized on the basis of individuals' preferences or even the intrinsic characteristics of the specific user like cognitive and emotional parameters, often referred as human factors. Both content and its way of presentation (modality, visual layouts, ways of interaction, structure) as well as functional elements of such communication environments may automatically adapt their behaviour according to the user needs and preferences enhancing the quality of service delivery and user satisfaction.

CHALLENGES

Mass customization should be more than just configuring a specific component (hardware or software), but should be seen as the co-design of an entire system, including personalized services, experiences and human satisfaction at the individual as well as at the community level. The main objective of this book is to focus on the latest research results on customization of services and communication environments that provide adaptive content and functionality advancing the levels of user satisfaction and providing a total redefinition of the way goods and services are created or sold and customers and vendors interact. It presents the research results produced in this area covering a wide spectrum of strategies, applications, systems and architectures starting from the higher level of modelling human factors and mass communication strategies used and then presenting the lower level issues of mass customization systems and the adaptivity of content and functionality. Special emphasis is given to the integration of Human Factors with traditional factors supporting a built-in flexibility embedded in the product or service. This embedded flexibility will provide high levels of product adaptability and intelligent behaviour of service or product interface so that it will be able to react and automatically adapt its response in changes of user behaviour or the sorrounding environment (i.e. changing system requirements, availability of resources, variation of bandwidth, loose connections, network congestion etc.). Human factors and users characteristics carry the most important role during the entire design and implementation of a product or a service which has the inherent ability to interact with its environment and the user and transparently adapt its behaviour using intelligent techniques, reaching high levels of usability, user satisfaction, effectiveness and quality of service presentation.

ORGANIZATION OF THE BOOK

This book is composed of four sections, with a total of fifteen chapters, each of which is described briefly below:

Section 1: Mass Customization in Products and Services

Chapter 1 argues that service stores most often offer standardized services, which may not hit the customers' demands. As a new possibility to customize service offerings the life event cycle is introduced, which builds on traditional lifecycle concepts but refines them by a stronger individual perspective. It is shown that all marketing instruments could be used to enhance individualization of services and to respect the implications of the life event cycle.

Chapter 2 suggests that a better understanding of consumer responses to mass customization can help companies to more successfully introduce mass customization strategies in new products. It discusses the specific conditions that affect the relative value of a mass-customized product. Based on this understanding, several strategies are presented on how companies could implement mass customization in order to optimize consumer responses and thus offer consumers the greatest value.

Chapter 3 explores the relationship between the capabilities of a manufacturing system and the participation of end-users in order determination. Using a simulated customer-direct mode for the customization of selected wood products, it is examined the manufacturing of system attributes that enhance direct interaction with customers. It is further discussed the strategic implications of the choice of customization-mode on fundamental resource requirements, and set out practical recommendations for deploying mass customization as a competitive strategy.

Chapter 4 underlines that electronic markets and Web-based content have improved traditional product development processes by increasing the participation of customers and applying various recommender systems to satisfy individual customer needs. It introduces a multi-agent system to support customized product family design by recommending customers' preferences in dynamic electronic market environments. Through experiments, it illustrates that the proposed recommender system can determine the preference values of products for customized recommendation and market segment design in various electronic market environments.

Chapter 5 proposes a standard-based framework to assist industrial organizations to develop interoperability in mass customization Information Systems. After identifying the major challenges for business and information systems in mass customization, the authors propose an innovative standard-based conceptual architecture for a combined model-driven and services-oriented platform stimulating the adoption of mass customization concepts.

Chapter 6 suggests that configurable products are an important way to achieve mass customization. Configurators are information systems that support the specification of product individuals and the creation and management of configuration knowledge, therefore being prime examples of information systems supporting mass customization. However, since there is no systematic review of literature on how mass customization with configurable products and use of configurators affect companies, this chapter provides such a review, focusing on benefits that can be gained and challenges which companies may face, identifying also benefits and challenges from the customer perspective.

Section 2: Mass Customization Meets Personalization: The Case of Adaptive and Intelligent User Interfaces

Chapter 7 realizes that mass customization should be more than just configuring a specific component (hardware or software), but should be seen as the co-design of an entire system, including services, experiences and human satisfaction at the individual as well as at the community level. The main objective of this chapter is to introduce a framework, smartTag, for the dynamic reconstruction of Web content based on human factors. It presents initial results of the evaluation conducted, proving that the proposed framework do not degrade the efficiency (in terms of speed and accuracy) during the Web content adaptation process as well as increases users' satisfaction and efficiency of information processing (both in terms of accuracy and task completion time), while users navigating in the personalized condition rather than the original one.

Chapter 8 underlines that popularisation of mass customization and the need for integration of the user needs into the design, production and marketing phases has called for more innovative methods to be introduced into this area. The integration of ubiquitous computing technologies with machine learning and data mining techniques, which has been popular in personalization techniques, will serve to bring about innovative changes in this area.

Chapter 9 supports that personalized services and products are only successful when the usage context is taken into consideration. For interactive TV services, where usage is typically taking place in a living room, the question on how to develop an interaction technique to enable personalization is central. Based on an extensive literature review a set of requirements for personalized iTV services was developed, applied on a case study, called vocomedia, showing the development of an interaction concept for interactive TV supporting personalization by using a fingerprint recognition.

Section 3: Innovative Applications and Services with Customized Adaptive Behaviour

Chapter 10 argues that the fulfillment of affective customers needs may award the producer extra premium in gaining a competitive edge. This entails a number of technical challenges to be addressed, such as, the elicitation, evaluation, and fulfillment of affective needs, as well as the evaluation of capability of producers to launch the planned products. To tackle these issues, this research proposes an affective human factor design framework to facilitate decision-making in designing product ecosystems. A case study of designing living room ecosystem is reported with dual considerations of customers' perceptions and producer's capacities.

Chapter 11 suggests that psychological customization systems can customize the experiences of users of various information technology-based products and services. In this context customization entails the intelligent automatic or semi-automatic adaptation of information per user profile, which may systematically manipulate transient psychological states of the user such as emotion or cognition. The chapter presents the psychological and technological fundamentals of psychological customization and discusses an example of an application area in emotionally adapted games.

Section 4: Case Studies and Evaluations of Mass Customization

Chapter 12 supports that product configuration systems (PCS) are a technology well suited for mass customization and support the task of configuring the product to the individual customer's needs. PCS are at the same time complex software systems that may be tailored to solve a variety of problems for a firm. It further reports findings from a study of 12 Danish firms, revealing that expected and realized benefits are consistent within the given investigation context.

Chapter 13 discusses that usability and user experience are two important factors in the development of mass-customizable personalized products. A broad range of evaluation methods is available to improve products during an user-centered development process. This chapter gives an overview on these methods and how to apply them to achieve easy-to-use, efficient and effective personalized products that are additionally fun to use. Eventually, it presents a case study on the development of a new interaction technique for interactive TV helping to understand how to set up a mix of evaluation methods to cope with some of the limitations of current usability and user experience evaluation methods.

Chapter 14 underlines that product customization is an important facility that e-commerce offers to its users. On the Web, choiceboard systems have become quite prevalent as the means by which users are able to customize their products. In this context, of choiceboard environment, this research examines the impact of system and information quality and information presentation on interface satisfaction and decision satisfaction. Further, it examines the impact of the latter two satisfaction factors on overall user satisfaction and intention to use. The research reveals that improved system quality, vis-à-vis choiceboards, leads to better information and decision satisfaction on the part of the users.

IN SUMMARY

The contribution of this book may be considered innovative and multi-fold since it brings together many research areas to the benefit of the end-user. This book aims at providing relevant theoretical foundations, principles, methodologies, frameworks, best practices and the latest research findings for the design and development of mass customization of traditional products as well as eServices with personalized features based on user preferences and human factors to professors, researchers, graduate and undergraduate students, and practitioners working on fields related to computer science, human computer interaction, e-business, software engineering, electrical and computer engineering, Web technology, information systems, e-commerce, e-marketing as well as to business leaders and consultants.

xviii

This book is a useful tool for academics, teachers and researchers, professionals in the field of mass customization and Web personalization, and to people that belong to the broader field of the information communication technologies (ICT). It provides pragmatic references, analysis, new methodologies, and architectures that tend to approach the subject more comprehensively providing latest suggestions and solutions.

Constantinos Mourlas and Panagiotis Germanakos
Athens, 2009

Acknowledgment

We would like to truly thank and express our deepest gratitude to the people involved for the successful completion of this project. Without their tireless, continuous engagement and constant assistance, this book would likely not have realized.

We would like to thank all authors for their dedication, interest and excellent work. This book is successfully completed due to their timely responses to the strict deadlines imposed throughout the process as well as patience during the editing, corrections and communications.

Also, we would like to thank all reviewers for their constructive, comprehensive comments and objective suggestions. Their role has been instrumental in allowing this book to mature.

Furthermore, we would like to thank our colleagues from the Laboratory of New Technologies, Faculty of Communication & Media Studies – National & Kapodistrian University of Athens and the Department of Computer Science, University of Cyprus for their facilitation, availability, feedback and invaluable insights throughout the implementation of this book.

Finally, we would like to thank the publishing team at IGI Global for discussing this project and giving us their full support from the inception of this idea to the final publication. In particular, many thanks to Mehdi Khosrow-Pour, Rebecca Beistline and Julia Mosemann for their invaluable assistance and guidance.

Most important, this book would be impossible to conclude without the support, patience, love and understanding of our families and beloved friends.

Constantinos Mourlas and Panagiotis Germanakos
Athens, Hellas
January, 2009

Section 1
Mass Customization in Products and Services

Chapter 1
The Life Event Cycle:
A Special Management Tool for Mass Customization of Services

Florian U. Siems
RWTH Aachen University, Germany

Dominik Walcher
Salzburg University of Applied Sciences, Austria

ABSTRACT

In this chapter it is argued that service stores most often offer standardized services, which may not hit the customers' demands. As a new possibility to customize service offerings the life event cycle is introduced, which builds on traditional lifecycle concepts but refines them by a stronger individual perspective. In the first part of the chapter, a short introduction in service management, kinds of services and the relevance of a long term customer relationship for service stores is given. Then the idea of life cycles is shown in general, before in the main part the life event cycle is explained. It is shown that all marketing instruments could be used to enhance individualization of services and to respect the implications of the life event cycle. The chapter ends with limitations and future trends.

INTRODUCTION: MANAGEMENT OF SERVICES

The management of services has become more and more important in practice and science within the last 20 years (Lovelock & Wirtz, 2004, pp. 4-8; Bruhn & Georgi, 2006, p. xvi; Zeithaml & Bitner & Gremler, 2006, p. 2). The definitions and classifications of service providers are as heterogeneous as the definitions of services themselves (Lovelock, 1983). In 1999 Tim Davis published his

classification of service firms (Davis, 1999). Based on a well founded criticism on other definitions, Davis classified service providers regarding to the two dimensions

(1)   Service task (routine / knowledge) and
(2)   Service delivery (decoupled / integrated).

The distinction between routinized and knowledge based service tasks can also be found at several other classifications (Lovelock, 1983), the distinction between decoupled and integrated service delivery however can be seen as new. This factor

DOI: 10.4018/978-1-60566-260-2.ch001

Figure 1. Four types of service firms

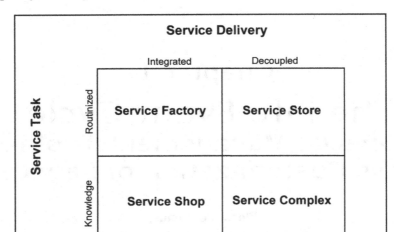

deals with the horizontal dimension of work – the core process or how services are delivered. Basically the service delivery dimension refers to the distance between the majority of tasks within the service firm and the customers. Thus, the majority of tasks of a fast food restaurant or a car repair station is closer to the customer than the tasks of a hospital or a insurance company (Davis, 1999, p. 23). Combining these two dimensions four types of service firms emerge (shown in figure 1).

(1) *Service Factories* have routine processes that are tightly integrated in delivery, such as fast food restaurants or car rental firms. (2) *Service Shops* carry out non-routine knowledge or craft work that is closely integrated in delivery, such as auto repair stations or small consulting offices. (3) *Service Complexes* engage in non-routine knowledge work that is decoupled in delivery, such as hospitals, large consulting firms or large advertising agencies. (4) *Service Stores* provide a variety of routine services that are decoupled or disintegrated in delivery, such as insurance companies or banks. At *Service Stores* it can be found that the level of service customization most often is very low. In order to stay cost efficient the standardization of services is pushed ("one type fits all") at the price of not addressing the individual needs of the customer. In this paper it is argued that the possibilities of professional service customization can be exploited by *Service Stores* to a much higher extent by systematically applying a refined lifecycle concept - the life event cycle.

In the last decade marketing for services (Bruhn & Georgi, 2006) as well as customization of services (Ahlström & Westbrook 1999; Mills & Morris 1986; Piller 2003; Piller & Meier & Reichwald 2002; Piller & Stotko 2002; Tseng & Piller 2003; Winter 2001) has become more and more important. It was shown that especially in the service industry a long term relationship between provider and customer is responsible for a company's success (Gummesson 1987; Reinartz & Kumar, 2000; Grönroos, 2000). Reichheld and Sasser (1990) for instance demonstrated in the 90ties, that increasing profits of a service provider can be traced back to long term relationships causing

(1)   increasing purchases,
(2)   cross- and up-selling-activities,
(3)   reduced operating costs,
(4)   customer as referrals and
(5)   increasing acceptance of premium prices.

Considering these effects of a long-term relationship for services, a new marketing perspective was born: The "Relationship Marketing", which is focused especially on the retention of customers and customer satisfaction as important antecedent (see e.g. Gummesson, 1994; Heskett & Sasser & Schlesinger, 1997; Hennig-Thurau & Hansen, 2000; Bruhn, 2003). For new approaches in this research area, some existing theories of traditional marketing also can be used, but often some modifications seem necessary. In the following, one of such modifications of a traditional marketing tool – the lifecycle – is shown. The kind of modification we show follows the idea of mass customization. It is demonstrated, how this modified tool can be used for services to enhance the intensity of the relationship between a service company and his customers.

BACKGROUND: LIFE CYCLE THEORIES

The use of lifecycles is a traditional method of strategic planning in marketing (Cox, 1967; Catry & Chevalier, 1974; Day, 1981; Kotler & Armstrong, 2006, pp. 290). The idea of these traditional concepts is to show the development of special marketing issues over time. The development of marketing objectives like the number of sales or the total revenue for instance can be used to identify stages like introduction, growth, maturity and decline (Cox, 1967, pp. 377). This differentiation helps to control the intensity of marketing instruments in the different phases (Clifford, 1965; Catry & Chevalier, 1974; Kotler & Armstrong, 2006, pp. 290). For example it is said that in the beginning of the product-lifecycle communication is the most important instrument, in the end however the marketing instrument price is more effective. The concept was tested in several industries (Brockhoff, 1967; Dodge & Fullerton, 1984) and critically discussed by many researches (Crawford, 1992). The lifecycle

concept was applied almost exclusively within the consumer goods industry. Figure 2 shows such a traditional product lifecycle (rf. Thomas & Pettigrew & Whittington, 2002, p. 213, respectively Kotler & Armstrong, 2006, pp. 290).

Considering the new developments in marketing, especially the new relationship marketing perspective shown before, other lifecycle concepts were developed, which focus especially on the relationship aspect. The customer relationship lifecycle for instance describes the intensity of the relationship between a company and a customer over time (Bruhn, 2003, pp. 41). Following this lifecycle marketing objectives and marketing instruments can be differed into the phases

(1) Recruitment,
(2) Retention and
(3) Recovery of customers

as shown in Figure 3. Thus a service has to (1) attract new customers, (2) bind the customers to the company and (3) recapture customers, if they do not want to receive the service any longer or if they have already changed the provider.

The Life Event Cycle: A Special Management Tool for Mass Customization of Services

Another life cycle concept which focus especially on the relationship aspect and on service customization and which should be illustrated in the following is the Life Event Cycle (in the few existing publications also named "customer requirements life cycle", see e.g. Bruhn 2003). The idea is as follows: The quantitative and qualitative needs concerning a service are changing over time, which can be traced back to different events in the life of a customer. Sometimes these events are defined as stages of family phases (e.g. young singles, young married couples without children, couples with children etc.). Thus the event approach sometimes

Figure 2. Traditional product lifecycle

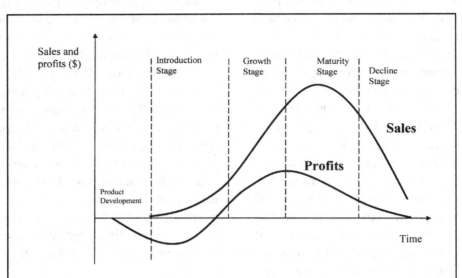

is called "family life cycle" (see e.g. Hollensen 2003, p. 129; Kotler & Armstrong, 2006, p. 144). In this paper, it is assumed that the family stages can be important events, but there can be also other events in the lifetime of customer which are influencing requirements and needs (e.g. new job, new house, increasing salary). So the family life cycle can be seen as a subset of the general life event cycle (Siems & Walcher, 2008) which is depicted in the following.

With the help of a banking example, a typical Service Store representative, this can be illustrated: At the beginning the customer – being a child – needs only limited financial services, i.e. only a simple account opened by parents or grandparents. Growing up other financial services becomes

Figure 3. Customer Relationship Lifecycle (Adapted from Bruhn, 2003, p. 46)

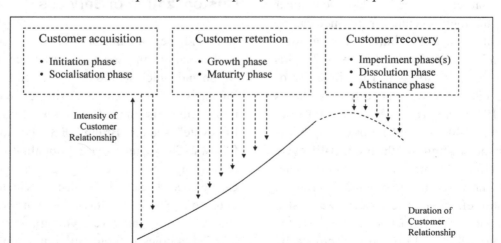

Figure 4. Showcase life event cycle for financial services

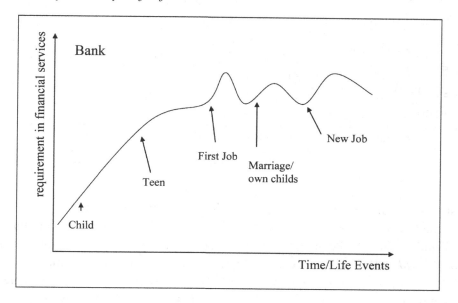

more important. The customer needs for instance a credit when starting to study. Having a job the customer wants to invest money – and so on. To marry, getting children, building a house, changing jobs or getting divorced are other important events. Thus service customization is needed depending on the life events of the customer (as shown in figure 4).

For a lot of other services similar curves can be generated. The differences between the tops and the downs and the number of the tops and the downs are depending on two determinants: The kind of service and the kind of customer. For example, the owner of an old car has high requirements for repairing the car, which causes short periods between the necessary repairs. After buying a new car there are no repairs for the first years. When the car gets older the cycle starts again - and so on. Figure 5 shows this example and others.

To realize a long term relationship, it is necessary to systematically manage this life event cycle: It must be avoided that the customer changes the company because a life event changes the requirements. This means life-event-cycle-based service

customization. Especially *Service Stores* mostly offer standardized services, which may not hit the customers' life event demands and thus can endanger a long term relationship.

To realize such a "Life Event Cycle Management", more than (traditional) segmentation seems necessary: The life events can differ from customer to customer: Some people get married when they are 18 years old, others when they are 30 years old. For each customer, the curve of life events could be different.

Based on this problem, it seems necessary, to realize an individualization, concerning all marketing instruments. To show how this can be done, we demonstrate a showcase in the following.

Showcase Financial Services: Individualization following the Life Event Cycle

An individualization following the life cycle can be done by a differentiation of the marketing instruments for different stages of a phase in which a customer is. We want to demonstrate this shortly for a bank in Switzerland, using the traditional

Figure 5. Customer life event cycles at different services

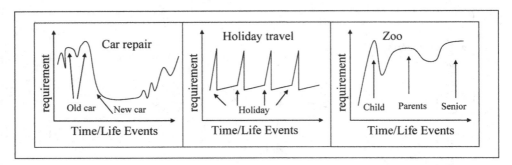

marketing instruments (the "four Ps", product, promotion, price and place). These instruments are enriched by the additional "P" "People" following the idea of *Magrath* (1986), that for services, extensions like this for the traditional marketing instruments seem useful.

People: At services employees play an important part of the customers' quality perception (Bruhn & Georgi, 2006 pp. 304). Thus the requirements for employees can be different in different stages of the customers' life event cycle: The bank therefore can try to manage that customers get service personal of the same age and with similar life experiences.

Product: The bank offers services for different life stages like special products for teens, twens and older people. At the homepage of this bank, customers can select their life phase with the help of an easy to use online-configurator to find the right offer. Especially the selection of funds follows the cafeteria-principle: customers can create own funds, at which they can choose the kind of fund, the different constituents and the risk diversification individually.

Promotion: In different life phase different kinds of communication and different intensity of communication are necessary. In some stages the customer needs information about how to invest money, in other stages more information about how to get money from the bank. Thus the customer can select on the internet page the actual segment in his life cycle (for example: just married) and

gets the fitting information for this stage. Especially for life event cycles with long differences between the tops (=high requirement) it is very important to use communication to remember the customer: So the bank sends memos to their customers regularly to remember that they should check their financial issues again.

Price: The Life Event Cycle can be used to offer different prices for different segments depending on the stage of the cycle. For example the bank offers the same service for a lower price while a customer is student at a University and increases the price for this customer after finishing the study. Thus the life event cycle can be used as base for different kinds of price differentiation integrating the customer to identify the segment and to get the fitting price.

Place: The requirement for or preferences for the distribution channel can also differ from stage to stage in the Life Event Cycle: For example, a student has different requirements concerning the office hours of a bank than he has after his studies, being a manager. Or there can be different requirements for the use of online services depending on the stage of the life cycle. Here it is also possible to offer different ways for different segments and to let the customer choose the – concerning his Life Event Stage – fitting way.

FURTHER RESEARCH AND CONCLUSION

In this paper it is argued that Service Stores most often offer standardized services, which may not hit the customers' demands. The life event cycle could be a helpful concept to refine and customize the service offerings. The short example of the Swiss Bank shows that there are first attempts.

Further research questions are:

- How can the life event cycle concept can be adapted to different other service stores?
- How can the life event cycle concept itself be refined?
- How does the customer interaction process look like?
- How can this interaction process be supported by IT?
- How can we use (existing or new) tools of mass customization to realize an individualization following the life events of a customer?
- Do investments in this concept really pay off (= is there an increasing long term relationship between company and customers?)

These further questions show the limitations of our research today: In practice, only a few companies are still using the concept of the life event cycle, in a lot other companies this tool is just introduced in this year. So – unfortunately – we cannot extend our experiences or give real evidence. It will be interesting to see what will be happened in the next years and how the questions we have shown above can be answered.

In addition to that, we must admit that this chapter follows a marketing perspective and is limited on it, but also other perspective seems useful. For example, it can be interesting if and how the life event cycle can be extended especially to the Human Resource Management: The life events of an employee can be interesting for his superiors, e.g. to fit the working conditions over time to the life events of an employee for generating a higher motivation and enhancing the efficiency of the employee.

It seems also interesting to link the idea of the life event cycle to other research areas, e.g. Human-Computer Interaction, Software-Engineering and Psychology.

In sum, we have seen that the Life Event Cycle and the mass customization for service are a new and important field where a lot of research still can be done in the future to optimize a long-term relationship of customers or other stakeholder.

REFERENCES

Ahlström, P., Westbrook, R. (1999). Implications of mass customization for operations management: an exploratory survey. *International Journal of Operations & Production Management, 19* (Jg. H. 3), 262-274.

Brockhoff, K. (1967). A Test for the Product Life Cycle. *Econometrica, 35*(3-4), 472–484. doi:10.2307/1905649

Bruhn, M. (2003). *Relationship Marketing*. Harlow, UK: Pearson.

Bruhn, M., & Georgi, D. (2006): Services *Marketing. Managing The Service Values Chain*, Harlow, UK: Pearson.

Catry, B., & Chevalier, M. (1974). Market Share Strategy and the Product Life Cycle. *Journal of Marketing, 38*(4), 29–34. doi:10.2307/1250388

Clifford, D.K. (1965). Managing the Product Life Cycle. *Management Review, Tge McKinsey Quarterly*, Spring, 34-38.

Cox, W. E. (1967). Product Life Cycles as Marketing Models. *The Journal of Business, 40*(4), 375–384. doi:10.1086/295003

Crawford, C. M. (1992). Business Took the Wrong Life Cycle from Biology. *Journal of Product and Brand Management, 1*(1), 5–11. doi:10.1108/10610429210036690

Davis, T. R. V. (1999). *Different service firms, different core competencies*. Bloomington, IN: Business Horizons.

Day, G. S. (1981). The Product Life Cycle: Analysis and Application Issues. *Journal of Marketing, 45*(4), 60–67. doi:10.2307/1251472

Dodge, H. R., & Fullerton, S. (1984). Copy Length Across the Product Life Cycle. *Current Issues and Research in Advertising, 7*(1), 149–158.

Grönroos, C. (2002). *Service Management and Marketing. A Customer Relationship Management Approach,* (2nd Ed.). West Sussex, UK: Wiley & Sons.

Gummesson, E. (1987). Marketing – A Long Term Interactive Relationship. *Long Range Planning, 20*(4), 10–20. doi:10.1016/0024-6301(87)90151-8

Gummesson, E. (1994). Making Relationship Marketing Operational. *International Journal of Service Industry Management, 5*(5), 5–20. doi:10.1108/09564239410074349

Hennig-Thurau, T., & Hansen, U. (Eds.). (2000). *Relationship Marketing. Gaining Competitive Advantage Through Customer Satisfaction and Customer Retention*. Berlin: Springer.

Heskett, J. L., Sasser, W. E., & Schlesinger, L. A. (1997). *The Service Profit Chain. How leading Companies Link Profit and Growth to Loyalty, Satisfaction, and Value*. New York: Free Press.

Hollensen, S. (2003). *Marketing Management: A Relationship Approach*. Prentice Hall: Harlow.

Kotler, P., & Armstrong, G. (2006). *Principles of Marketing,* (11th Ed.). Upper Saddle River, NJ: Pearson.

Lovelock, C., & Wirtz, J. (2004). *Services Marketing. People, Technology, Strategy,* (5th Ed.). Upper Saddle River, NJ: Pearson.

Lovelock, C. H. (1983). Classifying services to gain strategic marketing insights. *Journal of Marketing, 47*(3), 9–20. doi:10.2307/1251193

Magrath, A. J. (1986). When Marketing Services, 4 Ps Are Not Enough. *Business Horizons, 29*(3), 44–50. doi:10.1016/0007-6813(86)90007-8

Mills, P. K., & Morris, J. H. (1986). Clients as "Partial" Employees of Service Organizations: Role, Development in Client Participation. *Academy of Management Review, 11*(4), 726–735. doi:10.2307/258392

Piller, F. (2003). Turning products into Sustainable Service Businesses. In A. Tukker, M. Charter, (Eds.), *Proceedings of the Conference "Sustainable Product-Service Systems: State of the Art,"* (p. 51-60), Amsterdam.

Piller, F., Meier, R., & Reichwald, R. (2002). eService Customization. In M. Bruhn, & B. Stauss, (Hrsg.), *Handbuch Dienstleistungsmanagement,* (pp. 225-242). Wiesbaden, Germany: Gabler.

Piller, F. T., & Stotko, C. (2002). Four approaches to deliver customized products and services with mass production efficiency. In T. S. Durrani, (Ed.), *Proceedings of the IEEE International Engineering Management Conference. Managing Technology for the New Economy,* Cambridge University, Cambridge, UK, (p. 773-778).

Reichheld, F. F., & Sasser, W. E. (1990). Zero Defections: Quality Comes to Services. *Harvard Business Review,* (September/October): 105–111.

Reinartz, W. J., & Kumar, V. (2000). On the Profitability of Long-Life Customers in a Noncontractual Setting: An Empirical Investigation and Implications for Marketing. *Journal of Marketing, 64*(4), 17–35. doi:10.1509/jmkg.64.4.17.18077

Siems, F., & Walcher, D. (2008). Modularity as base for efficient life event cycle management. In F. Piller (Ed.), *Proceedings of The World Conference on Mass Customization & Personalization (MCPC 2007)*. Boston: Massachusetts Institute of Technology (MIT).

Thomas, H., Pettigrew, A. M., & Whittington, R. (2002). *Handbook of Strategy and Management*. London: Sage Publications.

Tseng, M., & Piller, F. T. (2003). *The Customer Centric Enterprise: Advances in Mass Customization and Personalization*. New York: Springer.

Winter, R. (2001). Mass Customization and Beyond - Evolution of Customer Centricity in Financial Services. In C. Rautenstrauch, R. Seelmann-Eggebert &K. Turowski (Eds.), *Moving into Mass Customization: Information Systems and Management Principals*. Berlin: Springer.

Zeithaml, V. A., Bitner, M. J., & Gremler, D. D. (2006). *Services Marketing. Integrating the Customer Focus Across the Firm*, (4th Ed.). Boston: McGraw Hill.

Chapter 2
Optimizing Consumer Responses to Mass Customization

Ruth Mugge
Delft University of Technology, The Netherlands

Jan P. L. Schoormans
Delft University of Technology, The Netherlands

ABSTRACT

A better understanding of consumer responses to mass customization can help companies to more successfully introduce mass customization strategies in new products. Only if consumers believe that the value of the mass-customized product significantly exceeds that of an off-the-shelf product, consumers are willing to mass customize a product. In this chapter, the authors discuss the specific conditions that affect the relative value of a mass-customized product. Characteristics of the consumer who is performing the customization task, the product category that is mass customized, and the specific mass customization process can affect the perceived benefits and drawbacks of mass customization. Based on this understanding, several strategies are presented on how companies could implement mass customization in order to optimize consumer responses and thus offer consumers the greatest value.

INTRODUCTION

Many marketplaces are moving from a mass-orientation to an individualization of offerings. In doing so, it is acknowledged that consumers' tastes and preferences are often highly heterogeneous, leaving many unfulfilled with standard goods or services (Franke & Piller, 2004; Piller & Müller, 2004; Weightman & McDonagh, 2003). A business strategy aimed at addressing this growing demand

DOI: 10.4018/978-1-60566-260-2.ch002

of individualization is to offer consumers the opportunity to mass customize products. In mass customization, consumers take active part in the design process and act as (co-)designers of their own products. Mass customization can provide consumers with important benefits, because it allows them to purchase a unique product that fits their individual preferences. Nevertheless, nowadays, mass-customized products take up only a small percentage of the total market of consumer durables. Although mass customization is not yet implemented often, the concept is not new. Pine presented the concept of mass customization in 1993 (Pine II, 1993) and Toffler already suggested in 1980 that consumers will be replaced by 'prosumers'; individuals who are both the producer and the consumer of a product (Toffler, 1980).

There are several reasons why only a relatively small number of companies have implemented mass customization in products so far. From a technical perspective, the implementation of mass customization is generally complex and costly. Moreover, consumers may not always be interested in mass-customized products, which may have contributed to the current small market share as well. To successfully implement mass customization in products, companies need to understand and know how to optimize consumer responses to mass customization. The goal of this chapter is twofold. First of all, we provide an extensive overview of the literature on consumer responses to mass customization. Specifically, we explore why consumers may (not) appreciate mass customization and under which conditions consumers' evaluation becomes more positive or negative. Second, based on this understanding, we present several strategies for companies to optimize consumer responses to mass customization.

The chapter is organized as follows. We start with a discussion of the potential benefits (e.g., better fit to preferences) and the potential drawbacks (e.g., complexity) that mass customization may bring about for consumers. In the subsequent sections, we discuss the different conditions that may affect consumers' appreciation of mass customization. Specifically, we explore which consumers are more willing to mass customize products, which product categories are the most attractive to mass customize, and how the mass customization process should be implemented in order to achieve the greatest value for the consumer. Based on this understanding, several strategies are discussed that may help companies to optimize consumer responses by either stimulating the benefits of mass customization or avoiding its

drawbacks. Finally, some suggestions for future research are presented.

THE BENEFITS AND DRAWBACKS OF MASS CUSTOMIZATION FOR CONSUMERS

Past research concluded that mass customization through consumer co-creation/co-production can increase value perceptions of and overall satisfaction with a product (Bendapudi & Leone, 2003; Kamali & Loker, 2002). The potential benefits of mass customizing products for the consumer are twofold. First, the consumer can mass customize the product in such a way that it better fits his/her utilitarian and aesthetic preferences than a standard off-the-shelf product does (Franke & Piller, 2003; Schreier, 2006). Franke and Piller (2004) showed that consumers have highly heterogeneous preferences: in their study, 165 consumers designed a total of 159 different watches, suggesting that standard off-the-shelf products may not optimally correspond to consumers' individual preferences. Consumers can mass customize the functionality and/or appearance of a product. Mass customization of a product's functionality results in a product that fits an individual's utilitarian desires. For example, a Dell computer (http://www.dell.com) can be customized to fit one's preferences with respect to a personal computer and an Adidas shoe (http://www.miadidas.com) can be customized to improve the fit to one's feet. In addition, mass customization enables consumers to choose the specific functionalities they will use, without having to pay for unwanted functions/options (Bardakci & Whitelock, 2004). If the product's appearance is mass customized (e.g., Nike ID shoes, http://nikeid.nike.com; Timbuk2 bags, http://www.timbuk2.com; 121Time watches, http://www.121time.com), the product is perceived as better fitting to the consumer's aesthetic preferences. Furthermore, mass customization of product aesthetics offers consumers an immense variety of products, which facilitates a person's differentiation from others (Franke & Schreier, 2008). Accordingly, past research concluded that products that are customized along aesthetic dimensions are perceived as more self-expressive of one's identity than standard off-the-shelf products (Blom & Monk, 2003; Kiesler & Kiesler, 2005; Mugge, Brunel, & Schoormans, 2007; Mugge, Schoormans, & Schifferstein, 2009a). This is further enhanced by the fact that consumers perceive a mass-customized product to be unique (Fiore, Lee, & Kunz, 2004; Franke & Schreier, 2008; Schreier, 2006).

In addition to the enhanced fit to one's preferences, consumers may also derive benefits from the process of mass customization. The process of 'doing it yourself' is by many consumers perceived as self-rewarding. Consumers may experience joy during the co-design task as a result of the fulfillment of an intrinsically rewarding, artistic, and creative act (Csikszentmihalyi, 1996; Fiore et al., 2004; Franke & Piller, 2003; Schreier, 2006). Related to this issue is the benefit of 'pride of authorship'. The positive outcome of having created a satisfactory product on their own during the co-design process (instead of purchasing a standard off-the-shelf product) provides consumers with positive feedback, which gives a feeling of pride. As a result, the mass-customized product is valued more than consumers would value an identical off-the-shelf product (Fischer, 2002; Schreier, 2006).

Past research showed that creating a product partly yourself may also result in the development of a stronger emotional bond with this product (Mugge et al., 2009a). Both the effort invested during the co-design process and the self-expressive value positively affect the strength of the emotional bond the consumer experiences with this product (Mugge et al., 2009a). The consequence of experiencing a strong emotional bond with a product is that this product gains meaning beyond the functional and becomes extraordinary. In ad-

dition, when people are asked to list the emotions they experience towards products with which they feel emotionally bonded, more positive emotions (e.g., happiness, love, warmth, pride, and joy) are reported than for products with which they do not feel emotionally bonded (Schultz, Kleine, & Kernan, 1989).

As a result of the benefits of mass customization, companies can gain a competitive advantage by implementing mass customization strategies in products and consumers are willing to pay a premium price for mass-customized products. Past research showed that the willingness to pay for a self-designed product can in some cases even be twice as high as for standard off-the-shelf products (Franke & Piller, 2004; Piller & Müller, 2004; Schreier, 2006). It is likely that mass customization may also bring about favorable behaviors during ownership, such as more positive word of mouth.

Although mass customizing a product can offer consumers several benefits, mass customization might have a downside as well. First of all, mass customization requires the consumers' investment of time and effort (Mugge et al., 2009a). During the co-design task offered by mass customization, consumers have to make much more choices with respect to the product than in an ordinary purchase situation. As a result, consumers have to direct more time and attention to the purchase of a mass-customized product than to that of an off-the-shelf product. Consumers are only motivated to invest their time and effort if they feel that the ultimate value of the mass-customized product significantly exceeds the value of a standard off-the-shelf product. Otherwise, consumers will prefer an off-the-shelf product that does not require this investment.

The second drawback of mass customization is that consumers may perceive the task of designing one's own product as complex and risky. Mass customization allows consumers to create their own product by making selections among a great number of options. Consequently, consumers may become overwhelmed by the increased number of possibilities at their disposal (Dellaert & Stremersch, 2005; Huffman & Kahn, 1998; Piller, Koch, Möslein, & Schubert, 2003; Zipkin, 2001). Because human capacity to process information is limited, offering a great number of customization options will increase the number of cognitive steps and the effort needed in the decision making process (Bettman, Johnson, & Payne, 1990). This might lead to negative affective reactions, such as confusion, regret, or frustration. As consumers get confused by the increased number of choices, they might feel insecure about their own edibility to decide on the right alternative amongst that large potential set of options and designs. If consumers perceive the mass customization process as complex and risky, this will result in a less favorable evaluation of mass customization and, consequently, in a reduction of the willingness to purchase the mass-customized product (Dellaert & Stremersch, 2005; Mugge et al., 2007).

We believe that these drawbacks may have contributed to the lack of success of mass customization, so far. The market share of mass-customized products will only increase if consumers believe that the benefits of mass customization counterbalance its drawbacks. Only then, the relative value of a mass-customized product will outweigh that of a standard off-the-shelf product. Specific conditions related to the consumer, product, and mass customization process may affect this balance and, consequently, consumers' appreciation of mass customization.

Do All Consumers want to Mass Customize their Products?

Although past research suggested that many consumers are innovative (von Hippel, (2005): 10%-30% of all consumers have modified or created a product for personal use) and thus capable to co-design their own products, it is likely that certain groups of consumers will gain relatively more benefits from mass customization and/or

will perceive less drawbacks. As a result, these consumers will respond more positively towards mass customization and will be more eager to purchase mass-customized products than others. First, demographic variables may influence consumer responses to the mass customization process. Goldsmith and Freiden (2004) concluded that younger, well-educated people with higher incomes are more likely to purchase mass-customized products. Probably, the Internet usage of these consumer groups can partly explain this relationship. People who often make use of the Internet and have purchased products online in the past, will be more likely to purchase mass-customized products. In contrast, people who have no Internet access or who consider purchasing products online risky and undesirable will evaluate mass customization more negatively. Second, several personality characteristics are likely to affect the mass customization evaluation. Consumers with a high optimum stimulation level (OSL) tend to seek more exciting experiences. Consequently, the process benefits of mass customization are more valuable for high OSL consumers, resulting in a stronger willingness to mass customize products (Fiore et al., 2004; Fiore, Lee, Kunz, & Campbell, 2001). Another personality characteristic that can enhance the perceived benefits of mass customization is consumers' need for uniqueness, which is defined as an "individual's pursuit for differentness relative to others that is achieved through the acquisition, utilization, and disposition of consumer goods" (Tepper Tian, Bearden, & Hunter, 2001, p. 50). As discussed, a mass-customized product is perceived to be unique and can facilitate a person's differentiation from other people. Consequently, consumers with a high need for uniqueness will value the opportunities provided by mass customization more than consumers with a low need for uniqueness (Franke & Schreier, 2008).

Finally, consumers may differ in their skills, knowledge, and expertise to design their own product in the way they want to. In this respect, consumers' creativity (Burroughs & Mick, 2004) may influence consumer responses to mass customization. Creative people may be more able to customize a product in such a way that it fulfills their needs. In addition, it is likely that creative people experience more joy during the mass customization process, because the design process allows them to use their creativity. As a result, creative people will gain more benefits from mass customization. The specific skills of consumers may also reduce the perceived drawbacks of mass customization. Dellaert and Stremersch (2005) found that for the mass customization of utilitarian features, consumers with high levels of product expertise consider mass customization toolkits less complex than consumers with low levels of product expertise do. Similarly, we believe that for the mass customization of product aesthetics, consumers' centrality of visual product aesthetics (Bloch, Brunel, & Arnold, 2003) may reduce the complexity and risk of mass customizing products' appearances. Centrality of visual product aesthetics (CVPA) represents the overall level of significance that visual aesthetics hold for a particular consumer in his/her relationships with products. Accordingly, high CVPA consumers can be considered experts with respect to product design.

Before implementing mass customization, companies should first explore whether their target group is interested in mass-customized products and sufficiently skilled to accomplish the co-design task.

Which Products do Consumers want to Mass Customize?

In addition to the individual differences between consumers, the product category may play a role in consumers' appreciation of mass customization. For certain product categories, mass customization may offer consumers relatively more value than for others. The first product-related factor that affects the value of mass customization

for consumers is visibility. Mugge, Brunel, and Schoormans (2007) concluded that regarding product aesthetics consumers more strongly prefer to mass customize a product if the customized elements are visible to others. As discussed, mass customization of product aesthetics can provide products with more self-expressive value than standard off-the-shelf products, due to which the owner can communicate one's unique identity to others. However, inferences about others are mainly driven by the objects that are publicly consumed (Bearden & Etzel, 1982). Accordingly, the relative benefit of self-expressiveness is enhanced if the outcome of the mass customization process is more publicly visible, either because the mass-customized product is visible to others or because the mass-customized elements of the product (e.g., exterior of a car vs. its interior) are clearly visible to others. Conversely, consumers may be reluctant to invest their time and effort in the mass customization process if the product is only privately consumed and may prefer an off-the-shelf product instead.

The second product-related factor that can influence the value of a mass-customized product in comparison to an off-the-shelf product is the degree of usage. Consumers prefer mass customization for products that are used relatively often, because frequent usage of a product intensifies the importance of the benefits that mass customization can offer (Blom & Monk, 2003; Kaplan, Schoder, & Haenlein, 2007).

Third, consumers should feel a certain degree of involvement with the product category to perceive the mass customization process sufficiently valuable to invest their time and effort in it. Accordingly, we believe that mass customization is more valuable for durable products than for fast-moving consumer goods.

For companies interested in implementing mass customization in a product, it is important to determine whether consumers are truly interested in mass customization for this particular product category. Based on the former arguments, we propose that mass customization is especially valuable for durable products that are used relatively often and serve as means to support consumers' individuality. For example, it is more interesting to mass customize apparel (e.g., clothing, footwear, jewelry, bags, watches) and lifestyle products (e.g., cars, furniture, mobile phones, MP3-players) than utilitarian products (e.g., screwdrivers, lawn mowers, washing machines).

How Should Companies Design the Mass Customization Process?

The particular mass customization process that is applied can affect consumer responses to mass customization as well. In order to increase the relative value of a mass-customized product in comparison to a standard off-the-shelf product, companies should design the mass customization process in such a way that either the perceived benefits of mass customization are enhanced and/or the drawbacks of mass customization are avoided.

To enhance the perceived benefits of mass customization, companies should make certain benefits more explicit in the mass customization process. Then, the relative value of the mass-customized product may increase. In this respect, Franke and Schreier (2008) suggested that during the mass customization process consumers could receive affirmative feedback concerning the scarcity of the mass-customized product in order to enhance the perceived uniqueness as a value driver. For example, the toolkit may indicate the number of consumers who have purchased the same or a similar design. This is especially interesting for consumers with a high need for uniqueness. Another possibility to make the mass customization values more explicit is to deliberately provide positive feedback on the fact that the consumer has created the product himself/herself in order to stimulate the pride-of-authorship benefit. An example is Nike ID that allows consumers to

'sign' their own pair of shoes by placing a name or tag on the back.

Increasing consumers' design freedom in the mass customization process may also help companies to enhance the perceived benefits of mass customization. In some mass customization offerings, consumers' design freedom is small, because consumers are only offered a limited number of choices (e.g., selecting the color of a shoe from four colors), whereas in other cases they might be offered greater design freedom by having a larger number of product parts that they can customize (e.g., selecting the color for different parts of a shoe) and/or by being able to make selections amongst more options for each product part (e.g., 10,000 colors and patterns for each part). Greater design freedom in the mass customization process allows consumers to create a greater number of possible products, which enhances the product's fit to one's personal preferences (both utilitarian and aesthetic) and its uniqueness (Dellaert & Stremersch, 2005; Franke & Piller, 2003; Mugge et al., 2007). As a result, consumers will evaluate these mass customization offerings more positively. In this respect, Schreier (2006) showed that when comparing three different mass customization offerings the highest consumers' willingness to pay was found for the mass customization offering with the greatest degree of design freedom. Although providing consumers a large set of options strongly reduces the chance that other people will own an identical product, such mass-customized products are still not entirely unique. It remains possible for other consumers to create an identical product again. Accordingly, it may be interesting to create mass customization offerings with an even greater degree of freedom by allowing consumers to personally design (parts of) their own product (e.g., create a personal design pattern for the fabric used to make a shoe), as opposed to just choosing amongst a set of alternatives. This allows consumers to be truly creative and to create a unique product that no one else owns. An

Figure 1. Freitag website © 2008 Freitag. Used with Permission.

example of a mass customization offering with an extended degree of freedom is Freitag (see Figure 1). Freitag sells customized bags made out of recycled truck tarpaulins. On the website (http://www.freitag.ch), consumers can create their own unique bag by positioning the various stencils on the tarpaulins that are available at that moment. During the design process, the consumer can see which pieces of the tarpaulins are still available and which are already used for other bags. Because each part of each tarpaulin can only be used for one bag, every bag is different. Furthermore, the process feels more creative than merely selecting colors for the different parts of the bag. In comparison to most mass customization offerings, the benefits for the consumer are thus enhanced (Mugge & Schoormans, 2005). Because production facilities are often set up to produce a number of predetermined product variants, offering consumers a great degree of design freedom may have considerable consequences for the implementation at the company. Nevertheless, the Freitag example shows that it is in some

cases possible to produce truly unique products at relatively low costs. When implementing mass customization, companies should explore the possibilities to offer a great degree of design freedom within their current production facilities.

The specific toolkit that consumers make use of during the co-design task plays an important role in the mass customization process. Hence, another strategy to stimulate the benefits and/or avoid the drawbacks of mass customization is to improve the toolkit's interface. By improving the usability and visualization of the toolkit's interface, consumers are guided in their design process, perceive less risk and complexity, and, consequently, experience more satisfaction with the mass customization process and outcome. In this respect, Vink (2003) concluded that mass customization toolkits should constantly provide vivid and accurate information on the selected product, should show all customizable product attributes simultaneously, should start with choosing the most important product characteristic, should include interactivity, and should stimulate a trial-and-error process. Moreover, toolkits can offer consumers module libraries with a number of standards for several product parts. Instead of starting the design from scratch (with hundreds or millions of options), this allows consumers to focus their design process on the relevant aspects and choose standard solutions for the other aspects (Dellaert & Stremersch, 2005; Thomke & Von Hippel, 2002). This guarantees an efficient investment of time and effort. Furthermore, consumers can creatively use these standards as a starting point to create one's own unique product while restricting the required risk. An example of a company that offers a useful toolkit is the Nokia 3220 mobile phone. The web-based toolkit (http://www. qa.nokiausa.com/fun/3220/1,9186,~swQt,00. html) allows consumers to personally design their own cut-out cover using their creativity, instead of merely choosing one among several predetermined options. In addition to the possibility to upload one's own image, the toolkit provides several basic elements (e.g., backgrounds, stencils, and colors) that consumers can use in their design. This provides consumers with the opportunity to create a more personal and unique product, while reducing complexity.

By designing a mass customization process and toolkit, companies should also consider the target group and their specific needs, experience, and capabilities. In this respect, Randall, Terwiesch, and Ulrich (2007) found that, in the context of PC purchasing, consumers who are experts prefer to use a parameter-based mass customization system that allows them to directly specify and fine tune the desired design elements for the product (e.g., a PC's processor or internal memory). In contrast, novices created better outcomes with a needs-based mass customization system. In a needs-based system, consumers merely specify the importance of their needs (e.g., PC is for storing music or for playing 3D-games), based on which the system provides them with the product that fits their needs best.

Another strategy to stimulate the relative value of mass customization is the implementation of more flexibility in mass customization by allowing consumers to customize their product over and over again (Mugge, Schoormans, & Schifferstein, 2009b). An example is the customization of a mobile phone by changing the cover. Nowadays, most mass-customized products are inflexible. After the consumer finishes the mass customization and decides to order the mass-customized product, the features of the mass-customized product are fixed. Nevertheless, a high degree of flexibility provides consumers with an important benefit: It offers the possibility to change and improve the product design later in time. This may reduce the perceived risk of spoiling the product during the mass customization process and may make consumers less uncertain about the final outcome. However, most consumers will only change the product design if the flexible customization process will take them only little time and effort. We acknowledge that implementing flexibility in mass customization may have some negative consequences, due to which this strategy may not be feasible in all situations. First of all, implementing flexibility will often result in an increase in the production costs and thus in a more expensive product. Consequently, it is impossible to implement flexibility for all components, and companies need to examine for which component(s) the added value will be the highest. Companies also need to determine at which point in time the flexible components are offered to consumers. If consumers have to select the different flexible components directly at purchase, the selected components may not fit their future preferences, because their preferences may change in time. In addition, storing the additional components of the product may annoy consumers in time. On the other hand, if consumers have to purchase the flexible components during ownership, they may perceive the flexibility as less interesting, because most consumers do not want to postpone the usage of specific product features. Furthermore, this may result in a complex and costly logistic process for the company.

The relative value of a mass-customized product may also be stimulated by the implementation of online communities for collaborative co-design (Jeppesen, 2005; Piller, Schubert, Koch, & Möslein, 2005). An example of such an online community is the virtual design environment of Lego (http://www.lugnet.com), where users can exchange models and ideas how to use standard Lego building blocks for individual models. In an online community, consumers can discuss, exchange, and rate their product designs and provide each other with feedback. Online communities may help consumers in several ways. First, consumers may use the designs of peers as a starting point in their own design process. By using the input from other consumers the amount of choices an individual has to make reduces, which makes it possible for him/her to focus specifically on his/her personal details. As a result, peer input stimulates more systematic problem solving behavior, which in turn leads to a superior outcome of the mass customization process, that is a mass-customized product that fits the preferences of the consumer more effectively (Franke, Keinz, & Schreier, 2008). Furthermore, an online community enables consumers to discuss their design with peers before the purchase is made. By giving each other constructive feedback on their design solutions, the ultimate product's quality will increase. In addition, consumers do not just follow their own individual taste, but are often influenced by peers and the taste of a community (Piller et al., 2005). Consequently, input from peers during the mass customization process can help consumers to develop an individual design that is likely to appeal to their peers and, therefore, the perceived risk of the mass-customization process is reduced. In order to take advantage of the benefits of an online community for consumers, companies can set up such a community themselves and link it to their mass customization website. Although personally maintaining an online community will cost a company time and money, it can provide additional benefits. First of all, maintaining the online community allows companies to control the topics that are being discussed. Discussions that may harm the company can then be banned from the community. If necessary, companies can also add comments and suggestions, which will further enhance the product quality. Second, companies can benefit from an online community, because the discussions in such a community may provide valuable input for the improvement of the mass customization toolkit and for new product development (Füller, Bartl, Ernst, & Mühlbacher, 2006). We believe that the discussed benefits of online communities for both consumers and the company are significant. Especially for toolkits that offer a great degree of design freedom, these benefits will compensate the costs needed for setting up and maintaining the online community.

FUTURE TRENDS

So far, the number of successful mass customization examples is small. Nevertheless, we believe that now the time seems right for companies to implement mass customization in more products. At present, the Internet is increasingly available for many consumers in developed countries. Furthermore, large groups of consumers in these countries are willing to purchase products online and the number of purchases that are done online is rapidly increasing. Furthermore, online communities grow in popularity and many people use these communities as ways to present and discuss opinions, problems, ideas, stories, photos, etc. We believe that online communities can provide a powerful means to enhance the relative value of a mass-customized product in comparison to an off-the-shelf product.

Future research in the field of mass customization should investigate how companies can make use of such online communities in order to offer mass customization toolkits that provide the greatest benefits for consumers. In this respect, we need an understanding of how mass customization toolkits should be designed in order to facilitate interaction through an online community.

In addition to online communities, it may in some cases also be worthwhile to implement a mass customization toolkit offline, for example, in a warehouse. An example is the Puma Mongolian BBQ. The Puma Mongolian BBQ consists of several bins that are placed in the Puma store. The bins contain pieces of fabric that differ in colour and material, and correspond to the various shoe parts. Consumers can choose different pieces of fabric to design and assemble their unique pair of shoes. In contrast to more common mass customization toolkits (e.g., Nike ID), consumers are physically active and have a tangible interaction with (parts of) their future Puma shoes. Such an offline mass customization toolkit offers several advantages. First, the offline toolkit allows them to hold, touch, and see (parts) of the product in real life, which may be crucial for certain product categories (Peck & Childers, 2003). This may reduce consumers' uncertainty concerning the mass-customized product as well. Second, when using an offline toolkit, consumers can immediately receive feedback on their design from the sales person and/or peers. Third, the experience of jointly designing a product with a group of friends using an offline toolkit may be more engaging, due to which the flow experience may be enhanced (Schoormans, Morel, & Zheng, 2006). For companies, an offline toolkit suggests that the mass-customized products are sold through two different distribution channels. For certain companies, this may be business as usual, but other mass customization companies, like 121Time, may lack experience in selling products through physical stores. Accordingly, the costs for implementing an offline toolkit will differ considerably. Furthermore, companies need to consider how much value an offline mass customization can bring for the specific product category and target group.

CONCLUSION

This chapter provides an overview of some of the specific conditions that affect consumer responses to mass customization. Specifically, we propose that conditions related to the consumer (e.g., demographics, need for uniqueness, creativity, expertise), the product (e.g., public visibility, degree of usage, involvement), and the mass customization process (e.g., usability and visualization of the toolkit) may affect the benefits and drawbacks that mass customization may bring about. Depending on these conditions, the relative value of a mass-customized product will (not) outweigh that of a standard off-the-shelf product. Companies need to understand and know how to optimize consumer responses towards mass customization to take full advantage of the mass customization market potential. Only when the outcome of the mass customization process provides the target group with enough value to counterbalance its drawbacks, mass customization can be a success. In order to optimize consumer responses, several strategies for the implementation of mass customization (e.g., flexibility, online communities) were presented to help companies to accomplish this difficult task. For the success of their mass customization offerings, it is important that companies continue to compare the relative value of their mass-customized product with that of standard off-the-shelf products.

REFERENCES

Bardakci, A., & Whitelock, J. (2004). How "ready" are customers for mass customisation? An exploratory study. *European Journal of Marketing*, *38*(11/12), 1396–1416. doi:10.1108/03090560410560164

Bearden, W. O., & Etzel, M. J. (1982). Reference group influence on product and brand purchase decisions. *The Journal of Consumer Research, 9*(September), 183–194. doi:10.1086/208911

Bendapudi, N., & Leone, R. P. (2003). Psychological implications of customer participation in co-production. *Journal of Marketing, 67*(January), 14–28. doi:10.1509/jmkg.67.1.14.18592

Bettman, J. R., Johnson, E. J., & Payne, J. W. (1990). A componential analysis of cognitive effort in choice. *Organizational Behavior and Human Decision Processes, 45*(1), 111–139. doi:10.1016/0749-5978(90)90007-V

Bloch, P. H., Brunel, F. F., & Arnold, T. J. (2003). Individual differences in the centrality of visual product aesthetics: Concept and measurement. *The Journal of Consumer Research, 29*(March), 551–565. doi:10.1086/346250

Blom, J. O., & Monk, A. F. (2003). Theory of personalization of appearance: Why users personalize their PCs and mobile phones. *Human-Computer Interaction, 18*, 193–228. doi:10.1207/S15327051HCI1803_1

Burroughs, J. E., & Mick, D. G. (2004). Exploring antecedents and consequences of consumer creativity in a problem-solving context. *The Journal of Consumer Research, 31*(September), 402–411. doi:10.1086/422118

Csikszentmihalyi, M. (1996). *Creativity: Flow and the psychology of discovery and invention.* New York: HarperCollins Publishers.

Dellaert, B. G. C., & Stremersch, S. (2005). Marketing mass-customized products: Striking balance between utility and complexity. *JMR, Journal of Marketing Research, 42*(May), 219–227. doi:10.1509/jmkr.42.2.219.62293

Fiore, A. M., Lee, S.-E., & Kunz, G. (2004). Individual differences, motivations, and willingness to use a mass customization option for fashion products. *European Journal of Marketing, 38*(7), 835–849. doi:10.1108/03090560410539276

Fiore, A. M., Lee, S.-E., Kunz, G., & Campbell, J. R. (2001). Relationships between optimum stimulation level and willingness to use mass customisation options. *Journal of Fashion Marketing and Management, 5*(2), 99–107. doi:10.1108/EUM0000000007281

Fischer, G. (2002). Beyond 'couch potatoes': From consumers to designers and active contributors. *First Monday (Peer-Reviewed Journal on the Internet), available at*http://firstmonday.org/issues/issue7_12/fischer/.

Franke, N., Keinz, P., & Schreier, M. (2008). Complementing mass customization toolkits with user communities: How peer input improves customer self-design. *Journal of Product Innovation Management, 25*(6), 546–559. doi:10.1111/j.1540-5885.2008.00321.x

Franke, N., & Piller, F. T. (2003). Key research issues in user interaction with user toolkits in a mass customisation system. *International Journal of Technology Management, 26*(5/6), 578–599. doi:10.1504/IJTM.2003.003424

Franke, N., & Piller, F. T. (2004). Value creation by toolkits for user innovation and design: The case of the watch market. *Journal of Product Innovation Management, 21*(6), 401–415. doi:10.1111/j.0737-6782.2004.00094.x

Franke, N., & Schreier, M. (2008). Product uniqueness as a driver of customer utility in mass customization. *Marketing Letters, 19*(2), 93–107. doi:10.1007/s11002-007-9029-7

Füller, J., Bartl, M., Ernst, H., & Mühlbacher, H. (2006). Community based innovation: How to integrate members of virtual communities into new product development. *Electronic Commerce Research, 6*(January), 57–73. doi:10.1007/s10660-006-5988-7

Goldsmith, R. E., & Freiden, J. B. (2004). Have it your way: Consumer attitudes toward personalized marketing. *Marketing Intelligence & Planning, 22*(2), 228–239. doi:10.1108/02634500410525887

Huffman, C., & Kahn, B. E. (1998). Variety for sale: Mass customization or mass confusion. *Journal of Retailing, 74*(4), 491–513. doi:10.1016/S0022-4359(99)80105-5

Jeppesen, L. B. (2005). User toolkits for innovation: Consumers support each other. *Journal of Product Innovation Management, 22*(4), 347–362. doi:10.1111/j.0737-6782.2005.00131.x

Kamali, N., & Loker, S. (2002). Mass customization: On-line consumer involvement in product design. *Journal of Computer-Mediated Communication, 7*(4).

Kaplan, A. M., Schoder, D., & Haenlein, M. (2007). Factors influencing the adoption of mass customization: The impact of base category consumption frequency and need satisfaction. *Journal of Product Innovation Management, 24*(2), 101–116. doi:10.1111/j.1540-5885.2007.00237.x

Kiesler, T., & Kiesler, S. (2005). My pet rock and me: An experimental exploration of the self extension concept. In G. Menon & A. Rao (Eds.), *Advances in Consumer Research* (Vol. 32, pp. 365-370). Provo, UT: Association for Consumer Research.

Mugge, R., Brunel, F. F., & Schoormans, J. P. L. (2007). Psychological and behavioral consumer responses to the mass customization of product aesthetics. In W. Mitchell, F. T. Piller, M. M. Tseng, R. Chin & B. L. McClanahan (Eds.), *2007 World Conference on Mass Customization and Personalization*. Cambridge: MIT.

Mugge, R., & Schoormans, J. P. L. (2005). Product personalisatie. Kan de consument zijn eigen product ontwerpen? (Product personalization. Can a consumer design his own product?). *Product, November,* 9-11.

Mugge, R., Schoormans, J. P. L., & Schifferstein, H. N. J. (2009a). Emotional bonding with personalized products. *Journal of Engineering Design, 20*(5), 467–476. doi:10.1080/09544820802698550

Mugge, R., Schoormans, J. P. L., & Schifferstein, H. N. J. (2009b). Incorporating consumers in the design of their own products: The dimensions of product personalisation . *CoDesign, 5*(2), 79–97. doi:10.1080/15710880802666416

Peck, J., & Childers, T. L. (2003). Individual differences in haptic information processing: The "need for touch" scale. *The Journal of Consumer Research, 30*(December), 430–442. doi:10.1086/378619

Piller, F., Koch, M., Möslein, K., & Schubert, P. (2003). *Managing high variety: How to overcome the mass confusion phenomenon of customer co-design.* Paper presented at the EURAM 2003 Conference, Milan, Italy.

Piller, F., & Müller, M. (2004). A new marketing approach to mass customisation. *International Journal of Computer Integrated Manufacturing, 17*(7), 583–593. doi:10.1080/0951192042000273140

Piller, F., Schubert, P., Koch, M., & Möslein, K. (2005). Overcoming mass confusion: Collaborative customer co-design in online communities. *Journal of Computer-Mediated Communication, 10*(4). http://jcmc.indiana.edu/vol10/issue14/piller.html.

Pine, B. J., II. (1993). *Mass customization. The new frontier in business competition.* Boston, MA: Harvard Business School Press.

Randall, T., Terwiesch, C., & Ulrich, K. (2007). User design of customized products. *Marketing Science, 26*(2), 268–280. doi:10.1287/mksc.1050.0116

Schoormans, J. P. L., Morel, K. P. N., & Zheng, Y. (2006). Consumer chatting during online shopping: An exploratory study. In G. J. Avlonitis, N. Papavassiliou & P. Papastathopoulou (Eds.), *Proceedings of the 35th EMAC conference.* Athens: EMAC.

Schreier, M. (2006). The value increment of mass-customized products: An empirical assessment and conceptual analysis of its explanation. *Journal of Consumer Behaviour, 5*(July-August), 317–327. doi:10.1002/cb.183

Schultz, S. E., Kleine, R. E., & Kernan, J. B. (1989). 'These are a few of my favorite things.' Toward an explication of attachment as a consumer behavior construct. In T. Scrull (Ed.), *Advances in Consumer Research* (Vol. 16, pp. 359-366). Provo: UT: Association for Consumer Research.

Tepper Tian, K., Bearden, W. O., & Hunter, G. L. (2001). Consumers' need for uniqueness: Scale development and validation. *The Journal of Consumer Research, 28*(June), 50–66. doi:10.1086/321947

Thomke, S., & Von Hippel, E. (2002). Customers as innovators. A new way to create value. *Harvard Business Review, 80*(4), 74–81.

Toffler, A. (1980). *The third wave.* New York: Bantam Books.

Vink, N. Y. (2003). *Customization Choices.* Delft: Delft University of Technology.

von Hippel, E. (2005). *Democratizing innovation.* Cambridge: The MIT Press.

Weightman, D., & McDonagh, D. (2003). People are doing it for themselves. In B. Hanington & J. Forlizzi (Eds.), *International Conference on Designing Pleasurable Products and Interfaces (DPPI'03)* (pp. 34-39). Pittsburgh, PA.

Zipkin, P. (2001). The limits of mass customization. *Sloan Management Review, 42*(3), 81–87.

Chapter 3
Resource Implications of Manufacturer– Customer Interactions in Mass Customization

Emmanuel T. Kodzi Jr.
Strathmore Business School, Kenya

Rado Gazo
Purdue University, USA

ABSTRACT

This chapter explores the relationship between the capabilities of a manufacturing system and the participation of end-users in order determination. Using a simulated customer-direct mode for the customization of selected wood products, the authors examine manufacturing system attributes that enhance direct interaction with customers. The authors discuss strategic implications of the choice of customization-mode on fundamental resource requirements, and set out practical recommendations for deploying mass customization as a competitive strategy. End-user participation in configuring customized products requires that beyond desirable attributes such as agility in manufacturing systems, compelling service capability be developed to enhance customer experience.

INTRODUCTION

Given a specific mode of customization, an organization's ability to engage customers in collaborative order determination is a function of the resources it possesses or develops (Brown and Bessant, 2003; Hart, 1995). The desired resources for mass customization include the capability to manage the increased levels of complexity associated with inte-

grating individual customer preferences into product offerings in a cost-effective way (Mok et al, 2000). To enhance successful collaboration, market-driven organizations must also posses the capability for linking customers effectively (Day, 1994). Relative to a scenario where the order-determination process is moderated by retail channels, a manufacturing system that interfaces directly with the end-user may require a more comprehensive deployment of resources. However, though customization may be

DOI: 10.4018/978-1-60566-260-2.ch003

offered through retailers (especially where product options may be selected and incorporated at the point of sale) retail-driven customization may not always be an attractive proposition from the standpoint of managing a manufacturer's brand. The opportunity to leverage customers' loyalty to a brand, and its implications for trust and long-term relationships, may provide sufficient basis for a manufacturer to consider direct collaboration with the customer (Berger et al, 2005). Thus, the complexity inherent in direct collaboration must be recognized and managed proactively through building the necessary capabilities.

In a study of a customer-direct offer of customized signage, Kubiak (1993) outlined how the iterative co-design process for determining and fulfilling customer preferences slowed down operations and increased costs as a company expanded its hitherto successful offering. The inability of the company to provide guidance for customers severely eroded earlier competitive gains; cross-training of employees needed to support the consultation for co-design was found to be lacking. We consider the proposition that specifying the key resource interactions that exist at the onset of the customization offer, can facilitate a more systematic translation of the essential mass customization principles in the growth phase of the business. From a resource development perspective, any competitive gains from an initial offer of customization could then be more easily retained as the company's operations expand.

Resources and capabilities are critical considerations in formulating a strategy that might deliver a sustained competitive advantage to any company. The resource-based view of the firm essentially highlights the role of strategic resources and capabilities in driving economic value and sustainable competitive advantage (Barney, 1991; Conner 1991; Grant, 1991). Specific resources such as customer relationship networks, supplier relationship networks, reputation, market knowledge, materials management, and a com-

petent manufacturing workforce are important considerations in resource development (Rangone, 1999). However, to contribute to a sustainable competitive advantage, these resources must also be harnessed in ways that differentiate how specific companies fulfill customer needs; incorporate features that are difficult to imitate; and have the potential to generate long-term benefits as the company exploits the associated advantages in the marketplace (Collis and Montgomery, 1995). For example, resources that are integrated with the knowledge-base of an organization may be considered to be significant contributors to competitive advantage because they cannot be easily imitated. This "knowledge-based view" of the firm expands the resource-based view by focusing on knowledge-based capabilities as an organization's most critical resource for sustaining superior performance (Spender 1996; Grant 1996; Nonaka 1995; Kogut and Zander 1992). The literature also addresses the "relational view" of the firm and recognizes that a firm's critical resources may be rooted in inter-firm relationships (Das and Teng, 2000; Afuah, 2000; Araujo et al., 1999; Dyer and Sing 1988). Macpherson et al (2004) suggest that the "relational elements of inter-firm transactions provide entrepreneurs with the opportunity to expand their organizational capabilities". Thus, a firm's critical resources may possibly be external to the firm itself. However, it is not our intention in this paper to address this extended resource-based view of the firm (Squire et al, 2006; Mathews, 2003). Neither do we specifically discuss the "relational view" nor the "knowledge based view" of the firm. Rather, we limit our scope to the resource interactions that are required for customization in a customer-direct mode at the firm level. The value in studying resource interactions within this limited scope lies in the fact that regardless of exogenous network factors, firms seeking to pursue mass customization in any form need to harness the contribution of specific capabilities within their manufacturing systems to be effective (Brown and Bessant, 2003). This study uses a simplified customer-direct model to examine *elemental forms* of these resource interactions. Our expectation is that a simplified model that provides the opportunity to focus on the very basic issues will be useful for deriving general application, with the applied contextual caveats.

The objective of the study is to assess the extent to which direct end-user participation constrains, or is constrained by, the resources within a manufacturing system. We examine what manufacturing system attributes enhance this direct interaction, and explore interdependencies between customer participation in order determination and the capabilities of a manufacturing system. Based on the dynamics of customer interactions in a simulated customizing scenario for selected wood products, this study provides research insights on manufacturer-customer interactions, given a strategic choice of collaboration mode.

Methods

This exploratory study was conducted in 2006 with the help of a team of faculty and students from the Wood Research Laboratory at Purdue University. The study design was informed by Gilmore and Pine's (1997) four approaches to mass customization – collaborative, transparent, adaptive and cosmetic customization. Given the limitation of test-scale resources at the Wood Research Laboratory, cosmetic customization was the most reasonable form of customization to simulate because it presents the least complex scenario for customer involvement. In cosmetic customization a standard product is fundamentally unchanged for different customers; however, the product is represented in different ways to reflect the preferences of each customer within the limits of the product offering itself. The study context was the fulfilling of customized orders for engraved wooden nameplates and cutting boards; it was timed to coincide with an open day hosted by the Department of Forestry and Natural Resources as a way of enlisting the participation

of a wide variety of visitors to contemporaneous campus-wide activities. Patrons were invited to personalize three sizes of nameplates or two sizes of cutting boards by having an inscription of their choice engraved on them. Thus, though the basic product types were fundamentally unchanged, every finished order met the expressed preferences of particular customers.

Study Design

The study was designed to offer an affordable personalized product by facilitating seamless linkage between a standardized base structure and a customized engraving operation - in line with Kubiak's (1993) study of customized company signs. Interaction between customers and the manufacturing system was promoted by presenting customers with the opportunity to select size and lettering parameters for the nameplates or cutting board types they chose. The applicability of this simulation project to furniture customization, which informed our study context, relates to the process of selecting options from a range of components for a given product family. This customization model is used by some acclaimed mass customizers of furniture[1], though a wider range of configurable options and other ramifications are involved. The selection options are limited in this simulated study, but the principles are comparable.

In spite of the simplicity of our approach, this study also made provision for the requirement that to implement mass customization effectively, products need to be "designed in synergistic families around standardized parts, with minimal setup variation, and for machining by Computer Numeric Control (CNC) programmable machine tools" (Andersson, 2004). In this case, the two different products (nameplates and cutting boards) were designed in such a way as to eliminate variation in the setups for a CNC router and to use similar tooling while giving customers the opportunity to personalize the final product.

Figure 1. Simplified schematic of production stages

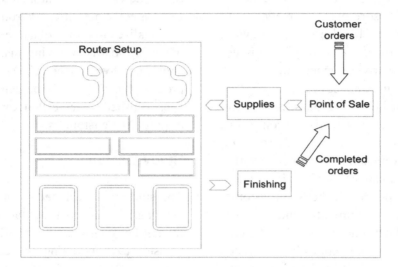

The main machines used were a CNC Router (3-Axis Turret Head) and a desktop computer. These two machines represent the functions of machining centers, and order-capturing centers; the computer station functioned as the point of sale at which customers placed orders, while a major part of the manufacturing operation was completed on the CNC router. The concurrent use of these centers of operation facilitated an examination of how manufacturing and service delivery could be integrated effectively in a real life situation.

Orders received were entered into a computer-aided design (CAD) program and a code was generated by the computer-aided manufacturing (CAM) system. Based on the electronic input from the point of sale, customer preferences were then executed on the CNC router. Our recognition of information technology (IT) as an interface tool for coordinating the customization process under-scored its critical role in this study; IT complements the interaction of key elements in customer-centric business strategies (Tiwana, 2001). The flow process for orders is represented by Figure 1 below. "Supplies" include the wood blanks that were used to manufacture the products, and "finishing"

involves the final operations that enhance their aesthetic appeal. The "router setup" shows only a scaled schematic of 11 preconfigured settings on the router table for cutting out the products (2 and 3 units each of two types of cutting boards, and 2 units each of three sizes of nameplates could be manufactured simultaneously).

The customer was allowed to observe the entire process, as a way of prompting additional feedback. Observations from the customization project were documented and reviewed with members of the project team. Implications of these observations and reflections were then analyzed in the context of customer demand versus resource adequacy, and compared with earlier studies such as Kubiak (1993) to explore key insights.

Project Details

The detailed actions involved in this study are now presented under the sub-headings "Preparation", "Perception" and "Processing" using the approach of Kodzi's (2006) 3P Operational Model for Mass Customization. This model basically shows that in a market environment that reflects changing customer preferences and business pressures, manufacturers need to develop functional combinations of **preparation**, **perception**, and **processing** to offer customization on a sustainable basis. We apply the model to this project description under the following sub-headings:

i.   Preparation - activities that preceded the public phase of the study, including raw material selection and specification, setup of manufacturing centers, and training of personnel

ii. Perception - specific efforts to improve the customer experience by highlighting distinctive features of the product offering, and by leveraging proactive service capability in direct interaction with customers

iii. Processing - the stepwise route from receiving variable batch size orders, until the finished product was delivered to the customer.

Preparation

This section highlights efforts aimed at allowing customers the flexibility to personalize the product in a utility-maximizing fashion, while preserving the technical and distinctive attributes of our product offering. We researched wood properties and production detailing for the products offered to ensure optimal raw material specification, and to enhance process flow on the router. We selected hard maple (*Acer saccharum*) as the basic raw material because it imparts no taste to food, and has a high resistance to abrasion and wear[2] – useful properties for cutting boards. Its close, fine, uniform texture and its different hues of reddish brown also make it an attractive wood for nameplates. This instance of dual application for the same basic raw material is an early expression of deriving economies of scope in customer-specific applications. The design of nameplates and cutting boards thus took into account complementary requirements that enhance the customization process:

- the need to offer more options to customers (not only in lettering size and style but also in edge detailing and finish)
- the need to reduce complexity within the manufacturing system (by the use of standardized raw material inputs and processes), and
- the need to take advantage of scope economies (by using similar processes to simultaneously manufacture different products).

All the boards were planed and edged to predetermined dimensions (a thickness of 0.625″ had been previously specified through tests), and then sanded for final thickness and surface quality. The boards were arranged in workshop bins for easy identification, and to facilitate a spontaneous supply of standardized raw material inputs.

Order-entry personnel received training to enable them to take orders using a defined format, and to accurately enter order information into the CAD software. The training step recognizes the role of human resource at the customer interface, and increases the chances of the entire setup running without incident. A limitation was placed on the maximum number of letters that customers could specify for each of the five possible base products; this was clearly stipulated on the order form along with prices for each option, and a range font types and sizes.

Perception

Prior to receiving orders at the beginning of the customization project some initial runs were conducted, and their outputs displayed for advertisement. The customizable nameplates and cutting boards were thus introduced to visitors and the first few orders were placed, after which there was a practically steady flow of orders till the close of business. The customization setup presented to the public was perceived by visitors as a means by which some of their needs/wants – perhaps not previously conceived – could be fulfilled. The possibility of personalizing the offered products and the attractiveness of the wood species we offered now formed the basis for inviting customers to configure their lettering parameters and other options. Customers showed a willingness to work with the project team to clarify their preferences for each unique product.

Processing

This section details the stepwise process from receiving an order till the finished product was delivered to the customer. Customer preferences received at the point of sale, were programmed for subsequent routing using a two-stage process. The first stage included complete cutting, routing and shaping of the boards, with a process-orientation allowing similar operations on all eleven boards to be completed simultaneously as illustrated in Figure 1 above. The tailored engraving of letters according to the specification of the customer was done in the second stage. The modular approach adopted allowed for new customer-specific preferences to be superimposed efficiently over basic logic embedded in subroutines. The two stages of the routing process could run with a time lag, or they could run sequentially, depending on the length of the order queue. The manufacturing system was designed to work with variable batch sizes, including one.

The intended product was rendered in 2D and 3D formats during the programming step for the joint review of customers and order-entry personnel. The involvement of the customer at this point also improved the feedback loop, and allowed for double-checking specification accuracy before the routing code was generated. The order entry and programming steps were synchronized with the routing settings such that information transfer between the two workstations required no additional adjustments. It was important to establish this seamless transfer of information to enhance system efficiency.

The routed pieces were finished according to the specification of the customer, and the final product delivered after checking that payment had been made in full. The finishing operation was simple, though it also highlighted the need to establish an effective connection between the order entry step and the finishing operation. In a more complex situation, immediate transfer of finishing information would allow the finishing cell to anticipate the resources that would be required for an order that has recently entered the production system. Details of how each item is to be finished, would then be provided when the item or group of items are received from the router, to facilitate an accurate match of order specifications. The value of such prompt and complete sharing of information is in reducing the variation in lead time (and increasing the service level) – thereby eliminating the possibility having an order delivered without the specified finish, or conversely to have a finish on an item that was specified unfinished.

Key Observations and Insights

In this section we explore the applicability of some key insights following team debriefing, and a discussion of the observed interactions between customers and the manufacturing system. This study recorded 44 completed unique orders by the end of the project, representing an average rate of one processed order every eight minutes (this rate would be higher if outright sales of the routed, but non-lettered blanks were included). Within the scope of the study, each completed order represents a learning opportunity for interaction-driven resource development.

Customers had been allowed the freedom to select the specific wood blank used for their orders, and some customers took the trouble to further enhance the aesthetic appeal of their finished products by selecting boards with curly or "fiddle back" grain patterns. This freedom served to improve the customer experience with the customization project, though it also highlighted the challenge of satisfying individualized needs in a mass market. Customers generally selected the size of nameplate or cutting board, and determined what inscription to engrave on it, based on the available options. However, fourteen percent of all the orders placed specified parameters that were beyond the initial configuration range offered - some orders required different positioning of letters, different fonts, and a different styling of word groups. The incidence of customers specifying parameter changes beyond the designated configuration range suggests that our offer of lettering options stimulated thought processes in certain customers that generated new ideas and possibilities beyond what we initially offered. This is the essence of customer innovation (Thomke and Von Hippel, 2002). Basically, by equipping customers with the tools to co-design products of their choice, manufacturing companies encourage customer innovation, rather than view it as a distraction. In this customization study, the design discovery process of some customers included particular cases of 'above-average' time invested to explore several font possibilities and obtain the one that was 'just right', not to mention the different size specification that came with it. Taking cognizance of the "moment of truth" concept in service industries, we engaged these 'above-average-customers' in collaborative exploration of the customization window to clarify their preferences and to locate the region of convergence between our offering and their expectations.

The collaborative exploration discussed above underscores the need for expert input at the point of sale, without which the preferences of this group of more sophisticated customers would not have been fulfilled. It appears that by their offer of customization, companies implicitly invite customers to interact more directly with the manufacturing system. The responsibility associated with this invitation must be recognized and managed. For example, the increased involvement by potential buyers in specifying the product resulted in greater variability in the order process and a reduction of the process speed for the project under study. These effects may have been construed as an unwelcome interruption by some members of our team. However, the pre-established rule was to guide customer choices objectively at the point of sale rather than react adversely to their stringent demands, and to explore a "solution space" that would fit customer expectations. Practically, given the uniqueness and variety that accompanies individual customer desires, it is necessary to develop both the relational skills and the competence of company associates to accommodate variation without significantly reducing the process rate. Obviously, not all products require human interaction during the configuration process as may be the case for wooden furniture. However, the customization experience must minimize frustration and shore up confidence in the customer regarding attributes of the final product to be purchased, regardless of whether the customization process is executed online or at a physical point of sale. If a company possesses a service capability that is commensurate with the anticipated levels of direct customer involvement, then collaborative interaction in the co-design process is encouraged. Additionally, if the customizing company has taken the time to conduct the necessary background research to assure high levels of performance-in-service, the option to personalize a product can be expected to increase the attachment of the customer to the product in the long term. In this way, the business defines its market identity using both the distinctive features of its product offering, and its service capability. Thus, an effective customization offer could potentially translate into positive customer perception of the company's brand (Shocker et al, 1994).

The extended time spent with the 'above-average' customers did not attract a price premium to cover the associated overhead cost. Customers had accepted the prices of the nameplates and cutting boards at the point of sale, and there was no possibility for an increase. Kodzi *et al*, (2007) indicate that the cost of a customized product must not communicate a penalty for the level of personalization or order size within a given solution space. Thus, the implications of customer involvement must be accounted for ahead of time in a fixed-price offer, given the market perception of what price is reasonable for a particular product configuration. It is of interest though, to explore the tradeoffs in this set up between the cost of service rendered at the manufacturing interface and the satisfaction of the client. The obvious limitation of not continuing this operation beyond one day leaves to conjecture the potential impact of immediate customer satisfaction on loyalty. However, an important indication of customer satisfaction that we were unaware of during the public phase of the study was that one of the more demanding customers did send us a 'thank you note' the next business day. The opportunity for building trust and long-term brand loyalty within a given market segment, or for increasing customer frustration on the other hand, is inherent in this type of interaction.

It was possible, within the manufacturing setup, not only to change font specifications as we have previously noted, but also to change the edge detailing of the different board configurations based on available tooling. However, to simplify the range of choices available, the stipulated tooling configurations were not presented upfront as negotiable. In this particular case, edge detailing may not have been a critical feature for customization because no customers required profile or dimensional changes during the production runs. This observation suggests that the customization window (the range of configuration options) must be specified carefully to include the features that are critical for a particular customization offer, yet posses the capability to incorporate other 'minor' features as might be requested in the context of an ongoing business.

The process bottleneck at the point of sale resulting from variability in the order patterns could be a function of the simplicity of the study. Process speed would be less constrained if orders were taken in parallel, as would have been the case in a real-life enterprise. However, the earlier manufacturing setup using a postponement mode also compensated for variation in the order-flow rate. Such a system improvement is a great help to company associates, and a means by which manufacturers offering customization could develop flexible capabilities. These observations are pointers to internal challenges that might limit responsiveness in a manufacturing system. They also highlight the learning curve benefits that could play a defining role in a customization environment.

Between production cycles it was possible to increase the stock of the standard profiled nameplates and cutting boards, some of which were bought as is. However, overstocking led to a markdown for the sale of excess inventory at the close of business. Had this been an ongoing enterprise, there would have been no attempt to quickly dispose of a day's excess inventory. The setups on the router were made to accommodate several production runs such that the excess inventory would have been used subsequently. Furthermore, in a real-life enterprise in which material flows are governed by a kanban system, the inventory levels would have been raised only to a predetermined maximum.

A manufacturing setback occurred in one particular order when a program to write 'KITCHEN', though spelled correctly in the order software, appeared as 'KITCHFN' leaving out one line. It appears that the post-processor malfunctioned, so the software was restarted to continue the process. However, for customer satisfaction, this anomaly implied that the defective piece had to be re-programmed and re-cut. Re-work is costly and constitutes an opportunity loss. Investment in appropriate technology is one way to achieve high quality and accuracy. Thus, a real-life enterprise needs to evaluate the trade-off between reworking a single product or part if necessary, and assuring consistent overall quality. The foregoing statement begs the question, what is the value of additional investment in state of the art equipment, relative to long term savings in quality-related costs. Two other instances of rework resulted from a specification error at the point of sale and a wrong process detail in routing specifications. Obviously, the interface between humans and machines is an important quality consideration that must not be ignored in the manufacturing system. Further research could investigate the role of rework management in a customization environment.

Lessons Learned

The key principles arising from this customization study include:

- A context must be defined for the customized offering that a company desires to make public. A mass customizing company cannot advertise that it will do 'any and everything' the customer specifies. The technical and other resource constraints must be considered carefully in defining the extent of configuration opportunity.
- By offering the opportunity to customize, manufacturers sharpen the sense of choice of end-users and invite them to interact more directly with the manufacturing system. By this means, manufacturers can derive benefits from the creativity of end-users. However, this interaction could potentially evoke dissatisfaction if the manufacturer does not develop a proactive service capability.
- This study confirms the need for a configuration toolkit that effectively captures and incorporates customer preferences within a customization window, for a mass-market situation. Such configuration software, under-girded with expert technical detailing, better disposes manufacturers to endorse

customer innovation. The manufacturing window might be re-sized through feedback analysis, to focus on those attributes that are critical to customize for a given product.

- Human capacity constraints introduce challenges at each non-automated transition point of the customization process in terms of collating, processing and transferring relevant information and item parts to other work cells. Specialized training could compensate somewhat for inadequate expert systems. The order capturing software at the point of sale must also have parallel processing ports to reduce queue lengths; the software must interface seamlessly with the manufacturing setup to minimize process bottlenecks.
- The manufacturing processes must be carefully monitored to avoid any glitches – as in malfunctioning of post processors. Quality control cannot be done at the end of production, but must be integrated into each stage of the process.

SUMMARY AND CONCLUSION

This study examined how resource demands are imposed on the manufacturing system by direct end-user participation. There is a clear need to develop a compelling service capability in the customization of certain products, and this is not without real-life application. In the wooden furniture context, for example, purchasing decisions appear to be influenced more by physical products than by virtual representations. Although customers could explore options online and make a decision, it is useful to have customers directly experience the sample item – as in "tactile evaluation" at local stores (Oh et al, 2004). Through the feedback inherent in mass customization, manufacturers could then refine their customization window for better satisfaction of customer requests. Some companies have a policy of directly interacting with customers in exploring possible options and exchanging ideas for the purpose of personalizing the purchasing decision for customized furniture. Similarly, other companies acknowledge the downsides of not "seeing or feeling your furniture till it is delivered to your door". Some also present their virtual showrooms as a place to "gather ideas, to dream, and to get familiarized" with the offered range of products[3]; however, potential buyers are encouraged to complete the product configuration at a designated point of sale, and personally experience the dynamics of purchasing furniture. The customer experience is a significant success factor in the process of customizing furniture, and resources must be deployed to that end. It is conceivable that there are several other product types for which managing customer interaction is critical.

A resource-based view of customization modes clearly highlights the need to develop specific capabilities that might be otherwise unimportant to a manufacturer linked only to traditional distribution chains. For example, proactive service capability has the potential to allow for the fulfillment of customer needs in ways that differentiate a company from its competitors.

In this chapter we have drawn attention to issues like background preparation in terms of building capacity to offer customization effectively in the chosen mode, including developing a response plan to expressed customer innovation at the point of sale. We have also underscored the need to understand the characteristics of the actual product being customized, and which features are important to customers; and to identify and mitigate potential constraints such as human expertise, system design, and technological appropriateness. As previously mentioned, our scope in this study limits the investigation of the contribution of resources such as customer relationship networks, supplier relationship networks, reputation, market knowledge, and materials management to enhancing customer loyalty though we have alluded to the

issues in the forgoing discussion. It is clear, however, that the enrichment of the knowledge-base of a company that goes through such a structured customization process is not trivial. Thus, we also leverage this expectation of knowledge-based capability development as a link to the dimensions of sustainable competitive advantage discussed by Collis and Montgomery (1995). In this regard we refer to (knowledge-based) resources being difficult to imitate or substitute due to features such as physical uniqueness, path dependency, casual ambiguity, and economic deterrence; and fulfilling customer needs in ways that differentiate the company from its competitors. Our research insights on manufacturer-customer interactions do support the view of developing specific skill-sets in response to a chosen generic mode of collaboration. Given that these findings emerged from a very simplified customization model, we expect strong applicability in other situations with the applied contextual caveats. Further research will examine how these issues play out in a real-life furniture customization enterprise, and draw comparisons with other industries such as customized banner-printing, which use methods similar to those described in this chapter.

REFERENCES

Afuah, A. (2000). How much do your co-opetitors' capabilities matter in the face of technological change? *Strategic Management Journal*, *21*, 387–404. doi:10.1002/(SICI)1097-0266(200003)21:3<397::AID-SMJ88>3.0.CO;2-1

Anderson, D.M. (2004). *Build-to-Order & Mass Customization, the Ultimate Supply Chain and Lean Manufacturing Strategy for Low-Cost On-Demand Production without Forecasts or Inventory*. Cambria, CA: CIM Press.

Araujo, L., Dubois, A., & Gadde, L. E. (1999). Managing interfaces with suppliers. *Industrial Marketing Management, 28*, 497–506. doi:10.1016/S0019-8501(99)00077-2

Barney, J. B. (1991). Firm resources and sustained competitive advantage. *Journal of Management, 17*(1), 99–120. doi:10.1177/014920639101700108

Berger, C., Möslein, K., Piller, F. T., & Reichwald, R. (2005). Cooperation between Manufacturers, Retailers, and Customers for User Co-Design: Learning from Exploratory Research. *European Management Review, 1*, 70–87. doi:10.1057/palgrave.emr.1500030

Brown, S., & Bessant, J. (2003). The manufacturing strategy-capabilities links in mass customization and agile manufacturing – an exploratory study. *International Journal of Operations & Production Management, 23*(7), 707–730. doi:10.1108/01443570310481522

Collis, D. J., & Montgomery, C. A. (2005). *Corporate Strategy: A Resource-Based Approach*, (2nd Ed.). Boston: McGraw-Hill/Irwin.

Conner, K. R. (1991). A Historical Comparison of the Resource-Based Theory and Five Schools of Thought Within Industrial Organization Economics: Do We Have a New Theory of the Firm? *Journal of Management, 17*(1), 121–154. doi:10.1177/014920639101700109

Das, T. K., & Teng, B. S. (2000). A resource-based theory of strategic alliances. *Journal of Management, 26*(1), 31–61. doi:10.1016/S0149-2063(99)00037-9

Day, G. S. (1994). The Capabilities of Market-Driven Organizations. *Journal of Marketing, 58*(4), 37–52. doi:10.2307/1251915

Dyer, J. H., & Singh, H. (1998). The Relational View: Cooperative Strategy and Sources of Interorganisational Competitive Advantage. *Academy of Management Review, 23*(4), 660–679. doi:10.2307/259056

Gilmore, J. H., & Pine, B. J. (1997). The Four Faces of Mass Customization. *Harvard Business Review, 75*(1), 91–101.

Grant, R. M. (1991). The Resource-Based Theory of Competitive Advantage: Implications for Strategy Formulation. *California Management Review, 33*(3), 114–135.

Grant, R.M., (1996). Toward a Knowledge-Based Theory of the Firm. *Strategic Management Journal* (17), Winter Special Issue, 109-122.

Hart, C. H. L. (1995). Mass customization: conceptual underpinnings, opportunities and limits. *International Journal of Service Industry Management, 6*(2), 36–45. doi:10.1108/09564239510084932

Kodzi, E. T., Jr. (2006). *Mass Customization as a Framework for Manufacturing Transformations in the US Furniture Industry*. West Lafayette, IN: Purdue University, Department of Forestry and Natural Resources.

Kodzi, E. T. Jr, Lihra, T., & Gazo, R. (2007). Process Transformation Mandates for Manufacturing Customized Furniture. *Journal of Forest Products Business Research, 4*(8).

Kogut, B., & Zander, U. (1992). Knowledge of the Firm, Combinative Capabilities, and the Replication of Technology. *Organization Science, 3*(3), 383–397. doi:10.1287/orsc.3.3.383

Kubiak, J. (1993). A Joint Venture in Mass Customization. *Planning Review, 21*(4), 25.

Macpherson, A., Jones, O., & Zhang, M. (2004). Evolution or revolution? Dynamic capabilities in a knowledge-dependent firm. *R & D Management, 34*(2), 161–177. doi:10.1111/j.1467-9310.2004.00331.x

Mathews, J. A. (2003). Competitive dynamics and economic learning: an extended resource-based view. *Industrial and Corporate Change, 12*(1), 115–145. doi:10.1093/icc/12.1.115

Mok, C., Stutts, A. T., & Wong, L. (2000). Mass Customization in the Hospitality Industry: Concepts and Applications. In *Proceedings of the Fourth International Conference, Tourism in Southeast Asia & Indo-China: Development marketing and sustainability* (pp. 123-139), Singapore.

Nonaka, I., & Takeuchi, H. (1995). *The Knowledge-Creating Company: How Japanese Companies Create the Dynamics of Innovation.* New York: Oxford University Press.

Oh, Y., Yoon, S., & Hawley, J. (2004). What Virtual Reality can offer to the Furniture Industry. *Journal of Textile and Apparel Technology and Management, 4*(1).

Rangone, A. (1999). A Resource-Based Approach to Strategy Analysis in Small-Medium Sized Enterprises. *Small Business Economics, 12*(3), 233–248. doi:10.1023/A:1008046917465

Shocker, A. D., Srivastava, R. K., & Ruekert, R. W. (1994). Challenges and Opportunities Facing Brand Management: An Introduction to the Special Issue. *JMR, Journal of Marketing Research, 31*(2), 149–158. doi:10.2307/3152190

Spender, J. C., (1996). Making Knowledge the Basis of a Dynamic Theory of the Firm. *Strategic Management Journal,* (17), Special Issues, 45-62.

Squire, B., Cousins, P. D., & Brown, S. (2006). Collaborating for customization: an extended resource-based view of the firm. *Int. J. Productivity and Quality Management, 1*(1/2), 8–25.

Thomke, S., & Von Hippel, E. (2002). Customers as Innovators: A New Way to Create Value. *Harvard Business Review, 80*(4).

Tiwana, A. (2001). *The essential guide to knowledge management: e-business and CRM applications.* Upper Saddle River, NJ: Prentice Hall.

ENDNOTES

[1] For example http://www.canadel.com/

[2] American Harwood Information Center http://www.hardwood.org/species_guide/

[3] See http://www.lofgrens.com/CustomService/FAQ.html; http://www.boxxelements.com/; and http://www.furnituredepot.com/ for examples

Chapter 4
A Multi–Agent System for Recommending Customized Families of Products

Seung Ki Moon
Texas A&M University, USA

Timothy W. Simpson
The Pennsylvania State University, USA

Soundar R.T. Kumara
The Pennsylvania State University, USA

ABSTRACT

Electronic markets and web-based content have improved traditional product development processes by increasing the participation of customers and applying various recommender systems to satisfy individual customer needs. This chapter introduces a multi-agent system to support customized product family design by recommending customers' preferences in dynamic electronic market environments. In the proposed system, a market-based learning mechanism is applied to determine the customers' preferences for recommending appropriate products to customers in the product family. The authors demonstrate the implementation of the proposed recommender system using a multi-agent framework. Through experiments, they illustrate that the proposed recommender system can determine the preference values of products for customized recommendation and market segment design in various electronic market environments.

1. INTRODUCTION

Mass customization depends on a company's ability to provide customized products based on economical and flexible development and production systems (Silveria et al., 2001). Electronic markets

DOI: 10.4018/978-1-60566-260-2.ch004

and web-based content have improved traditional product development processes by increasing the participation of customers and applying various recommender systems to satisfy individual customer needs. With the potential of reducing transaction costs between providers and customers, the applications of electronic markets are dramatically increasing in various industries (Bakos, 1997).

The growing number of electronic markets for product development has significantly increased information related to design and the complexity of transactions, making it difficult to control the electronic markets with human resources (Padovan et al., 2002). In recent years, agents and multi-agent systems have become a powerful and prevalent methodology to investigate and develop complex systems integrating human factors (Ezzedine et al., 2005; Monticino et al., 2007).

The division of a market into homogenous groups of consumers' preference is known as market segment (Meyer and Lehnerd, 1997). Because market segment provides guidelines for determining and directing customer requirements, it can be used to identify the criteria for designing product family more accurately and non-hypothetically (Simpson et al., 2005). In an electronic market environment, customers' preferences can be determined by information related to customers' purchasing patterns and evaluations for products. Product family planning is a way to achieve cost-effective mass customization by allowing highly differentiated products to be developed from a common platform while targeting products to distinct market segments (Simpson et al., 2005).

The objective of this chapter is to introduce a multi-agent system to recommend customized families of products in dynamic electronic market environments. The architectures of agents in a multi-agent system (MAS) are described including specifying their roles and knowledge. The proposed recommender system uses a market-based learning mechanism to determine customers' preference for recommending appropriate products to customers in a distributed and dynamic electronic market environment. In the proposed system, product preference values are identified from customers' preferences and are used to provide customers with customized product recommendations. A market-based learning mechanism is applied to determine the customers' preferences for recommending appropriate products to cus-

tomers in the product family. We demonstrate the implementation of the proposed recommender system using a multi-agent framework.

2. BACKGROUND

A product family is a group of related products based on a product platform, facilitating mass customization by providing a variety of products for different market segments cost-effectively (Simpson et al. 2005). A product platform is the set of features, components or subsystems that remain constant from product to product, within a given product family. A successful product family depends on how well the trade-off between the economic benefits and performance losses incurred from having a shared platform are managed. There are two recognized approaches to product family design (Simpson et al., 2001): (1) a *top-down (proactive platform) approach* and (2) a *bottom-up (reactive redesign) approach*. In the top-down approach, a company's strategy provides a guide line for developing a family of products based on a product platform and its derivatives. Meanwhile, the bottom-up approach is focused on redesigning and/or consolidating a group of distinct products to standardize components for sharing and reusing. In platform-based product development, two common types for product families are *module-based product family* and *scale-based product family* (Simpson et al., 2001). Products in a module-based product family are obtained by adding, substituting, and/or removing one or more modules from the platform. In a scale-based product family, products are created by scaling one or more variables related to the platform design to satisfy a variety of market niches.

A multi-agent system is an appropriate tool to design and implement a system for integrating information in a distributed environment because of its flexibility, scalability, and adaptability (Blecker et al., 2005; Lee et al., 2003; Monostori, et.al., 2006; Symenonidis et al., 2003). An agent has access to at least one and potentially many information sources and is able to collate and manipulate information obtained from these sources in order to answer queries posed by users and other information agents (Wooldridge, 2002). Since information integration for product design can be achieved through task decomposition, collaboration, and negotiation (Shen et al., 2001), agent-based technologies provide a natural way to achieve information integration in a distributed environment (Liang & Huang, 2002).

Agent-based systems based on agents' roles and tasks can provide appropriate methods to solve product design problems by recommending and managing design knowledge and information (Blecker et al., 2005; Chira et al., 2006). Agents have been used extensively in product design and can be used in product family design if developed properly (Shooter et al., 2005). Madhusudan (2005) proposed a flexible agent-based coordination framework for new product development in a distributed design process system. A centralized decision-making and task sharing approach was used to coordinate design activities for flexible management of knowledge-intensive workflows. Jia et al. (2004) presented an agent-based system for coordinated product development and manufacturing that is able to execute all the tasks in a coordinated and flexible way. In the proposed system, they introduced two type agents: (1) a management agent and (2) various functional agents that represented domain experts in product development. They also defined specific performatives to support agent communications in the proposed system. Tan et al. (1996) developed a multi-agent framework to provide information that helps designers, engineers, and managers work together to improve initial designs by satisfying a wider variety of concerns. An intelligent agent network was integrated into the framework to provide flexibility in modeling individual's perspective as task knowledge for a concurrent design environment. Chira et al. (2006) proposed an agent-based architecture to support

the designer's decision making process based on ontologies related to current design standards in a distributed design environment. They used the set of cooperative agents to manipulate ontological instances and facilitate knowledge management in the proposed architecture. Moon et al. (2008) introduced a dynamic multi-agent system to support product family design by determining an appropriate platform level using a market-based negotiation mechanism in an electronic market environment.

In agent-based electronic markets, reinforcement learning algorithms were used to evaluate agent's behaviors or reputation based on transactions (Padovan et al., 2002; Tran and Cohen, 2002). Zacharia et al.(2001) presented a framework for agent-mediated knowledge marketplaces in which agents' reputations are established by dynamic pricing algorithms. Padovan et al. (2002) described the prototypical implementation of an automated subsequent treatment of reputation information in a multi-agent system. Tran and Cohen (2002) proposed a reinforcement learning and reputation-based algorithm for buyers and sellers in agent-based electronic marketplaces that maximized expected value of goods for buyers and expected profit for sellers. In his chapter, a reputation mechanism is applied to determine agents' preference values in an electronic market environment.

3. AN AGENT-BASED RECOMMENDER

Most of the previous research efforts related to product design and multi-agent systems have been focused on the agents' roles and tasks in a deterministic manufacturing environment. In product family design for mass customization, a method to produce a variety of products should be considered for dynamic and various market segments to reflect a variety of customer needs and preferences. In addition, dynamic factors, like

Figure 1. The Process of Developing a Family of Products

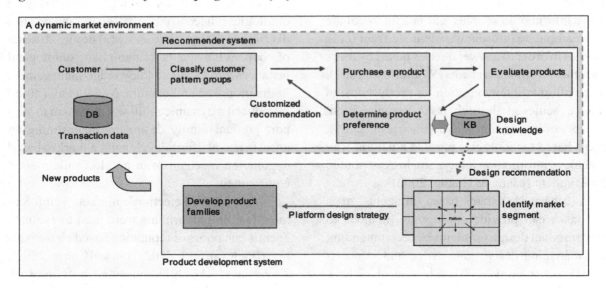

customer needs and trends, companies' strategies, and technologies, should be considered to increase customer's satisfaction in developing a family of products. Therefore, we need to address how to capture the dynamic factors for developing customized families of products in an agent-based recommender system. A market-based learning mechanism is one way to reflect various and dynamic market environments in a multi-agent system.

Figure 1 shows how the proposed recommender system supports the process of developing a family of products in a dynamic market environment. In the initial phase, customers are classified into groups based on their characteristics and preferences. Products are also clustered as groups for recommending to customers. Using transaction data and evaluation related to customers' purchases, we can identify product preferences for each customer group, and then products are recommended to customer groups based on these preferences. Product preference information can help develop market segmentation for product family design by identifying an initial platform based on functional requirements and trends among the recommended products. For example, Meyer and Lehnerd (1997)

introduced three platform leveraging strategies based on market segments within the gird during a conceptual design phase. The market segmentation grid is useful for both platform development and product family consolidation.

Based on the above mentioned recommender system, we propose a multi-agent system (MAS) architecture for determining product preferences in an electronic market environment. In this chapter, a multi-agent system (MAS) architecture is introduced by integrating an e-market environment and an agent-based recommender system as shown in Figure 2. The proposed architecture has two levels: (1) an electronic market (e-market) and (2) an agent-based recommender system. The e-market represents a dynamic market environment and the recommender system gives recommendations to determine products' preference using a market-based learning mechanism. These two levels are elaborated in the following two sections.

3.1 Electronic Market and Preference Value

A dynamic environment follows rudimentary e-market features such as business behaviors

Figure 2. Agent-Based Recommender System Architecture

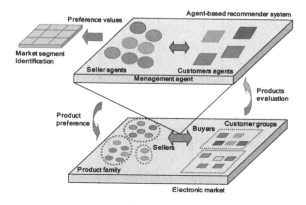

between buyers and sellers, dynamic pricing, and alternative selections (Padovan et al., 2002; Tran & Cohen, 2002). This e-market provides an agent environment where agents are economically motivated. The nature of an e-market allows economic agents (buyers and sellers) to freely enter or leave the e-market and negotiate with each other to obtain economic benefit. As shown in Figure 2, there are two types of agents for recommendation in an e-market: buyers and sellers. Buyers can be defined as auctioneers and sellers as bidders, and their goal is to maximize their own benefit. Depending on their strategy and market conditions, buyers and sellers purchase and provide products, respectively. Buyers can access all relevant sellers by querying information from them.

In this chapter, product preference values are defined as the degree of customers' preferences in relation to the product in an e-market. Customers' preferences are represented by the variation of their selections in the market and can be affected by their satisfaction, design technology and trends, price, and the quality of the products. A product having a high preference value in a family of products will be more strongly recommended to a customer. This customer can be related to a particular group having similar purchasing behavior. To determine a preference value effectively, we propose a learning algorithm that incorporates a

market mechanism. The next section introduces the proposed agent-based recommender system in detail.

3.2 A Multi-Agent System Architecture

To facilitate the process of recommending products, a multi-agent system (MAS) is proposed based on an electronic market environment. As shown in Figure 2, there are three types of agents in the proposed MAS: (1) a manager agent (MA), (2) customer agents (CAs), and (3) seller agents (SAs). The main task in the proposed MAS is to determine product preference values using a market-based learning algorithm for customized recommendation in a family of products. The MA provides an interface between the e-market and the MAS, and manages information related to customers and products in the e-market. The MA also classifies customers and products into groups based on their characteristics and assigns them to CAs and SAs by their roles and tasks, respectively. The MA manages CAs, SAs, the CA's requirements, and the SA's products. The MA supplies the product preferences for recommending customers to select a specific product in the e-market. Based on an auction mechanism, the CAs fulfill the requested tasks with SAs and return the result to the MA. The number of CAs is determined by the number of customer groups. After CAs perform their tasks, the information of the product preference is translated into new knowledge for identifying market segments. SAs can provide various products in terms of price and quality according to SAs' strategy or market situation. Therefore, a preference value can be used to recommend a specific product to a customer.

In the proposed MAS, agents use knowledge to decide actions for performing their roles. The knowledge can consist of constraints, functions, rules, and/or facts, which are associated with products and the system environment. Since agent activities are determined by their knowledge,

knowledge must be related to the overall system tasks and be accessible in an appropriate form (Chandra & Kamrani, 2003). Knowledge related to product preference is stored in a knowledge base and used to define agents' activities and tasks. The roles and knowledge of each agent are summarized in Table 1. In this chapter, reasoning about knowledge is used for inference and to capture knowledge in a distributed environment.

3.3 Learning Algorithm for Decision-Making

A preference value for a product can be affected by customer's preference and satisfaction, design technologies and trends, price, and quality. In this chapter, the quality and price of a product are used as the preference factors related to customers' preference and satisfaction. For determining the preference value in the proposed MAS, the approach of Tran and Cohen (2002) is applied to develop a learning mechanism, because the approach is suitable for an electronic market environment that consists of economically motivated agents.

To explain the process of determining the preference value in the proposed MAS, suppose that a CA requests a set of products to select an appropriate one for the customer. Let M be the set of product families, P be the set of prices, and I be the set of all CAs, and D be the set of all SAs in the marketplace. M, P, I, and D are finite sets. A CA determines the preference of all SAs in the market using the function $r^{CA}: D \mapsto (-1, 1)$, which is called the *CA's preference function*. The preference can be described as the value of the function according to customers' satisfaction. A preference value is set to 0 initially and updated based on transactions. To recommend a product and update the preference of a SA, a CA uses a utility function (u_i) that is computed from the difference between the expected product value (f_i) and the true product value (v_i):

Table 1. Agents' Roles and Knowledge for the Proposed Multi-Agent System

Agent	Roles	Knowledge
Manager Agent (MA)	• Interface with e-market and agent system • Classification for customers and products • Management for CAs and SAs	• Customer, MAs, and SAs information • Products information • Inference algorithm
Customer Agents (CAs)	• Decision-making: select a product • Product preference update • Evaluation for the quality of products	• Products information • Strategy for negotiation • Learning algorithm • SAs reputation and MA information
Seller Agents (SAs)	• Products sale	• Products information • Strategy for negotiation • MA information

$$u_i = v_i - f_i \tag{1}$$

where f_i is estimated by an expected product value function $f_i : M \times P \times D \mapsto \Re$. The real number $f_i(m,p,d)$ represents the CA's expected product value of recommending product m from SA_d paying price p. Meanwhile, v_i is determined by examining the quality of the product offered by the SA_d and estimated by a true product value function $v_i : M \times P \times Q \mapsto \Re$, where Q is a finite set of real values representing product function (quality). Since SAs may offer product m with different functions (qualities) and a SA may alter the quality of its products based on its market strategy, the CA trusts SAs with a high preference value and chooses the SA with the maximum expected product value among the SAs. The utility value is used for learning the expected product value function through a reinforcement learning mechanism:

$$f_i(m, p, d) \leftarrow f_i(m, p, d) + \alpha u_i \tag{2}$$

where α is the learning coefficient ($0 \leq \alpha \leq 1$). If $u_i \geq 0$, then the expected product value is updated with the same or a greater value than before. In this case, a chance to choose SA_d is increased if the SA_d provides the same valued product m at price p in the next auction. Otherwise, if $u_i < 0$, then the expected product value is updated with a smaller value than before.

The preference rating of a SA is defined as the amount of the increasing or decreasing preference value and is updated when the expected product value is updated. Let $p_i(m) \in \Re$ be the product value that a CA demands for the product m. To reflect differences when increasing and decreasing updated preference values, the approach proposed by Yu and Singh (2000) is used for preference updating (Tran & Cohen, 2002):

If $v_i(m,p,q) - p_i(m) \geq 0$, then the preference rating $r^{CA}(d)$ is increased by:

$$r^{CA}(d) \leftarrow \begin{cases} r^{CA}(d) + \beta(1 - r^{CA}(d)) & \text{if } r^{CA}(d) \geq 0 \\ r^{CA}(d) + \beta(1 + r^{CA}(d)) & \text{if } r^{CA}(d) < 0 \end{cases} \tag{3}$$

where β is a positive factor called the cooperation factor ($\beta > 0$) that is defined as:

$$\beta = \begin{cases} \dfrac{v_i(m, p, q) - p_i(m)}{\Delta v_i} & \text{if } \dfrac{v_i(m, p, q) - v_i(m)}{\Delta v_i} > v_{\min} \\ \beta_{\min} & \text{otherwise} \end{cases} \tag{4}$$

where $\Delta v_i = v_{i,\max} - v_{i,\min}$ with $v_{i,\max}$ and $v_{i,\min}$ being the maximum and minimum values of the true product function, respectively. If $v_i(m,p,q) = p_i(m)$, then the value $\beta_{\min}$ is used to prevent β from becoming zero.

If $v_i(m,p,q) - p_i(m) < 0$, then the preference rating $r^{CA}(d)$ is decreased by:

$$r^{CA}(d) \leftarrow \begin{cases} r^{CA}(d) + \gamma(1 - r^{CA}(d)) & \text{if } r^{CA}(d) \geq 0 \\ r^{CA}(d) + \gamma(1 + r^{CA}(d)) & \text{if } r^{CA}(d) < 0 \end{cases} \tag{5}$$

where γ is a negative factor called the non-cooperation factor ($\gamma < 0$), which is defined as:

$$\gamma = \lambda \left(\frac{v_i(m, p, q) - p_i(m)}{\Delta v_i} \right) \tag{6}$$

where λ is a penalty factor ($\lambda > 1$). To ensure that a preference is difficult to increase and easy to decrease, $|\lambda|$ should be greater than $|\beta|$. According to the result of updating the preference rate, a SA is reallocated to the new set of the preference with a new preference rating.

SAs' decision-making and learning algorithms are used to update their product price and quality to reflect the result of the transactions. SAs estimate their expected profit using an expected profit function, $k_d : M \times P \times I \mapsto \Re$. The real number $k_d(m,p,i)$ represents the SA's expected profit when providing product m if CA$_i$ selects product m with price p. Let $c_d(m,i)$ be the cost of SA$_d$ to provide product m for CA$_i$. SAs choose a price greater than or equal to the cost of providing the product to maximize their expected profit. The expected profit function is learned by a reinforcement learning mechanism:

$$k_d(m, p, i) \leftarrow k_d(m, p, i) + \alpha(t_d(m, p, i) - k_d(m, p, i))$$
(7)

where $t_d(m,p,i)$ is the true profit of the SAs and is defined as follows (Tran and Cohen, 2002):

$$t_d(m, p, i) = \begin{cases} p - c_d(m,i) & \text{if SA is determined as the provider of a product} \\ 0 & \text{otherwise} \end{cases}$$
(8)

In the next section, the proposed MAS is implemented to determine preference values for recommending products using a scenario and experiments.

3.4. Implementation and Experimentation

To demonstrate the proposed MAS, we implemented a multi-agent framework using JADE[1] (Java Agent Development framework) and JARE[2] (Java Automated Reasoning Engine). JADE is a software framework to develop agent applications that use FIPA specifications to manage agent communication. JARE is an environment for doing logical inference in Java. JARE can be used to model an agent's knowledgebase. The implementation focuses on recommendation between a CA and SAs to select a product.

3.4.1 Scenario and Agent Development

To evaluate the proposed MAS, two scenarios are considered for experimentation. The first scenario is developed for determining whether the proposed learning mechanism is used to select the proper product in the same customers' preference. The second scenario uses the learning mechanism to determine a proper product in different customers' preferences. Based on these scenarios, we consider an electronic market populated with one manager agent (MA), two customer agents (CAs), and four seller agents (SAs). Since JADE is a type of middleware and a framework to develop multi-agent systems, we can use JADE's capabilities to perform the functions of a MA instead of developing a MA separately. Two CAs are developed and have two different customers' preferences to choose an appropriate product. In these scenarios, a product's price, cost, and quality are considered as preference factors for determining a product preference value in the e-market. The cost and price of each product depends on its quality. In order to compare alternative products from different SAs, four SAs are developed based on different product design strategies. The knowledge of each agent is developed based on the role of that agent (refer to Table 1), which is used for capturing information and inference. Experimentation shows that a CA using the preference value is trying to determine appropriate products for customized recommendation. In this chapter, following scenarios are focused on determining product preference values in the proposed MAS.

3.4.2 Scenario 1 and Results

For the first scenario, there are two CAs that purchase products in a product family. One CA

Figure 3. System Architecture for CAs and SAs

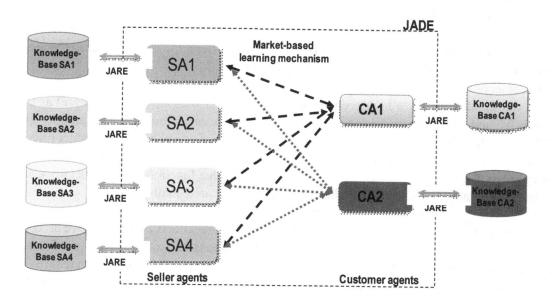

uses a product preference value to select a product and the other CA does not. Products can be designed by four different strategies that affect its quality. A product is selected by the customer's preferences.

Based on the scenario, six agents were developed as CAs and SAs for the experiment of selecting products in an e-market as shown in Figure 3. In the experiment, two CAs purchased the same product 100 times from four SAs and learned from the transaction history. Each experiment was performed 20 times to compare and analyze the behavior of the two CAs. For the price, finite and discrete values were used and varied randomly from 100 to 2000. The quality is proportional to the cost of the product. Let us assume that the product quality has a normal distribution with mean 1000 based on the cost range. The CAs' strategies and the SAs' alternative product design strategies are:

- CA1 uses reinforcement learning along with product preference.
- CA2 uses reinforcement learning without product preference.

- SA1: adjusts product's quality based on request and initial quality is 1000.
- SA2: provides a product with a fixed average quality value ($q=1000$).
- SA3: provides a product with quality chosen randomly from the interval [100, 2000].
- SA4: first tries to attract a CA with high quality ($q=1500$) and then cheats them with very low quality ($q=300$).

In this experiment, product preferences are categorized based on the value of preference function: (i) high preference ($r^{CA} \geq \Theta, 0 < \Theta < 1$), (ii) low preference ($r^{CA} \leq \theta, -1 < \theta < 0$), and (iii) non-preference ($\theta < r^{CA} < \Theta$), where Θ is a high preference threshold and θ is a low preference threshold. Non-preference means that a CA does not determine the preference of a SA because of insufficient information. The preference value is set to 0 initially and updated based on each transaction. If there are no SAs that have high preference, then CA randomly chooses a SA with a small probability among SAs with the non-preference. Parameters related to the learning mechanism are defined as follows:

- The product value function is: (*2×quality–price*), i.e., product quality is twice as important as product price.
- The threshold value for a high preference SA is 0.3 and a low one is -0.3.
- The learning rate α and exploration rate *e* are both 0.9999, and they decrease until they reach 0.1.
- The penalty factor is 1.5, which makes increasing the preference 50% harder than decreasing it.

After the experiment was performed, the number of purchased products by SAs with different product design strategies was obtained as shown in Figure 4. Based on the SAs' preference values, CA1 preferred to purchase products from SA1 and SA2. The random strategy of SA3 worsened its preference. SA4 should have the worst average preference; so, the number of purchases from SA4 is the lowest. CA2 used reinforcement learning without preference value. CA2 selected more modules from SA2 and SA3 than SA1 and SA4, since the average product qualities of SA2 and SA3 are higher than the others. The results show that CA1 has more ability to select appropriate SAs than CA2 does.

One-way Analysis of Variance (ANOVA) was performed to determine whether any significant differences existed between selecting products with different strategies based on these results. In this test, the level of significance (*p*-value) is 0.05. Table 2 shows the results of ANOVA for CA1 and CA2. In Table 2, the *p*-value of CA1 is less than 0.05; therefore, we conclude that there are *significant differences* in selecting products whether CAs use the proposed learning mechanism.

3.4.3 Scenario 2 and Results

For the second scenario, consider two CAs that have different customers' preferences as follows:

- CA1 uses (*2×quality – price*) as the product value function, i.e., product quality is twice as important as product price.
- CA2 uses (*quality – price*) as the product value function, i.e., product price and quality are equally important.

For the second experiment, we used the same conditions and parameters as in the first scenario. Figure 5 shows the number of purchases between SAs. CA1 selected more modules from SA1 and SA2 than SA3 and SA4 since the average product quality of SA1 and SA2 is higher than the others. CA2 also preferred to purchase products from SA1 and SA2.

One-way Analysis of Variance (ANOVA) was performed to determine whether any significant differences existed between selecting products with different customers' preferences based on the experimental results. Table 3 shows the results of ANOVA for CA1 and CA2. In Table 3, the *p*-values of CA1 and CA2 are less than 0.05; therefore, we conclude that there are *significant differences* in selecting products with different product design strategies according to customers' preferences.

The experiment demonstrated that CAs selected products properly according to product preference values in an electronic market. Therefore, the proposed learning mechanism can provide an appropriate method to support decision-making in the proposed MAS for determining a proper product in a product family that can be adapted to dynamic e-markets. The product preference values from the results of recommendation can provide designers with guide-lines for market segment design by identifying a platform based on customer preference trends in dynamic electronic

Figure 4. Number of Products Selected by CAs in Scenario 1

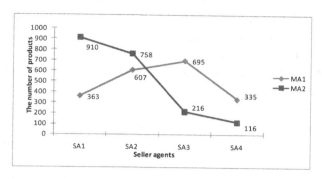

Table 2. The Result of ANOVA for CA1 and CA2 in Scenario 1

Agent	Source	DF	SS	MS	F-value	P-value
CA1	Factor	3	23139	7713	8.47	0.00
	Error	76	69183	910		
	Total	79	92322			
CA2	Factor	3	4773	1591	1.58	0.201
	Error	76	76447	1006		
	Total	79	81220			

Figure 5. Number of Products Selected by CAs in Scenario 2

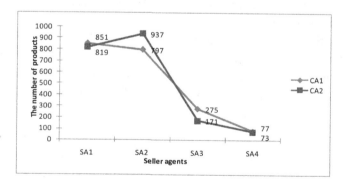

Table 3. The Result of ANOVA for CA1 and CA2 in Scenario 2

Agent	Source	DF	SS	MS	F-value	P-value
	Factor	3	22048	7349	7.47	0.00
CA1	Error	76	74792	984		
	Total	79	96840			
	Factor	3	29165	9722	12.37	0.00
CA2	Error	76	59731	786		
	Total	79	88896			

market environments. For example, a platform for a product family can be designed based on the functional requirements of a product with a high preference value in different market segments. In scenario 2, SA2's design strategy is considered as platform design for satisfying two different customers' preferences.

4. FUTURE TRENDS

In a dynamic electronic market environment, a successful recommendation for products depends on how to determine customers' preferences that are represented by the variation of their selections in the market. Therefore, various preference factors related to customer's preferences and satisfaction are identified to facilitate the preference values for determining robust and flexible design strategies in dynamic and uncertain market environments. To support customized product design effectively, preference values should provide information for market segment design. We need to develop a method that can design market segment using preference values for customized products. Since the market segment is sensitive to factors related to identify customers' preference, the factors should be determined by the products' characteristics, the relationships between company's and customers' preferences, and a market environment.

5. CONCLUSION

This chapter introduced an agent-based design recommender system to support customized recommendations for products based on market mechanisms. The agent architecture for the proposed system was described, including each agent's specific roles and knowledge. A market-based learning mechanism was used to determine a preference value and support decision-making for recommending appropriate products. We have implemented the proposed MAS using JADE and

JARE to demonstrate how the proposed learning mechanism determines products based on customers' preferences. Through two experiments, the proposed MAS can be used to determine proper products according to selections based on product preference values in an electronic market environment. Therefore, the proposed MAS can provide an appropriate method to support decision-making for recommending customized families of products by identifying customers' preferences in dynamic electronic market environments.

ACKNOWLEDGMENT

This work was funded by the National Science Foundation through Grant No. IIS-0325402. Any opinions, findings, and conclusions or recommendations presented in this chapter are those of the authors and do not necessarily reflect the views of the National Science Foundation.

REFERENCES

Bakos, J. Y. (1997). Reducing Buyer Search Costs: Implications for Electronic Marketplaces. *Management Science*, *43*(12), 1676–1692. doi:10.1287/mnsc.43.12.1676

Blecker, T., Friedrich, G., Kaluza, B., Abdelkafi, N., & Kreutler, G. (2005). *Information and Management Systems for Product Customization*. New York: Springer Science Business Media Inc.

Chandra, C., & Kamrani, A. K. (2003). Knowledge Management for Consumer-Focused Product Design. *Journal of Intelligent Manufacturing*, *14*(6), 557–580. doi:10.1023/A:1027358721819

Chira, O., Chira, C., Roche, T., Tormey, D., & Brennan, A. (2006). An Agent-based Approach to Knowledge Management in Distributed Design. *Journal of Intelligent Manufacturing*, *17*(6), 737–750. doi:10.1007/s10845-006-0042-0

Ezzedine, H., Kolski, C., & Peninou, A. (2005). Agent-oriented design of human-computer interface: application to supervision of an urban transport network. *Engineering Applications of Artificial Intelligence*, *18*(3), 255–270. doi:10.1016/j.engappai.2004.09.013

Jia, H. Z., Ong, S. K., Fuh, J. Y. H., Zhang, Y. F., & Nee, A. Y. C. (2004). An adaptive and upgradeable agent-based system for coordinated product development and manufacture. *Robotics and Computer-integrated Manufacturing*, *20*(2), 79–90. doi:10.1016/j.rcim.2003.08.001

Lee, Y. H., Kumara, S. R. T., & Chatterjee, K. (2003). Multiagent based dynamic resource scheduling for distributed multiple projects using a market mechanism. *Journal of Intelligent Manufacturing*, *14*(5), 471–484. doi:10.1023/A:1025753309346

Liang, W. Y., & Huang, C. C. (2002). The agent-based collaboration information system of product development. *International Journal of Information Management*, *22*(3), 211–224. doi:10.1016/S0268-4012(02)00006-3

Madhusudan, T. (2005). An agent-based approach for coordinating product design workflows. *Computers in Industry*, *56*(3), 235–259. doi:10.1016/j.compind.2004.12.003

Meyer, M. H., & Lehnerd, A. P. (1997). *The Power of Product Platforms: Building Value and Cost Leadership*. New York: The Free Press.

Monsotori, L., Vancza, J., & Kumara, S. R. T. (2006). Agent Based Manufacturing Systems. *Annals of CIRP*, *55*(2), 667–696. doi:10.1016/j.cirp.2006.10.003

Monticino, M., Acevedo, M., Callicott, B., Cogdill, T., & Lindquist, C. (2007). Coupled human and natural systems: A multi-agent-based approach. *Environmental Modelling & Software*, *22*(5), 656–663. doi:10.1016/j.envsoft.2005.12.017

Moon, S. K., Park, J., Simpson, T. W., & Kumara, S. R. T. (2008). A Dynamic Multi-Agent System Based on a Negotiation Mechanism for Product Family Design. *IEEE Transactions on Automation Science and Engineering*, *5*(2), 234–244. doi:10.1109/TASE.2007.896902

Padovan, B., Sackmann, S., Eymann, T., & Pippow, I. (2002). A Prototype for an Agent-Based Secure Electronic Marketplace Including Reputation-Tracking Mechanisms. *International Journal of Electronic Commerce*, *6*(4), 93–113.

Shen, W., Norrie, D. H., & Barthès, J. A. (2001). *Multi-agent Systems for Concurrent Intelligent Design and Manufacturing*. New York: Taylor & Francis.

Shooter, S. B., Simpson, T. W., Kumara, S. R. T., Stone, R. B., & Terpenny, J. P. (2005). Toward an Information Management Infrastructure for Product Family Planning and Platform Customization. *International Journal of Mass Customization*, *1*(1), 134–155. doi:10.1504/IJMASSC.2005.007354

Silveria, G. D., Borenstein, D., & Fogliatto, F. S. (2001). Mass Customization: Literature review and research directions. *International Journal of Production Economics*, *72*(1), 1–13. doi:10.1016/S0925-5273(00)00079-7

Simpson, T. W., Maier, J. R. A., & Mistree, F. (2001). Product platform design: method and application. *Research in Engineering Design*, *13*(1), 2–22. doi:10.1007/s001630100002

Simpson, T. W., Siddique, Z., & Jiao, J. (2005). *Product Platform and Product Family Design: Methods and Applications*. New York: Springer.

Symenonidis, A. L., Kehagias, D. D., & Mitkas, P. A. (2003). Intelligent Policy Recommendations on Enterprise Resource Planning by the Use of Agent Technology and Data Mining Techniques. *Expert Systems with Applications*, *25*(4), 589–602. doi:10.1016/S0957-4174(03)00099-X

Tan, G. W., Hayes, C. C., & Shaw, M. (1996). An Intelligent-Agent Framework for Concurrent Product Design and Planning. *IEEE Transactions on Engineering Management, 43*(3), 297–306. doi:10.1109/17.511840

Tran, T., & Cohen, R. (2002). A Reputation-Oriented Reinforcement Learning Strategy for Agents in Electronic Marketplaces. *Computational Intelligence, 18*(4), 550–565. doi:10.1111/1467-8640.t01-1-00203

Wooldridge, M. (2002). *An Introduction to Mulitagent Systems*. Chichester, UK: John Wiley & Sons Inc.

Yu, B., & Singh, M. P. (2000). A Social Mechanism for Reputation Management in Electronic Communities. In *The 4th International Workshop on Cooperative Information,* (pp. 154-165). Berlin: Springer-Verlag.

Zacharia, G., Evgeniou, T., Moukas, A., Boufounos, P., & Maes, P. (2001). Economics of Dynamic Pricing in a Reputation Brokered Agent Mediated Marketplace. *Electronic Commerce Research, 1*(2), 85–100. doi:10.1023/A:1011523612549

ENDNOTES

[1]   http://jade.tilab.com

[2]   http://jare.sourceforge.net

Chapter 5
Developing Interoperability in Mass Customization Information Systems

Ricardo Jardim-Goncalves
Universidade Nova de Lisboa, Portugal

António Grilo
Universidade Nova de Lisboa, Portugal

Adolfo Steiger-Garcao
Universidade Nova de Lisboa, Portugal

ABSTRACT

This chapter proposes a standard-based framework to assist industrial organizations to develop interoperability in mass customization Information Systems. After identifying the major challenges for business and information systems in mass customization, the authors propose an innovative standard-based conceptual architecture for a combined model-driven and services-oriented platform. The chapter concludes by describing a global methodology for integration of models and applications, to enhance an enterprise's interoperability in the support of mass customization practices, keeping the same organization's technical and operational environment, but improving its methods of work and the usability of the installed technology through harmonization and integration of the enterprise models in use by customers, manufacturers, and suppliers. Its platform aims to stimulate the adoption of mass customization concepts and improve those practices through proper integration and harmonization of information system models, knowledge, and data.

INTRODUCTION

The advance of mass customization principles can only be sustainable if supported with changes in how value is created, namely in the way goods and services are defined, and how logistics, operations, and customer interaction are designed. These changes must occur both internally, within organizations value chain, and also in the network wherein companies are embedded, further exploiting relationships with suppliers, distributors, and consumers. Nevertheless, all these changes in business can only occur if enabled by adequate interoperable information systems.

Nowadays, many enterprises already have information technology that can fulfill their mass customization requirements in each activity and with external organizations, like, for example, suppliers and customers. Also, in an industrial environment, many applications are available to support operating the product life cycle (PLC) stages. However, organizations typically acquire their applications with an aim to solve focused needs, without an overall view of the global enterprise's system integration. This essentially results from the way companies are organized, with internal departments usually adopting different frameworks. Even when enterprise models are interoperable, when information has to be exchanged, very often difficulties arise with respect to data semantics, since common reference models are not in place.

Mass customization and interoperability can be identified as key factors for enterprise success on a constantly-changing global custom-driven environment, enabling companies to act in networked partnership to strengthen their position facing the market. However, due to the difficulty of maintaining and integrating existing heterogeneous information systems, languages, and applications, the interoperable platforms are urging to emerge.

Applications developed using standard-based architectures present a systematic approach to enterprise integration and promotion of interoperability among different enterprises. Several reference models designed and developed using standard methodologies and techniques have already been developed for covering many industrial areas and related application activities, from design to production and sales, for example, ISO 10303 STEP, ebXML, EDI. Also, proposals for standardized architectures have been evolving, and they are expected to be shown as the standard way of handling middleware and infrastructure development for enterprise systems groups, like the model-driven architecture (MDA) and service-oriented architecture (SOA).

However, implementing new technology in organizations is a complex task that must be developed according to a suitable methodology supported by a proper and easy-to-implement platform. The advent of continuous technological evolution and business challenges makes companies unable to be constantly updated, and such dynamics have a recognized impact in organizations' strategies and resources with costs that they cannot afford.

This chapter proposes a framework to enhance an enterprise's interoperability in the support of mass customization practices, keeping the same organization's technical and operational environment, but improving its methods of work and the usability of the installed technology through harmonization and integration of the enterprise models in use by customers, manufacturers, and suppliers. Its platform aims to stimulate the adoption of mass customization concepts and improve those practices through proper integration and harmonization of information system models, knowledge, and data.

CHALLENGES FOR BUSINESS IN MASS CUSTOMIZATION

Mass customization implementation in companies requires intervention at business processes, production network, and information systems. Integrating the value chain, together with a flexible supply chain management, and supported by an information-rich supply and distribution chains is crucial for the success of companies in the advent of mass customization practices.

Integrated Value Chain

Mass customization principles promote the individual possibilities and unique features for the customer, and this must be supported accordingly by design, production, and sales processes. To compete in a mass customization strategy, companies must have capacities, competencies, and resources to cope with evolving product configurations, variable output frequency, and dynamic customer profiles, providing thus product and services that will differentiate from commodity type of products (Gilmore & Pine, 1997; Pine, 1993).

Diverse solutions have been considered to sustain these business demands, like product platforms, modularity, commonality, or postponement (Anderson & Pine, 1997; Da Silveira, Borenstein, & Fogliaatto, 2001; O'Grady, 1999). These solutions imply greater efficiency of internal business processes, and effective coordination mechanisms between its different functions.

Competition in highly-dynamic and agile production environments require a significant reduction of setup time in the production cycle to deal with flexible order-taking from customers. As companies reverse their traditional market push systems to market pull systems, it is the consumer who drives product configuration requirements. Thus, organizations must have new methods of work, where more precise and evolving forecasting models have to be deployed, based on the late interaction and marketers' fine analysis of consumer patterns. This implies the use of advanced algorithms for aggregate planning

based on a generic and intelligent bill of materials. Additionally, demands are posed in inbound and outbound logistics, and in the way stocks are managed; also, the manufacturing systems need to assemble the production basic blocks according to a set of evolving rules (Robertson & Ulrich, 1998; Simpson, 2005).

More than simple mass personalization of products and services that occurs in the late stages of the whole PLC, mass customization requires that the value chain's primary and secondary activities are linked together dynamically according to the product and customer profiles. These links need to be seamlessly established and error free. Since clients require highly-specific product or specific requirements, companies must be able to design products that both satisfy clients and are easily manufactured (Cusumano & Nobeoka, 1998; Liker, 2004). Thus, products must be designed to be manufactured.

These operations management challenges cannot be fulfilled if not supported by specialized computer applications, together with automation in the production line. To achieve agile and flexible response, these applications need to be integrated. Commercial ERP systems promise this integration, but real-world practice shows that too often companies choose fragmented, vertical, and functionally-oriented specialized applications rather than complete commercial ERP solutions (empírica GmbH, 2005). This poses challenges for information integration and therefore systems interoperability, as many applications run on disparate operating systems and use heterogeneous reference models and technologies.

Flexible Supply Chain Management

A mass customization paradigm requires enhanced flexible and efficiency in the supply chain, supported by seamless data exchange (Cusumano & Nobeoka, 1998; Hegge & Wortmann, 1991; Huang, Zhang, & Lo, 2005). Flexibility in the supply chain is necessary to respond to more complex products configuration and their fast-changing characteristics. However, this flexibility cannot compromise the efficiency of the businesses interaction, but rather increase it. Simultaneous flexibility and efficiency of the supply chain management can only be achieved through simplification. This requires standardization, automatic resupply mechanisms, and rationalization (Anderson, 2004).

Most products are designed without considering the benefits of using standardization. Thus, contrary to common practice, mass customization does not imply proliferation of elements to build products and services, if a focus on reuse of elements is considered since the design phase. Parts, components, and material diversity can be significantly reduced through standardization techniques. Automatic resupply is now well known and being used by many firms, as modern *kanban* or just-in-time techniques. Still, many firms are adverse to these techniques, as they do not recognize its benefits, and maintain the traditional issue of expensive time and resource-consuming purchase orders of parts, components, and materials. Also, it is fundamental that companies rationalize their product line to eliminate or make the outsourcing of the unfrequent, unusual, and low-volume products and services that marginally contribute to the profitability of the company.

Therefore, the supply chain simplification should be focused on reducing the variety of parts, components, and materials, in order to enable automatic and pull-based procurement of supplies. Also, it should reduce the number of qualified suppliers, developing partnerships to move away from price-based supplier competition, rather to flexibility and time- and quality-response selection (Anderson, 2004).

The enhanced flexibility and efficiency through supply chain simplification can only be achieved if electronic platforms are deployed, linking suppliers, producers, distributors, and customers. These e-platforms can have informational, collaborative, or transactional functions, enabling the definition of product characteristics, implementing joint product development, and sustaining distributed collaborative demand forecasting and stock management (Balakrishman, Kumara, & Sundaresan, 1999).

The success or failure of the adoption of these e-platforms is very much dependent on many business factors, like: (i) companies' individual business and IT strategies, processes, resources, and infrastructure; (ii) business relationships exchange episodes and atmosphere; and (iii) the characteristics of the production network governance structure and its input-output structure (Grilo & Jardim-Goncalves, 2005). However, to overcome hurdles posed by these business factors, it is important to develop interoperability between systems beyond the value chain, that is, at an inter-organizational dimension.

Information-Rich Supply and Distribution Chains

In traditional business approaches, the conventional value creation process implied that companies and consumers had distinct roles of production and consumption. Products and services contained value, and markets exchanged this value, from the producer to the consumer, that is, the value creation occurred outside the markets.

Mass customization allows a different process, a move towards cocreation of value, where consumers engage in the process of both defining and creating value. This approach is based on individual-centered cocreation of value between consumers and companies, grounded on the experience of the individual, whether as an individual consumer or as a "consumer" from an institutional client (Prahalad & Ramaswamy, 2004).

Thus, companies that wish to be competing in the market need to understand well the personalized experiences of consumers. Then, they need to extract the real attributes that are relevant for value creation, and modularize or define product platforms that can be mass-produced (Schooler, 2005). Definition of meta-data enables that a personalized user experience focused on certain attributes can go one step further in creating a customized user experience based on products and their attributes, and sharing that information across the production network. This requires that information systems are able to support not only the interaction between the parties but also have the capability to acquire and share knowledge on collaborative networks of people and companies (Balakrishman et al., 1999, Prahalad & Ramaswamy, 2004).

Hence, mass customization requires the existence of an information-rich enterprise system, where data is stored and processed on product types, rates, features, promotions, distribution channels, or customer interaction arrangements. This implies that sales and servicing people must be supported by integrated information systems that are able to give adequate answers to customer interaction.

To implement systems that can support global seamless information flow across the value chain, its heterogeneous and fragmented applications must be integrated. In such an environment, the information systems must: (1) support client personalization, enabling them to interact with design, production, and delivery systems in order to do the planning of what, when, and where to deliver; (2) have rule-based functionality that bound clients' choices to companies' production capabilities and eventual regulatory and legal constraints; and (3) provide a customer interaction system that records each individual interaction and purchase, for fine-tuned sales forecasting, production, and supply planning. Personal details, tastes, and opinions should also be kept and then analyzed through data mining techniques.

CHALLENGES FOR INFORMATION SYSTEMS IN MASS CUSTOMIZATION

Mass customization implementation in companies requires integrated information systems. Today, a principal driver to reach this aim is enterprises interoperability, through the use of reference models and ontology in open platforms.

Interoperability Driver

According to the IEEE Standard Computer Dictionary, interoperability is "the ability of two or more systems or components to exchange information and to use the information that has been exchanged". In 2002, the European Group for Research on Interoperability informed the European Commission's Information Society Directorate General of the fact that "enterprise systems and applications need to be interoperable to achieve seamless operational and business interaction, and create networked organizations".

Recent observations state: "30-40% of companies' IT budget is spent on integration [Gartner and AMR], 30% of entire IT budget is spent on building, maintaining, and supporting application integration [Forrester], 61% of CIOs consider integration of systems and processes a key priority [CIOMagazine], $29 billion by 2006 for application integration by IT professional services [Gartner Group]".

While some companies have been able to master a mass customization approach with the support of an adequate information system infrastructure, large-scale improvements in the use of IT will come only when the networked production systems engendered by technology allows for the realization of positive network externalities to their fullest extent.

Part of the reason why organizations looking for mass customization practices have not yet been able to exploit the positive network externalities comes from their lack of full interoperability. As SMEs are often the largest part of the manufactures' supplier base in disparate industries, this issue becomes more severe due to the inexistence of internal know-how and resources to solve it (Fenves, Sriram, Choi, Elm, & Robert, 2004; Fenves, Sriram, Choi, & Robert, 2003).

Recent studies have uncovered the cost of interoperability barriers of the IT systems used in engineering and manufacturing in the U.S. auto industry, estimated to be of the order of $1 billion per year (Gregory, 1999). Similarly, for the construction industry, a study prepared for NIST by RTI International and the Logistic Management Institute, to identify and estimate the efficiency losses in the U.S. capital facilities industry resulting from inadequate interoperability among computer-aided design, engineering, and software systems estimates the cost of inadequate interoperability in the U.S. capital facilities industry to be $15.8 billion per year (Gallaher, 2004). These studies are an indication of the industry's inability to exploit IT to realize its full benefits. It is in this context that standards for information exchange are also critical in the mass customization paradigm.

Reference Model Driver

Many standard-based application protocols (APs) and business objects (BOs) are available today. They cover most of the major manufacturing and business activities, and come from ISO, UN, CEN, or OMG. However, most of these standards are not widely adopted, either by lack of awareness or due to private commercial interests of the software developers. Moreover, when they are selected, they are frequently used inadequately in most of the situations, due to an imprecise interpretation of the scope. This results in difficulties in achieving interoperability with others and introduces limitations in potential future reuse and model extensibility when creating new components (Jardim-Goncalves & Steiger-Garcao, 2002a).

However, a standard for data representation cannot usually cover all the range of activities one application needs to handle. As it is often the case that several of the enterprise's applications must operate side by side (horizontally), it is necessary to pay strong attention to the integration and cooperation of multiple standard application protocols and business objects.

The adoption of a strategy to help develop and implement architectures to support horizontally-oriented applications and to reuse vertically-developed APs and BOs, stimulates the intensive use and extensive reuse of existent standards. It also stimulates development of methodologies to specify and design flexible supportive architectures (Motta, 1999).

Hopefully, this will result in a framework to support extensive interoperability between standard models, based on the development of meta-protocols aimed to represent the overall organization structure and business activities in open platforms. This framework can also be a basis for the development of components.

Recently, XMI, one of the most promising tools for metamodel representation, revealed very able to assist on integration based on the concept of extending and reusing existent objects, and also on the development of compilers and code generators to assist in the development of new components (Jardim-Goncalves & Steiger-Garcao 2002b).

Complementing this, ISO13584 PLib is the standard suggested for representation of catalogues of objects and components (e.g., units of functionality, application objects and assertions, integrated resources, data access interfaces, object business data types, etc.), with direct link with a multi-level, multi-language ontology system. This multi-level characteristic also assists with the development of hierarchical components, while the multi-language mechanism will provide the adequate description of the objects and components in many native languages, for an easier understanding and better usage.

The architecture of standards for data exchange is typically complex. Due to its extent, it is a long and arduous task to fully understand a standard. This fact has been observed as one of the main obstacles for the adoption of standard models by the software developers. For this reason, even when software developers are aware of a standard which fits the scope for which they are looking, often they prefer to not adopt it, but rather to create a new specific framework.

However, most of the standards for data exchange contain a framework that includes a language for data model description, a set of application reference models, libraries of resources, mechanisms for the data access, and representation in neutral format. Examples are the DOM for XML, or the Part 21 of standard STEP (DOM, 2006; ISO10303-1, 1994).

Open Platform Driver

Generally, a standard data access interface (SDAI) is defined for each standard. Although it is of major importance to motivate implementers to adopt one standard, very low level interfaces were made available, with all the complexity of the standard's architecture to be managed and controlled by the user. Such interfaces require a significant effort from the implementers to use, and it has been a source of systematic errors. When functionalities for data access are very similar with slight differences in attribute names or data types, errors often occur.

Automatic code generators are state-of-the-art and can stimulate implementers to adopt the standards and implement them with more ease, minimizing the already-mentioned problems. These generators automatically produce code ready to be linked to the applications. The generated methods for data access act as a high-level interface on the top of the standard data access interface, offering a simpler interface that hides the detailed complexity of the standard architecture.

The code generated represents an abstract data type (ADT) as an implementation of the conceptual standard description of the standard model. The interface offered by the ADT virtualizes the complexities of the standard architecture, which will instantiate the ADT structure through the set of methods for putting and getting data in its attributes, and import and export data to the neutral format.

Using these generators, the applications become less exposed for coding errors once the code generator has itself been validated. Having them available for several platforms further enables applications to adopt the standards with relative ease. Should the generated interfaces be universally harmonized and adopted as a reference for data access, independently of the standard and platform in use, this will enable the construction of very powerful configurable architectures, offering the flexibility that systems nowadays desire in order to face the rapid changes in the business requirements.

With this methodology, changing one of the adopted standards for data exchange will not imply updating the interfaces. Only the low level library, which interfaces with the data in neutral format and is linked with the generated code, needs to be substituted.

If the platform stores a repository with several implementations of standard data access interfaces, the implementer can multiplex the one he would like to use for the specific case, and keep using the higher level because the SDAI is not changed. In this case, the adoption of the new interface will be automatic, and the access to the new standard will be immediate.

To avoid the explosion on the number of required translators to cover all the existing standard data models, this methodology proposes the use of standard metamodel descriptions, that is, the Metamodel, using a standard Meta language, for example, XMI, to link the generators with this Metamodel information.

ONTOLOGY DRIVER

Ontology is the study of the categories of things within a domain and reflects a view of a segment of the reality. Its definition comes from philosophy and provides a logical framework for research on knowledge representation, embracing definition, classification, and relationships of concepts (IDEAS Project, 2003).

In this context, two or more communities (e.g., organizations, teams), operating in the same domain, may use different terminologies and have different views on the same concept, leading to different underlying ontologies, and consequently conducting to problems of interoperability. At a first level, this problem comes out in the communication between humans, then between humans and computer systems, and finally between computer systems.

For example, when a client talks with suppliers searching for a specific customization, they all need to understand each other. If for any reason this is not the case, humans are able to use reasoning and combine their knowledge, attempting to converge to a common understanding and, hence, to communicate. In opposition to this interactive and intelligent human-to-human process, computer systems communicate under a well-established syntax, through rigid communication protocols. However, the inclusion of semantics in the communication protocol under a well-established classification mechanism, making use of knowledge modeling components described according established semantic representation paradigms, complements the information exchanged contributing for an enhanced understanding between the systems.

Therefore, an interoperable system that seamlessly communicates and understands each other requires the comprehensive understanding of the meaning of the data exchanged within the domains which are involved. This can be realized, if the communication process is supported by an ontol-

ogy developed under global consensus (Jardim-Goncalves, 2004; JTC 1/SC 7/WG 17, 2006).

To obtain this consensual model, it is necessary to classify and merge the concepts from the different sources within the domain of applicability, describing them in a unique harmonized structure of classes, attributes, relationships, knowledge components, and definitions. Through a combining procedure, the harmonized classification is defined, structuring the various suppliers' information from different sources and for diverse product categories.

CONCEPTUAL IS ARCHITECTURES FOR INTEROPERABILITY

With the large diversity of today's software applications, models, data repositories, programming languages, and operating systems, developers face difficulties to produce applications enabled to interoperate with any other. Therefore, to design their applications, they need to search for a common reference architecture that can guarantee interoperability with the others.

The Model-Driven Architecture

The Object Management Group (OMG) has been proposing the model-driven architecture (MDA) as a reference to achieve wide interoperability of enterprise models and software applications (JTC 1/SC 7/WG 17, 2006). MDA provides specifications for an open architecture appropriate for the integration of systems at different levels of abstraction and through the entire information systems' life cycle (Mellor & Balcer, 2002; Miller & Mukerji, 2001). Thus, this architecture is designed to incite interoperability of the information models independently of the framework in use (i.e., operating system, modeling and programming language, data servers, and repositories).

The MDA comprises three main layers (AlMellor, 2004; MDA, 2006). The Computation-

Independent Model (CIM) is the top layer and represents the most abstract model of the system, describing its domain.

A computation independent model (CIM) is a stakeholders-oriented representation of a system from the computation-independent viewpoint. A CIM focuses on the business and manufacturing environment in which a system will be used, abstracting from the technical details of the structure of the implementation system.

The middle layer is the platform-independent model (PIM), and defines the conceptual model based on visual diagrams, use-case diagrams, and meta-data. For that it uses the standards UML (unified modelling language), OCL (object constraint language), XMI (XML metadata interchange), MOF (metaobject facility) and CWM (common warehouse metamodel). Thus, the PIM defines an application protocol in its full scope of functionality, without platform dependencies and constraints. For an unambiguous and complete definition, the formal description of the PIM should concern using the correct business vocabulary, choosing the proper use-cases and interface specifications.

The platform-specific model (PSM) is the bottom layer of the MDA. It differs from the PIM as it targets a specific implementation platform. Therefore the implementation method of the MDA,

also known as model-driven development (MDD), is achieved through a transformation that converts the PIM to the PSM. This procedure can be done through automatic code-generation for most of the system's backbone platforms, considering middleware-specific constraints, for example, CORBA, .NET, J2EE, Web Services. Figure 1 depicts the Model-Driven Architecture, compared with the traditional scenario.

Catalysis is one example of a method adopting MDA (D'Souze & Wills, 1998). Based on one extension of the UML, it was initially conceived by Desmond D'Souza and Alan Wills to model businesses processes. It describes and documents business models and collaborative processes, developing patterns to be employed as a reference and assist the applications to achieve interoperability (Trireme International, 2006).

The research community is also developing and validating other proposals, like those known as *executable UML*. With it, the abstract models described in UML are implemented and tested at a conceptual level, that is, PIM, before transforming them to be implemented in the targeted platform (AlMellor, 2004).

Recently, the ISO TC184 SC4 community has been developing the parts 25 and 28 of the standard ISO10303, known as STEP, the STandard for the Exchange of Product model data (ISO TC184/SC4

Figure 1. The model-driven architecture

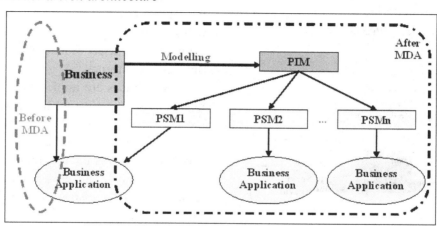

2006). These two new parts are reinforcing the implementation of STEP Application Protocols according to MDA.

Indeed, part 25 of STEP provides the specification for the XMI binding of EXPRESS schemata. The part 28 specifies the implementation method of ISO10303 product data according to XML. With them, a STEP Application Protocol can be implemented using a MDA, with the PIM represented in EXPRESS and transformed to XMI and UML according to Part 25 of this standard, and implemented in a specific platform in XML according to Part 28.

The Service-Oriented Architecture

The World Wide Web Consortium (W3C) refers to the service-oriented architecture (SOA) as "a set of components which can be invoked, and whose interface descriptions can be published and discovered" (W3C, 2006). Also, according to Microsoft, the goal for SOA is a world-wide mesh of collaborating services that are published and available for invocation on a service bus (SOA, 2006).

SOA does not consider the services architecture just from the technology perspective, but also proposing a normalized service-oriented environment (SOE) offering services' description, registration, publication, and search functionalities (Figure 2). Placing emphasis on interoper-

ability, SOA combines the capacity to invoke remote objects and functions, that is, the services, with standardized mechanisms for dynamic and universal service discovery and execution.

The service-oriented architecture offers mechanisms of flexibility and interoperability that allow different technologies to be dynamically integrated, independently of the system's platform in use. This architecture promotes reusability, and it has reduced the time to put available and get access to the new system's functionalities, allowing enterprises to dynamically publish, discover, and aggregate a range of Web services through the Internet.

Thus, SOA encourages enterprises to be focused on their business and services, not constrained by the specificities of the applications and platforms. This is an essential requirement for organizations to achieve information technology independence, business flexibility, agile partnership, and seamless integration in dynamic collaborative working environments and in digital ecosystems.

Some known service-oriented architectures are Microsoft's DCOM, IBM's DSOM protocol, or the OMG's Object Request Brokers (ORBs) based on the CORBA specification. Nowadays, the use of W3C's Web services is expanding rapidly as the need for application-to-application communication and interoperability grows. They can implement a business process integrating services developed internally and externally to the company, providing a standard means of communication among different software applications running on a variety of heterogeneous platforms through the Internet.

Web services are implemented in XML (extended markup language). The network services are described using the WSDL (Web services description language), and the SOAP (simple object access protocol) is the communication protocol which is adopted. The registration of the services is in the UDDI registry (universal description, discovery, and integration).

Figure 2. Service oriented environment based on SOA

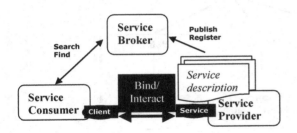

Although providing a significant contribution, the SOA alone is not yet the answer to achieve seamless interoperability between applications. For example, despite the efforts done to ensure compatibility between all the SOAP implementations, currently there is no unique standard. The Web Services Interoperability Organization (WS-I) is a good example of an organization supporting Web services interoperability across platforms, operating systems, and programming languages, and that has been developing efforts for the convergence and support of generic protocols for the interoperable exchange of messages between Web services (WS-I, 2006).

Combining MDA and SOA

Most of the standards contain a framework including a language for data model description, a set of application reference models, libraries of resources, mechanisms for the data access, and representation in neutral format. However, its architecture is typically complex. Especially due to its extent, to understand and dominate a standard completely is a long and arduous task (Bohms, 2001; Dataform EDIData, 1997; IAI/IFC, 1997; ISO10303-1, 1994).

This fact has been observed as one of the main obstacles for the adoption of standard models by the software developers. Even when they are aware of a standard which fits the scope of what they are looking for, quite often they prefer not to adopt it, and instead, create a new framework of their own (aecXML, 2006; Berre, 2002; CEN/ISSS, 2006; Clements, 1997).

Generally, the standard data access interfaces are described at a very low level. Moreover, they are made available with all the complexity of the standard's architecture to be managed and controlled by the user. This circumstance requires a significant effort from the implementers to use it, and is a source of systematic errors of implementation, for instance when there are functionalities for data access very similar with slight differences in attributes, names, or data types (ENV 13550, 2006; Pugh, 1997; Vlosky, 1998).

To avoid the explosion in the number of required translators to cover all the existent standard data models, an extension of this methodology proposes the use of standard metamodel descriptions, that is, the metamodel, using a standard metalanguage, and putting the generators to work with this metamodel information (Jardim-Goncalves & Steiger-Garcão, 2001; Umar, 1999)

With this methodology, changing one of the adopted standards for data exchange does not imply an update of the interface with the application using it, where only the low-level library linked with the generated code needs to be substituted. If the platform stores a repository with several implementations of standard data access interfaces, the implementer can choose the one that he would like to use for the specific case, for example, through a decision support multiplexing mechanism. In this case, the change for the new interface will be done automatically, and the access to the new standard will be immediate.

A proposal to contribute to face this situation considers the integration of SOA and MDA to provide a platform-independent model (PIM) describing the business requirements and representing the functionality of their services. These independent service models can then be used as the source for the generation of platform-specific models (PSM), dependent of the Web services executing platform.

Within this scenario, the specifications of the execution platform will be an input for the development of the transformation between the MDA's PIM and the targeted Web services platform. With tools providing the automatic transformation between the independent description of the Web services and the specific targeted platform, the solution for this problem could be made automatic and global.

PROPOSED CONCEPTUAL PLATFORM FOR INTEROPERABILITY

An integration platform (IP) is characterized by the set of methods and mechanisms capable of supporting and assisting in the tasks for integration of applications. When the data models and toolkits working for this IP are standard-based, they would be called Standard-based Integration Platforms (Boissier, 1995; Nagi, 1997).

The architecture of an IP can be described through several layers, and proposes using an *onion layer model* (Figure 3). Each layer is devoted for a specific task, and intends to bring the interface with the IP from a low to a high level of abstraction and functionality. The main aim of this architecture is to facilitate the integration task, providing different levels of access to the platform and consequently to the data, covering several of the identified requirements necessary for integration of the applications (Jardim-Goncalves & Steiger-Garcao, 2002b).

Figure 3. Layers of an integration platform

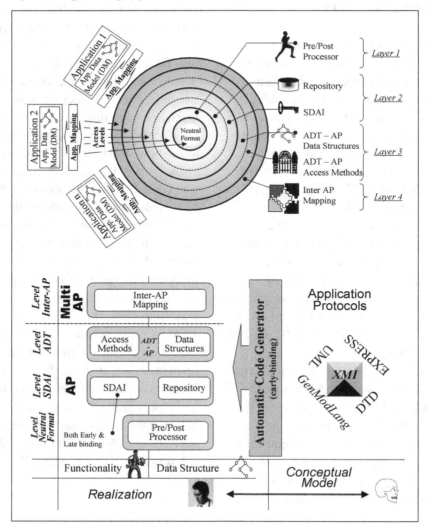

Layer 1 (L1) is the lowest of this architecture, and is the one dealing with the representation of data in neutral format (NF). L1 provides the possibility for applications to translate its own data to the NF using a Pre/Post Processor and use this format as the means for data exchange. IPs must adopt for its set of available NFs those from the set of available standards, for example, ISO10303, Part 21 (STEP neutral format representation of data) or XML, and include in the IP the correspondent Pre/Post Processor.

The standard data access interface (SDAI) Layer comprehends the set of commands to handle and manage the data in NF. The SDAI acts as a low-level interface for Applications willing to handle Neutral Format data, using the repository as its support for handle and management of data and meta-data. Examples of components of a SDAI layer are the bindings for programming languages of ISO10303, Part 22, and the document object model (DOM). The repository could be any database or engine with persistence capabilities, although most SDAIs are released bundled with a proprietary database.

Nevertheless, to have SDAI with a standard interface to the repository (e.g., SQL) is a very important added value, though users become independent of any proprietary system (Loffredo, 1998). The low-level interface of SDAI has shown to be one of the main obstacles for the integration of Application in IPs. To provide higher-level interfaces using latest generation programming languages would make the development of translators easier and would stimulate users to plug in such platforms and consequently adopt the standards.

The Layer 3 (L3), abstract data type – application protocol, provides a higher-level interface on top of SDAI, developed in one of the popular programming languages. This layer offers to the applications' integrators Data Structures and Access Methods. They act as an early binding mapping from the application protocols used in the scope of the platform and described in a standard language for model representation (e.g., ISO10303, Part 11-EXPRESS, XMI) (ISO10303-11, 1998; XMI, 2006).

The need to plug into an IP is most often related with the usage of one application in an inter-cross industrial environment. Layer 4 (L4) deals with this issue. In this case, the use of a unique AP is often considered not enough, once APs are developed for a specific scope of industrial use. Thus, harmonization from more than one AP is necessary to cover all needs.

To develop interfaces for applications integrating such inter-cross platforms requires an additional effort to map, develop, and implement those APs required for the target integrated system. To facilitate this task, such mapping should be done in a descriptive high-level language (e.g., ISO10303, Part14 - EXPRESS-X), and generate automatically code in a program language ready to be linked with the Layer below, that is, L3.

However, to enable one application to be integrated in such an environment, not all layers are required to be implemented in its integrator interface. The interface can be developed at a lower or higher level, depending at what level the application intends to connect with the IP. For instance, if one application already adopts the same SDAI as the IP, the integration can be done at this level, avoiding the bi-directional translation down to the neutral format level, and up in the way back.

Levels of Integration of an Integration Platform

The described layered architecture of IPs renders to the integrator several levels of integration corresponding to the many ways to access to the standard-based data. When an application is integrated through a neutral format access level, it accesses to data in NF using the translator as a pre/post processor to generate/parse the neutral format data based on the AP from/to the application's internal data structure.

The use of the SDAI level for integration implies the direct use of a SDAI by the application using SDAI's set of commands to handle the data and communicate through it. Because the commands of SDAI allow the management of the SDAI's repository at data and meta-data level, and include direct connection to the generator and parser for neutral format data, the interface of the application dealing with SDAI should read/write the data from/to the repository using the SDAI commands, and commit/revoke such data in the repository to keep it updated with the exchanged information.

Integration at ADT level means that the applications use the high-level interface to establish communications and exchange data with third parties. Because the ADT data structures are a mapping resulting from the early-binding code generation from the AP in use, the integrator should create and instantiate objects correspondent to the entities in the conceptual model. It should access to its attributes by putting and getting the required data using the ADT access methods, and thus call the import and export methods to access to the neutral format data.

Figure 4. Two views of the levels of integration in an IP

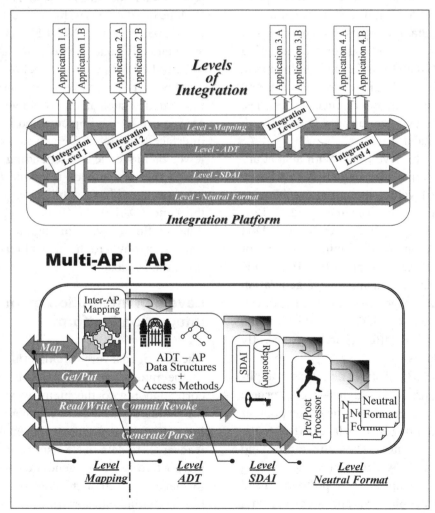

Whenever inter-APs mapping is required for the integration of one application, this should be done at the mapping access level. This integration level releases the mapping interface generated through the inter-AP mapping description to applications, thus establishing the links between the several data structures corresponding to entities from the APs in use by the IP, and the application's internal data structure.

These present four levels of access conduct to the statement of four levels of integration (Figure 4) dependent on the selected access levels. These levels of integration let the integrator decide how deep he would like to go to enable the change of the standard-based data with the platform. For instance, an integration of one application in the IP at a Level 3 – ADT, means that the integrator does not need to understand all the details related with the commands and functionalities of the SDAI nor the syntax of the neutral format to enable his application to communicate via IP. To handle and manage all issues at ADT level should be enough.

Execution and Entry Point Level of IP

The realization of an application integration task in an IP is conducted by one of the presented integration levels, through one of its levels of access to data. The IP's levels of execution and entry point are the gates that provide entrance to the mechanism for the execution of commands and information exchange between the applications and the platform, and therefore among applications.

Each level of data access makes available different execution and entry point levels at which its functionality depends directly on the intended level of integration, with a specific level of abstraction. Figure 5 describes many execution and entry point levels that could be identified in an IP, in the extent of the levels of integration.

For the neutral format level, the entry point for execution is the sum of the mechanisms that allow writing and reading the information in NF. For instance, in the case of STEP Part 21, or XML, those are the commands that enable applications

Figure 5. Execution and entry point levels of IP

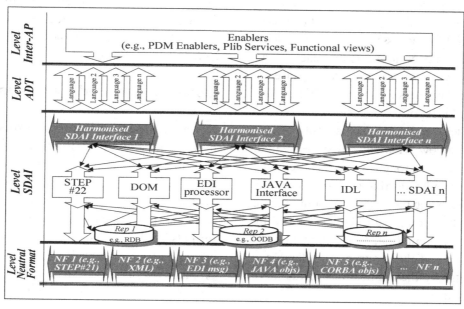

to read and write characters and strings in the syntax defined by the standard. In the case of Java or Corba objects, they are those that generate and handle directly the representation of the instances of these objects at its very low level (e.g., in binary format, under its data structure).

The entry point at SDAI level offers executable commands suitable to handle and manage repositories of data and meta-data compatible with the APs adopted by the IP, and to import and export such data in neutral format. The main aim of these commands is to virtualize the data represented in neutral format, providing to the integrators a unique interface independent of the standard adopted to represent the data. Since in the market there are several libraries that can be adopted with the role of a SDAI, there is a need to harmonize such interfaces, defining a new one on top of them which represents those commands that are universal to a set of SDAIs, and which applications can use universally.

Adopting this approach, one application can, for example, move immediately from one neutral format in STEP Part 21 to XML, by just changing the library of software, that is, by just changing SDAI. At this level, the kind of repository used is also very important to give persistence to the data in the IP. The ideal scenario would be the one where a unique repository is used and accessed using a standard data access mechanism, like SQL. In fact, what has been found is that each SDAI uses its property repository, not providing an easy connection to the others for sharing. This implies a propagation of repositories inside the IPs.

The ADT level makes available a set of methods that allows the new AP's objects to be created, instantiating them through its access methods, and importing and exporting such objects to the neutral format, using methods that communicate with one of the harmonized SDAIs adopted by the IP. For implementation, ADTs should be developed in some of the programming language in frequent use by the applications to facilitate immediate usage.

The high-level nature of the methods provided by the ADT's classes of objects, designed to be a steady mapping from their conceptual representation in the AP, provides a natural and easier way for integrators to handle the integrated data. Using the execution and entry points at the ADT level provide to the integrators an interface independent of the SDAI and consequently to the neutral format adopted by the IP.

When a mapping between ADTs is required, the mapping rules should be coded and made available to the integrator as a set of commands that allows it to easily instantiate the attributes of the required objects at once. This level of execution and entry points enables the integrator to see the global IP designed as a metaprotocol, in which its constituents are APs or parts of linked APs based on mapping and transformation rules between them. Working on the top of ADTs, this meta-AP could be accessed and handled independently of the SDAI or neutral format which has been adopted.

Using the inter-AP level raises the level of the IP to the one where access to it is done by mechanisms assigning data to the related APs. When reference between data from different standards is required, mechanisms to support this link should be supported. Examples are the STEP's PLib services and the Plib's view exchange protocols to join the standards STEP and PLib (Fowler, 2000; PLib, 2000).

Metadata and Model Morphisms

Nowadays UML is a main framework supported by toolkits in the market (Rumbaugh, 1998). However, major standard models are not represented using it, as are the cases of the ISO10303-STEP application protocols. To avail the existent models and reuse and put them in the market in popular formats like UML, a solution could be to develop model translators to UML. But the kernel of the problem still persists, since UML models are described in proprietary formats depending on the tools managing them. There is no established neutral way to represent them.

The Object Management Group (OMG) released a proposal entitled XML metadata interchange (XMI) with the intention of providing a common mechanism for interchange of models. Today, XMI has been universally accepted as a standard for metamodel representation. Major groups involved with electronic data exchange, and most of the popular toolkits available in the market, have been adopting XMI as the standard for import/export of modeling information, supporting direct translation of major modeling technologies like UML and UMM (XMI, 2006).

Contradictory facts:
There is huge investment in developing models using standard-based methodologies, for example, STEP.

There is a technology that is very well accepted by the market, using methodologies like the unified modeling language (UML) that, besides the modeling features provided, also offers others like process design or system's deployment (Rational, 2006; Rumbaugh, 1998).

Question:
How can we take the large number of existing models described in languages like EXPRESS or XML and reuse them and put them in the market in a popular format like UML?

One immediate answer could be to develop model translators to UML, but the core of the problem still persists. Once UML models are represented in proprietary internal formats depending on the tools managing them, there is still not an established neutral way to represent them.

To translate from one modeling *Language 1* (e.g., EXPRESS) to XMI, first the model should be compiled, using the parser to populate a Meta-dictionary repository according to the processed information. For each language considered for the translation process, for example, EXPRESS

and XMI, a library of commands to handle the meta-data dictionary repository will be provided. This library acts as a meta-SDAI for each language, and it is the bridge between the model in one language and its representation in the meta-dictionary repository.

Hence, the access to the repository should be done using the meta-SDAI for the model language. Afterwards, the Mapping module is executed, translating the metadata from *Language 1*'s repository format, to XMI's repository language format. To have a mapping and translators from XMI to all languages in which models developed by the major standards exist, as are the cases of STEP APs or several of the registered DTDs, would be an important step to assure reusability and acceptance of these models.

The mapping between such languages is not direct, and therefore complete translations are sometimes difficult to achieve (Breton & Bézivin, 2001). To give a practical example identified during one of the real implementations of this framework, one of the difficulties found in translating an EXPRESS model to UML via XMI is related with the *classtoclass* relationship. While in EXPRESS this is represented using an attribute value, in UML it could be represented using aggregation or association mechanisms. There is no way to automatically infer from the EXPRESS model which is the correct semantic in order to translate it according to UML.

A mapping specification should document the correspondence between the information requirements defined by the reference model of an AP and how the requirements are satisfied by the objects in the integrated format. The mapping specification is established through analysis of the information requirements and the definition of a mapping for each application object, application object attribute, and application object assertion. It takes into account the scope and context of the AP, semantics of the application objects and resource constructs, together with the definition of constraints on the population of the resource constructs used in the integrated model. Therefore, the mapping specification should be understood as defining the complete correspondence between instances in the reference model and instances in the integrated model.

When the mapping module is executed, it translates the metadata from *Language 1*'s repository format to XMI's repository language format. One the other side, a generator will interpret the metadata in the XMI's repository, and generates the XMI model. Standards for data model exchange and inter-model mapping, like XMI or EXPRESS-X, together with code generators for mapping and high-level interfaces, have shown potential to be an ever increasing reference adopted by industry in general. Figure 6 gives an example of a translation between EXPRESS, UML, DTD, and XMI.

This platform is designed based on the concept of model morphisms (MoMo), which addresses the problem of mapping and transformation of models. The research community identifies two core classes of morphisms: nonaltering morphisms and model altering morphisms. In nonaltering, given two models, source and target model, a mapping is created relating each element of the source with a correspondent element in the target, leaving the two models intact. In model-altering morphism, the source model is transformed using some kind of transformation function which outputs the target model.

The proposed framework is according to the altering morphism class, as it gets the mapping rules already defined. As well, the framework is designed with extensibility in mind, so one can easily plug in other translators according to specific needs, as long as their implementations follow specific rules. Some of the proposed outputs to be available in the framework are XMI, XML, OWL, RDB, and visualization formats of EXPRESS schemas.

Figure 6. Translation between EXPRESS, UML, DTD, and XMI

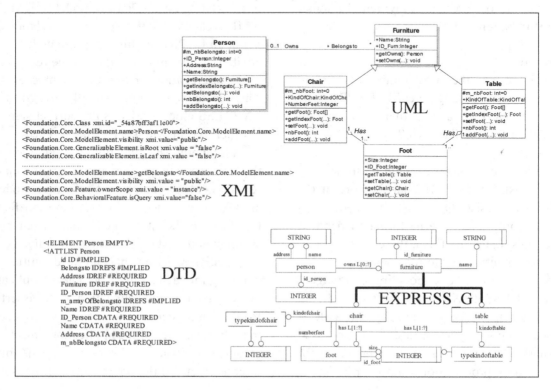

GLOBAL METHODOLOGY FOR INTEGRATION OF MODELS AND APPLICATIONS

After selecting the AP to be used as integrator of one application in an IP using an AP, the next stage is the development of its translator, and, as presented in a previous section, different levels of integration and levels of access to the platform become possible. In order to accelerate the development of these translators, and consequently the integration of the application in the IP, code can be generated based on the model adopted, thus providing faster development and better conformance of data and interoperability of applications with the IP.

For the implementation of inter-modeling mapping and generation of the ADT from a XMI model description, the architectures described in Figure 7 and Figure 8 are proposed. The modules to be considered are those directly related with the programming language selected for the code generation. Nevertheless, the mapping in this case is specialized in the generation of implementable

Figure 7. Architecture for inter-modeling mapping

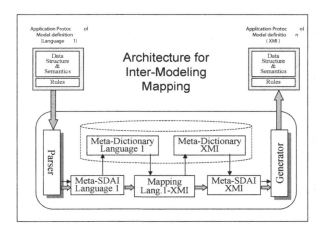

Figure 8. Architecture for ADT generation and early-binding SDAI

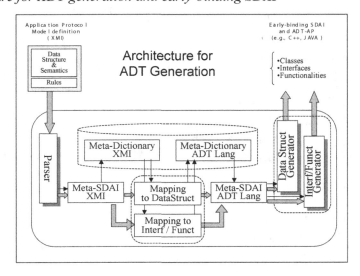

data structures and methods from the conceptual model. These methods will provide the functionalities to access to the class members, and virtualize the low-level layers of the IP architecture, as are the SDAI and the neutral format generators.

To have a complete system able to generate interfaces for several programming languages, and to have a general architecture supporting a flexible code generation, the requirement is that each programming language provides its meta-SDAI ADT, data structure, and interface/functionalities mapping, altogether with the respective generators.

The basis for the inter-AP mapping is the description of the mapping between the APs using a specialized language, like EXPRESS-X or XSLT. The architecture to support the inter-AP mapping generation is an extension of the two

Figure 9. Architecture for inter-AP mapping

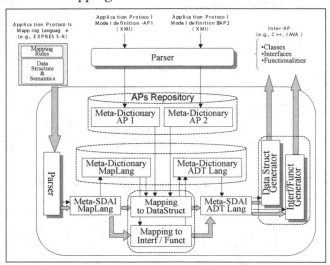

Figure 10. Methodology for integration of applications using general APs

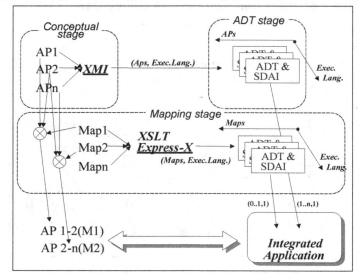

architectures previously presented (Figure 9). The procedure to execute the inter-AP mapping should first compile the mapping description and store it in the repository. For that, a parser to this language, together with a meta-SDAI, should be plugged in the system.

In this architecture, the mapping is the core module. It runs by analyzing the mapping rules stored in the inter-AP mapping repository, together with the meta-dictionary information of the two APs and the one for the target ADT language. Therefore, this module will generate the data structure and functionalities to support the mapping between the models described in XMI.

To produce accurate mapping, the mapping tool needs to have knowledge about the mechanism for interoperability between the standards that originate the model in XMI, in order to implement in the translators the inter-reference mechanisms, accordingly with such standards. For instance, the reference from one model described in STEP to PLib should be done using the PLib services, as recommended by the ISO TC184/SC4 community (Staub, 1998).

The usage of the general architecture presented for inter-AP modeling, inter-AP mapping, and code generation must be driven by a methodology for the integration of applications in IPs (Jardim-Goncalves & Steiger-Garcao, 2002b).

The proposed methodology is described in four stages by Figure 10. They are:

Conceptual stage:
a.   Select the APs and models to be used as support for the integration of the application in the IP;
b.   Select the parser, meta-SDAI, and mapping module for each of the selected AP's language; and
c.   Translate those conceptual models to XMI.

ADT stage:
d.   Select the programming languages to be used for the implementation of the translators;
e.   Select the ADT generator, meta-SDAI, and mapping module for each of the selected programming language; and
f.   Generate for each AP the correspondent ADT in the set of selected programming languages.

Mapping stage:
g.   Select the set of APs that is required for the mapping;
h.   Define the mapping rules between them, using EXPRESS-X;
i.   Select the ADT generator, meta-SDAI, and Mapping module for each of the selected programming languages; and
j.   Generate for each mapping the correspondent inter-model mapping ADT, in the set of selected programming languages.

=» *Integrate the Application in the IP using the generated code.*

CONCLUSION

Companies need to fulfill a customer's expectations in terms of product and service specifications, price, and quality, in a dynamic environment, where products life cycle is dramatically reduced and competitors appear from everywhere, anytime. The globalization process of the last decade has exposed companies to wider markets, with an increasing number of potential clients. Competition on a global market means that clients are becoming more demanding, either through producing and selling products and services across the world, or by selling locally but competing with global players.

Mass customization is a rational way for firms to cope with this continuously-evolving business environment. To be able to produce based on the mass customization paradigm, companies must change the way they innovate and produce, requiring an increased productivity and enhanced flexibility, that must be sustained through the integration of their value chain, flexibility in the supply chain management, and exploitation of the information-rich supplier and distribution chain.

The required business changes must be enabled by adequate support of information systems and technology, along with an appropriate methodology. In the last decade, companies have made heavy investments in IT, both to support their internal business and manufacturing systems and to take advantage of new business opportunities in the emergence of the Internet.

Yet most of these implemented systems are unlikely to automatically exchange services and data, not only between internal applications but especially with trading partners' applications. This mainly results due to incompatibility of data formats, reference models, and semantics between the components to be exchanged between the systems. Indeed, the identified interoperability problems between applications are typically related with data model compatibility and mapping, different languages and methodologies for model representation, correctness in the semantics of the data being exchanged, and lack of accurate conformance and interoperability checking.

Companies are thus often facing a dilemma. They must respond to the demands posed by global competition and the need to mass-customize their production which needs to be supported by interoperable IT systems. But usually, even after large investments in IT applications, they are still not able to communicate and exchange data, information, and knowledge with other applications. Companies cannot afford to scrap everything and deploy new IT systems that are interoperable. Ideally they, require plug-and-play solutions that overcome existing technical barriers.

Despite this, there are an increasing number of specialized and complementary software applica-

tions working for each industry, together with a strong support for reuse, integration, and extension of already-existent application protocols, intending to cover the needs for inter-cross industrial scope, and trying to save most of the existent standardized work. Hence, mass customization can only be a viable manufacturing paradigm for companies having traditional operations management systems and IT systems, if they start investing in the development of interoperability for their business and information systems.

Conceptual IS architectures for interoperability are the foundation for the development of platforms for mass customization. The emerging model-driven architectures, combined with the promising service-oriented architectures, seem to be an adequate proposal to face seamless communication between systems and applications, integrating internal and external organizations. Also, reference models, like the standard ISO10303 STEP application protocols, and standard technologies for data representation, like XML, are today available to integrate the product life cycle.

However, even with such variety of available tools and methods, their adoption requires skilled expertise, usually not available in traditional organizations. Thus, to motivate the adoption of these available technologies, a proper methodology, supported by a set of tools that can facilitate the integration of these models using the proper technology, needs to be used. These should be part of the framework based on a conceptual platform to develop interoperability in mass customization information systems.

The presented work has been developed and applied in the scope of the intelligent manufacturing systems (IMS) SMART-fm programme (www.ims.org) and European ATHENA IP and INTEROP NoE projects (www.athena-ip.org, www.interop-noe.org), under real industrial environments.

ACKNOWLEDGMENT

The authors would like to thank all the national and international organizations that have been supporting and funding, during the last fifteen years, a significant number of international projects in the area of interoperable systems, which resulted in the framework presented in this chapter.

Major organizations are the European Commission, CEN/ISSS, Ministry of Industry of Portugal, Ministry of Economy of Portugal, Portuguese Foundation for Science and Technology, Portugal/USA Foundation for Development, IPQ, and the Portuguese Standardization Body.

Also, we express our recognition for the project partners that work and contribute substantially in the mentioned projects.

REFERENCES

aecXML (2006). Retrieved March 22, 2006, from http://www.iai-na.org/aecxml/mission.php

AlMellor (2004). *Introduction to model-driven architecture.* Addison-Wesley.

Anderson, D. (2004). *Build-to-order and mass customization: The ultimate supply chain and lean manufacturing strategy for low-cost on-demand production without forecasts or inventory.* CIM Press.

Anderson, D. M., & Pine II, B. J. (1997). *Agile product development for mass customization.* Chicago: Irvin Publishers.

Balakrishman, A. Kumara, S., & Sundaresan, S. (1999). Manufacturing in the digital age: Exploiting information technologies for product realization. *Information Systems Frontiers, 1,* 25-50.

Berre, A. (2002). Overview of international standards on enterprise architecture. *SINTEF.*

Böhms, M. (2001). Building construction extensible markup language (bcXML) description: E-construct bcXML. *A Contribution to the CEN/ISSS eBES Workshop, Annex A, ISSS/WS-eBES/01/001.*

Boissier, R. (1995). Architecture solutions for integrating CAD, CAM and machining in small companies. In *Proceedings of the IEEE/ECLA/IFIP International Conference on Architectures and Design Methods for Balanced Automation Systems* (pp. 407-416). London: Chapman & Hall.

Breton, E., & Bézivin, J. (2001). Using meta-model technologies to organize functionalities for active system schemes. In *Proceedings of the 5th International Conference on Autonomous Agents,* Canada.

CEN/ISSS (2006). *European Committee for Standardisation - Information Society Standardization System.* Retrieved March 22, 2006, from http://www.cenorm.be/isss

Clements, P. (1997). Standard support for the virtual enterprise. In *Proceedings of the International Conference on Enterprise Integration Modeling Technology – ICEIMT'97, Torino, Italy.* Retrieved March 22, 2006, from http://www.mel.nist.gov/workshop/iceimt97/pap-cle2/stdspt2.htm

Cusumano, M. A., & Nobeoka, K. (1998). *Thinking beyond lean.* New York: Free Press.

D'Souza, D., & Wills, A., (1998). *Objects, components, and frameworks with UML: The catalysis.* Addison-Wesley. Retrieved March 23, 2006, from http://www.catalysis.org

Da Silveira, G., Borenstein, D., & Fogliaatto, F. S. (2001). Mass customization: Literature review and research directions. *International Journal of Production Economics, 72*(1).

DATAFORM EDIData (1997). *UN/EDIFACT Release 93A.*

DOM (Document Object Model) (2006). Retrieved March 23, 2006, from http://www.w3.org/TR/REC-DOM-Level-1

empirica GmbH (2005). *The European e-Business Report: A portrait of e-business in 10 sectors of the EU economy, 2005 edition*. Retrieved March 23, 2006, from http://www.ebusiness-watch.org/resources/documents/Pocketbook-2005_001.pdf

ENV 13 550 (1995). *Enterprise Model Execution and Integration Services (EMEIS)*. Brussels, Belgium: CEN.

Fenves, S. J., Sriram, R. D., Choi, Y., & Robert, J. E. (2003). *Advanced Engineering Environments for Small Manufacturing Enterprises, 1*.

Fenves, S. J., Sriram, R. D., Choi, Y., Elm, J. P., & Robert, J. E. (2004). *Advanced Engineering Environments for Small Manufacturing Enterprises, 2*.

Fowler, J. (2000). *Co-operative use of STEP and PLib*. Retrieved March 22, 2006, from http://www.nist.gov/sc4

Gallaher, M. (2004). *Cost analysis of inadequate interoperability in the U.S. capital facilities industry* (NIST GCR 04-867). Washington, DC: National Institute of Standards and Technology, Department of Commerce.

Gilmore, J. H., & Pine II, B. J. (1997). The four faces of mass customization. *Harvard Business Review*, (January-February).

Gregory, T. (1999). *Interoperability cost analysis of the U.S. automotive supply chain* (99-1 Planning Rep.). Washington, DC: National Institute of Standards and Technology, Department of Commerce.

Grilo, A., & Jardim-Goncalves, R., (2005). Analysis on the development of e-platforms in the AEC sector. *International Journal of Internet and Enterprise Management, 3*(2).

Hegge, H. M., & Wortmann, J. C. (1991). Generic bill-of-material: A new product model. *International Journal of Production Economics, 23*.

Huang, G. Q., Zhang, X. Y., & Lo, V. H. (2005). Optimal supply chain configuration for platform products: Impacts of commonality, demand variability, and quantity discount. *International Journal of Mass Customization, 1*(1).

IAI/IFC (1997). *IFC End User Guide. International Foundation Classes Release 1.5. IAI*.

IDEAS Project (2003). Ontology state of the art - Final report.

ISO TC184/SC4 Standards (2006). Retrieved March 23, 2006, from http://www.tc184-sc4.org

ISO1030-1 (1994). ISO 10303 - Standard for the exchange of product data, Part 1, Overview and fundamentals principles. *International Organization for Standardization*.

ISO10303-11 (1998). ISO 10303 Standard for the exchange of product data (STEP), Part 11, Description methods, The EXPRESS language reference manual. *International Organization for Standardization*.

ISO10303-22 (2001). ISO 10303 Standard for the exchange of product data (STEP), Part 22. *International Organization for Standardization*.

Jardim-Goncalves, R. (2004). Ontology-based framework for enhanced interoperability in networked industrial environments. In *Proceedings of the 11ᵗʰ IFAC Symposium on Information Control Problems in Manufacturing, INCOM2004*. Salvador, Brazil.

Jardim-Goncalves, R., & Steiger, A. (2002). Integration and adoptabilidade of APs – The role of ISO TC184/SC4 standards. *Special issue: Applications in Industry of Product and Process Modelling Using Standards International Journal of Computer Applications in Technology*.

Jardim-Goncalves, R., & Steiger-Garcão, A. (2001). Supporting interoperability in standard-based environments - Towards reliable integrated systems. Advances in Concurrent Engineering. In *Proceedings of the 8th ISPE International Conference on Concurrent Engineering (CE2001)*, Anaheim, CA.

Jardim-Goncalves, R., & Steiger-Garcão, A. (2002a). Implicit hierarchic metamodeling - In search of adaptable interoperability for manufacturing and business systems. In *Proceedings of the 5th IEEE/IFIP BASYS2002*, Mexico.

Jardim-Goncalves, R., & Steiger-Garcão, A. (2002b). Implicit multi-level modeling to support integration and interoperability in flexible business environments. *Communications of ACM, Special Issue on Enterprise Components, Services, and Business Rules*, 53-57.

JTC 1/SC 7/WG 17 (2006). *ISO - International Organization for Standardization*.

Liker, J. (2004). *The Toyota way*. McGraw Hill.

Loffredo, D. (1998). *Efficient database implementation of EXPRESS information models*. PhD thesis, Rensselaer Polytechnic Institute, Troy, NY.

MDA (2003). *Model Driven Architecture, MDA Guide Version 1.0.1, June 2003*. Retrieved March 23, 2006, from http://www.omg.org/mda

Mellor, S., & Balcer, M. (2002). *Executable UML - A foundation for model-driven architecture*. Addison-Wesley.

Miller, J., & Mukerji, J. (2001). *Model driven architecture white paper*. Retrieved March 23, 2006, from http://www.omg.org/cgi-bin/doc?ormsc/2001-07-01

Motta, E. (1999). *Reusable components for knowledge modelling*. Amsterdam, The Netherlands: IOS Press.

Nagi, L. (1997). Design and implementation of a virtual information system for agile manufacturing. *IIE Transactions on Design and Manufacturing, Special issue on Agile Manufacturing, 29*, 839-857.

O'Grady, P. (1999). *The age of modularity*. Iowa City, IA: Adams and Steele Publishers.

Pine II, B. J. (1993). *Mass customization: The new frontier in business competition*. Boston: Harvard Business School Press.

PLib (2000). ISO 13584 Parts Library, ISO TC184/SC4, Part 102, View Exchange Protocol: View Exchange Protocol by ISO10303 conforming specification. *International Organization for Standardization*.

Prahalad, C. K., & Ramaswamy, V. (2004). *The future of competition: Co-creating unique value with customers*. Boston: Harvard Business School Press.

Pugh, S. (1997). *Total design: Integrated methods for successful product engineering*. Wokingham: Addison-Wesley.

Rational (2006). Retrieved March 22, 2006, from http://www.rational.com/uml

Robertson, D., & Ulrich, K. (1998). Planning product platforms. *Sloan Management Review, 39*(4).

Rumbaugh, J. (1998). *UML - The unified modeling language*. Addison-Wesley.

Schooler, S. B. (2005). Toward a multi-agent information management infrastucture for product family planning and mass customization. *International Journal of Mass Customization, 1*(1).

Simpson, T. W. (2005). Product platform design and customization: Status and promise. *Special Issue on Platform Product Development for Mass Customization, AIEDAM, 18*(1).

SOA (2006). *The Service-Oriented Architecture.* Retrieved March 23, 2006, from http://msdn.microsoft.com/architecture/soa/default.aspx

Staub, G. (1998). ISO TC184/SC4QC N068, *Interpretation of PLib Services-Guideline for the common interpretation of the "services" provided by PLib using the STEP IR.*

Trireme International (2006). Retrieved March 23, 2006, from http://www.trireme.u-net.com/catalysis

Umar (1999). A framework for analyzing virtual enterprise infrastructure. In *Proceedings of the 9ᵗʰ International Workshop on Research Issues in Data Engineering - IT for Virtual Enterprises, RIDE-VE'99* (pp. 4-11). IEEE Computer Society.

Vlosky, R. P. (1998). Partnerships versus typical relationships between wood products distributors and their manufacturer suppliers. *Forest Products Journal, 48*(3), 27-35.

W3C (2006). *World Wide Web Consortium.* Retrieved March 23, 2006, from http://www.w3c.org

WS-I (2006). Web services interoperability organization. *WS-I.* Retrieved March 23, 2006, from http://www.ws-i.org

XMI, XML Meta-data Interchange (2006). Retrieved March 23, 2006, from http://www.omg.org/technology/xml/index.htm

This work was previously published in Mass Customization Information Systems in Business, edited by T. Blecker; G. Friedrich, pp. 136-161, copyright 2007 by Information Science Reference (an imprint of IGI Global).

Chapter 6
Mass Customization with Configurable Products and Configurators:
A Review of Benefits and Challenges

Mikko Heiskala
Helsinki University of Technology, Finland

Juha Tihonen
Helsinki University of Technology, Finland

Kaija-Stiina Paloheimo
Helsinki University of Technology, Finland

Timo Soininen
Helsinki University of Technology, Finland

ABSTRACT

Configurable products are an important way to achieve mass customization. A configurable product is designed once, and this design is used repetitively in the sales-delivery process to produce specifications of product individuals meeting customer requirements. Configurators are information systems that support the specification of product individuals and the creation and management of configuration knowledge, therefore being prime examples of information systems supporting mass customization. However, to the best of our knowledge, there is no systematic review of literature on how mass customization with configurable products and use of configurators affect companies. In this chapter, we provide such a review. We focus on benefits that can be gained and challenges which companies may face. A supplier can move to mass customization and configuration from mass production or from full customization; we keep the concerns separate. We also review benefits and challenges from the customer perspective. Finally, we identify future research directions and open challenges and problems.

INTRODUCTION

Today, customers are demanding products that will better meet their increasingly diverse needs. *Mass customization* (MC) has been proposed (Pine, 1993a) as a more cost-efficient solution to this challenge than *full customization* (FC), a term we use in this chapter for craft production of one-of-a-kind, bespoke products. MC is the ability to provide products tailored to individual customer needs on a large scale at, or close to, mass production (MP) efficiency, using flexible processes (Da Silveira, Borenstein, & Fogliatto, 2001; Hart, 1995; Pine, 1993a). One way to implement MC is through *configurable products* (CP). The design of a configurable product specifies a set of pre-designed elements and rules on how these can be combined into valid product individuals (Salvador & Forza, 2004; Tiihonen & Soininen, 1997). Such knowledge is called *configuration knowledge*. The design of a configurable product is used repetitively, in a routine manner without creative design, in the sales-delivery process to produce specifications of product individuals that meet the requirements of particular customers. Defining a valid, error-free (sales) specification of a customer-specific product individual can be difficult because the product elements often manifest complex interdependencies and incompatibilities. Some companies have addressed this difficulty by employing information systems called *product configurators* (or configurators, for short) as support in the task of defining a sales specification (Barker & O'Connor, 1990; Forza & Salvador, 2002a, 2002b). A *configurator* is an information system that supports the creation and management of configuration knowledge and the specification of product individuals (Sabin & Weigel, 1998; Tiihonen & Soininen, 1997).

However, to the best of our knowledge, there is no systematic review of literature on how configurators affect the operations and business of companies pursuing mass customization with configurable products. The majority of papers de-

scribe the introduction and use of a configurator in a single-case company. A significant set of papers describes issues of MC, CP, and configurators. This review aims to provide a summary.

The rest of this chapter is structured as follows. Next, the overall framework of the literature review is described. The following section then contemplates the benefits and challenges of MC and CP for the supplier and customer, first compared with MP and then compared with FC.

This section is followed by a discussion of configurator benefits, how they may overcome or alleviate the MC and CP challenges, and then moves on to configurator challenges. Also in this section, the supplier perspective is discussed before the customer perspective. Before suggestions for future research directions, discussion, and conclusions end this chapter, the rationale for a company to move to MC are briefly discussed.

LITERATURE REVIEW METHODS AND FRAMEWORK

For the literature review, we first identified the benefits and challenges attributed to MC, configurable products, and configurators. Second, we studied how configurators have been used to meet the challenges related to MC with configurable products. Third, we identified unmet challenges and remaining problems in configurator-supported MC and derived suggestions for future work. The framework for our literature review reflects this process and illustrates our viewpoints (see Figure 1). We classified benefits and challenges according to whom they concern (supplier or customer) and the direction of a move to MC. A supplier can move to MC (Duray, 2002; Lampel & Mintzberg, 1996; Svensson & Barfod, 2002) and CP (Tiihonen & Soininen, 1997) from either the direction of MP or FC. The latter classification is not visible in Figure 1.

We used electronic scientific databases with search terms such as mass customization, customization, product configuration, configurator, configurable products, benefits, challenges, opportunities, threats, limitations, problems, and drawbacks. From the yield of hundreds of articles, books, and conference papers, we browsed the abstracts and selected about 75 publications for closer examination. Further selection left some of them out of this chapter. For readability, we omit a full list of references to a benefit or challenge from the text. All references are shown in tables at the end of each subsection. The tables also show whether a reference belongs to MC or CP literature, when applicable.

MASS CUSTOMIZATION AND CONFIGURABLE PRODUCTS

Supplier Benefits Compared with Mass Production

In this section, we discuss the benefits for a supplier from MC or CP compared with MP. The benefits and references are summarized in Table 1.

In general, MC refers to the ability to effectively fulfill a wider range of customer needs than with MP (Pine, 1993a), an idea often incorporated into definitions of MC.

Perhaps the most cited benefit of MC and CP is the reduction in inventories of finished goods and work-in-progress, tying less capital compared to build-to-forecast MP (Pine, 1993a). Less inventory handling and management is necessary (Broekhuizen & Alsem, 2002) and improvements in inventory turnover are implied (Beaty, 1996). Similarly, MC can eliminate or reduce the need to sell aging models and seasonal products by discount as MC products are less subject to product obsolescence and fashion risk (Kotha, 1995). MC often involves modular products. An inventory of modules is less subject to fashion and technological obsolescence than differentiated inventory (Berman, 2002). As a result, the supplier does not have to include markdowns or

high inventory accumulation in its pricing (Berman, 2002).

In MC and also with CP, the customer participates in the specification of the product. Customers may enjoy the participation in design and it can increase customer satisfaction in the finished good as well (Huffman & Kahn, 1998). Further, the effort spent and information accumulated and stored in the specification process can become a switching cost for the customer (Pine, Peppers, & Rogers, 1995). Switching to competition would mean spending the effort again. However, this benefit can be realized fully only if the interactions or repurchases with the customers are frequent enough (Broekhuizen & Alsem, 2002; Pine et al., 1995). As customers need to express their needs, the supplier has an opportunity to gather more accurate customer information (Pine et al., 1995) and develop a deep understanding of the customer's needs (Berman, 2002). This and engaging the customer in a continuous dialog (Berman, 2002) and learning relationship (Pine et al., 1995) makes it more difficult for competitors to accumulate the same depth of customer knowledge and entice customers away. Moreover, information on actual orders directly reflects current market information (Berman, 2002). This may enable quicker product development response to changes in overall customer needs (Berman, 2002; Slywotzky, 2000). However, Kakati (2002) argues that all customer needs cannot be captured with tracking choices on physical product elements. The customers must also be willing to share their preferences and purchase patterns with the supplier on an ongoing basis if the supplier is to be able to use them for their own purposes (Wind & Rangaswamy, 2001).

MC can enable premium pricing (Kotha, 1995) due to the better fit of the product to customer needs and due to the difficulty of comparison-shopping of customized products (Agrawal, Kumaresh, & Mercer, 2001, see Table 8). Ability to participate in design may also increase willingness to pay

Table 1. Summary of supplier benefits compared with mass production

Benefit	References	MC/ CP
Efficient way to fulfill a wider range of customer needs	Pine, 1993a; Hart, 1995; Da Silveira et al., 2001 (*MC has been usually defined in a similar vein.*)	MC
	Tiihonen, Soininen, Männistö, and Sulonen, 1996; Tiihonen and Soininen, 1997; Tiihonen,, Soininen, Männistö, and Sulonen, 1998; Bonehill and Slee-Smith, 1998	CP
Reduction in inventories	Pine 1993a; Kay, 1993; Kotha, 1995; Ross, 1996; Beaty, 1996; Gilmore and Pine, 1997; Radder and Louw, 1999; Slywotzky, 2000; Zipkin, 2001; Agrawal et al., 2001; Wind and Rangaswamy, 2001; Berman, 2002; Broekhuizen and Alsem, 2002; Svensson and Barfod 2002; Piller, Moeslein, and Stotko, 2004; Piller and Müller, 2004	MC
	Tiihonen and Soininen, 1997; Tiihonen et al., 1998	CP
Reduction in product model obsolescence, fashion risk	Kotha, 1995; Agrawal et al., 2001; Zipkin, 2001; Berman, 2002; Piller et al., 2004; Piller and Müller, 2004	MC
Customer participation in design: satisfaction, effort spent, and switching cost	*Satisfaction*: Huffman and Kahn, 1998; Wind and Rangaswamy, 2001; Bardacki and Whitelock, 2003. *Switching costs*: Pine et al., 1995; Broekhuizen and Alsem, 2002; Bardacki and Whitelock, 2003; Piller et al., 2004; Piller and Müller, 2004	MC
More accurate customer information	Pine et al., 1995; Hart, 1995; Åhlström and Westbrook, 1999; Slywotzky, 2000; Agrawal et al., 2001; Kakati, 2002; Broekhuizen and Alsem, 2002; Berman, 2002; Brown and Bessant, 2003; Bardacki and Whitelock, 2003; Piller et al., 2004; Franke and Piller, 2004	MC
Potential for premium pricing	Kotha, 1995; Ross, 1996; Agrawal et al., 2001; Berman, 2002; Broekhuizen and Alsem, 2002; MacCarthy and Brabazon, 2003; Piller and Müller, 2004; Piller et al., 2004; Franke and Piller, 2004	MC

for the self-designed, customized final product (Franke & Piller, 2004).

Supplier Challenges Compared with Mass Production

In the following, we discuss the supplier challenges from MC or CP compared with MP from a number of viewpoints.

Business

See Table 2 for a summary of the supplier business challenges which we discuss in this section.

MP products have to be developed or adjusted to be suitable for MC. MC tends to be more costly than MP (Kotha, 1995). One of the key challenges for MC with CP for the supplier is to find the right amount of customization to offer that balances the costs of added complexity and increased customer value (Beaty, 1996). The offered customization range has to be matched to customer needs of the targeted segment(s). A mismatch reduces sales potential and can lead to excessive one-of-a-kind design (Tiihonen & Soininen, 1997; Tiihonen et al., 1998). Excessive customization increases the specification complexity both for the supplier and the customer, and may strain the production process too far (Berman, 2002). Further, development of a product to be easy to configure ("design for configuration") can be a significant effort (Tiihonen & Soininen, 1997; Tiihonen et al., 1998).

MC products often are modular and possibly share components across product lines or families. Component sharing may cause customers to see the products as overly similar (Pine, 1993b) and create confusion over the "true" customiza-

Table 2. Summary of supplier business challenges compared with mass production

Challenge	References	MC/CP
Producing customized products often costs more than MP	Kotha, 1995; Åhlström and Westbrook, 1999; Zipkin, 2001; Berman, 2002; Broekhuizen and Alsem, 2002; Kakati, 2002; Bardacki and Whitelock, 2003; Piller et al., 2004; Piller and Müller, 2004	MC
Finding right amount, balance of offered customization	Beaty, 1996; Svensson and Barfod, 2002; Berman, 2002; MacCarthy and Brabazon, 2003; Piller and Müller, 2004	MC
	Tiihonen and Soininen, 1997; Tiihonen et al., 1998	CP
Component sharing across product lines may cause customer to see the products as overly similar	Pine, 1993b; Berman, 2002; Kakati, 2002	MC
Possible channel conflicts with retailers	Wind and Rangaswamy, 2001; Broekhuizen and Alsem, 2002	MC
Elicitation difficulties can cause lost business, image, and lower customer and dealer loyalty and satisfaction.	Huffman and Kahn, 1998	MC
	Fohn et al., 1995; Heatley et al., 1995; Yu and Skovgaard, 1998; Forza and Salvador, 2002a	CP

tion level of the product (Berman, 2002; Kakati, 2002).

MC may cause channel conflicts (Broekhuizen & Alsem, 2002; Wind & Rangaswamy, 2001) as retailers may be unwilling to participate in fear of the supplier bypassing them in the future, and they may also be reluctant to take on more specification tasks. Difficulties of eliciting customer needs and creating sales specifications (discussed in section Specification Process below) can cause severe challenges. These include loss of confidence from

customers (Fohn, Liau, Greef, Young, & O'Grady, 1995), lost sales, customers, and repeat business (Fohn et al., 1995; Heatley, Agraval, & Tanniru, 1995), and decreased customer satisfaction (Forza & Salvador, 2002a; Heatley et al., 1995). Further, the problems and complexity of specifying a product individual, and dissatisfaction in the shopping process are often attributed to the retailer (Huffman & Kahn, 1998). Elicitation difficulties, resulting order errors, and delays may also lower dealer loyalty (Yu & Skovgaard, 1998).

Table 3. Summary of supplier organizational and operational challenges compared with mass production

Challenge	References	MC/CP
Extent of operational changes large	Pine et al., 1993; Hart, 1995; Kotha, 1995; Ross, 1996; Agrawal et al., 2001; Zipkin, 2001; Berman, 2002; Broekhuizen and Alsem, 2002	MC
	Tiihonen & Soininen, 1997	CP
Increased information management	Åhlström and Westbrook, 1999; Da Silveira et al., 2001; Zipkin, 2001; Berman, 2002; Broekhuizen and Alsem, 2002; Kakati, 2002; MacCarthy and Brabazon, 2003; Brown and Bessant, 2003; Piller et al., 2004; Comstock et al., 2004	MC
	Forza and Salvador, 2002a; Salvador and Forza, 2004	CP
Extent of organizational and cultural changes large	Pine et al., 1993; Kay, 1993; Ross, 1996; Åhlström and Westbrook, 1999; Slywotzky, 2000; Agrawal et al., 2001; Kakati, 2002; Berman, 2002	MC
	Tiihonen and Soininen, 1997	CP

Organization and Operations

The organizational and operational challenges for the supplier which we contemplate here are summarized in Table 3. The extent of operational changes required is large (Pine et al., 1993). Sales and marketing has to increase interaction with the customers (Kakati, 2002) and learn new specification tasks (Tiihonen & Soininen, 1997). MC requires more manufacturing and logistics flexibility (discussed in section Manufacturing below).

A commonly-cited challenge in MC is that it increases the need for information management (Åhlström & Westbrook, 1999). What an MC supplier basically does is that it takes the customer requirements, that is, information, and translates them to a manufactured product (Da Silveira et al., 2001). The information about the customer requirements flows through the supplier organization from sales to manufacturing and distribution, crossing organizational boundaries, until the customer-specific product is finally delivered to the customer. This increases both the amount of information transferred and the information flows (or paths) in the supplier organization. Both operations flow information, and customer information need to be managed by the supplier (Broekhuizen & Alsem, 2002). MC also increases the need for product data and variant handling (Comstock, Johansen, & Winroth, 2004).

The extent of required organizational and cultural changes is large (Pine et al., 1993). Functional silos are a hindrance to MC (Pine et al., 1993). It can be difficult to create company-wide understanding of the benefits of MC with CP. Effort spent and effects felt may occur at different places. Developing well-managed and documented configuration knowledge takes effort in the product process but helps sales. Producing error-free and complete sales specifications takes extra effort at sales but helps to reduce fire-fighting in manufacturing (Tiihonen & Soininen, 1997). Highly-skilled, more costly sales staff and increased training may be required for eliciting customer needs, specification tasks, and verification of specifications (Berman, 2002). Achieving the required skills is more difficult if the supplier does not own the sales companies (Broekhuizen & Alsem, 2002; Tiihonen et al., 1996) or if the turnover in sales is high (Berman, 2002).

Specification Process

In this section, we discuss the supplier challenges related to the specification process; for a summary, see Table 4. The most-often cited challenge with MC and CP is the difficulty of customer needs elicitation and defining corresponding valid sales specifications (Ross, 1996) as customization increases both the complexity and amount of required information. Sales often have incomplete or out-of-date configuration knowledge, which is one contributing factor to the specification errors. This issue is discussed in detail in section Long-Term Management of Configuration Knowledge below.

Several specification error types have been identified. (1) The specified product individual cannot be produced at all or it would not work properly (Aldanondo, Véron, & Fargier, 1999; 2000). Such errors cause iterations in the sales-delivery process (Wright, Weixelbaum, Vesonder, Brown, Palmer, Berman, & Moore, 1993) between the customer and supplier or sales and manufacturing because specifications have to be reconsidered. (2) The specification might not meet customer needs optimally (Aldanondo et al., 1999; Forza & Salvador, 2002a). One reason may be the different terminology or level of abstraction in expressing customer requirements and technical specifications (Tiihonen & Soininen, 1997; Tiihonen et al., 1998). Communicating customization possibilities of a very flexible product to the customer may also be hard (Tiihonen & Soininen, 1997). Technical experts consulted for specification feasibility may not communicate with the customer at all, which may be a cause for mismatch as well (Tiihonen &

Table 4. Summary of the supplier challenges in the specification process compared with mass production

Challenge	References	MC/CP
Difficulty of customer needs elicitation and definition of a corresponding, complete, and error-free sales specification	Ross, 1996; Huffman and Kahn, 1998; Åhlström and Westbrook, 1999; Zipkin, 2001; Wind and Rangaswamy, 2001; Berman, 2002; MacCarthy and Brabazon, 2003; Piller et al., 2004; Comstock et al., 2004	MC
	Sviokla, 1990; Wright et al., 1993; Heatley et al., 1995; Fohn et al., 1995; Tiihonen et al., 1996; Tiihonen and Soininen, 1997; Tiihonen et al., 1998; McGuinness and Wright, 1998; Sabin and Weigel, 1998; Yu and Skovgaard, 1998; Vanwelkenheysen, 1998; Aldanondo et al., 1999; Aldanondo et al., 2000; Forza and Salvador, 2002a, 2002b; Salvador and Forza, 2004	CP
Can specified product individual be produced/ manufactured, and will it work properly?	Aldanondo et al., 1999; Aldanondo et al., 2000	CP
Errors noticed after sales specification phase lead to iterations in sales-delivery process	Wright et al., 1993; Heatley et al., 1995; Fohn et al., 1995; Tiihonen and Soininen, 1997; Tiihonen et al., 1998; Sabin and Weigel, 1998; Aldanondo et al., 2000	CP
Does the specified product individual fit customer needs optimally?	Aldanondo et al., 1999; Forza and Salvador, 2002a	CP
Erroneous, smaller price than effective cost for the specified product individual.	Wright et al., 1993; Fohn et al., 1995; Aldanondo et al., 1999; Aldanondo et al., 2000; Salvador and Forza, 2004	CP
Erroneous delivery time	Salvador and Forza, 2004	CP
Sales staff create repertoires of typical specifications, valid but not optimal in fit with customer needs	Sviokla, 1990; Heatley et al., 1995; Salvador and Forza, 2004	CP
Two sales persons may produce different specifications for identical customer orders	Sviokla, 1990	CP
Technical experts deeply involved in verifying specifications	Tiihonen et al., 1998; Forza and Salvador, 2002a; Salvador and Forza, 2004	CP

Soininen, 1997). Further, it is difficult to identify intangible preferences like the preferred fit of a shoe (tight/loose) (Wind & Rangaswamy, 2001). (3) Pricing errors: for example, a specification might define a smaller price than the effective cost of producing the product individual (Wright et al., 1993). If pricing information is not available during the specification task, the sales staff is not able to "guide" the customer to more profitable options, nor inform the customer of costly options (Salvador & Forza, 2004). (4) An erroneous delivery time could also be specified (Salvador & Forza, 2004).

To avoid difficulties of specification, sales staff may create repertoires of typical sales specifications that are valid but not necessarily optimal in

fit with customer needs (Sviokla, 1990). Therefore, the full customization potential of the product is not offered to the customer (Salvador & Forza, 2004). Specification task complexity may also cause sales persons to produce different specifications for identical orders (Sviokla, 1990). To counter the difficulties of sales staff, technical experts are often deeply involved in verifying specification validity (Tiihonen et al., 1998), which detracts them from other tasks like product development (Forza & Salvador, 2002a), and also increases the lead-times in order processing (Wright et al., 1993). The validity checks are often bypassed under time pressure, which results in more errors (Forza & Salvador, 2002a; 2002b).

Table 5. Summary of supplier manufacturing challenges compared with mass production

Challenge	References	MC/CP
Difficulties in achieving the required production process flexibility	Kotha, 1995; Åhlström and Westbrook 1999; Slywotzky, 2000; Zipkin, 2001; Kakati 2002; Berman 2002; Piller et al. 2004	MC
	Tiihonen and Soininen, 1997; Tiihonen et al., 1998; Forza and Salvador, 2002a	CP
May require expensive investments in flexible machinery and acquiring highly-skilled staff.	*Machinery:* Piller and Müller, 2004 *Staff:* Kotha, 1995	MC
Fire-fighting in manufacturing from sales specification errors	Heatley et al., 1995; Tiihonen et al., 1996; Yu and Skovgaard, 1998; Forza and Salvador, 2002a; Salvador and Forza, 2004	CP

Manufacturing

The manufacturing challenges for the supplier are summarized in Table 5. The manufacturing of customer-specific products requires more manufacturing and logistics flexibility, which can be difficult to achieve (Kotha, 1995). It is difficult to reach lead times (Åhlström & Westbrook, 1999; Comstock et al., 2004; Svensson & Barfod, 2002) and consistent quality (Svensson & Barfod, 2002) comparable to MP. Further, the supplier has to handle variable costs instead of fixed costs (Hart, 1995). To operate efficiently, an MC supplier needs to produce, sort, ship, and deliver small quantities of highly-differentiated products (Berman, 2002), which increases the complexity of production planning and quality control (Piller et al., 2004). Achieving the flexibility can require investments in expensive flexible machinery (Piller & Müller, 2004) and hiring and training highly skilled staff (Kotha, 1995).

Specification errors that reach manufacturing cause fire-fighting activities (Heatley et al., 1995) that can take up to even 80% of the order-processing time (Tiihonen et al., 1996) to manage incorrect bills-of-materials (BOMs) and production orders, missing parts, rush deliveries from part suppliers at an extra cost, and missed delivery dates (Forza & Salvador, 2002a).

Long-Term Management of Configuration Knowledge

For a summary of the challenges we discuss here, see Table 6. MC based on CP requires up-to-date configuration knowledge, stressing the importance of its management. The long-term management and maintenance of configuration knowledge is a major task and its level in companies often poor (Wright et al., 1993). This contributes to the sales specification errors discussed earlier. Sales may not know the variation possibilities because configuration knowledge is not systematically documented (Tiihonen et al., 1996; Tiihonen et al., 1998). Product development rarely creates configuration knowledge and if it does, extracting the knowledge to sales is problematic and the transfer rarely systemized (Tiihonen et al., 1996; Wright et al., 1993). Knowledge transfer to retailers is even more challenging (Tiihonen et al., 1996). A compounding factor is that the configuration knowledge is often dispersed among a variety of sources across the supplier organization, like manufacturing, assembly, and marketing (Haag, 1998; McGuinness & Wright, 1998; Wright et al., 1993). This impedes knowledge acquisition in maintenance and update situations (McGuinness & Wright, 1998).

A further problem is that the configuration knowledge often changes frequently (Tiihonen & Soininen, 1997), which together with the transfer problems means that the configuration knowledge used in sales is often not up-to-date

Table 6. Summary of supplier challenges in long-term management of configuration knowledge compared with mass production

Challenge	References	MC/CP
Long-term management of configuration knowledge	Wright et al., 1993; Tiihonen et al., 1996; Tiihonen and Soininen, 1997; Tiihonen et al., 1998; Yu and Skovgaard, 1998; McGuinness and Wright, 1998; Haag, 1998; Fleischhanderl et al., 1998	CP
Transferring updated configuration knowledge to sales force	Wright et al., 1993; Tiihonen et al., 1996	CP
Configuration knowledge changes frequently	Tiihonen and Soininen, 1997; Fleischanderl et al., 1998; McGuinness and Wright, 1998	CP
Long-term management of delivered product individuals and reconfiguration	Tiihonen et al., 1996; Tiihonen and Soininen, 1997; Tiihonen et al., 1998; Yu and Skovgaard, 1998; Sabin and Weigel, 1998	CP

(Wright et al., 1993). The workarounds that sales staff sometimes invent to curb the elicitation complexity, like the aforementioned repertoires of typical specifications, are especially easily outdated (McGuinness & Wright, 1998). Reasons for configuration knowledge changes can be shifts in customer requirements and marketing strategies (Fleischanderl et al., 1998; Tiihonen & Soininen, 1997), product and component evolvement (Tiihonen et al., 1996), and added or removed product functionalities (Tiihonen & Soininen, 1997).

Long-term management of delivered product individuals (Tiihonen et al., 1996) is a related challenge. Information on the product type and product individual is needed when changes have to be made to an existing product individual for maintenance and servicing reasons, or when new or better functionality is added (Sabin & Weigel, 1998; Tiihonen & Soininen, 1997). This reconfiguration is problematic and prone to errors as it involves adding and removing components that may have complex interdependencies (Sabin & Weigel, 1998; Tiihonen & Soininen, 1997) and the required configuration knowledge may have to be retrieved from various sources and has to bridge temporally-different versions of the configuration knowledge base (Tiihonen & Soininen, 1997; Tiihonen et al., 1996, 1998).

Customer Benefits Compared with Mass Production

This section presents the customer benefits as compared with MP; see Table 7 for a summary. The customer viewpoint has received relatively little attention in literature.

The main benefit from MC is the better product fit with customer needs (Pine, 1993a) which applies to CP as well. Customers may also find participation in the design and specification enjoyable in itself (Huffman & Kahn, 1998), and it can also increase satisfaction in the final product (Bardacki & Whitelock, 2003).

Customer Challenges Compared with Mass Production

Next, the customer challenges from MC and CP compared with MP are discussed; a summary can be seen in Table 8. As for benefits, the customer viewpoint of the challenges appears to have received little attention in CP literature.

In MC, customers have to express their preferences for the product and may suffer from the complexity of the specification (Pine, 1993a). They may be overwhelmed by the number of options, sometimes referred to as "mass confu-

Table 7. Summary of customer benefits compared with mass production

Benefit	References	MC/CP
Improved fit with customer needs	Pine, 1993a; Kotha, 1995; Radder and Louw, 1999; Agrawal et al., 2001; Wind and Rangaswamy, 2001; Berman, 2002; Broekhuizen and Alsem, 2002; Bardacki and Whitelock, 2003; MacCarthy and Brabazon, 2003	MC
Enjoyable participation in specification and design	Huffman and Kahn, 1998; Wind and Rangaswamy, 2001; Bardacki and Whitelock, 2003; Piller and Müller, 2004; Franke and Piller, 2004	MC

Table 8. Summary of customer challenges compared with mass production

Challenge	References	MC/CP
Complexity of design and specification	Pine, 1993a; Pine et al., 1993; Pine et al., 1995; Beaty, 1996; Gilmore and Pine, 1997; Huffman and Kahn, 1998; Berman, 2002; Wind and Rangaswamy, 2001; Zipkin, 2001; Svensson and Barfod, 2002; Broekhuizen and Alsem, 2002; Piller et al., 2004; Dellaert and Stremersch, 2005	MC
	Forza and Salvador, 2002a	CP
Time and effort spent in design and specification	Gilmore and Pine, 1997; Berman, 2002; Broekhuizen and Alsem, 2002; Kakati, 2002; Bardacki and Whitelock, 2003	MC
Feeling of invaded privacy	Pine, 1993a; Pine et al., 1995; Wind and Rangaswamy, 2001; Broekhuizen and Alsem, 2002	MC
Waiting for the finished product	Radder and Louw, 1999; Agrawal et al., 2001; Zipkin, 2001; Svensson and Barfod, 2002; Bardacki and Whitelock, 2003; MacCarthy and Brabazon, 2003	MC
Need to trust supplier to deliver exactly as specified	Berman, 2002; Broekhuizen and Alsem, 2002	MC
Increased price of products	Hart, 1995; Radder and Louw, 1999; Wind and Rangaswamy, 2001; Zipkin, 2001; Agrawal et al., 2001; Broekhuizen and Alsem, 2002; Kakati, 2002; Svensson and Barfod, 2002; Bardacki and Whitelock, 2003; Piller and Müller, 2004	MC
More difficult comparison-shopping, limited transparency of product	Wind and Rangaswamy, 2001; Broekhuizen and Alsem, 2002; Piller et al., 2004	MC

sion" (Huffman & Kahn, 1998). Customers can be unsure of their needs and have trouble both in deciding what they want and in communicating their decisions precisely (Gilmore & Pine, 1997; Zipkin, 2001). Further, some needs are unarticulated (Gilmore & Pine, 1997). Customers may also feel uncertainty about whether they have been exposed to all alternatives and have complete information about the options (Huffman & Kahn, 1998). Specification difficulties are compounded if the customers lack sufficient product expertise (Huffman & Kahn, 1998). Moreover, due to the time and effort customers have to spend in specification, expressing preferences is an added drawback (Gilmore & Pine, 1997) compared to picking a product "off-the-shelf" as in MP. Some

customers may feel that expressing preferences invades their privacy (Pine, 1993a), especially in Internet (Wind & Rangaswamy, 2001).

In MC, the customers usually have to wait for the finished product (Radder & Louw, 1999) as it is produced for order. Moreover, customers must trust the supplier to deliver exactly according to the specification (Berman, 2002; Broekhuizen & Alsem, 2002). Customized products tend to be more expensive (Hart, 1995). The limited transparency of products, their complexity, and the uniqueness of individual products make comparison-shopping and judging whether the product is good value for money more difficult (Wind & Rangaswamy, 2001). On the other hand, customization raises customer expectations, which can backfire as more severe disappointment if the end product does not meet the higher expectations (Berman, 2002). Further, customers may fear that the customized products have more inconsistent quality (Svensson & Barfod, 2002).

Supplier Benefits Compared with Full Customization

This section discusses the supplier benefits (summarized in Table 9) from MC or CP compared with FC. Literature on moving to MC from FC and on associated benefits and challenges is limited to Svensson and Barfod (2002) while CP literature gives a bit more attention.

Svensson and Barfod (2002) mention several benefits that a FC supplier can gain from switching to MC. They all seem to stem from increased standardization. The benefits are increased efficiency and more controlled production, improved and more uniform product quality, shorter lead-times, and lower costs. These benefits are mentioned in CP literature as well. A reason for improved control of production is the use of a relatively small number of components to produce a large variety of end products (Tiihonen et al., 1996). A cause for quality improvements can be the use of a standard, modular design, which reduces incorrect assemblies (Bonehill & Slee-Smith, 1998). Lead-time reductions can result from quality improvements, and from the reduced need for customer-specific design of components or end products (Tiihonen et al., 1998). This also may free expert engineering resources to other tasks like product development (Tiihonen et al., 1998). Reduced effort also contributes to lower costs.

Lead-times may also be reduced by easier selling. For a configurable product, the sales options have been defined in advance. Choosing from existing options rather than beginning from scratch brings two benefits: it is easier to arrive at a sales specification and to price the product (Tiihonen et al., 1998). This may allow retailers or even customers to do specification themselves (Salvador & Forza, 2004). Customers who are engaged in the specification process may accept

Table 9. Summary of supplier benefits compared with full customization

Benefit	References	MC/CP
Increased efficiency, more controlled production	Svensson and Barfod, 2002	MC
	Tiihonen et al., 1996; Tiihonen and Soininen, 1997; Tiihonen et al., 1998	CP
Improved, more uniform quality	Svensson and Barfod, 2002	MC
	Tiihonen et al., 1996; Tiihonen and Soininen, 1997; Tiihonen et al., 1998; Bonehill and Slee-Smith, 1998; Salvador and Forza, 2004	CP
Shorter lead-times, more accurate on-time delivery	Svensson and Barfod, 2002	MC
	Tiihonen et al., 1996; Tiihonen and Soininen, 1997; Tiihonen et al., 1998	CP
Lower costs	Svensson and Barfod, 2002	MC
	Bonehill and Slee-Smith, 1998	CP
Reduced design effort…		
…which freed expert engineering to other tasks like R&D	Tiihonen et al., 1998; Bonehill and Slee-Smith, 1998; Salvador and Forza, 2004	CP
Easier to do specifications, even by customers or retailers themselves, easier selling	Tiihonen et al., 1998; Salvador and Forza, 2004	CP
Easier pricing	Tiihonen et al., 1998	CP

more responsibility for the product's fit to their needs (Salvador & Forza, 2004).

Supplier Challenges Compared with Full Customization

Next, the supplier challenges from MC or CP compared with full customization are contemplated. The challenges are summarized in Table 10. It seems that MC has not been compared with FC in terms of benefits and challenges as often as with MP.

Compared to FC, MC with CP requires changes in operations and organization that can be significant (Tiihonen & Soininen, 1997). Achieving more uniform quality and repeatable production may be a difficult challenge (Svensson & Barfod, 2002). For FC suppliers, the main challenge in MC is the shift from managing the product and processing materials (which they master) to systematically managing and processing information involved in customer-specific orders, product documentation, and so forth, according to Svensson and Barfod (2002). This requires a cultural change that can be difficult to achieve. Finding the right amount of offered customization is equally important (Beaty, 1996), as when compared with MP. A balance must be found between the added stan-

dardization, uniform quality, and lowered costs, and compromising the optimal fit of a fully-customized product.

Customer needs elicitation and error-free specification is still a challenge (Svensson & Barfod, 2002). Sales specification errors cause similar problems in manufacturing, as when compared to MP. The sales force must learn not to offer changes to the product that would require customer-specific design (Tiihonen & Soininen, 1997).

For product development, it is a challenge and a big effort to develop a design for the configurable product, with a modular structure of reusable, replicable product components (Tiihonen & Soininen, 1997) and clearly-defined module interfaces. On the other hand, Pine (1993a; 1993b) has expressed the fear that modular designs are easier to reverse engineer and copy than unique designs.

Customer Benefits Compared with Full Customization

Here, the customer benefits compared with full customization are contemplated. However, the literature is scant. Nevertheless, the benefits for the supplier (see Table 9) could also generate benefits for the customers like shorter delivery times, more

Table 10. Summary of supplier challenges compared with full customization

Challenge	References	MC/CP
Requires changes in operations and organization	Tiihonen and Soininen, 1997; Tiihonen et al., 1998	CP
Achieving uniform quality	Svensson and Barfod, 2002	MC
Systemizing information management	Svensson and Barfod, 2002	MC
Finding right amount and balance of offered customization	Beaty, 1996; Berman, 2002; Svensson and Barfod, 2002; MacCarthy and Brabazon, 2003	MC
	Tiihonen and Soininen, 1997; Tiihonen et al., 1998	CP
Customer needs elicitation, specification	Svensson and Barfod, 2002	MC
Sales staff must not offer changes outside pre-designed customization possibilities	Tiihonen and Soininen, 1997; Tiihonen et al., 1998	CP
Systemizing product design from configuration viewpoint a big effort	Tiihonen and Soininen, 1997; Tiihonen et al., 1998	CP
Reverse engineering of modular designs	Pine, 1993a, 1993b	MC

predictable deliveries, better serviceability, more communicable product specifications, improved spare part stock management, better and more consistent quality, more affordable products, better accessibility to products, and the like. Further, customers may prefer the easier specification by choosing from existing options and receive better product documentation than for an FC product.

Customer Challenges Compared with Full Customization

The literature we studied seems not to have examined the customer challenges compared with full customization. However, it is probable that explicit specification is difficult for customers, as it is a complex task nevertheless. Customers may also have to compromise on the optimal fit of the product, and the customer service experience may not feel personal enough, as with FC the customers are used to get exactly what they want.

CONFIGURATORS

Overview

A configurator checks the specification of a product individual, that is, a *configuration*, for *completeness* (i.e., that all the necessary selections are made) and *consistency* (i.e., that no rules are violated) with respect to the configuration knowledge, stored in configuration models in configurators (Tiihonen & Soininen, 1997). Configurators also support the user in specifying a product individual, called a configuration task. Depending on the configurator, additional functionality such as price and delivery time calculation, layout drawing and document generation, and so forth, may be provided. Configurators are also used to create and manage the configuration models and configuration knowledge embedded in them.

In the rest of this section, the benefits and challenges related to configurators are discussed. The discussion is divided into supplier and customer viewpoints. The supplier perspective is further divided to issues concerning the business, organization, specification process, manufacturing, product development, and long-term management of configuration knowledge perspectives. The benefits are related to configurator use compared with MC with CP prior to configurator introduction. Challenges relate to configurator use. The benefits are also discussed in terms of whether they alleviate or overcome some challenges related to MC with CP.

Supplier Benefits

This section discusses the benefits configurators can bring to the supplier and if they overcome challenges related to MC with CP. The benefits are summarized in Tables 11-17.

Business

In this section, we review the business benefits of configurators for the supplier. They are summarized in Table 11. In some circumstances configurators can enable premium pricing. Heatley et al. (1995) document a case where a sixfold shortening of the order throughput cycle brought a competitive advantage that enabled premium pricing. They also observed that configurator-supported sales engineers sold more complex products, often commanding a high premium. In a similar vein, Yu and Skovgaard (1998) claim increased sales due to (partially) configurator induced shorter delivery times and product flexibility. Heatley et al. (1995) report that products that were at the borderline of profitability prior to the configurator because of order delays, pricing errors, and rework costs became attractive as the configurator reduced these costly problems. Overall, avoidance of errors, related rework, and production problems seem to reduce costs. Fleischanderl et al. (1998) report of a case where

Table 11. Summary of business benefits for the supplier

Benefit	References	Challenges met?
Better price from products, in some situations	Heatley et al., 1995	Higher costs of producing customized products
Increased sales from shorter delivery times and product flexibility.	Yu and Skovgaard, 1998	Higher costs of producing customized products
Products at borderline of profitability can become more attractive	Heatley et al., 1995	Higher costs of producing customized products
Reduction of costs in many areas	Fleischanderl et al., 1998	Higher costs of producing customized products
Improved customers' satisfaction, perception	Barker and O'Connor, 1989; Heatley et al., 1995	Low customer satisfaction, lost image from elicitation difficulties
Customer "lock-in" from configurator usage; dealer and retailer loyalty	*Lock-in:* Forza and Salvador, 2002b. *Loyalty:* Heatley et al., 1995; Yu and Skovgaard, 1998	Low dealer and customer loyalty from elicitation difficulties
Improve tracking of purchases and sales; mining of customer orders and preferences from configurator for future strategy	McGuinness and Wright, 1998; Bramham and MacCarthy, 2004	

configuration-related costs were reduced 60% over the product life cycle.

Barker and O'Connor (1989) and Heatley et al. (1995) argue that customer satisfaction increases as many of the configurator-induced benefits affect customers' perceptions positively. Giving the configurator to customers to use had the effect of "tying" customers to the company in the case reported by Forza and Salvador (2002b). The configurator reduced the time that customers needed for defining product specifications. Dealer and retailer loyalty may be improved by configurators (Heatley et al., 1995; Yu & Skovgaard, 1998) due to less errors and subsequent hassles, and as configurators can enable selling products with a higher premium. Further, configurators can boost customer relationship management by enabling storage and mining of customer orders and preferences for cues to future strategy, forecasting, and supply chain management (Bramham & MacCarthy, 2004) and improve tracking of purchases and sales (McGuinness & Wright, 1998). This can be an enabling factor for realizing a benefit of MC, getting access to real-time, more accurate customer information (Table 10).

Organization

Next, we discuss the benefits from configurators to the organization; for a summary, see Table 12. As configurators ensure the consistency of configurations and reduce manufacturing problems, they allow for the use of less skilled workers in sales (Bramham & MacCarthy, 2004) and in production (Sviokla, 1990). This probably lowers employment costs, as skilled labor tends to be more expensive. In a similar vein, customers (Forza & Salvador, 2002b) or retailers (Yu & Skovgaard, 1998) may do the specification themselves with configurators. Further, technical experts are no longer needed for consistency checks or technical consulting during sales (McGuinness & Wright, 1998), or preparing customer-specific documentation (Forza & Salvador 2002a); see also Table 4. This frees them to other tasks like new product development (Bonehill & Slee-Smith, 1998; Forza & Salvador 2002a) or, less personnel may be necessary in general (Barker & O'Connor, 1989; Sviokla, 1990). Work satisfaction increases as configurators obviate the need to working with mundane details, like verifying specifications,

Table 12. Summary of supplier benefits in organization

Benefit	References for benefit	Challenges met?
Allows for less-skilled workers in sales and production	*Sales:* Bramham and MacCarthy, 2004; Salvador and Forza, 2004. *Production:* Sviokla, 1990	Higher costs of producing customized products.
Allows for specification by retailers or even customers themselves	*Retailers:* Yu and Skovgaard, 1998. *Customers:* Forza and Salvador, 2002b	Technical experts deeply involved in verifying specifications
Technical experts needed less in specification → freed to other tasks, like R&D	Barker and O'Connor, 1989; Sviokla, 1990; McGuinness and Wright, 1998; Bonehill and Slee-Smith, 1998; Forza and Salvador, 2002a	Technical experts deeply involved in verifying specifications
Configurators eliminate some tasks, even parts of organization related to consistency checks	McGuinness and Wright, 1998; Forza and Salvador, 2002b	
Work satisfaction increases as configurators reduce working with mundane details, and more time may be devoted to challenging cases	Heatley et al., 1995; Tiihonen and Soininen, 1997	

and more time may be devoted to intellectually challenging cases (Heatley et al., 1995).

Specification Process

For a summary of the benefits, see Table 13 and Table 14. The ability of configurators to ensure the consistency and completeness of sales specifications by managing the complex interdependencies and incompatibilities between choices brings a number of benefits to the specification process. Configurators can reduce or even eliminate the errors in sales specifications (Barker & O'Connor, 1989) meaning also that the specified product individuals can be manufactured. Further, configurators also help to eradicate the errors noticed after sales, thus reducing or eliminating the iterations between sales and manufacturing (Wright et al., 1993), and help sales staff to promptly give either correct or good estimates of delivery times (Vanwelkenheysen, 1998) and prices (Barker & O'Connor, 1989). As configurators ensure the specifications are error-free, sales staff can devote more time to actual selling instead of doing consistency checks (Heatley et al., 1995) and technical staff need not do consistency checks anymore either (McGuinness & Wright, 1998).

The support configurators lend to the specification process, making it less difficult and complex. Therefore, the sales staff can more freely and efficiently explore the alternatives, which can help to optimize the specification to customer needs (Tiihonen & Soininen, 1997). This also enables the sales staff to sell more complex products that often are more expensive as well (Heatley et al., 1995). Configurators also reduce the effort needed in the specification (Wright et al., 1993) by taking care of consistency checks and supporting the specification task, and often automatically generating documents that previously had to be produced manually. All this also results in shorter lead-times in order-processing before manufacturing (Barker & O'Connor, 1989) and in an increase in the volume of processed quotations and orders without increasing sales staff (Sviokla, 1990).

With configurator support, the repertoires of typical specifications sales staff invented to workaround the specification process complexity should become unnecessary. Further, as configuration knowledge and therefore the customization range of configurable products are "built-in" to configurators, they standardize specification results: It is not possible to specify product individuals outside the customization range or to

Table 13. Summary of supplier benefits in the sales specification process (Part 1)

Benefit	References for benefit	Challenges met?
Reduce or eliminate errors in sales specifications	Barker and O'Connor, 1989; Sviokla, 1990; Fohn et al., 1995; Heatley et al., 1995; Ariano and Dagnino, 1996; Tiihonen and Soininen, 1997; Bonehill and Slee-Smith, 1998; Fleischhanderl et al., 1998; Vanwelkenheysen, 1998; Günter and Kühn, 1999; Yu and Skovgaard, 1998; Aldanondo et al., 1999; Aldanondo et al., 2000; Forza and Salvador, 2002a; Pedersen and Edwards, 2004	Difficulty and complexity of specification; repertoires of typical specifications; specified individuals that cannot be manufactured
Reduce or eliminate iterations between sales and manufacturing	Wright et al., 1993; Heatley et al., 1995; Tiihonen and Soininen, 1997; Vanwelkenheysen, 1998; Aldanondo et al., 1999; Aldanondo et al., 2000	Errors noticed after sales lead to iterations in the sales-delivery process
Correct delivery time, or good estimate	Vanwelkenheysen, 1998; Forza and Salvador, 2002a	Incorrect delivery time
Correct price, or good estimate	Barker and O'Connor, 1989; Heatley et al., 1995; Ariano and Dagnino, 1996; Vanwelkenheysen, 1998; Forza and Salvador, 2002a	Incorrect, smaller price than effective cost
Sales can devote more time to selling	Heatley et al., 1995; Tiihonen and Soininen, 1997; Vanwelkenheysen, 1998	Difficulty and complexity of specification
Technical staff need not check consistency	McGuinness and Wright, 1998; Yu and Skovgaard, 1998; Forza and Salvador, 2002a, 2002b	Technical experts deeply involved in verifying specifications

Table 14. Summary of supplier benefits in the sales specification process (Part 2)

Benefit	References for benefit	Challenges met?
More free exploration or product alternatives; helps to optimize to customer needs	Tiihonen and Soininen, 1997; Bonehill and Slee-Smith, 1998; McGuinness and Wright, 1998; Hvam, Malis, Hansen, & Riis, 2004; Pedersen and Edwards, 2004	Does specified product individual meet customer needs optimally?
Reduce specification effort	Wright et al., 1993; Heatley et al., 1995; Ariano and Dagnino, 1996; McGuinness and Wright, 1998; Yu and Skovgaard, 1998; Aldanondo et al., 1999; Aldanondo et al., 2000; Forza and Salvador, 2002a; Hvam et al., 2004; Pedersen and Edwards, 2004	Customer has to spend time in specification and wait for the finished product.
Shorter lead-times in order-processing	Barker and O'Connor, 1989; Sviokla, 1990; Wright et al., 1993; Heatley et al., 1995; Fohn et al., 1995; Ariano and Dagnino, 1996; Tiihonen and Soininen, 1997; Bonehill and Slee-Smith, 1998; Günter and Kühn, 1999; Vanwelkenheysen, 1998; Aldanondo et al., 1999; Aldanondo et al., 2000; Forza and Salvador, 2002a, 2002b; Hvam et al., 2004; Pedersen and Edwards, 2004	Customer has to spend time in specification and wait for the finished product.
Increases volume of quotations and orders processed, without increasing staff	Sviokla, 1990; Tiihonen and Soininen, 1997; Vanwelkenheysen, 1998; Pedersen and Edwards, 2004	
Standardize specification results	Sviokla, 1990; Tiihonen et al., 1996; Vanwelkenheysen, 1998; Forza and Salvador, 2002b	Sales force must not offer changes outside pre-designed customization options. Different specifications for identical customer order

Table 15. Summary of supplier benefits in manufacturing

Benefit	References for benefit	Challenges met?
Ordered products can be manufactured; less production problems, stoppages, fire-fighting	Heatley et al., 1995; McGuinness and Wright, 1998; Forza and Salvador, 2002a, 2002b	Fire-fighting in manufacturing from specification errors
More reliable and on-time delivery	Forza and Salvador, 2002a; Pedersen and Edwards, 2004	
More accurate planning and scheduling of production	Heatley et al., 1995; Bonehill and Slee-Smith, 1998; Yu and Skovgaard, 1998; McGuinness and Wright, 1998; Forza and Salvador, 2002a	Achieving uniform quality
Configurators guide to more standard solutions → easier production	McGuinness and Wright, 1998; Forza and Salvador, 2002b; Pedersen and Edwards, 2004	
Lower (buffer) inventories	Barker and O'Connor, 1989; Yu and Skovgaard, 1998; McGuinness and Wright, 1998; Forza and Salvador, 2002a	Higher costs of producing customized products

specify different product individuals for identical customer orders.

Overall, configurators improve the productivity of sales, quoting, and engineering for the aforementioned reasons. Moreover, customers may perceive the quality of operations to be higher, as a single contact produces a manufacturable specification, often with a price and delivery time (or estimate), and in a prompt manner. Further, configurators lower the costs due to less effort required in specification, and the reduced rework and iterations due to elimination of specification errors (Wright et al., 1993; Vanwelkenheysen, 1998).

Manufacturing

This section discusses the benefits configurators can bring to manufacturing. Summary of the benefits can be found in Table 15. The main benefits for manufacturing stem from the error-free, manufacturable sales specifications (Heatley et al., 1995). Without errors there are less production problems, stoppages, and firefighting due to, for example, missing or wrong parts. Consequently, the reliability of deliveries improves (Forza & Salvador, 2002a) and planning and scheduling of production become more accurate (Heatley et al., 1995). Moreover, as configurators guide cus-

tomers to ordering within the supplier's normal product range there is less variation to handle, making production easier overall (McGuinness & Wright, 1998). The aforementioned manufacturing benefits meet or alleviate the challenges of firefighting in manufacturing and help in achieving uniform quality. Finally, improved predictability of production and reduced order-processing time also allow reduction of buffer inventories at the factory (Barker & O'Connor, 1989).

Product Development

The benefits from configurators to product development, summarized in Table 16, are discussed next. As configurators improve the complexity-handling capabilities of the supplier in sales and production, more complex products with competitive features can be developed (Heatley et al., 1995) and increased variety can be offered (Sviokla, 1990).

Configurators require explicit definition, that is, modeling, of the configuration knowledge. This can initiate a better understanding of company's products (Ariano & Dagnino, 1996) or redefinition of the products to better suit the market and reduce unnecessary complexity, according to Forza and Salvador (2002a). Forza and Salvador (2002a) also argue that configuration modeling

Table 16. Summary of supplier benefits in product development

Benefit	References
Increased complexity handling capability → products with a wider customization range can be developed	Sviokla, 1990; Heatley et al., 1995
Explicit configuration modeling may initiate better understanding of the products, or redefining them to meet markets better	Ariano and Dagnino, 1996; Forza and Salvador, 2002a
Configuration modeling may provide a way to represent architectural product knowledge	Forza and Salvador, 2002a
Configurators free resources to product development from consistency checks and ongoing management of configuration knowledge	*Checks:* Barker and O'Connor, 1989; Sviokla, 1990; McGuinness and Wright, 1998; Bonehill and Slee-Smith, 1998; Forza and Salvador, 2002a *Management:* Yu and Skovgaard, 1998

may provide ways to describe architectural product knowledge. Further, more resources may be available for product development because configurators free the technical experts from doing consistency checks (Barker & O'Connor) and ongoing management of configuration knowledge (Yu & Skovgaard, 1998).

Long-Term Management of Configuration Knowledge

For a summary of the configurator benefits discussed here, see Table 17. Configurators support centralized configuration knowledge maintenance and management (Sviokla, 1990). Without a configurator, configuration knowledge can be dispersed in the supplier organization, and transferring up-to-date configuration knowledge within it can be problematic. With configurators, up-to-date configuration knowledge is easily available in the organization (Barker & O'Connor, 1989), in sales and for customers as well.

Having systematic configuration knowledge embedded in the configurator may help in training new employees to become productive (Fleischanderl et al., 1998). Further, configuration knowledge managed centrally in a configurator helps to turn individual knowledge into organizational knowledge, reducing the need of the organization to rely on (few) knowledgeable individuals

(Günter & Kühn, 1999) and supports systematic management of information.

Supplier Challenges

Business

The business challenges of the supplier, discussed next, are summarized in Table 18. Taking a configurator into use is a significant investment, as developing, deploying, and maintaining a configurator represents a significant cost, requires a significant effort, can take a considerable time, and can widely affect the organization and its functions. The cost may include software licenses, software development and integration, hardware, consultation, product modeling, and long-term maintenance (Tiihonen at al., 1997). Case experiences of costly configurator implementation and deployment projects taking a lot of effort and time have been reported in Aldanondo et al. (2000); Forza and Salvador (2002a, 2002b); Hvam et al. (2004); and Pedersen and Edwards (2004). Investment into a configurator must be paid back in its repetitive use. Thus, a high enough volume is needed to justify the costs (Pedersen & Edwards, 2004).

Problems related to configurator introduction or long-term management might delay new product introductions or product improvements (Barker& O'Connor, 1989; Tiihonen et al., 1996).

Table 17. Summary of supplier benefits from configurator in long term maintenance of configuration knowledge

Benefit	References for benefit	Challenges met?
Support to maintain configuration knowledge, centrally	Sviokla, 1990; Tiihonen and Soininen, 1997; Yu and Skovgaard, 1998; McGuinness and Wright, 1998; Fleischhanderl et al., 1998; Forza and Salvador, 2002a	Long-term management of configuration knowledge; systemizing information management; dispersed configuration knowledge in the organization
Correct, up-to-date configuration knowledge available in the organization	Barker and O'Connor, 1989; Sviokla, 1990, Wright et al., 1993; Tiihonen et al., 1996; Tiihonen and Soininen, 1997; Fleischanderl et al., 1998; Bonehill and Slee-Smith, 1998; McGuinness and Wright, 1998; Vanwelken-heysen, 1998; Yu and Skovgaard, 1998	Transferring updated configuration knowledge to sales force
Availability of systematic configuration knowledge helps in training new employees to become productive	Fleischanderl et al., 1998; Bonehill and Slee-Smith, 1998; Salvador and Forza, 2004; Pedersen and Edwards, 2004	
Centralized configuration knowledge in a configurator helps to turn individual knowledge into organizational	Günter and Kühn, 1999; Forza and Salvador, 2002a; Bramham and MacCarthy, 2004; Pedersen and Edwards, 2004	Systemizing information management.

Table 18. Summary of business challenges of the supplier

Challenge	References
Configurator development and maintenance takes considerable time and represents significant cost and effort.	*Cost:* Tiihonen at al., 1997; Pedersen and Edwards, 2004. *Effort:* Barker and O'Connor, 1989; Sviokla, 1990; Aldanondo et al., 2000; Forza and Salvador, 2002b. *Time:* Forza and Salvador, 2002a; Hvam et al., 2004
Challenges of long-term management may delay product introductions or improvements	Barker and O'Connor, 1989; Tiihonen et al., 1996
Risk of becoming over-dependent of configurator and knowledge in it	Sviokla, 1990
The necessary alignment of business needs and processes, and scope of configurator-support is challenging.	Barker and O'Connor, 1989; Tiihonen et al., 1996; Forza and Salvador, 2002a; Bramham and MacCarthy, 2004; Hvam et al., 2004; Pedersen and Edwards, 2004
Business process re-engineering may be required	Tiihonen and Soininen, 1997; Tiihonen et al., 1998; Hvam et al., 2004
Multiple sales processes and channels may have to be supported	*Processes:* Tiihonen et al.1996; Tiihonen and Soininen, 1997; Reichwald et al., 2004. *Channels:* Reichwald et al., 2004
Effective distribution of the configurator to the sales force	Heatley et al., 1995; Tiihonen et al., 1996; Tiihonen and Soininen, 1997

The supplier may end up being over-dependent of the configurator and the knowledge embedded in it (Sviokla, 1990). Thus the configurator becomes a mission-critical application.

A major challenge in configurator implementation is aligning the business needs and processes of the supplier and the configurator. It is necessary and challenging to integrate the configurator to the company's business processes (Bramham & MacCarthy, 2004). Business, not technologists, should guide the implementation (Barker & O'Connor, 1989). The scope of support provided by a configurator must be determined according to business needs. It may be feasible to leave the most complex products out to reduce the complexity of systemizing and managing configuration knowledge, as was done due to limited volume in a case reported by Forza and Salvador (2002a).

Aligning the processes with the configurator may require business process re-engineering to achieve full benefits (Tiihonen & Soininen, 1997). The sales process, especially, may have to be systemized or streamlined. The need for different sales-delivery processes after the deployment of a configurator should be determined. For example, separate processes may be needed for mass-produced products, configurable products, and products that require case-specific engineering in addition to configurable parts (Tiihonen et al., 1996). A manual configuration process may have to be retained even when a configurator is deployed. For example, in less-developed areas, the availability or price of computers and data communications or the computer illiteracy of sales-persons may limit the use of a configurator (Tiihonen et al., 1996). Further, multiple sales channels may have to be supported, for example, in-shop "off-line" configuration, and online self-service in Web (Reichwald, Piller, & Mueller, 2004).

Effective distribution of the configurator to the entire sales force, especially to retailers, may be problematic (Heatley et al., 1995). When the supplier does not own or control the sales channel, configurator use cannot be enforced (Tiihonen et al., 1996). Retailers, possibly having low volumes, may be unwilling to adopt a configurator due to the cost of the system or training (Tiihonen & Soininen 1997).

Organization

Next, the supplier challenges involving the organization are reviewed. The challenges are outlined in Table 19.

Introducing a configurator can significantly change an organization (Barker & O'Connor, 1989), making it harder to implement than anticipated (Ariano & Dagnino, 1996). Configurators can reduce or eliminate the need for consistency checks, consulting technical staff during sales, part-list creation, and other tasks related to creating specifications. This changes personnel roles (Barker & O'Connor, 1989) and may make organizational units involved in the tasks redundant (Barker & O'Connor, 1989).

Cooperation between different parts of the organization is required to align the configurator with business needs (Barker & O'Connor, 1989), as well as for configuration knowledge acquisition and modeling (Sviokla, 1990). Configuration knowledge can be dispersed in the organization between different units and personnel. Some modeling decisions are business decisions. It can be challenging to have prompt access to individuals who have the necessary authority and knowledge to make these decisions (Vanwelkenheysen, 1998). The required work in implementing and maintaining a configurator and the challenges it alleviates may touch different parts of the organization (Tiihonen & Soininen, 1997), which may hamper cooperation and cause resistance towards the configurator.

Resistance in the organization towards the configurator can also be caused by changes in personnel roles (Bonehill & Slee-Smith, 1998) and organization (Forza & Salvador, 2002a). Further, personnel may see the configurator as a menace

Table 19. Summary of organizational challenges of the supplier

Challenge	References
Significant organizational changes may be necessary and harder to implement than anticipated.	Barker and O'Connor, 1989; Ariano and Dagnino, 1996; Aldanondo et al., 2000; Forza and Salvador, 2002b
Roles of individuals change, and some people delegate part of their tasks to configurator.	Barker and O' Connor, 1989; Bonehill and Slee-Smith, 1998; Forza and Salvador, 2002a
Organizational cooperation required to align configurator with business needs, and in configuration knowledge acquisition	Barker and O'Connor, 1989; Sviokla, 1990; Wright et al., 1993; Vanwelkenheysen, 1998; Forza and Salvador, 2002b
Benefits and challenges of the configurator and required work may touch different parts of the organization.	Tiihonen and Soininen, 1997
Potential for resistance towards configurator.	Heatley et al., 1995; Tiihonen et al., 1996; Bonehill and Slee-Smith, 1998; Forza and Salvador, 2002a
Configurator development and maintenance organization may be introduced and can become critical for company and individuals leaving a risk	Sviokla, 1990; Ariano and Dagnino, 1996; Vanwelkenheysen, 1998; Forza and Salvador, 2002b; Hvam et al., 2004.

to their position (Forza & Salvador, 2002a) or be unwilling to trust the decisions made by an automatic system (Tiihonen et al., 1996). In a case described in Heatley et al. (1995), achieving 100% usage had required an enforcing policy.

A new function responsible for configurator development and maintenance may be introduced (Ariano & Dagnino, 1996; Sviokla, 1990) as continuity in development and maintenance of the knowledge bases needs to be ensured (Vanwelkenheysen, 1998). This can cause subtle challenges. Configurator maintenance can be very critical (Sviokla, 1990) with configurator experts becoming vital to the company (Ariano & Dagnino, 1996; Forza & Salvador, 2002b). Expertise on configuration knowledge may shift to the configurator development and maintenance organization, whose people may not be good enough product experts (Sviokla, 1990). Management challenge may move from keeping staff up-to-date to keeping configurator software up-to-date (Sviokla, 1990).

Specification Process

In this section, the challenges related to the specification process are discussed. The challenges are summarized in Table 20.

Even with configurators, eliciting and understanding real customer needs may be difficult. It is possible that customers do not know their real needs (Blecker, Abdelkafi, Kreutler, & Friedrich, 2004; Franke & Piller, 2003), cannot express them (Blecker et al., 2004), or that the supplier may misinterpret customer requirements (Blecker et al., 2003; Tiihonen & Soininen, 1997). Customers may not want to part with all types of needed information (e.g., personal information affecting needs) during the specification task (Bramham & MacCarthy, 2004). These issues may be more serious in self-service settings where personal interaction with sales staff is not available. In some cases customers may prefer consultative selling where sales employees operate the configurator over self-service with Web-based configurator (Reichwald et al., 2004).

Configurators may fix interaction with the customer in general (Bramham & MacCarthy, 2004) or at the level of fixing the order of selections (Fohn et al., 1995). The customer interaction which the configurator enables is easily imitated and may yield the same offering as competitors (Bramham & MacCarthy, 2004). Franke and Piller (2003) discussed the need to support creative product specification during the configuration task instead of simply choosing from pre-designed options.

Table 20. Summary of supplier challenges in the specification process

Challenge	References
Obtaining and understanding real customer needs	Tiihonen and Soininen, 1997; Franke and Piller, 2003; Blecker et al., 2004
Personal service may remain preferable to self-service with a configurator.	Reichwald et al., 2004
Configurators may fix interaction with the customer	Fohn et al., 1995; Bramham and MacCarthy, 2004
Support for creative product specification	Franke and Piller, 2003
It may be difficult to modify created configurations	Sviokla, 1990; Männistö et al., 1999

Configurators support partially-configurable products that still involve some custom design, but they do it poorly (Tiihonen et al., 1998).

It may be difficult to modify created configurations (Sviokla, 1990). Most often reconfiguration is managed on a case-by-case basis, which cannot be efficiently supported by configurators (Männistö, Soininen, Tiihonen, & Sulonen, 1999).

Long-Term Management of Configuration Knowledge

In the following, we review the challenges related to configurators in long-term management of configuration knowledge. For a summary of the challenges, see Table 21.

Configuration knowledge often changes frequently due to product changes and for business related reasons like shifting customer needs and marketing strategies (Fleischanderl et al., 1998) and pricing changes. If the sales rely on configuration support, fast updating of configuration knowledge is important, even business-critical (Barker & O'Connor, 1989). Over time, configuration models grow and new ones are added to the configurator increasing the complexity of management (Barker & O'Connor, 1989; Bramham & MacCarthy, 2004). More complexity arises from regional differences in products and prices (Tiihonen & Soininen, 1997) and if reconfiguration needs to be supported (Männistö et al., 1999).

There must be means for deploying the updated configurator and/or configuration knowledge

Table 21. Summary of supplier challenges in long term management of configuration knowledge

Challenge	References
Fast updating and creating of configuration knowledge bases and configuration models	Barker and O'Connor, 1989; Wright et al., 1993; Tiihonen et al., 1996; Fleischanderl et al., 1998; Forza and Salvador, 2002b; Bramham and MacCarthy, 2004
Configuration models grow and new ones are introduced, increasing complexity	Barker and O'Connor, 1989; Bramham and MacCarthy, 2004
There must be mechanisms that distribute and take configurator and/or knowledge base updates to use in entire sales force and/or customers.	Tiihonen et al., 1998
Ensuring correctness of the configurator knowledge base may be challenging after updates	Tiihonen and Soininen, 1997; Felfernig, Friedrich, Jannach, and Stumptner, 2004
Updates can require both product and configurator expertise (*should need only product expertise*).	Fohn et al., 1995; Tiihonen and Soininen, 1997
Long-term management of configurators is both mission-critical and challenging.	Tiihonen and Soininen, 1997; Tiihonen et al., 1998

bases to the entire sales force and/or to customers (Tiihonen et al., 1998). The related challenges are different in different architectural scenarios. Configurators based on a centralized, for example, Web-based architecture require updates only to the centralized system and knowledge base. Stand-alone configurators require either a synchronization mechanism (e.g., a docking station with appropriate software) or actions by the user and cannot therefore guarantee that configuration knowledge updates will be taken into use. Ensuring the correctness of the configurator knowledge may be challenging after updates (Tiihonen & Soininen, 1997).

The challenges of dispersed configuration knowledge and diverse expertise possibly required in implementing configurators play their role in long-term management as well. To reduce these burdens, Fohn et al. (1995) and Tiihonen and Soininen (1997) propose that configuration modeling and maintaining the configurator knowledgebase should not require any configurator expertise. Rather, updates should be performable by product experts.

It can be concluded that long-term management of configurators is both mission-critical and challenging (Tiihonen & Soininen, 1997). Its failure may be a reason for many failed configurator projects. However, empirical evidence has not been published.

Development and Initial Introduction of a Configurator

Here we discuss the challenges related to the development and initial introduction of a configurator. For a summary, see Table 22.

Fleischanderl et al. (1998) point out that the development and introduction of a configurator is a demanding task. Configuration modeling requires knowledge acquisition from different parts of the company, which is not always easy or frictionless (Wright et al., 1993). The people with the required knowledge may be different individuals, located in different parts of the organization, also geographically (Barker & O'Connor, 1989). The gathered configuration knowledge must be systemized and formalized (Tiihonen et al 1998) to make it coherent and usable in the configurator. Thus, taking a configurator into use requires expertise both in the domain (products and industry) and in configurators (e.g., modeling, possibly programming) and related IT. However, validation and testing of configuration models is a challenge due to combinatorial nature of configurable products (Barker & O'Connor, 1989). Regional differences increase the complexity of configuration models and related information systems. Often all product options are not available everywhere, prices differ from one area to another, and there may be

Table 22. Summary of supplier challenges in configurator introduction

Challenge	References
Configuration knowledge acquisition	Wright et al., 1993, Tiihonen and Soininen, 1997; Forza and Salvador, 2002a
Configuration knowledge systemization and formalization	Tiihonen et al., 1998; Forza and Salvador, 2002a
Expertise in products and industry, in configurators, modeling, and IT required	Barker and O'Connor, 1989; Fleischanderl et al., 1998; Aldanondo et al., 2000
Validation and testing of configuration models	Barker and O'Connor, 1989; Heatley et al., 1995; Tiihonen and Soininen, 1997; Felfernig et al., 2004
Integration to other IT systems	Barker and O'Connor, 1989; Tiihonen et al., 1996; Tiihonen and Soininen, 1997; Tiihonen et al., 1998; Franke and Piller, 2003
Developing a good and suitable user interface	Aldanondo et al., 2000, Franke and Piller, 2003

several language versions to maintain (Tiihonen & Soininen, 1996).

It may be necessary to improve product modularization to enable configuring (Hvam et al., 2004). Tiihonen and Soininen (1997) argue that good long-term results in using a configurator can be expected only when the product has been designed to be easily configurable as it simplifies the configuration models.

Integration of a configurator to other systems may be necessary (Barker & O'Connor, 1989). Integration can facilitate efficient and error-free transfer of configurations (e.g., parts lists, drawings, connection information, etc.), price, delivery time or capacity, and product model information. Systems that could be integrated include sales and CRM tools, ERP, PDM, and CAD. However, the high cost and complexity of integrations calls for judgment. Integration to IT systems of retailers or customers may also be desirable (Tiihonen et al., 1998).

Developing an efficient, learnable user interface for a configurator can be difficult. Determining "the best and most logical" sequence of user prompts can be challenging (Aldanondo et al.,

2000). Additional concerns are the ability of the user interface to provide a satisfactory customer experience, which also provides integration into the company brand, and whether the configurator supports creative innovation by the customers (Franke & Piller, 2003).

Customer Benefits

Next, we discuss the customer benefits from configurators, summarized in Table 23. Because configurators check the consistency and enable rapid specification, it is possible to explore the alternatives and their impacts in a more thorough and free manner during sales (McGuinness & Wright, 1998). This increases the possibility to find a good match with needs and probably lessens the complexity of specification to some extent. Moreover, as sales staff need not worry about consistency checks, they can devote more time to the customer (Vanwelkenheysen, 1998). This increased advice available to customers should help alleviate the complexity of specification in customers' mind and increase the possibility of finding a suitable product. Some configurators can

Table 23. Summary of customer benefits from configurators

Benefit	References for benefit	Challenges met?
More product alternatives and their impact can be more freely inspected during specification → increase possibility to find a good product fit.	McGuinness and Wright, 1998; Forza and Salvador, 2002b; Salvador and Forza, 2004	Optimal product individual fit to customer needs; complexity of specification
Sales can devote more time for customer	Vanwelkenheysen, 1998	Complexity of specification; optimal product individual fit to customer needs
Configurator can help to explain to the customer why some alternative choices are not compatible	Aldanondo et al., 1999	Complexity of specification
Configurator makes company product language available to customer, which may make communication easier	Forza and Salvador, 2002b	Optimal product individual fit to customer needs
Customers can do the specification themselves, when they want (over the Web)	Forza and Salvador, 2002b; Salvador and Forza, 2004	
Save customer time in specification	Forza and Salvador, 2002b	Time and effort spent in specification
Possibility to use existing specifications as basis saves customer time	McGuinness and Wright, 1998	Time and effort spent in specification
Price and delivery time immediately	Vanwelkenheysen, 1998	

help to explain the incompatibilities and dependencies between product options to the customer (Aldanondo et al., 1999), alleviating the complexity in specification. Forza and Salvador (2002b) argue that communication may become easier as a configurator makes the company language available to customers. The differences in terms used by the customer and supplier to describe the preferred product could be reduced, alleviating the difficulty of finding an optimal product to customer needs.

A configurator can enable the customers to do the specification task themselves (Salvador & Forza, 2004) whenever they want (Forza & Salvador, 2002b) if the configurator is available on the Web or distributed to the customers. In general, configurators can save customer time during specification (Forza & Salvador, 2002b). Some configurators allow using existing configurations as a basis for specification, which also saves customer time (McGuinness & Wright, 1998). The price and delivery time (or estimates) may be available immediately (Vanwelkenheysen, 1998).

Customer Challenges

The challenges from the customer point-of-view have not been discussed much in literature. The challenges caused by configurators mostly relate to self-service configurators.

All customers may not want to use a self-service configurator. Selecting a suitable configurable product from the set of available products can be difficult, especially for non-expert customers typical to consumer e-commerce (Heiskala, Anderson, Huhtinen, Tiihonen, & Martio, 2003; Pargamin, 2002). Special product selection support may be needed (Heiskala et al., 2003). However, trusting recommendation(s) of a system can be a problem (Tiihonen et al., 1996). Self-service customers may find configurator user interfaces difficult, especially if the needs are not clear, or if there is a mismatch between configurator and customer

logic for preferences. A configurator may also restrain the interaction, making it too rigid for customers' liking.

Several customer challenges discussed for MC and CP probably apply, even with configurator support. The number of options may overwhelm the customer (Huffman & Kahn, 1998), who may not be able accept the risk of making wrong decisions (Berman, 2002). Additionally, the documentation of the customer's explicit preferences and personal information in the product specification process may feel as an invasion of privacy (Broekhuizen & Alsem, 2002). Even with a configurator, it may be difficult to judge whether the end product presents good value (Broekhuizen & Alsem 2002). Price in e-commerce is also an issue; it is difficult to know if personal contact could provide a better price. The challenges related to modifying created configurations, reconfiguration, and creative product specification are probably relevant as well.

RATIONALE FOR INTRODUCING MASS CUSTOMIZATION

In this section, we briefly discuss under what kind of conditions it does make sense to introduce an MC strategy to the company and when it does not. Naturally, the benefits we have listed provide motivation for a company to introduce MC. Further, the company probably should have capabilities in place to overcome or alleviate the challenges we have listed, at least to an extent that ensures that the benefits gained from MC outweigh the additional sacrifices, for both the company and its customers.

The necessary conditions and capabilities for MC have been discussed by several authors, again dominantly from an MP viewpoint (Bardacki & Whitelock, 2003; Berman, 2002; Broekhuizen & Alsem, 2002; Da Silveira et al., 2001; Hart, 1995; Kotha, 1995; Pine, 1993a, 1995; Radder & Louw, 1999; Zipkin, 2001). Berman (2002) and Radder and Louw (1999) provide checklists for practitioners to assess the soundness of an MC switch. An integrative overview of the conditions is given by Blecker et al. (2005, pp. 23-41), which we summarize here.

Blecker et al. (2005) categorize the conditions to ones relevant before and after moving to MC. Before the move, the company should assess the market conditions on a macro (demand and structural factors) and micro (customer demand for customization) levels. On the demand and structural factors, Blecker et al. (2005, p. 31) follow Pine's (1993a) market turbulence indicators, like unstable, unpredictable, and heterogeneous demand, uncertain and quickly-changing customer needs, low-price consciousness, but high quality and fashion/style consciousness and high level of pre- and post-sale service. Customer demand for customization must truly exist, and it is likely to be so only for a limited group of products (Blecker et al., 2005, p. 32; Svensson & Barfod, 2002). For luxury products (Pine, 1993a, p. 56) and business-to-business customers that arguably, in many markets, are more knowledgeable and demanding than consumers (MacCarthy & Brabazon, 2003), this might be more probable. The value of customization to customers must also overcome the challenges of possible higher prices, time to wait for the final product, effort spent in specification, and privacy concerns (Bardacki & Whitelock, 2003; Broekhuizen & Alsem, 2002). Blecker et al. (2005, p. 33) also state that possible first-mover advantages have to be taken into account. Pine et al. (1995) argue that frequent enough repeat business and interactions with the customer are positive conditions for MC to be a viable option. On the other hand, Spring and Dalrymple (2000) argue that on occasions that the price premium does not lead to increased profitability, there are still valid reasons to customize products: (1) to keep competition out, (2) to force the organization to learn and develop new capabilities, and (3) to enhance the company's standing/brand in the industry.

In addition to the external conditions, before moving to MC the company must assess whether it has or can acquire the capabilities necessary to customize its products (Blecker et al. 2005, p. 33). The company's value chain must be responsive and flexible and willing and able to meet the added challenges of MC (Blecker et al., 2005), and connected with an efficiently-linked information network (Da Silveira et al., 2001). The production processes of the company must be flexible to be able to produce a variety of products, and the products themselves must be customizable (Blecker et al., 2005, p. 35). A key ingredient for MC is customer needs elicitation capability of the company (Blecker et al., 2005, p. 35). MC with CP requires significant investment in product design, information management, and the like. Payback requires a high enough volume to cover the costs (Tiihonen & Soininen, 1997). This can be a challenge especially for those companies whose background is in FC with limited volumes.

When pursuing MC on a continuous basis, the company must maintain and improve its MC capabilities. These include the aforementioned customer needs elicitation, process flexibility, supply chain agility, and customer-oriented product design. Blecker et al. (2005, p.38) also emphasize the importance of having capabilities to manage the increased complexity and variety in products and production processes and of efficient knowledge-sharing throughout the company.

SUGGESTIONS FOR FUTURE RESEARCH DIRECTIONS

The customer view on mass customization, configurable products, and configurators is thin in the literature. Moving to MC with CP has been mainly documented from the direction of MP, especially in the MC literature. We call for research, especially empirical, on the customer benefits and challenges of MC with CP and on the move to MC from the direction of FC.

This review makes the same observation as Da Silveira et al. (2001) and Paloheimo, Miettinen, and Brax (2004) that services have received little attention in MC literature, at least as regards to the benefits and challenges. Literature on configurable service products and configurators is even scarcer. We therefore call for future research on MC, CP, and configurators in service settings. We also observed, as Franke and Piller (2003), that empirical findings on MC are limited.

Research on ways to overcome or alleviate the challenges, a collection of best practices, would probably be of interest to practitioners. A specific viewpoint could be avoiding the pitfalls in the initial move to MC with CP and in configurator introductions. The reviews of Broekhuizen and Alsem (2002) and Da Silveira et al. (2001) provide a good starting point. We would expect to find different necessary conditions, success factors, enablers, and best practices when switching from MP versus switching from FC. In literature, the configurator benefits are dominantly discussed with relation to the company not having a configurator. Comparative studies on what kinds of configurators are best for a given situation would be of interest.

Research on configurator introductions could benefit from literature on information system implementations and account for relevant differences. Is configuration knowledge acquisition different for technical knowledge and knowledge related to identifying optimal fit to customer needs? How tacit are these types of configuration knowledge? Is a configurator sufficient to transfer knowledge to sales? What are the challenges? In our view, especially empirical knowledge management research could provide interesting insights for MC and CP suppliers and configurator research. Further, empirical research on long-term management of modern configurators would be most welcome. How much effort is needed? What are the challenges? Can product experts do it? What are the costs versus the benefits?

We echo the notion of Franke and Piller (2003) that future research is needed on user interaction with configurators. This includes user interaction process patterns with configurators, user perception of "mass confusion", user satisfaction drivers with configurators, and how configurators affect customers' valuation of individualization. We would like to extend the perspective from self-service configurator use over the Web in consumer markets towards business-to-business (B2B) environments. In some B2B scenarios, the need to support consultative selling may be more important than self-service.

Configurators presently fail to provide support for ensuring that the created configuration models correspond to the real customization possibilities of the configurable product. Configurator vendors, for example, SAP (Haag, 2005) and Tacton (Orsvärn, 2005) call for research on methods and techniques to debug and diagnose configuration models. Significant steps towards diagnosis have been provided, for example, by Felfernig et al. (2004), who present a method that applies knowledge-based diagnosis techniques with configuration test cases for locating errors in configuration models. On a more basic level, using capabilities of inference engines could provide semantic level configuration model checking without writing test cases. For example, it could be possible to check if, any discrete configuration variable value can be present in a consistent configuration, or if any individual requirement that can be expressed can be satisfied. Future work on empirical evaluation on benefits versus sacrifices is required after such tools are in widespread use.

Another source of potential improvement is in user interfaces of configuration modeling tools that could apply ideas from Integrated Development Environments that are common in software development tools. This could provide model overview and navigation as well as immediate experimentation with the configuration model (Haag, 2005).

Although configurators do alleviate the complexity of specification, there is still room for improvement and future research. Configurators are not well-equipped to find optimal product fit with customer needs (Blecker et al., 2005, p. 92). Recommender or advisory system functionality could be included in configurators, or they could be integrated with such systems. Reconfiguration is also still a challenge (Manhart, 2005, Männistö et al., 1999).

DISCUSSION AND CONCLUSION

MC literature has been reviewed from a general perspective (Da Silveira et al., 2001), with the aim of recognizing the necessary conditions for successful MC (Blecker et al., 2005, p. 23; Broekhuizen & Alsem, 2002), and from the angle of customer sacrifices of MC (Bardacki & Whitelock, 2003). Franke and Piller (2003) have identified empirical research in the field of MC and discuss configurators among other user design toolkits for MC. The approaches to describe, model, and formalize configuration knowledge in configurators have been reviewed earlier (Günter & Kühn, 1999; Stumptner, 1997). Blecker et al. (2005, p. 80) have classified configurators to different categories. Our review has a different perspective and also synthesizes findings from MC, CP, and configurator literature. However, the scientific quality of the articles which we have reviewed varies. We chose to aim for broad identification of issues instead of concentrating only on the papers of highest scientific quality. The amount of references discussing an issue may be an indicator of the level of its importance.

Judging from the benefits that configurators can bring and the challenges that their use can overcome or alleviate, configurators truly are key enablers for mass customization with configurable products. However, only individual cases with more efficient and streamlined business processes have been reported, and conclusive evidence on

realized configurator benefits and whether the benefits outweigh the required sacrifices in a given situation is still lacking.

Configurator challenges remain. We believe our review, although by no means exhaustive, has been able to identify most of them, providing practitioners a useful checklist of issues that have to be taken into account when contemplating configurator-supported mass customization with configurable products.

Long-term management of configurators is claimed as one of the most significant challenges. The literature we examined does not provide a comprehensive answer on how difficult long-term management of configurators really is and to what extent it is easier with current configurators that do not require programming in configuration knowledge maintenance. Also, configurator introduction remains as a challenge, and configurators represent significant cost over the whole life cycle. Future opportunities and challenges remain in supporting customers in self-service settings; selecting a suitable product and appropriate technical specifications is a challenge, especially for customers who configure their products or services infrequently.

Applicability of the configurable products paradigm and configurators to services has received relatively little attention and remains a subject for future research.

REFERENCES

Agrawal, M., Kumaresh, T. V., & Mercer, G. A. (2001). The false promise of mass customization. *The McKinsey Quarterly, 3,* 62-71.

Åhlström, P. & Westbrook, R. (1999). Implications of mass customization for operations management: An exploratory survey. *International Journal of Operations & Production Management, 19*(3), 262-274.

Aldanondo, M., Véron, M., & Fargier, H. (1999). Configuration in manufacturing industry, requirements, problems, and definitions. In *Proceedings of the IEEE International Conference on Systems, Man, and Cybernetics: Vol. 6* (pp. 1009-1014).

Aldanondo, M., Rougé, S., & Vérnon, M. (2000). Expert configurator for concurrent engineering: Caméléon software and model. *Journal of Intelligent Manufacturing, 11*, 127-134.

Ariano, M., & Dagnino, A. (1996). An intelligent order entry and dynamic bill of materials system for manufacturing customized furniture. *Computers in Electrical Engineering, 22*(1), 45-60.

Bardacki, A., & Whitelock, J. (2003). Mass-customisation in marketing: The consumer perspective. *Journal of Consumer Marketing, 20*(5), 463-479.

Barker, V. E., & O'Connor, D. E. (1989). Expert systems for configuration at Digital: XCON and beyond. *Communications of the ACM, 32*(3), 298-318.

Beaty, R. T. (1996). Mass customisation. *IEE Manufacturing Engineer, 75*(5), 217-220.

Berman, B. (2002). Should your firm adopt a mass customization strategy? *Business Horizons, 45*(4), 51-60.

Blecker, T., Abdelkafi, N., Kreutler, G., & Friedrich, G. (2004). Product configuration systems: State of the art, conceptualization, and extensions, In A. B. Hamadou, F. Gargouri, & M. Jmaiel (Eds.), *Proceedings of the Eighth Maghrebian Conference on Software Engineering and Artificial Intelligence (MCSEAI 2004)* (pp. 25-36).

Blecker, T., Friedrich, G., Kaluza, B., Abdelkafi, N., & Kreutler, G. (2005). *Information and management systems for product customization.* New York: Springer.

Bonehill, E., & Slee-Smith, P. (1998). Product configurator. *IEE Workshop on Responsiveness in Manufacturing (Digest No.1998/213)*, 9/1-9/4.

Bramham, J., & MacCarthy, B. (2004). The demand-driven chain. *IEE Manufacturing Engineer, 83*(3), 30-33.

Broekhuizen, T. L. J., & Alsem, K. J. (2002). Success factors for mass customization: A conceptual model. *Journal of Market-Focused Management, 5*(4), 309-330.

Brown, S., & Bessant, J. (2003). The manufacturing strategy-capabilities links in mass customisation and agile manufacturing - An exploratory study. *International Journal of Operations & Production Management, 23*(7), 707-730.

Comstock, M., Johansen, K., & Winroth, M. (2004). From mass production to mass customization: Enabling perspectives from the Swedish mobile telephone industry. *Production Planning & Control, 15*(4), 362-372.

Da Silveira, G., Borenstein, D., & Fogliatto, F. S. (2001). Mass customization: Literature review and research directions. *International Journal of Production Economics, 72*, 1-13.

Dellaert, B. G. C., & Stremersch, S. (2005). Marketing mass-customized products: Striking a balance between utility and complexity. *Journal of Marketing Research, 42*(2), 219-227.

Duray, R. (2002). Mass customization origins: Mass or custom manufacturing? *International Journal of Operations & Production Management, 22*(3), 314-328.

Felfernig, A., Friedrich, G., Jannach, D., & Stumptner, M. (2004). Consistency-based diagnosis of configuration knowledge bases. *Artificial Intelligence, 152*(2), 213-234.

Fleischanderl, G., Friedrich, G., Haselböck, A., Schreiner, H., & Stumptner, M. (1998). Configuring large-scale systems with generative constraint satisfaction. *IEEE Intelligent System- Special issue on Configuration, 13* (7), 59-68.

Fohn, S. M., Liau, J. S., Greef, A. R., Young, R. E., & O'Grady, P. J. (1995). Configuring computer systems through constraint-based modeling and interactive constraint satisfaction. *Computers in Industry, 27,* 3-21.

Forza, C., & Salvador, F. (2002a). Managing for variety in the order acquisition and fulfilment process: The contribution of product configuration systems. *International Journal of Production Economics, 76,* 87-98.

Forza, C., & Salvador, F. (2002b.) Product configuration and inter-firm co-ordination: An innovative solution from a small manufacturing enterprise. *Computers in Industry, 49,* 37-56.

Franke, N., & Piller, F. (2004). Value creation by toolkits for user innovation and design: The case of the watch market. *Journal of Product Innovation Management, 21,* 401-415.

Franke, N., & Piller, F. T. (2003). Key research issues in user interaction with user toolkits in a mass customisation system. *International Journal of Technology Management, 26*(5/6), 578-599.

Gilmore, J. H., & Pine II, B. J. (1997). The four faces of customization. *Harvard Business Review, 75*(1), 91-101.

Günter, A. & Kühn, C. (1999). Knowledge-Based Configuration: Survey and future directions. *In XPS-99: Knowledge Based Systems, Proceedings of the 5th Biannual German Conference on Knowledge Based Systems. Springer Leture Notes in Artifical Intelligence 1570.*

Haag, A. (1998). Sales configuration in business processes. *IEEE Intelligent Systems, 13*(4), 78-85.

Haag, A. (2005). "Dealing" with configurable products in the SAP business suite. *Workshop on Configuration, International Conference on Artificial Intelligence (IJCAI 2005), Edinburgh, Scotland* (pp. 68-71).

Hart, C. W. L. (1995). Mass customization: Conceptual underpinnings, opportunities, and limits. *International Journal of Service Industry Management, 6*(2), 36-45.

Heatley, J., Agraval, R., & Tanniru, M. (1995). An evaluation of an innovative information technology - The case of carrier EXPERT. *Journal of Strategic Information Systems, 4*(3), 255-277.

Heiskala, M., Anderson, A., Huhtinen, V., Tiihonen, J., & Martio, A. (2003). A tool for comparing configurable products. *Workshop on Configuration, International Conference on Artificial Intelligence (IJCAI 2005), Acapulco, Mexico* (pp. 64-69).

Hvam, L., Malis, M., Hansen, B., & Riis, J. (2004). Reengineering of the quotation process: Application of knowledge-based systems. *Business Process Management Journal, 10*(2), 200-213.

Huffman, C., & Kahn, B. E. (1998). Variety for sale: Mass customization or mass confusion? *Journal of Retailing, 74*(4), 491-513.

Kakati, M. (2002). Mass customization - Needs to go beyond technology. *Human Systems Management, 21,* 85-93.

Kay, M. J. (1993). Making mass customization happen: Lessons for implementation. *Strategy & Leadership, 21*(4), 14-18.

Kotha, S. (1995). Mass customization: Implementing the emerging paradigm for competitive advantage. *Strategic Management Journal, 16,* 21-42.

Lampel, J. & Mintzberg, H. (1996). Customizing Customization. *Sloan Management Review, 38*(1), 21-30.

MacCarthy, B., & Brabazon, P. (2003). In the business of mass customisation. *IEE Manufacturing Engineer, 82*(4), 30-33.

Manhart, P. (2005). Reconfiguration – A problem in search of solutions. In D. Jannach & A. Felfernig (Eds.), *Configuration – Papers from the Configuration Workshop at IJCAI'05* (pp. 68-71).

McGuinness, D. L., & Wright, J. R. (1998). An industrial-strength description logic-based configurator platform. *IEEE Intelligent Systems, 13*(4), 69-77.

Männistö, T., Soininen, T., Tiihonen, J., & Sulonen, R. (1999). Framework and conceptual model for reconfiguration. *Configuration Papers from the AAAI Workshop* (AAAI Technical Report WS-99-05) (pp. 59-64). AAAI Press.

Orsvärn, K. (2005). Tacton configurator - Research directions. *Workshop on Configuration, International Conference on Artificial Intelligence (IJCAI 2005), Edinburgh, Scotland.*

Paloheimo, K. -S., Miettinen, I., & Brax, S. (2004). *Customer-oriented industrial services.* Espoo, Finland: Report Series –Helsinki University of Technology BIT Research Centre.

Pargamin, B. (2002). Vehicle sales configuration: The cluster tree approach. *ECAI 2002 Workshop on Configuration* (pp. 35-40).

Pedersen, J. L., & Edwards, K. (2004). Product configuration systems and productivity. In *Proceedings of International Conference on Economic, Technical and Organisational Aspects of Product Configuration Systems (PETO) 2004.*

Piller, F. T., Moeslein, K., & Stotko, C. M. (2004). Does mass customization pay? An economic approach to evaluate customer integration. *Production Planning & Control, 15*(4), 435-444.

Piller, F. T., & Müller, M. (2004). A new marketing approach to mass customisation. *International Journal of Computer Integrated Manufacturing, 17*(7), 583-593.

Pine, B. J. II (1993a). *Mass customization: The new frontier in business competition.* Boston: Harvard School Business Press.

Pine, B. J. II (1993b). Mass customizing products and services. *Strategy & Leadership, 21*(4), 6-13, 55.

Pine, B. J. II, Peppers, D., & Rogers, M. (1995). Do you want to keep your customers forever? *Harvard Business Review, 73*(2), 103-114.

Pine, B. J. II, Victor, B., & Boynton, A. C. (1993). Making mass customization work. *Harvard Business Review, 71*(5), 108-119.

Radder, L., & Louw, L. (1999). Research and concepts: Mass customization and mass production. *The TQM Magazine, 11*(1), 35-40.

Reichwald, R., Piller, F., & Mueller, M. (2004). A multi-channel interaction platform for mass customization – Concept and empirical investigation. *Workshop on Information Systems for Mass Customization (ISMC 2004), Fourth International ICSC Symposium on Engineering of Intelligent Systems (EIS 2004).*

Ross, A. (1996). Selling uniqueness. *IEE Manufacturing Engineer, 75*(6), 260-263.

Sabin, D., & Weigel, R. (1998). Product configuration frameworks – A survey. *IEEE Intelligent Systems & Their Applications, 13*(4), 42-49.

Salvador, F., & Forza, C. (2004). Configuring products to address the customization-responsiveness squeeze: A survey of management issues and opportunities. *International Journal of Production Economics, 91*(3), 273-291.

Slywotzky, A. J. (2000). The age of the choiceboard. *Harvard Business Review, 78*(1), 40-41.

Spring, M., & Dalrymple, J. F. (2000) Product customisation and manufacturing strategy. *International Journal of Operations & Production Management, 20*(4), 441-467.

Svensson, C., & Barfod, A. (2002). Limits and opportunities in mass customization for "build to order" SMEs. *Computers in Industry, 49,* 77-89.

Sviokla, J.J. (1990). An examination of the impact of expert systems on the firm: The case of XCON. *MIS Quarterly, 14*(2), 127-140.

Tiihonen, J., & Soininen, T. (1997). *Product configurators – Information system support for configurable products* (Tech. Rep. TKO-B137). Helsinki University of Technology, Laboratory of Information Processing Science. Also published in Richardson, T. (Ed.). (1997), *Using information technology during the sales visit.* Cambridge, UK: Hewson Group.

Tiihonen, J., Soininen, T., Männistö, T. & Sulonen, R. (1996). State-of-the-practice in product configuration—A survey of 10 cases in the Finnish industry. In T. Tomiyama, M. Mäntylä, & S. Finger (Eds.), *Knowledge Intensive CAD. Vol. 1* (pp. 95-114). Chapman & Hall.

Tiihonen, J., Soininen, T., Männistö, T. & Sulonen, R. (1998). Configurable products - Lessons learned from the Finnish industry. In *Proceedings of 2nd International Conference on Engineering Design and Automation (ED&A '98).* Integrated Technology Systems, Inc.

Vanwelkenheysen, J. (1998). The tender support system. *Knowledge-Based Systems, 11,* 363-372.

Wind, J., & Rangaswamy, A. (2001). Customerization: The next revolution in mass customization. *Journal of Interactive Marketing, 15*(1), 13-32.

Wright, J. R., Weixelbaum, E. S., Vesonder, G. T., Brown, K. E., Palmer, S. R., Berman, J. I., & Moore, H. H. (1993). A knowledge-based configurator that supports sales, engineering, and manufacturing at AT&T network systems. *AI Magazine, 14*(3), 69-80.

Yu, B., & Skovgaard, H. J. (1998). A configuration tool to increase product competitiveness. *IEEE Intelligent Systems, 13*(4), 34-41.

Zipkin, P. (2001). The limits of mass customization. *MIT Sloan Management Review, 42*(3), 81-87.

This work was previously published in Mass Customization Information Systems in Business, edited by T. Blecker; G. Friedrich, pp. 1-32, copyright 2007 by Information Science Reference (an imprint of IGI Global).

Section 2
Mass Customization Meets Personaliztion:
The Case of Adaptive and Intelligent User Interfaces

Chapter 7
A Dynamic User Centric Framework for Enhancing eServices Effectiveness Aiming at Mass Customization

Mario Belk
University of Cyprus, Cyprus

Panagiotis Germanakos
National & Kapodistrian University of Athens, Hellas and University of Cyprus, Cyprus

Nikos Tsianos
National & Kapodistrian University of Athens, Hellas

Zacharias Lekkas
National & Kapodistrian University of Athens, Hellas

Constantinos Mourlas
National & Kapodistrian University of Athens, Hellas

George Samaras
University of Cyprus, Cyprus

ABSTRACT

Mass customization should be more than just configuring a specific component (hardware or software), but should be seen as the co-design of an entire system, including services, experiences and human satisfaction at the individual as well as at the community level. The main objective of this chapter is to introduce a framework, smartTag, for the dynamic reconstruction of Web content based on human factors. Human factors and users' characteristics play the most important role during the entire design and implementation of the framework which has the inherent ability to interact with its environment and the user and transparently adapt its behaviour using intelligent techniques, reaching high levels of usability, user satisfaction, effectiveness and quality of service presentation. The initial results of the evaluation have proven that the proposed framework do not degrade the efficiency (in terms of speed

DOI: 10.4018/978-1-60566-260-2.ch007

and accuracy) during the Web content adaptation process as well as increases users' satisfaction and efficiency of information processing (both in terms of accuracy and task completion time), while users navigating in the personalized condition rather than the original one.

INTRODUCTION

Peoples' lives today are more turbulent and diversified. The "one size fits all" (Stonebraker and Çetintemel, 2008; Brown, 2004; Stonebraker, 2007) model could be considered out-of-date. People now want to be seen and treated as individuals and many are prepared to pay for this. They are better educated and informed; able and willing to make their own decisions (cyLEDGE Media, 2008).

Mass customization moves towards this direction and it aims to replace mass production, which is no longer suitable for today's chaotic markets, growing product variety, and opportunities for eCommerce and eServices (also referred to as eServices or On-line services) in general.

Mass customization is a broad term. It could be easily perceived as a working and profitable business model with a whole spectrum of ways and methodologies that can companies benefit from. At the most visible end of the spectrum, companies can mass customize products for individual customers.

However, with the rapid development of Internet technologies and the imminent change of business processes and services provision, there is always the question whether mass customization and internet can co-exist, or better is it actually happening (cyLEDGE Media, 2008)?

Nevertheless, we could perceive mass customization, together with personalization, as a combination that together tend to change the business information systems offering personalized service relationships as a way of connecting with customers over a number of platforms and of differentiating their services from those of competitors.

Mass customization should be more than just configuring a specific component (hardware or software), but should be seen as the co-design of an entire system, including services, experiences and human satisfaction at the individual as well as at the community level. It is widely acceptable that individuals differ in the way they think, feel, perceive and learn. Factors that could affect individuals' behavior range from cognitive and mental processes to visual and emotional characteristics liable to determine their degree of information assimilation and learning capacity at a given moment.

Henceforth, the research that is described in this chapter focuses on incorporating theories of individual differences in information processing within the context of eServices and the dynamic reconstruction and adaptation of any hypermedia content to the benefit of the unique user. Previous research of authors, in the field of adaptive eLearning, focused upon the enhancement of the quality of information presentation and users' interactions in the Web by matching their specific needs and preferences with the information space. It has been demonstrated that the incorporation of human information processing factors in eLearning environments leads to better comprehension on behalf of the users and increase of their academic performance (Germanakos et al., 2008a, Lekkas et al., 2008; Tsianos et al., 2008a). The comprehensive three-dimensional perceptual preferences model used comprises of the following human factors: Cognitive Style, Cognitive Processing Efficiency and Emotional Processing. The first dimension is unitary, whereas Cognitive Processing Efficiency is comprised of (a) Visual Working Memory Span (VWMS) (Baddeley, 1992) and (b) speed and control of information processing and visual attention (Demetriou et al., 1993). The emotional aspect of the model focuses on different aspects of anxiety (Cassady, 2004; Cassady and Johnson, 2002; Spielberger, 1983) and self-regulation.

Furthermore, since the WWW is by definition a huge resource of information, it would make much sense that individuals' information processing characteristics should be taken into consideration into this more generic context where constraints and challenges are radically differentiated. To that direction, our extended research efforts are focused on improving the effectiveness of Web services, and more broadly generic hypertext/hypermedia structures, by employing methods of personalization.

In our more recent work, a dynamic Web-based framework, called smarTag, for achieving mass customization on the Web based on human factors has been developed and evaluated. SmarTag is an easy to use framework that enables any entity, Web designer and/or developer to enhance their Web services (technology and language independent) with adaptive Web objects that adapt according to the users' cognitive factors. More specifically, given the users' individual differences, the same service content provided by an organization will be reconstructed and delivered differently based on the users' profile typologies. This way, we will increase information assimilation, accuracy on cognitive targets' searching activities and consequently enhance acceptability of the On-line services.

Therefore, the main objective of this chapter is to describe the smarTag architecture and its components as well as the involved theoretical implications. Towards this point, an overview of Web Personalization techniques and methods is presented and ways on how they can be integrated with Mass Customization of Web services and products are suggested. A high-level analysis of major Web services/sites with regards to the degree of customization based on the given cognitive framework (Tsianos et al. 2008a) is also outlined, as well as a comprehensive review of current Web Development Frameworks. Finally, an evaluation of the smarTag System concludes the chapter with the initial results being really encouraging for the future of the proposed conceptualization.

BACKGROUND

Mass Customization and Web Personalization are widely appreciated as viable and promising strategies, which aim to provide product and services that best serve individuals' personal needs with near mass production efficiency. Personalization is adapting or sequencing solutions to fit individual differences, expectations, and needs. In contrast, mass customization is adapting to fit common characteristics identified for groups of users.

Web Personalization

Web personalization is the process of customizing the content and structure of a Web-site to the specific needs of each user by taking advantage of the user's navigational behavior and specific perceptual characteristics. Being a multi-dimensional and complicated area a universal definition has not been agreed to date.

Many researches (Cingil et al. 2000; Blom, 2000; Kim, 2002; Wang and Lin, 2002) agree that the steps of the Web personalization process include: (1) the collection of Web data, (2) the modelling and categorization of these data (preprocessing phase), (3) the analysis of the collected data, and the determination of the actions that should be performed. Moreover, many argue that emotional or mental needs, caused by external influences, should also be taken into account.

Personalization could be realized in one of two ways: (a) Web-sites that require users to register and provide information about their interests, and (b) Web-sites that only require the registration of users so that they can be identified (De Bra et al., 2004). The main motivation points for personalization can be divided into those that are primarily to facilitate the work and those that are primarily to accommodate social requirements. The former motivational subcategory contains the categories of enabling access to information content, accommodating work goals, and accommodating individual differences, while the latter eliciting an emotional response and expressing identity (Wang and Lin, 2002).

Web Personalization can be detached into four main categories (Germanakos et al., 2004), these include: Link Personalization, Content Personalization, Context Personalization, Authorized Personalization and Humanized Personalization. The technologies that are employed in order to implement these processing phases are distinguished to: Content-based filtering, Rule-based filtering, Collaborative filtering, Web-usage mining, Demographic-based filtering, Agent technologies, Cluster Models.

Mass Customization

Traditionally customization and low cost have been mutually exclusive. Mass production provided low cost but at the expense of uniformity. Customization was the product of designers and craftsman. Its expense generally made it the preserve of the rich. To-day, new interactive technologies, like the Internet, allow customers to interact with a company and specify their unique requirements which are then manufactured by automated systems. Whilst this may at first seem complicated and beyond the average consumer, there are various ways to hide the technical details. In some cases the process will be handled by an organization's staff, a third party, or intermediary.

Mass customization is the customization and personalization of products and services for individual customers at a mass production price (cyLEDGE Media, 2008). It is actually a further step of enhancing an individual customers' relationship. It may not always be practical to support one user at a time or to build in total personaliza-

tion capabilities specific to one user. It may be preferable to start with a mass customized solution that identifies a few common critical success attributes that are key for improved performance. Based on recent technological advances it is possible to implement On-line services and communication environments accessed via Internet or Web technologies which may be personalized on the basis of individuals' preferences or even the intrinsic characteristics of the specific user like cognitive and emotional parameters, often referred to as human factors. Both content and its way of presentation (modality, visual layouts, ways of interaction, structure) as well as functional elements of such communication environments may automatically adapt their behavior according to the user needs and preferences enhancing the quality of service delivery and user satisfaction.

The greatest benefit of mass customization done well is technology's ability to make complex instruction easier by alternatively presenting content for a particular learner/user – what the user wants to see in the appropriate manner and at the appropriate time. A well-tested framework, based on sound scientific and design foundations, can help identify the capabilities, resources, issues, and content that is relevant, useful, and attractive to the targeted group of users. It also helps designers tailor products and services to satisfy the wide variety of requirements and capabilities (business, learning, educational, and personal goals).

Furthermore, mass customization raises the profits and lowers the costs. Whilst it is possible to manufacture at a mass produced price, there is the option to charge a premium whilst still retailing below the price of a custom product. This, in turn, will open a given product to a wider market. The uniqueness and profitability of customized products and services with the economies of scale and mass market penetration stemming from the mass production techniques that have to be adjusted and aligned with the current trends ruled by the dynamic contexts and environments, as is nowadays the Internet. World Wide Web introduces a new model of communication that differs from traditional media, since information is distributed in a variety of ways that enhances the proliferation of human networks (Mason & Hacker, 2003), regardless of their social, educational, economic or political orientation.

THE WEB TODAY: A HIGH-LEVEL ANALYSIS OF MAJOR WEB SERVICES SITES BASED ON A GIVEN COGNITIVE FRAMEWORK

A mass production technique is to devise a cognitive framework that is, could assist providers to develop Web-sites that will embrace intrinsic values of customers, tailoring their On-line services accordingly.

We have previously mentioned that cognitive factors have an important role in user satisfaction and identification of the products that are interested in. However, the way cognitive factors used today in order to design and develop Web services is considered unwisengly and principally based on provider's perception, without following particular rules that could achieve the appropriate mapping with selected content meta-characteristics; thus reconstructing any content to the benefit of the users.

In further support of the aforementioned concepts, one cannot disregard the fact that, besides the parameters that constitute the "traditional" user profile (composed of parameters like knowledge, goals, background, experience, preferences, activities, demographic information, socio-economic characteristics, device-channel characteristics etc., (Germanakos et al., 2007), each user carries his own perceptual and cognitive characteristics that have a significant effect on how information is perceived and processed. Information is encoded in the human brain by triggering electrical connections between neurons, and it is known that the number of synapses that any person activates each time is unique and dependant on many fac-

tors, including physiological differences (Graber, 2000). Since early work on the psychological field has shown that research on actual intelligence and learning ability is hampered by too many limitations, there have been a "number of efforts to identify several styles or abilities and dimensions of cognitive and perceptual processing" (McLoughlin, 1999]), which have resulted in what is known as learning and cognitive styles. *Learning and cognitive styles* can be defined as relatively stable strategies, preferences and attitudes that determine an individual's typical modes of perceiving, remembering and solving problems, as well as the consistent ways in which an individual memorizes and retrieves information (Pithers, 2002). Each learning and cognitive style typology defines patterns of common characteristics and implications in order to overcome difficulties that usually occur throughout the procedure of information processing. Therefore, in any Web-based informational environment, the significance of the aforementioned users' differences, both physiological and preferential, is distinct and should be taken into consideration when designing such adaptive environments.

It is true that nowadays, there are not main researches, to our knowledge, that move towards the consideration of user profiles that incorporate optimized parameters taken from the research areas of visual attention processing and cognitive psychology in combination and used effectively in generic hypermedia structures and On-line services. Some serious attempts have been made though on approaching eLearning systems providing adapted content to the students but most of them are lying to the analysis and design of methodologies that consider only the particular dimension of cognitive learning styles, including Field Independence vs. Field Dependence, Holistic-Analytic, Sensory Preference, Hemispheric Preferences, and Kolb's Learning Style Model (Yuliang & Dean, 1999), applied to identified mental models, such as concept maps, semantic networks, frames, and schemata (Ayersman &

Figure 1. Riding's Learning Styles Characteristics and Implications

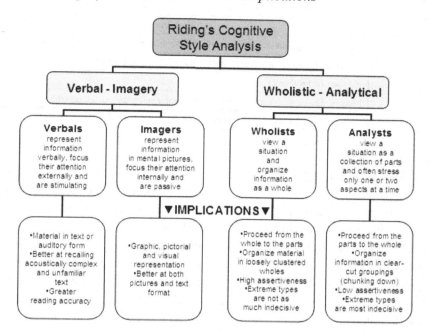

Reed, 1998; Reed et al., 1996]. In order to deal with the diversified students' preferences such systems are matching the instructional materials and teaching styles with the cognitive styles and consequently they are satisfying the whole spectrum of the students' cognitive learning styles by offering a personalized Web-based educational content.

In our research, a selection of the most appropriate and technologically feasible learning styles (those that can be projected on the processes of selection and presentation of Web-content and the tailoring of navigational tools) has been studied, such as Riding's Cognitive Style Analysis (Verbal-Imager and Wholistic-Analytical) (Riding, 2001), Felder / Silverman Index of Learning Styles (4 scales: Active vs Reflective, Sensing vs Intuitive, visual vs. Verbal and Global vs. Sequential) (Felder & Silverman, 1988), Witkin's Field-Dependent and Field-Independent (Witkin et al., 1977), and Kolb's Learning Styles (Converger, Diverger, Accommodator, and Assimilator) (Kolb & Kolb, 2005]), in order to identify how users transforms

information into knowledge (constructing new cognitive frames).

We consider that Riding's CSA (as well as in many cases Felder / Silverman's ILS) implications can be mapped on the information space more precisely, since they are consisted of distinct scales that respond to different aspects of the Web-space (see Fig. 1). Learning style theories that define specific types of learners, as Kolb's Experiential Learning Theory, have far more complex implications, since they relate strongly with personality theories, and therefore cannot be adequately quantified and correlated easily with Web objects and structures.

According to the theory behind CSA, individuals that are placed towards the edges of each axis have a strong preference for a specific method of information structure (Analyst/Wholist) or presentation (Imager/Verbalizer) - see Table 1.

Consequently, when an individual is required to process information in the Web, it is most likely that the matching of his/hers preference to the structure and method of presentation of

Table 1. Preferences of individuals according to cognitive style

Cognitive Style	Preference
Analyst	Internal (self-)guidance, non-linearity, index of interconnected concepts, view of situations in parts
Wholist	External guidance, linearity, defined framework, view of situations as a whole
Intermediate	No specific preference
Imager	Images, diagrams, schemes, better comprehension through visual representations.
Verbal	Predominance of text, better comprehension through verbal representations.

the Website would lead to better understanding, efficiency and satisfaction.

The first step to ground the need of personalization would be a preliminary inspection of the direction that major Web services sites are oriented to, with regards to cognitive style. For that reason, we selected five very deeply elaborated Web-sites of major commercial companies in the field of computers: www.dell.com, www.ibm.com, www.sony.com, www.apple.com, and www.hp.com. Due to the extreme breadth and depth of these sites, our analysis was limited to information related to the characteristics of computers that these companies offer, since this kind of information is factual and visitors are expected to understand and retain these data for further processing that could lead to commercial decisions.

In general, quite a few common patterns were observed: firstly, it is evident that in all five cases the lack of sequential organization and the extreme segmentation of the content require that the users should adopt an analytic path. External guidance is missing, and a general framework that would benefit Wholists is absent. Important information is available only through additional clicking and navigating.

Still, it is of high interest that when users successfully navigate to a specific product, the presentation is rather sequential, since information is provided without interconnections and links to concepts that would allow Analysts to form a deeper understanding; Wholists on the other hand would find this simplicity more to their liking.

It could as well be supported that this is not an intermediate approach, with all aspects of information processing being equally taken into account, but a mixed-mode that at instances may serve users' preferences in a random way. Of course, this is expected since Web-sites are not built around this kind of individual differences.

As it concerns the Imager/Verbalizer dimension, while all sites are aesthetically very pleasing with the inclusion of photos and banners, all significant information is mostly conveyed through text. The idea of schematically presenting important details is not actualized in any case; however, the Sony and Apple sites accompany many texts with relevant images that provide a somehow visual description of the information, as long as users are a little bit experienced with computers.

To this end, it could be supported that the 3 out of 5 sites are heavily suitable for Verbalizers; the remaining two adopt a rather intermediate approach which can be considered as balanced, even if this happens for aesthetical reasons.

At this point, the construct of working memory should be discussed. Working Memory (WM) has gained some popularity in terms of examining the interaction of WM span with different hypertext levels of complexity. DeStefano and LeFevre (Spielberger, 1983) reviewed 38 studies that address mainly the issue of cognitive load in hypertext reading, and working memory is often considered as an individual factor of significant importance, even at the level of explaining differ-

Figure 2. Mapping process

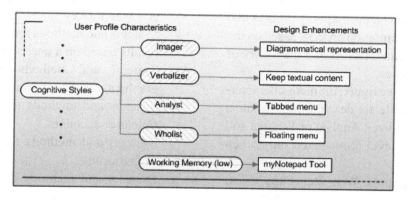

ences in performance. Lee and Tedder (De Bra et al., 2004) examine the role of working memory in different computer texts, and their results show that low working memory span learners do not perform equally well in hypertext environments. The term Cognitive Load Theory is often used when referring to guidelines for designing hypermedia applications, and it is often correlated with working memory span (Kim, 2002).

In all five sites, the amount of links and information is rather exhaustive. Especially at the first levels of the navigational structure, there are so many links to information resources that could burden users with low WM span. The lack of a coherent pattern or even better an adaptive mechanism that would adjust the availability of information to users' capabilities could as well reduce the efficiency of navigation through the site.

The most demanding task is to keep a track of the paths that lead to different resources in order to avoid disorientation; it seems that, according to the abovementioned studies, this task requires a satisfactory level of WM span. The way we approach methodologically this issue is discussed in a next section of this chapter.

In our opinion and in relation to our work in the field of adaptive educational hypermedia (Cingil, 2002), the sites that were inspected, though at a preliminary level, are not exactly biased towards specific preferences, neither well balanced. At

each instance, a mode of information presentation predominates, but this is not stable; it may as well change, for example when an actual product is shown. Perhaps Analysts/Verbalizers would find these Web-sites more comprehensible than Wholists/Imagers, but not at all times.

Consequently, our research interest is whether we could dynamically alter a section of a Web-site (the computer section in this case) by personalizing the content and the structure to specific users' cognitive preferences. This could be achieved by enriching the existing Web structures with further design enhancements and specific content transformations based on the adaptation mapping rules derived from selected cognitive factors. In the event that this would be proven successful and meaningful, individuals would learn better the information that is important to them.

Therefore, based on our previous research, the way cognitive styles could be used effectively within the context of any content reconstruction is to identify the way we will reconstruct the content. The adaptation process involves the transformation and/or enhancement of a given raw Web-based content (provider's original content) based on the impact the specific human factors have on the information space (Germanakos et al., 2008a; Tsianos et al., 2008a) (i.e., show a more diagrammatical representation of the content in case of an Imager user, as well as provide the user with extra navigation support tools). Figure

2 shows the possible Web content transformations/enhancements based on the mapping process that take place during adaptation process based on the influence of the human factors and the theory of individual differences.

Based on the above figure, the meta-characteristics of a user profile are deterministic (at most 3); Imager or Verbalizer, Analyst or Wholist and Working Memory level (considered only when low).

Today's most popular Web-sites (http://www.alexa.com/site/ds/top_500) like Google, Microsoft Live, Yahoo, Amazon, eBay, BBC news etc. do not heavily use the abovementioned cognitive considerations but they rather mostly employ customization techniques where the user has direct control; the user explicitly selects between certain options. On the other hand, personalization is driven by the system which tries to serve up individualized pages to the user according his profile and needs. Although, personalization is used by many of these popular Web-sites (especially Google), the techniques they maintain are lying under the predetermined customization of services or products and not to the actual personalization and dynamic reconstruction of content based on user preferences.

Personalization and Mass Customization Techniques used in Today's most Popular Web-Sites

Indicatively, two live cases under this category are Google and Amazon personalization methods.

Google Personalization Methods

Google Inc. uses several methods and techniques that look at personalization, and provide a system for collecting information from a searcher that may make it easier for the search engine to deliver search results to them that more closely match what they may be looking for than from a non-personalized search. Some of them are:

- Systems and methods for analyzing a user's Web history
- Systems and methods for modifying search results based on a user's history
- Systems and methods for providing a graphical display of search activity
- Systems and methods for managing multiple user accounts
- Systems and methods for combining sets of favourites
- Systems and methods for providing subscription-based personalization

Profile building is one of the most popular techniques Google uses for providing personalization. A lot of information is collected in this process, including clicks on search results pages, which pages are viewed, how long someone stays on different pages, how long ago these activities happened, and more. Different algorithms might be used to identify other types of data, including pages that are similar to ones that users have interacted with.

Amazon Personalization Methods

Amazon.com has a much-vaunted personalization element that gives each customer individualized recommendations of books. Even though this feature is far from perfect, it usually succeeds in including some relevant titles.

The book recommendations succeed for two reasons: (a) Users do not need to do anything to set it up, and (b) the system learns their preferences by recording what books they buy.

By watching millions of buyers, the system learns which books are similar. If many people who buy some user's books also buy i.e. Don Norman's books, then it is a good idea to recommend Norman's new book to somebody who has bought the user's books in the past, even if they have never bought any of his books.

We have to note at this point that both steps happen without imposing any extra work on the users. Also, the fact that somebody buys a book is a pretty strong signal that they have an interest in the book (much more reliable data than most preference settings one can collect from users).

Amazon also uses the similarity data to include hypertext links between related books. Thus, when users are browsing the page for one book, they see links to three other books they are likely to want. This use of the data is much better than the personal recommendation list because the hypertext links are embedded in the context of the users' natural behaviour. When the users go to a book page, they will be shown recommendations that match their specific interest in that moment (as opposed to being derived from a generic model of the users' average interests).

CURRENT WEB-BASED AUTHORING TOOLS

Nowadays, most semantic Web authoring tools (neither HTML editors, nor CMS), provide the Web developer with techniques and easy-to-use tools to create and generate descriptive ontologies of eServices' content. These authoring tools, as well as any other kind of Web editing tools (CMS, HTML Editors etc.) do not take into consideration adaptation and personalization techniques. Ideally, a combination of a Web authoring process of Web-based content and the adaptation of this content based on a given framework would give a more comprehensive approach to the personalization of content production.

To our knowledge, there has not been a Web Development Editor that takes into consideration the above issues for mass customizing and personalizing Web products and services. A comprehensive review of current Web Development Editors will be presented in this section.

Web-based authoring tools are becoming standard issue in modern content management systems. They range from simple text editors to high powered graphical authoring tools and con-

tent management systems. This section contains a listing of some noteworthy research oriented and commercial Web authoring tools. Many of the editors listed below are "What You See Is What You Get" (WYSIWYG) HTML editors, some of which have the option to view the HTML source code. These are quite popular due to the low learning curve, yet it is important to get some understanding of HTML since WYSIWYG HTML editors can be limiting.

Non-Commercial Oriented Web Authoring Tools

A selection of the most predominant non-commercial Web-based authoring tools is described below:

Protégé

Protégé (Noy, 2001) (http://protege.stanford.edu/) is a free, open-source platform that provides a growing user community with a suite of tools to construct domain models and knowledge-based applications with ontologies. At its core, Protégé implements a rich set of knowledge-modeling structures and actions that support the creation, visualization, and manipulation of ontologies in various representation formats. Protégé can be customized to provide domain-friendly support for creating knowledge models and entering data. Further, Protégé can be extended by way of a plug-in architecture and a Java-based Application Programming Interface (API) for building knowledge-based tools and applications.

An ontology describes the concepts and relationships that are important in a particular domain, providing a vocabulary for that domain as well as a computerized specification of the meaning of terms used in the vocabulary. Ontologies range from taxonomies and classifications, database schemas, to fully axiomatized theories. In recent years, ontologies have been adopted in many business and scientific communities as a way to share, reuse and process domain knowledge. Ontologies are now central to many applications such as scientific knowledge portals, information management and integration systems, electronic commerce, and semantic Web services.

Swoop: A Web Ontology Editing Browser

SWOOP ((http://code.google.com/p/swoop/) (Kalyanpur et al., 2005a; Kalyanpur et al., 2005b)) is a tool for creating, editing, and debugging OWL ontologies. It was produced by the MIND lab at University of Maryland, College Park, but is now an open source project with contributors from all over.

Swoop is built primarily as a Web Ontology Browser and Editor, i.e., it is tailored specifically for OWL ontologies. Thus, it takes the standard Web browser as the UI paradigm, believing that URIs are central to the understanding and construction of OWL Ontologies. The familiar look and feel of a browser emphasized by the address bar and history buttons, navigation side bar, bookmarks, hypertextual navigation etc are all supported for Web ontologies, corresponding with the mental model people have of URI-based Web tools based on their current Web browsers.

OntoStudio

OntoStudio (http://semanticWeb.org/wiki/OntoStudio) is an engineering environment for ontologies and for the development of semantic applications, with particular emphasis on rule-based modelling. It is the successor of OntoEdit which was distributed worldwide more than 5000 times. OntoStudio was originally developed for F-Logic but now also includes some support for OWL, RDF, and OXML. It also includes functions such as the OntoStudio Evaluator. The Evaluator is used for the implementation of rules during modelling; this procedure has been recently patented.

Commercial Web Authoring Tools

A selection of the most predominant commercial Web-based authoring tools is described below:

EditOnPro by RealObjects

RealObjects edit-on Pro (http://www.realobjects.com/) is a cross-platform WYSIWYG XHTML / XML editor as a Java applet, allowing individuals and teams to update, create, and publish Web content within Content Management, Knowledge Management, e-Learning or other Web-based systems.

The editor has an easy-to-use, intuitive user interface which provides word processor-like and XML editor-like features to Web based applications, empowering non-technical users to become content contributors without knowing HTML, XML or other cryptic mark-up languages.

It guarantees XHTML compliance of the contents created or pasted from other applications by validation. Thus corporate site standards for style, layout and code can uncompromisingly be enforced. The valid XHTML output assures portability, compatibility and interoperability. For example, content can easily be parsed and automatically be transformed using XSLT.

Cute Editor by Cute Soft

Cute Editor (http://cutesoft.net/) for ASP.NET is a WYSIWYG browser-based Online HTML Editor for ASP.NET (cyLEDGE Media, 2008). It is also available for PHP and ASP.

It enables ASP.NET Web developers to replace the Textarea in the existing content management system with a powerful, but easy to use WYSIWYG HTML editing component.

It empowers business users to make content updates easily and safely themselves while maintaining control over site design and content, all at an affordable price.

Figure 3. The smarTag Framework

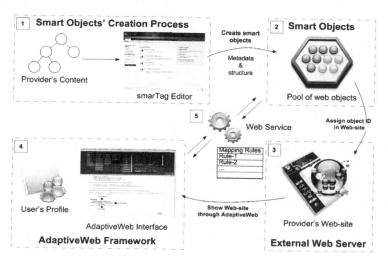

TinyMCE - Javascript WYSIWYG Editor

TinyMCE (http://tinymce.moxiecode.com/) is a platform independent Web based Javascript HTML WYSIWYG editor control released as Open Source under LGPL by Moxiecode Systems AB. It has the ability to convert HTML Textarea fields or other HTML elements to editor instances. TinyMCE is very easy to integrate into other Content Management Systems.

JXHTMLEdit by Tecnick

JXHTMLEdit (http://www.tecnick.com/) is a free Open Source browser-based HTML/XHTML content authoring tool based on the Java 2 Platform that allows WYSIWYG editing on multiple platforms (require the Sun JavaTM Plug-in 1.4 or higher installed on client).

It is a cross-platform WYSIWYG HTML/XHTML content authoring tool, a very small Java Applet based on the Java 2 Platform. JXHTMLEdit provides word processor-like user interface that allows users to edit the XHTML document directly in the final form (as will be rendered). This empowers non-technical users to become content contributors without any knowledge of HTML or XHTML.

JXHTMLEdit has been designed to offer great flexibility and could be used to easily integrate WYSIWYG authoring functionality into existing Websites, CMS, WMS or any other Web-based software. The Applet JAR archive is less than 150 KB and it's cacheable, so it loads very quickly.

A PROPOSED FRAMEWORK FOR ENHANCING MASS CUSTOMIZATION OF WEB SERVICES BASED ON HUMAN FACTORS

The smarTag framework (see Fig. 3) is an extension of the AdaptiveWeb (Germanakos et al., 2007; Germanakos et al., 2008a) framework aiming to improve the creation process of adaptive Web-pages based on given user's characteristics (cognitive factors). A visitor that wants to get personalized information of a Web services site (that has been enhanced under the smarTag framework) has to authenticate through the AdaptiveWeb System. The AdaptiveWeb System is responsible for the mapping process of the user's comprehensive profile and the smart Web objects created under the smarTag framework.

A user initially enters the Adaptive Web System and navigates through any Web-site available on the net. So far the user views the raw content of a Web-site without any personalization of content taking place. When the user wants to get personalized content he authenticates into his / her profile (initially created in the Profile Construction Component). If the current Web-site consists of smart objects, the Web-page will be reconstructed based on the user's profile; all the corresponding Web objects will be filtered out from the available pool of objects.

The smarTag framework is composed of five interrelated components[1], each one representing a stand-alone Web-based system. The idea behind the framework is to enhance any Web services page (technology and language independent) with adaptive Web objects that will adapt according to a given user's profile (user's cognitive characteristics).

Initially, authorized Web services developers create smart Web objects by characterizing them through the smarTag Web Editor. All the Web objects' information (metadata and structure) are stored on the system's server.

The Web developer will create specific sections (e.g. <div> sections) in the Web-page that will be mapped with a smart object that has been initially created in the smarTag Editor. When navigating through the Web-site, the user's characteristics will be mapped with the smart objects and the Web-page will be personalized accordingly.

A more detailed description and analysis of how the components in the smarTag framework interact and how the adaptation process works is presented in the following sections.

Authoring Smart Objects - The smarTag Editor

SmarTag Editor is a Web Development tool enabling a content provider to create smart objects. A smart object under the smarTag Framework is conceptually similar to the traditional XML objects: they too consist of attributes and content. The content can either be in textual or diagrammatical form in case of a Verbalizer and Imager user respectively. The smarTag attributes are special meta-characteristics describing the possible behavior the object can perform in its environment (Germanakos et al., 2008a). All the objects are stored on the smarTag Server which are used in the mapping process of a user's profile (Tsianos et al., 2008a), as well as the provider's external Web-page.

Since all the smart objects will be embedded as enhancements in an external Web-site, our main concern is to ensure openness and interoperability between the system's components and any external Web-site, as well as to ensure the Web security policies. In order to achieve this, the smart objects must be easily extendible and easy to handle. Using XML for implementing the smart objects' structure seems to be the best way to achieve this. Indeed XML[2] enables the extendibility we need and enhances interoperability and integration among systems' components. We have designed a Web Service (a software system designed to support interoperable Machine to Machine interaction over a network) for retrieving the smart objects. A more comprehensive description on this matter will take place in the following section.

Enhancing any Web-Site with smarTag Editor

Our main concern was to create an easy to use Web enhancement tool that enables any Web developer / designer to enhance divisions of his / her Web-site with mass customization and personalization techniques. More specifically, the traditional

Figure 4. Traditional Web-site development process

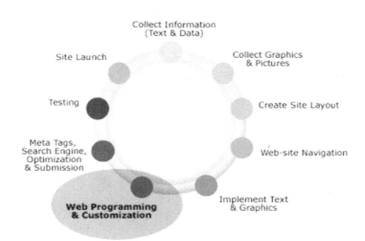

methods of Web Development will take place in the process; based on the main requirements of the end-users of the Web-site and mainly on the "design taste" of the Web Designer / Developer.

Fig. 4 depicts the Traditional Web-site development process. Initially, based on the Web-site requirements and specifications, all the needed information (text, data, graphics and pictures) of the Web-site is collected. The Web-site's layout and Navigation is then designed by the Web Designer and all the collected information is implemented in the Web-site.

So far, the Web-site's author will follow the traditional steps of the Web development process without the need of smarTag Editor. As mentioned before, smarTag is a Web enhancement tool. Accordingly, smarTag Editor is used in the Web Programming and Customization phase. The Web Developer will define specific divisions in the Web-site that will adapt according to individual characteristics (cognitive styles).

For a better understanding of how smarTag Editor works in practice, Fig. 5 shows a quick step process diagram for enhancing a Web-site with smart objects.

Based on the abovementioned figure, an authorized Web Developer will create a new adaptive Web object by storing the object's actual content (text or image) and characterizing (see Fig. 6) it based on the smarTag framework. A unique identifier will be assigned to this object and stored on the smarTag server. Based on the unique identifier, the Web Developer will map the corresponding object with a specific division in the Web-site created so far (Fig. 4). SmarTag will then generate a JavaScript file based on the provider's preferences and will be embedded in the Web-site. This JavaScript file is the core element for communication establishment between the smarTag Web Service and the provider's external Web-site as described below.

Adaptation and Mapping Process

We have designed an experimental setting in the application fields of eCommerce, by authoring smart Web objects and enhancing an existing commercial Web-site.

The eCommerce (Web) environment that has been developed used the design and information content of an existing commercial Web-site of IBM[3]. This Web-site provides products' specifica-

Figure 5. Enhancing Web-sites using smarTag Editor

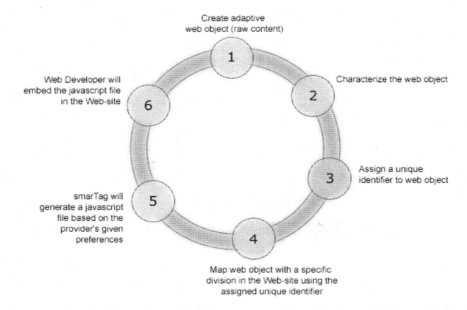

tions of the IBM Company. We have developed an exact replica of the IBM System Servers section in IBM.com using smart objects.

To get a better insight of the adaptation process and how data flows, we hereafter discuss how the personalized content interacts with the Comprehensive User Profile, using specific mapping rules. In Fig. 6, the Content and Structure Description Schema is shown, while Fig. 7 shows the whole adaptation process.

Figure 6. Content and Structure Description Schema

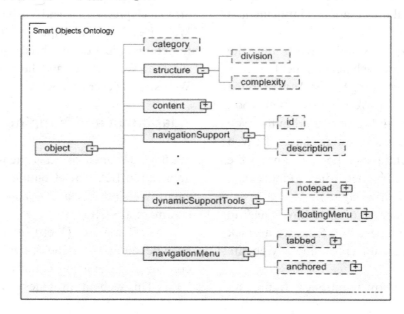

When users want to interact with the adapted and personalized content they have to provide their credentials for retrieving their profile using the AdaptiveWeb System (Germanakos et al., 2007). After the user's comprehensive profile is retrieved a cookie is created on the client browser with the username and password. Every time a Web-page is requested, unique user id is sent to the smarTag Web Service and specific Web objects are filtered out and shown to the user, based on his / her comprehensive profile.

In this particular example (see Fig. 7), the user happens to be an Imager / Analyst with regards to the Cognitive Style, has an average knowledge on

Figure 7. The Adaptation Process

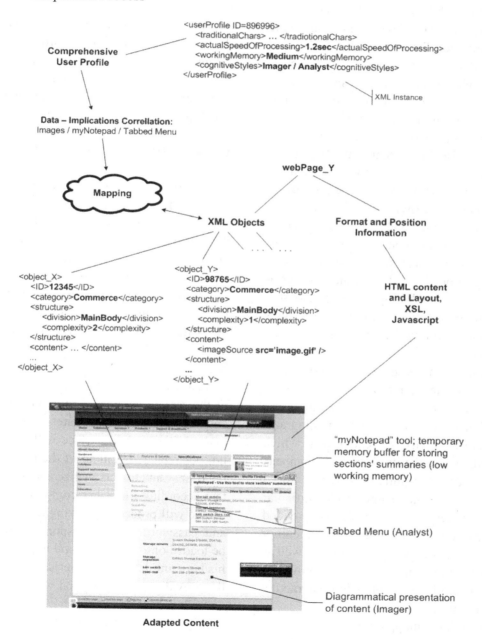

Adapted Content

the subject (computer knowledge) based on his traditional characteristics, has an Actual Cognitive Processing Speed Efficiency of 1200 msec and a low Working Memory Span (weighting 2/7). Using these preferences the data-implications correlation diagram is evaluated.

Every Web-page is detached into standalone objects, each one having special characteristics. In our example, the user visits the "WebPage_Y" Web-page. First, the main HTML document of this Web-page is retrieved which contains all the needed information for building the Web-page; that is, (i) the HTML Web-page itself which is a predefined HTML document (designed by the provider) keeping information of specified divisions / frames in the page for positioning each object, (ii) all objects (text, image, audio, video etc.) that comprise the content of the Web-page, and (iii) a generated JavaScript file from smarTag that is responsible for the proper integration of the smart objects into the divisions' Web-page.

At this point we have all the information we need for adapting the content; the data-implications correlation diagram based on the user's comprehensive profile and the content description of the particular Web-page. The next step is to map the implications with the Web-page's content, for assembling the final version of the provider's content.

The interpretation of the user's data-implications correlation diagram results in the following conclusions: (a) the user is an Imager, therefore the provision of visual information (diagrammatical representation) is predominant, which has an average complexity because he happens to have a medium cognitive processing speed efficiency, average knowledge of the particular subject (computer knowledge) (b) is provided with the "myNotepad" tool; temporary memory buffer for storing sections' summaries, as well as (c) extra navigation support tools are provided, devised to be more applicable while interacting with an eCommerce environment.

Fig. 8 shows the mapping process using our

example; explained in pseudo code. The XML documents do not provide any formatting information and/or any information about how XML documents should be displayed, unlike HTML documents that carry that information. For this purpose, the author designs the desired page and formats using XSL (eXtensible Stylesheet Language) and puts the objects in a specified subdivision of the Web-page (HTML layout document).

The subsection below will explain in more detail the AdaptiveWeb Environment, namely AdaptiveInteliWeb, where all personalized content is shown along with the extra navigation support and learner control that differ according to each user's profile and application area.

Viewing the Adapted Content

The AdaptiveWeb User Interface (Germanakos et al., 2008b), namely AdaptiveInteliWeb (see Fig. 9 a, b, c), is a Web application used for displaying the raw and/or personalized and adapted content on the user's device. This can be a home desktop, laptop or a mobile device.

The main concept of this component is to provide a framework where all personalized Web-sites can be navigated. Using this interface the users interact with the provider's content and based on their profile further support is provided to them with the use of a slide-in panel at the top of the screen, containing all navigation support and learner control attributes adjusted accordingly. Initially, the interface will show the raw, not personalized content of the provider. When the user wants to personalize and adapt the content according to his/her comprehensive profile he/she will proceed by giving his/her username and password. The corresponding profile will be loaded onto the server and in proportion with his/her cumulative characteristics the content of the provider will be mapped with the "Mapping Rules", as described before.

Fig. 9a depicts an exact replica of the IBM Web-

Figure 8. Mapping Process Example (pseudo code)

```
Algorithm : Mapping Process Phase
Input: User's data-implications correlation diagram
(diagrammaticalRepresentation, navigationTools, cognitiveStyles),
SmartObjects, XSL document, JavaScript document, HTML Web-page
content and layout
Output: Generate an Adapted and Personalized Web-page
Execute these steps (top-down):
  1) For each structure division (Introduction, MainBody, Conclusion)
     Filter out the WebObjects in ascending order based on their
     complexity (<complexity>);
  2) For each remained object, make a further filtering based on the
object's <type> tag
        if (cognitiveStyle1 == Imager)
           Provide diagrammatical representation of object;
        elseif (cognitiveStyle1 == Verbalizer)
           Provide textual representation of object;
        if (object has NavigationSupport Tag){
          if (cognitiveStyle2 == Analyst)
             Provide Tabbed Navigation Menu;
          elseif (cognitiveStyle2 == Wholist OR
               cognitiveStyle2 == Intermediate)
          Provide Floating Navigation Menu
        }
  3) Create "myNotepad" tool (temporary memory buffer)
     if (working memory == low)
        Provide the user with "myNotepad" tool for storing a section of
     the page and keep active information;
        Create a link next to each smart object, along with a unique id
     for the corresponding item;
        OnUserClick store the smart object's content into "myNotepad"
     tool;
  4) Format each smart object based on the XSL (eXtensive
Stylesheet) document
  5) Position each smart object in the right structure division based on
     the HTML layout document
```

site without any personalization made, while Fig. 9b and Fig. 9c shows the same Web-site after the personalization and adaptation process has been initiated, with the content to be adapted according to the user's comprehensive profile.

As we can easily observe, the original environment has been altered based on rules that define the typologies of the users in terms of content reconstruction and supportive tools. For example, a user might be identified as an "Analyst-Imager" with low working memory and therefore the Web environment during interaction time would be as in Fig. 9b. The information will be presented in a diagrammatic form (imager), will be enriched with menu tabs (analyst) to be easier accessible and with the "myNotepad" tool (temporary memory buffer) for storing sections' summaries (low working memory). In case that a user is

identified as "Wholist-Verbalizer" the content will be automatically reconstructed as in Fig.9c, where a floating menu with anchors (Wholist) have been added so to guide the users on specific parts into the content while interacting. In this case no diagrammatical presentation will be used because the user is a Verbalizer.

EXPERIMENTAL EVALUATION OF SMARTAG

The current environment and the dynamic transformation mechanism are currently at the evaluation stage. However, the whole procedure is driven by our previous findings (Germanakos et al., 2008a), whereby the alteration of presentation based on various cognitive factors has been proved efficient and effective. The predefined environment devised in this case concerns the Sony[4] company and the section of laptops' specifications. We have to emphasize that the main difference between the two experimental settings (IBM and Sony) is the implementation method of the reconstruction approach (automatic adaptation based on <csl> tag

and predefined environment for IBM and Sony, respectively).

Assessing System's Performance

To measure system's performance, functional behavior and efficiency of our system we have run

Figure 9. Content adaptation according to user's comprehensive profile (eCommerce)

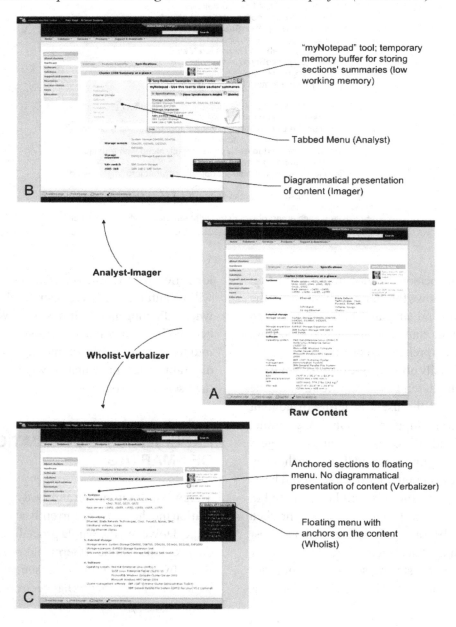

Figure 10. Raw Content and Adapted Content Scenarios

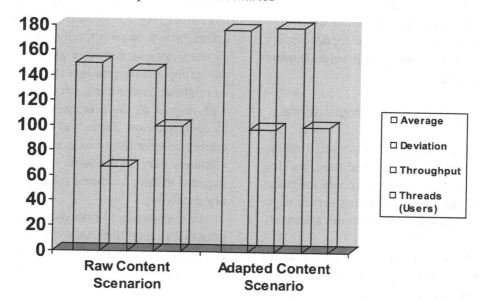

two different simulations with 100 threads (users) each: (a) users retrieving raw content without any personalization and adaptation taking place and (b) users interacting with adapted and personalized content. In the second scenario, there is a significant increase of functions and modules ran, compared to the first one (raw content scenario), like user profile processing, dynamic content adaptation, learner control dynamic tools, navigational support etc. Based on the simulations made (see Fig. 10) we assume the following: (i) Deviation for raw content is 67ms and for personalized content 98ms. This difference is expected since the system uses more functional components in the case of personalized content like profile loading, dynamic content, etc. Thus, this consumes more network resources, due to the enhanced/extended content, causing the deviation of our average to be greater than that of the raw content test.

The deviation is not considered to be significantly greater and thus this metric result is proving the system to be stable and efficient; (ii) the throughput for the raw content scenario was 144Kb/sec while for the personalized content was 179Kb/sec. Based on the latter results, the system

is again considered efficient mainly due to the fact that the difference in throughput between the two scenarios is minimal. Taking in consideration that major component functionality is used in the case of personalized content this small difference underlines the efficiency of the system; (iii) the same arguments are true in the case of the average response times. The average response time for the raw content scenario was 150ms while for the personalized content was 177ms. This difference is again marginal that proves the efficiency of the system.

Assessing the impact of Human Factors in Web Services Development Process

As mentioned above, previous research (Germanakos et al., 2008b; Germanakos et al., 2008a; Tsianos et al., 2008b) related to the use of human factors in the design and development of eServices/ eCommerce (as well as eLearning) systems, it has been proven to have a positive effect to the end user customer (increase satisfaction, easier navigation, faster completion of tasks/goals). Therefore, an extended version would include the measurement of satisfaction of the content provider, in terms of efficiency and effectiveness of use for developing and designing their products for promotion using the particular framework.

Methodology and Design Implications

In order to evaluate such an approach a within participants experiment was conducted, seeking out to explore if the personalized condition based on the particular cognitive factors serves users better at finding information more accurately and fast.

The number of participants was 89; they all were students from the Universities of Cyprus and Athens and their age varied from 18 to 21, with a mean age of 19. They accessed the Web environments using personal computers located at the laboratories of both universities, divided in groups of approximately 12 participants. Each session lasted about 40 minutes; 20 minutes were required for the user-profiling process, while the remaining time was devoted to navigating in both environments, which were presented sequentially (as soon as they were done with the first environment, the second one was presented).

The content was about a series of Sony laptops: general description, technical specifications and additional information were available for each model. We considered that the original (raw) version of the environment was designed without any consideration towards cognitive style preferences, and the amount of information was so high and randomly allocated that could increase the possibility of cognitive overload. The personalized condition addressed these issues by introducing as personalization factors both cognitive style and working memory span. The psychometric materials that were used are the following: i) Cognitive Style: Riding's Cognitive Style Analysis, ii) Working Memory Span: Visuospatial working memory test (Demetriou et al., 1993; Cassady, 2004).

In each condition, users were asked to fulfill three tasks: they actually had to find the necessary information to answer three sequential multiple choice questions that were given to them while navigating. All six questions (three per condition) were about determining which laptop excelled with respect to the prerequisites that were set by each question. There was certainly only one correct answer that was possible to be found relatively easy, in the sense that users were not required to have hardware related knowledge or understanding.

As soon as users finished answering all questions in both conditions, they were presented with a comparative satisfaction questionnaire; users were asked to choose which environment was better (1-5 scale, where 1 means strong preference for environment A and 5 for environment B), regarding usability and user friendliness factors.

The dependent variables that were considered as indicators of differences between the two environments were:

a) Task accuracy (number of correct answers)
b) Task completion time
c) User satisfaction

The within participants design allowed the control of differences and confiding variables amongst users.

Regarding the design implications in this eServices/eCommerce setting, the content enhancements and transformation considerations discussed in previous sections regarding users' particular typologies were followed. More specifically, users with low working memory received a "myNotepad" tool that allowed them to make entries of goal-related information, while as it concerns cognitive style Table 2 shows the implications for each preference.

Table 2. Implications for cognitive style preferences in the eCommerce environment

Imager	Verbalizer	Analyst	Wholist
Presentation of information is visually enhanced as to resemble a diagrammatical form of representation	The usage of text is predominant, unaccompanied by any visual enhancements	The structure of the environment is chunked to clear cut links, as to match the analytical way of thinking	The structure of the environment is less segmented and follows a more holistic pattern. Users are shown where they are and what they have viewed, while a more sequential approach is encouraged

Intermediates in both axes received a condition that was balanced between the opposite preferences.

Results

The most robust and interesting finding was the fact that users in the personalized condition were more accurate in providing the correct answer for each task. The same user in the raw condition had a mean of 1 correct answer, while in the personalized condition the mean rose to 1.9.

Since the distribution was not normal and the paired samples t-test assumptions were not met, Wilcoxon Signed Ranks Test was performed, showing that this difference is statistically significant at zero level of confidence (Z= -4.755, p=0.000). This is probably a very encouraging finding, implying that personalization on the basis of these factors (cognitive style and working memory span) benefits users within an eServices/eCommerce environment, as long as there are some cognitive functions involved of course (such as information seeking).

Equally interesting is the fact that users in the personalized condition were significantly faster at task completion. The mean aggregated time of answering all three questions was 541 seconds in the raw condition, and 412 in the personalized. A paired samples t-test was performed (t(88)=4.668, p=0.000) demonstrating significance at zero level of confidence. Again, this second dependent variable (time) shows that the personalized environment is more efficient.

As it concerns the satisfaction questionnaire, 31 users leaned towards the personalized environment, 38 had no preference while 20 preferred the raw. This descriptive statistic is merely indicative

of whether participants would consciously observe any positive or negative effects of the personalized condition. A considerable percentage leaned towards that condition (or at least users did not seem somehow annoyed by such a restructuring), but overall it cannot be supported that they were fully aware of their increase in performance, as shown by the abovementioned findings.

In sum, the specific experiment shows in a rather clear way that users performed better within the personalized environment, and these findings are statistically very robust. It could be argued of course that there is no way to be fully aware if information processing was more efficient at a deeper level, or users simply found the personalized condition more of their (perhaps unconscious) liking, thus devoting more conscious cognitive effort.

Nevertheless, such an increase in performance, which is consistent to the findings of previously conducted experiments in the field of eLearning (Lekkas et al., 2008), provides support for the further development and application of the particular cognitive factors in different Web-based services environments and generic hypertext/hypermedia contents.

CONCLUSION AND FUTURE TRENDS

The explosive growth in the size and use of the World Wide Web as a communication medium has been enthusiastically adopted by the mass market to provide an electronic connection between progressive businesses and millions of customers bringing to light the eCommerce sector. eCommerce aims to deliver better quality of eServices increasing productivity with focused services to be provided by various channels, at a lower cost and time and in a personalized style.

Research implications and challenges of the Web Personalization and mass customization concepts could be considered as an enabler of eCommerce services sustainability. To succeed this, customers must not be spatially disoriented and be able to have continuous and adapted access on information and services requested.

In this regards, the basic objective of this chapter was to present a framework, namely smarTag, for the dynamic reconstruction of any Web content based on human factors for providing a comprehensive personalized result. According to these attributes the main content of a Web-page will be adjusted to the various typologies of users (mainly presentation, flow of content as well as quantity of content based on users' working memory). This approach is liable of enhancing efficiency and effectiveness of users' interaction with eServices in terms of information assimilation and accuracy of finding their cognitive targets (products or services).

Based on previous findings, it has been proven that user's cognitive factors have an important impact in the information space and on specific content meta-characteristics. Accordingly, the smarTag system provides an easy to use framework for enhancing any Web-site with smart objects that take into consideration human factors for the adaptation of the content. The initial results of the system's evaluation have shown that the proposed framework do not degrade the efficiency (in terms of speed and accuracy) in the Web content adaptation process and could be efficiently used for targeting the mass market by encapsulating customers' distinct characteristics. Such a method could be considered nowadays fundamental for the provision of adapted and personalized eServices,

via any medium, increasing this way one-to-one service delivery and integrity, enabling businesses to retain their customers and therefore to gain a substantial competitive advantage.

Future and emerging trends include: Further analysis and testing of the current cognitive factors framework with the use of the IBM experimental setting and the automatic content reconstruction approach; a more detailed analysis of the current model as well as the relationship between its different sub-dimensions; further investigation of constraints and challenges arise from the implementation of such issues on mobile devices and channels; study on the structure of the metadata coming from the providers' side, aiming to construct a Web-based personalization architecture that will be based on human factors and will serve as an dynamic personalization filter in different domains and contexts.

REFERENCES

Ayersman, D. J., & Reed, W. M. (1998). Relationships among hypermedia-based mental models and hypermedia knowledge. *Journal of Research on Computing in Education*, *30*(3), 222–238.

Baddeley, A. (1992). Working Memory. *Science*, *255*, 556–559. doi:10.1126/science.1736359

Blom, J. (2000). *Personalization – A Taxonomy*. New York: ACM.

Brown, D. (2004). *Wave goodbye to the era of one-size-fits all*.

Cassady, J. C. (2004). The influence of cognitive test anxiety across the learning–testing cycle. *Learning and Instruction*, *14*(6), 569–592. doi:10.1016/j.learninstruc.2004.09.002

Cassady, J. C., & Johnson, R. E. (2002). Cognitive Test Anxiety and Academic Performance. *Contemporary Educational Psychology*, *27*(2), 270–295. doi:10.1006/ceps.2001.1094

Cingil I., Dogac A., & Azgin A. (2000). A broader approach to personalization. *Communications of the ACM, 43*(8). cyLEDGE Media (2008). *Disentangling Web 2 and Mass Customization.*

De Bra, P., Aroyo, L., & Chepegin, V. (2004). The next big thing: Adaptive Web-based systems. *Journal of Digital Information, 5*(1), 247.

Demetriou, A., Efklides, A., & Platsidou, M. (1993). The architecture and dynamics of developing mind: Experiential structuralism as a frame for unifying cognitive development theories. *Monographs of the Society for Research in Child Development, 58* (Serial No. 234), 5-6.

Felder, R. M., & Silverman, L. K. (1988). Learning and Teaching Styles in Engineering Education. *English Education, 78*, 674–681.

Germanakos, P., Mourlas, C., Isaia, C., & Samaras, G. (2005). An Optimized Review of Adaptive Hypermedia and Web Personalization - Sharing the Same Objective. In *Proceedings of the 1st International Workshop on Web Personalization, Recommender Systems and Intelligent User Interfaces (WPRSIUI 2005) of the 2nd International Conference on E-business and TElecommunications Networks (ICETE2005)*, Reading, October 3-8, (pp. 43-48).

Germanakos, P., Tsianos, N., Lekkas, Z., Mourlas, C., Belk, M., & Samaras, G. (2007). A Semantic Approach of an Adaptive and Personalized Web-based Learning Content - The case of Adaptive Web. In *Proceedings of the 2nd International Workshop on Semantic Media Adaptation and Personalization (SMAP 2007)*, London, UK, December 17-18, (pp. 68-73). Washington, DC: IEEE Computer Society.

Germanakos, P., Tsianos, N., Lekkas, Z., Mourlas, C., Belk, M., & Samaras, G. (2008a). Towards an Adaptive and Personalized Web Interaction using Human Factors. In M. Angelides (Ed.) *Advances in Semantic Media Adaptation and Personalization*, (Vol.2). San Francisco: Taylor & Francis Group, LLC.

Germanakos, P., Tsianos, N., Lekkas, Z., Mourlas, C., & Samaras, G. (2008b). Realizing Comprehensive User Profiling as the Core Element of Adaptive and Personalized Communication Environments and Systems. *The Computer Journal, Special Issue on Profiling Expertise and Behaviour.* Retrieved from doi:10.1016/j.chb.2007.07.010

Graber, D. A. (2000). *Processing Politics.* Chicago: The University of Chicago Press.

Kalyanpur, A., Parsia, B., & Hendler, J. (2005a). A Tool for Working with Web Ontologies. In . *Proceedings of the International Journal on Semantic Web and Information Systems, 1*(1).

Kalyanpur, A., Parsia, B., Sirin, E., & Cuenca-Grau, B., James Hendler. (2005b). Swoop: A 'Web' Ontology Editing Browser. *Journal of Web Semantics, 4*(2).

Kim, W. (2002). Personalization: Definition, Status, and Challenges Ahead. *JOT, 1*(1).

Kolb, A.Y., & Kolb, D.A. (2005). The Kolb Learning Style Inventory. *Technical Specifications, Experience Based Learning Systems, Inc.,* Version 3.1.

Lekkas, Z., Tsianos, N., Germanakos, P., Mourlas, C., & Samaras, G. (2008). The Role of Emotions in the Design of Personalized Educational Systems. In *Proceedings of the 8th IEEE International Conference on Advanced Learning Technologies (ICALT 2008).*

Mason, M. S., & Hacker, L. K. (2003). Applying Communication Theory to Digital Divide Research. *IT & Society, 1*(5), 40–55.

McLoughlin, C. (1999). The implications of the research literature on learning styles for the design of instructional material. *Australian Journal of Educational Technology, 15*(3), 222–241.

Noy, N., Sintek, M., Decker, S., Crubézy, M., Fergerson, R., & Musen, M. (2001). *Creating Semantic Web Contents with Protégé-2000*. Paolo Alto, CA: Stanford University.

Pithers, R., T. (2002). Cognitive Learning Style: a review of the field dependent- field independent approach. *Journal of Vocational Education and Training, 54*(1), 117–118. doi:10.1080/13636820200200191

Reed, W., M., Ayersman, D., J. & Liu, M. (1996). The effects of students' computer-based prior experiences and instructional exposures on the application of hypermedia-related mental models. *Journal of Educational Computing Research, 14*(2), 175–187.

Riding, R. (2001). *Cognitive Style Analysis – Research Administration.* Birmingham, UK: Learning and Training Technology.

Santader (2008). Cantabria, Spain, July 1-5, 2008, (pp. 886-890). Washington, DC: IEEE Computer Society Press.

Spielberger, C. D. (1983). *Manual for the State-Trait Anxiety Inventory (STAI).* Palo Alto, CA: Consulting Psychologists Press.

Stonebraker M. (2007). *One size fits all: A concept whose time has come and gone.*

Stonebraker, M., & Çetintemel, U. (2008). *"One Size Fits All": An Idea Whose Time Has Come and Gone.*

Tsianos, N., Germanakos, P., Lekkas, Z., Mourlas, C., & Samaras, G. (2008b). Incorporating Human Factors in the Development of Context-Aware Personalized Applications: The Next Generation of Intelligent User Interfaces. In D. Stojanovic (Ed.), *Context-Aware Mobile and Ubiquitous Computing for Enhanced Usability: Adaptive Technologies and Applications.* Hershey, PA: IGI Global.

Tsianos, N., Lekkas, Z., Germanakos, P., Mourlas, C., & Samaras, G. (2008a). User-centered Profiling on the basis of Cognitive and Emotional Characteristics: An Empirical Study. In *Proceedings of the 5th International Conference on Adaptive Hypermedia and Adaptive Web-based Systems (AH 2008),* Hannover, Germany, July 28 - August 1, (LNCS Vol. 5149, pp. 214-223). Berlin: Springer-Verlag.

Wang, J., & Lin, J. (2002). Are personalization systems really personal? – Effects of conformity in reducing information overload. In *Proceedings of the 36th Hawaii International Conference on Systems Sciences (HICSS'03).* Washington, DC: IEEE.

Witkin, H., Moore, C., Gooddenough, D., & Cox, P. (1977). Field- dependent and field- independent cognitive styles and their educational implications. *Review of Educational Research, 47,* 1–64.

Yuliang, L., & Dean, G. (1999). Cognitive Styles and Distance Education. *Online Journal of Distance Learning Administration, 2*(3).

Chapter 8
Adaptive Interaction for Mass Customisation

Gulden Uchyigit
University of Brighton, UK

ABSTRACT

The popularisation of mass customization and the need for integration of the user needs into the design, production and marketing phases has called for more innovative methods to be introduced into this area. At present the continuous growth of the world wide web and its rapid integration into people's everyday lives and the popularisation of new technologies such as ubiquitous computing making possible the computing everywhere paradigm, offers a more desirable alternative for vendors in reaching their customers using more innovative techniques in an attempt to provide each customer with a one-to-one design, manufacturing and marketing service. The integration of ubiquitous computing technologies with machine learning and data mining techniques, which has been popular in personalization techniques, will serve to bring about innovative changes in this area. In future years this may revolutionise the way in which vendors can reach their customers offering every customer a tailored one-to-one service from design, to manufacturing, to delivery. This chapter will present the state of the art techniques to enable the combination of machine learning, data mining and ubiquitous computing technologies which will serve to provide innovative techniques applications and user interfaces for mass customization systems. This is currently a field of intense research and development activity and some technologies are already on the path to practical application. This chapter will present a state of the art survey of these technologies and their applications.

INTRODUCTION

The notion of integrating user needs into the production and design process has had great im-

DOI: 10.4018/978-1-60566-260-2.ch008

portance in mass customization. This idea is a promising strategy for companies being forced to react to the growing individualization of demand (Franke & Piller, 2002). In mass customization concepts, goods and services are made to meet individual customer's needs produced with near mass production efficiency (Tseng & Jia, 2001). Mass customization embarks a new paradigm for manufacturing industries (Pine, 1993). It recognises each customer as an individual and provides each of them with tailor made features that can only be offered in the pre-industrial craft systems (Jiao & Tseng, 1999).

Mass customization (Shafer, Konstan & Riedl, 1999) was first popularised by Pine in 1993 (Pine 1993). In his book Pine argues that companies need to shift from the old world of mass production where "standardized products, homogeneous markets, and long product life and development cycles were the rife, to the *new* world where the variety and customization supplant standardized products." Pine argues that building one product is simply not adequate any more. Companies need to be able to at a minimum, develop multiple products that meet the multiple needs of multiple customers.

With the ever increasing popularity of the World Wide Web in recent years Rheingold (Rheingold, 2002) states that Web software holds the promise of mass customization and further states that a software's ability to fulfil an individual's needs necessitates the application to be aware of several factors such as, the user's profile, his/her current task or goal, and additional factors such as location, time or device used. The combination of all relevant factors can be termed *context* and thus a web application which takes them into account is a context-aware application (Kaltz, Wolfgang, Ziegler & Lohmann, 2005).

In this paper we present an overview of how the different techniques in personalization, data mining and ubiquitous computing in particular context-sensitive systems can be integrated with mass customization of services and products to bring innovation in this field of research.

BACKGROUND

Web Personalisation and E-Commerce

The World Wide Web has created a challenging arena for e-commerce: with on-line shops, products and services offered to on-line customers. In this context, two specific strategic goals must be addressed (Meirer & Werro, 2007). First, to attract new on-line customers, or lost customers that have to be re-acquired, these customers have attractive market and resource potential. The second strategic goal is to maintain and improve customer equity, this can be achieved by cross-selling and up-selling, and through programs aimed at lifetime customer retention (Blattberg, Getz, & Thomas, 2001). Managing on-line customers as an asset requires measuring them and treating them according to their true value. With the sharp customer classes of conventional marketing methods this is not possible.

In recent years web personalization technologies have revolutionised e-commerce, enabling the one-to-one marketing practice. Personalisation technologies are an important tool to the service provider/vendor and to the end user the customer. Web personalization tools are able to assist in the complex process of information/product discovery. There are numerous benefits to the vendors these include attracting new visitors, turning visitors into buyers increasing revenues, increasing advertising efficiency, and improving customer retention rate and brand loyalty (Kobsa, 2001). Nielsen (Kobsa, 2001) reports that e-commerce sites offering personalised services convert significantly more visitors into buyers than e-commerce sites that do not offer personalised services. An important aspect of a web site is its ability to guide the user through its complex structure and in effect assist the user while interacting with the web site. The benefits to the user are improved usability and faster information/product discovery time, the benefits to the vendor are better understanding of user needs, so it can design its web site to better fit its customers' needs, it is also able to provide the user with what they are looking for, so in particular with e-commerce web sites this is of particular importance because they can increase their sales and gain a competitive edge if they are able to sell to every customer that interacts with their site. Web personalization plays an important role here because it is able to equip the web site with the tools in order to help a site better understand its customer and help the user whilst navigating the site. In other words web personalization aims at customizing a web site to the user's preferences and to guide the customer to the products or services of interest. Personalization is increasingly used for customer relationship management (Kobsa, Koenemann, & Pohl, 2001) The single most important way to provide value to a customer is to know them and serve them as individuals. The terms micro marketing and one-to-one marketing are being used to describe this business model (Peppers & Rogers, 1993; Peppers & Rogers, 1997).

Web Personalisation techniques generally follow a similar method of operation, a data representation technique is used to represent the domain data and the user's preferences, a technique for matching the domain data with the user's preferences to make personalised suggestions to the user. Mobasher (Mobasher, 2005) classifies web personalization into 3 groups. Manual decision rule systems, content-based filtering agents and collaborative filtering systems. Manual decision rule systems allow the web site administrator to specify rules based on user demographics or static profiles (collected through a registration process).

User Modelling

User modelling is an important component in computer systems which are able to adapt to the user's preferences, knowledge, capabilities and to the environmental factors. According to Ko-

bsa (Kobsa, 2001) systems that take individual characteristics of the users into account and adapt their behaviour accordingly have been empirically shown to benefit users in many domains. Examples of adaptation include customized content (e.g. personalized finance pages or news collections), customized recommendations or advertisements based on past purchase behaviour, customized (preferred) pricing, tailored email alerts, express transactions (Kobsa, 2001).

According to Kay (Kay 2000), there are three main ways a user model can assist in *adaptation*. The first is the interaction between the user and the interface. This may be any action accomplished through the devices available including an active badge worn by the user, the user's speech via audio input to the system etc. The user model can be used to assist as the user interacts with the interface. For instance, if the user input is ambiguous the user model can be used to disambiguate the input. The second area where the user model can assist the adaptation process is during the information presentation phase. For instance, in some cases due to the disabilities of the user the information needs to be displayed differently to different users. More sophisticated systems may also be used to adapt the presented content. A considerable amount of work has been done in this area, this area is also known as adaptive hypermedia. Finally, the user model can drive internal actions of the system. This is the goal of the system that filter information on behalf of the user.

Kay (Kay 2000), describes the first of the user modelling stages as the *elicitation* of the user model. This can be a very straight forward process for acquiring information about the user, by simply asking the user to fill in a multiple choice form of their preferences, interest and knowledge, or it can be a more sophisticated process where elicitation tools such concept mapping interface (Kay, 1999) can be used. Elicitation of the user model becomes a valuable process under circumstances where the adaptive interface is to be used by a diverse population.

As well as direct elicitation of the user model, the user model can also be constructed by observing the user interacting with the system and automatically inferring the user's model from his/her actions. The advantage of having the system automatically infer the user's model is that the user is not involved in the tedious task of defining their user model. In some circumstances the user is unable to correctly define their user model especially if the user is unfamiliar with the domain.

Stereotypes is another method for constructing the user model. Groups of users or individuals are divided into stereotypes and generic stereotype user models are used to initialise their user model. The user models are then updated and refined as more information is gathered about the user's preferences, interest, knowledge and capabilities. A comprehensive overview of generic user modelling systems can be found in (Kobsa, 2001)

Recommender Systems

The movement towards E-commerce has allowed companies to provide customers with more options (Shafer, Konstan & Riedl, 1999). However, in expanding to this new level of customization, businesses increase the amount of information that customers must process they are able to select which items meet their needs, one solution to this information overload problem is the employment of recommender systems (Shafer, Konstan & Riedl, 1999). Over the past decade recommender systems have become very successful in assisting with the information overload problem. They have been very popular in applications including e-commerce, entertainment and news. Recommender systems fall into three main categories collaborative, content-based and hybrid systems. Their distinction relies on the nature in which the recommended items are derived. These distinctions are formalised by the methods in which the items are perceived by a community of users, how the content of each item compares with the user's profile or a combination of both methods.

Collaborative based systems take as input user ratings from a community of users and make recommendations to an active user based on how he/she rated similar items with the community of users, content-based systems utilize the user's individual profiles to make recommendations and finally hybrid systems combine both the content and collaborative based techniques.

Content based systems automatically infer the user's profile from the contents of the item the user has previously seen and rated. These profiles are then used as input to a classification algorithm along with the new unseen items from the domain. Those documents which are similar in content to the user's profile are assumed to be interesting and recommended to the user.

A popular and extensively used document and profile representation method employed by many information filtering methods, including the content based method is the so called *vector space representation* (Chen & Sycara, 1998; Mladenic, 1996; Lang, 1995; Moukas, 1996; Liberman, 1995; Kamba & Koseki, 1997; Armstrong et al., 1995). Content based systems have their roots in text filtering, many of the techniques. The content-based recommendation method was developed based on the text filtering model described by (Oard 1997). In (Oard, 1997), a generic information filtering model is described as having four components: a method for representing the documents within the domain; a method for representing the user's information need; a method for making the comparison; and a method for utilising the results of the comparison process. The vector space method (Baeza-Yates & Ribeiro-Neto, 1999) consider that each document (profile) is described as a set of keywords. The text document is viewed as a vector in n dimensional space, n being the number of different words in the document set. Such a representation is often referred to as *bag-of-words*, because of the loss of word ordering and text structure (see Figure 2). The tuple of weights associated with each word, reflecting the significance of that word for a given document, give the document's position in the vector space. The weights are related to the number of occurrences of each word within the document. The word weights in the vector space method are ultimately used to compute the *degree of similarity* between two feature vectors. This method can be used to decide whether a document represented as a weighted feature vector, and a profile are similar. If they are similar then an assumption is made that the document is relevant to the user. The vector space model evaluates the similarity of the document d_j with regard to a profile p as the correlation between the vectors d_j and p. This correlation can be quantified by the cosine of the angle between these two vectors. That is,

$$sim(d_j, p) = \frac{d_j \bullet p}{|d_j| \times |p|} = \frac{\sum_{i=1}^{t} w_{i,j} \times w_{i,p}}{\sqrt{\sum_{i=1}^{t} w_{i,p}^2 \times \sum_{i=1}^{t} w_{i,j}^2}}$$

Content-based systems suffer from shortcomings in the way they select items for recommendations. Items are recommended if the user has seen and liked similar items in the past.

Collaborative-based systems (Terveen et al., 1997; Breese et al., 1998; Knostan et al., 1997; Balabanovic & Shoham, 1997) were proposed as an alternative to the content-based methods. The basic idea is to move beyond the experience of an individual user profile and instead draw on the experiences of a population or community of users. Collaborative-based systems (Herlocker et al., 1999; Knostan et al., 1997; Terveen et al., 1997; Kautz et al., 1997; Resnick & Varian, 1997) are built on the assumption that a good way to find interesting content is to find other people who have similar tastes, and recommend the items that those users like. Typically, each target user is associated with a set of nearest neighbour users by comparing the profile information provided by the target user to the profiles of other users. These users then act as recommendation partners for the target user, and items that occur in their profiles

can be recommended to the target user. In this way, items are recommended on the basis of user similarity rather than item similarity. Collaborative recommender systems have several shortcomings one of which is that the users will only be recommended new items only if their ratings agree with other people within the community. Also, if a new item has not been rated by anyone in the community if will not get recommended.

To overcome, the problems posed by pure content and collaborative based recommender systems, hybrid recommender systems have been proposed. Hybrid systems combine two or more recommendation techniques to overcome the shortcomings of each individual technique (Balabanovic, 1998; Balabanovic & Shoham, 1997; Burke, 2002; Claypool et al., 1999). These systems generally, use the content-based component to overcome the new item start up problem, if a new item is present then it can still be recommended regardless if it was seen and rated. The collaboration component overcomes the problem of over specialization as is the case with pure content based systems.

Adaptive Hypermedia Systems

Adaptive Hypermedia Systems (AHS) have been popularised since the early 90's. Since that time they have been extensively employed on a varied range of applications including e-commerce, and educational systems. According to Brusilovsky's (Brusilovsky, 1996) definition of adaptive hypermedia systems three criteria needs to be satisfied: the system should be based on hypertext or hypermedia technologies; a user model should be applied; the system should be able to adapt the hypermedia by using the user model. Brusilovsky (Brusilovsky, 2001) presents a comprehensive review of existing adaptive hypermedia systems.

Brusilovsky (Brusilovsky, 2001) distinguishes between two different types of AHS depending on their adaptation methods. These adaptation techniques are based on content-level and link-level.

The groups of systems which use these types of techniques are known as *adaptive presentation* systems and *adaptive navigation support* systems respectively. Techniques which provide adaptation based on the content can be adapted to various details, difficulty, and media usage to satisfy users with different needs, background knowledge, interaction style and cognitive characteristics. Techniques which provide adaptation based on links provide direct guidance, adaptive hiding or re-ordering of links, link annotation, map adaptation, link disabling and link removal (Kinshuk & Lin, 2003). The introduction of hypermedia and the Web has had a great impact on adaptive web systems but there are some limitations of AHS. De Bra (De Bra, 2000) states, that if prerequisite relationships are omitted or are just wrong, the user may be directed to pages that cannot be understood because the lack of necessary prior knowledge in the domain. Other issues include users interacting with a different interface due to the adaptation of the user model which may lead to confusion.

Data Mining for Mass Customisation

The importance of data mining approaches for mass customization has been recognised in recent years. Data mining techniques can be used for predicting the customers purchasing behaviour, preferences and needs. These patterns can be useful in analysing the varying customers which may fall into different purchasing groups, this information can be utilised in the designing and manufacturing products for specific group of customers. Utilising data mining algorithms in this manner makes it possible for vendors to practice more individualised marketing. In this section we present the data mining approaches which may be used to determine customer needs for one-to-one marketing.

Fuzzy Systems

A number of fuzzy classification (Meirer & Werro, 2007) approaches have been proposed in the marketing literature. Hruschka (Hruschka, 1986) proposed a segmentation of customers using fuzzy clustering methods.

Fuzzy systems deal with representation of classes whose boundaries are not well defined. The key idea is to associate a membership function with the elements of a class. The function takes values in the interval [0, 1] with 0 corresponding to no membership and 1 corresponding to full membership. Membership values between 0 and 1 indicate marginal elements in the class.

Fuzzy systems have been very popular in the analysis of consumer habits in the marketing literature. Hsu's Fuzzy Grouping Positioning Model (Hsu, 2000) allows an understanding of the relationship between consumer consumption patterns, and the company's competitive situation and strategic positioning. The modelling of fuzzy data in qualitative marketing research was also described by Varki (Varki et al 2000). Finally, a fuzzy Classification Query Language (fCQL) for customer relationship management was proposed by Meier et al. (Meier et al. 2005). Most of the cited research literature applies fuzzy control to classical marketing issues. Up to now, fuzziness has not yet been adapted for e-business, e-commerce, and/or e-government. In (Meirer & Werro, 2007) the power of a fuzzy classification model is used for an electronic shop. On-line customers will no longer be assigned to classical customer segments but to fuzzy classes. This leads to differentiated on-line marketing concepts and helps to improve the customer equity of on-line shop users. A prototype system has been implemented on the Internet that demonstrates the proposed fuzzy mass customization concept. Through examples of wine glass and furniture design, it can be seen that the proposed system is effective for products of simple shape or when only a few critical parameters of a complex product are frequently customized. In (Chen et al, 2001) a new design approach, namely fuzzy mass customization, which allows most household consumers, who are not familiar with both mechanical design and sophisticated CAD software, to customize some parameters of a product using preferred linguistic information such as small, normal, big, very big, and so on. A family of products is represented using a set of parameters that is divided into two types: user-defined parameters and deduced parameters. All parameters are defined as fuzzy variables. The user-defined parameters are input by a user. The deduced parameters are determined by the user-defined parameters using fuzzy reasoning. A prototype system (Chen et al, 2001) is implemented on a web client/server architecture, namely CyberFGC, which consists of a fuzzy geometric customization (FGC) program, Virtual Reality Modelling Language (VRML), and common gateway interface (CGI) programs. In this system, household consumers can customize products using their preferred linguistic description such as big, small, normal, etc., over the World Wide Web. Here a fuzzy model is proposed for the classification of on-line customers. With fuzzy classification, an on-line customer can be treated as a member of a number of different classes at the same time. Based on these membership functions, the on-line shop owner can devise appropriate marketing programs for acquisition, retention, and add-on selling.

Clustering Algorithms

Clustering algorithms are important for determining patterns within consumer purchasing habits. They can be used to cluster consumers into groups based on their purchasing behaviour. In e-commerce clustering techniques are used to analyse shopping basket history, click stream data etc. They function by clustering the instances together based on their similarity. The clustering algorithms can be divided into *hierarchical* and *non hierarchical* methods. Hierarchical methods

construct a tree where each node represents a subset of the input items, where the root of the tree represents all the items in the item set. Hierarchical methods can be divided into the *divisive* and *agglomerative* methods. Divisive methods begin with the entire set of items and partition the set until only an individual item remains. Agglomerative methods work in the opposite way, beginning with individual items, each item is represented as a cluster and merging these clusters until a single cluster remains. At the first step of *hierarchical agglomerative clustering* (HAC) algorithm, when each instance represents its own cluster, the similarities between each cluster are simply defined by the chosen similarity method rule to determine the similarity of these new clusters to each other. There are various rules which can be applied depending on the data; some of the measures are described below:

Single-Link: In this method the similarity of two clusters is determined by the similarity of the two closest (most similar) instances in the different clusters. So for each pair of clusters S_i and S_j,

$$sim(S_i, S_j) = \max\left\{\cos(d_i, d_j) \middle| d_i \in S_i, d_j \in S_j\right\}$$

Complete-Link: In this method the similarity of two clusters is determined by the similarity of the two least similar instances of both clusters. This approach can be performed well in cases where the data forms the natural distinct categories, since it tends to produce tight (cohesive) spherical clusters. This is calculated as:

$$sim(S_i, S_j) = \min\left\{\cos(d_i, d_j)\right\}$$

Average-Link or *Group Average*: In this method, the similarity between two clusters is calculated as the average distance between all pairs of objects in both clusters, i.e. it's an intermediate solution between complete link and single-link. This is unweighted, or weighted by the size of the clusters. The weighted form is calculated as:

$$sim(S_i, S_j) = \frac{1}{n_i n_j} \sum \cos(d_i, d_j)$$

where n_i and n_j refer to the size of S_i and S_j respectively.

Rule Learning Algorithms

These are algorithms that learn *association* rules or other attribute based rules. The algorithms are generally based on a *greedy search* of the attribute-value tests that can be added to the rule preserving its consistency with the training instances. Apriori algorithm is a simple algorithm which learns association rules between objects. Apriori is designed to operate on databases containing transactions (for example, the collections of items bought by customers). As is common in association rule mining, given a set of item sets (for instance, sets of retail transactions each listing individual items purchased), the algorithm attempts to find subsets which are common to at least a minimum number S_c (the cut-off, or confidence threshold) of the item sets. Apriori uses a bottom up approach, where frequent subsets are extended one item at a time (a step known as candidate generation, and groups of candidates are tested against the data. The algorithm terminates when no further successful extensions are found.

Ubiquitous (Pervasive) Computing: Context-Aware Systems

The notion of a ubiquitous network society where computing devices provide users with assistance in all areas of their everyday lives will continue to be a common theme amongst the popular technologies in future trends and will find their way to assist the user's in their everyday tasks (Baldauf & Dustdar, 2004).

The term pervasive computing was first introduced in 1991 by Weiser (Weiser, 1991). Pervasive computing is the integration of technological de-

vices into the user's everyday environment, such that the user is not aware of their existence and the user is able to function in the environment without any interference into the user's everyday situation. An area of pervasive computing which has been popularised over the recent years is the so called context-aware systems. Context-sensitive systems are able to adapt to the environment without user intervention thus aiming to improve usability and effectiveness by taking environment factors into account (Baldauf & Dustdar, 2004)

There have been several different attempts at the definition and use of context aware systems. Shildt and Theimer (Shildt & Theimer, 1994) define context as location, identities of people in the vicinity, and objects within the environment. Ryan et al (Ryan et al. 1997) referred to context as the user's location, environment, identity and time. (Dey, 1998) defines context as the user's emotional state, focus of attention, location, orientation, date and time. Hull et al (Hull et al 1997) describe context as the aspects of the current situation. Brown (Brown, 1996) defines context to be the current elements of the user's environment. But the one definition which has been used repeatedly is that of (Dey and Abowed, 2000b) "They define context as any information that can be used to characterise the situation of entities (i.e whether a person, place or object) that are considered relevant to the interaction between the user and the application including the user and the application themselves."

The context information is retrieved in a variety of ways including embedding sensors into the environment, using network information, device status and using user profiles. The history of context aware systems started when Want (Want et al 1992) introduced the active badge location system in 1991. The active badge signal emitters were embedded in communal areas such as main corridors, staff rooms in office buildings. The badges, which emit infrared signals, were worn by members of staff. The active badge location system was used to emulate a telephone receptionist. People were located depending on where they were in the building and their calls were routed to the nearest phone. Although an interesting idea this concept was not considered to be favourable amongst the staff members, since some of their meetings had different priority levels and preferred not to be disturbed. Some years later the importance of such location aware devices became popular with popularity of small hand held devices such as PDA's. A similar technology is the one introduced in (Harter et al 1999), here an infrastructure to determine the movement of people in buildings is presented. Bats and sensor stations emit and transmit signals to detect the location of people. A fine grained sensor system which provides up to date location information offers a finer granularity than the Active badge system and also enables more context information to the application. Also, a spatial monitoring service which enables event based location-aware application.

Personalised Context Aware Systems and Applications

One of the future deployments of context-aware systems and application is to successfully integrate context information with the user model in order to have personalised context aware systems. Such systems will present more usable information systems. For instance the system can present to the user favourite theatre shows depending on their location.

User modelling has an important role in ubiquitous computing. It is essential for the personalization of user environments and it will be the repository of information that might be collected about a user from ubiquitous sensors. As ubiquitous computing is quickly becoming increasingly important, it is timely to explore the nature of the user model representations for ubiquitous personalisation (Kay et al 2003). Kay et al (Kay et al 2003) present a distributed architecture for ubiquitous computing applications for distributed

personalisation. Each application which the device interacts with has its own partial model of the user's model (see Figure 1)

There is a great demand to combine context-aware computing with personalization services. Combination of these two areas can improve interaction and usability of the system. Dey and Abowed (Dey & Abowed, 2000b) distinguish between systems which use context and systems which adapt to context. This distinction is important if they are to be fully integrated into applications. In Zakarias (Zakarias et al. 2001) adaptation of context refers to: awareness of the environment where the user interacts (location, time, whether condition, noise, companions, description of the surrounding area); awareness of the system to a particular device in use and proper response/ communication; awareness and reconciliation of bandwidths of the station of wireless communication (Chervest, 1998) of switching between network providers.

Personalization and integration of user models into context-aware systems is a relatively new area. These two approaches are very close to each other since they both aim to provide the user with assistance and to improve the ease of usability. The integration of the two research areas is still relatively new with very little research being done. Byun and Ceverst (Byun & Ceverst, 2001) highlight the notion of integrating context aware systems and user modelling and present a system which is able to act as a context aware personal activity planner which is able to assist the user as they are walking. eg return library book if due date etc. Byun and Ceverst (Byun & Ceverst, 2001) present a comparison of context models and user modelling. Further they state that user models should be integrated into the application since the context module in some context aware systems shield the details of context acquisition from the user and is built into the application. Further generic user models can be used to be integrated into the applications. They state that the representation of the user model can be both

Figure 1. The Architecture for distributed personalization U, single user model for each person, A are the different applications, I, are the local inference sources, s represent the sensor data coming in and u, are the partial user models owned by the different applications (Kay 2000b).

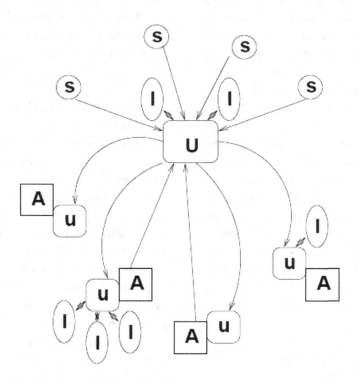

a data model or a behaviour model or a combination of both. The contextual information is used as soon as it is captured where as with the user model there is some initialisation period before the user model is ready to be used.

Zakarias (Zakarias et al. 2001) present the PALIO (Personalised access to local information services for tourists) framework which combines contextual information with a user model to provide a personalised service. This framework provides a location aware information system delivering fully adaptive information to a wide range of devices, including mobile devices. It presents a provision of services integrated in open source personalised information from local databases. PALIO framework is adaptable to user preferences in different contexts. Pignotti and Edwards (Pignotti & Edwards, 2004) present a

recommender system (RECO) which takes into consideration context with the recommendation system. A recommendation is given depending on the user's location. If the user is at a cinema watching their favourite film then the nearest restaurant of their best food preference is given as the recommendation of the restaurant. Moon et al [Moon et al, 2007] present the CAMUS system which has a middleware context-aware infrastructure. In this system sensors are embedded into the house environment. The system is also integrated with a recommendation engine, which uses feature vectors for modelling the user's interests. The system is operational in the TV domain. The sensors around the house are able to track the rooms which the user is in and turn on the TV and present the user with programs which they would be interested in watching. The system is also integrated with voice recognition software for controlling the system. The system also uses software agent technology.

Context-Aware Architectures

It is desirable for mobile devices to react effectively to the environment which it is present in. This involves taking into consideration the devices time, location etc. The challenging aspects of these technologies are rapid change and adaptation of the device when the person is on the move and the space limitation of the hand held device (Baldauf & Dustdar, 2004).

One of the important issues with context aware systems is the architecture of the system. Generally, the design of the architecture depends on the availability of sensors and the availability and acquisition of the context-aware data. Chen et al present three different ways in which context aware data can be collected:

Context-aware systems can be implemented in many ways. The approach depends on special requirements and conditions such as the location of sensors (local or remote), the amount of possible users (one user or many), the available resources of the used devices (high-end-PCs or small mobile devices) or the facility of a further extension of the system. Furthermore, the method of context-data acquisition is very important when designing context-aware systems because it predefines the architectural style of the system at least to some extent. Chen (2004) presents three different approaches on how to acquire contextual information: *Direct sensor access* - Sensors are built into the device. These systems do not have an additional component for collecting the sensor data. The application program directly collects the sensor data from the sensors. In (Baldauf & Dustdar, 2004) the authors comment that it is not suited for distributed systems due to its direct access nature which lacks a component capable of managing multiple concurrent sensor accesses.

Middleware infrastructure - This approach introduces a layered architecture to context-aware systems and hides the low-level sensing details. *Context server* - The next logical step is to permit multiple clients access to remote data sources. This distributed approach extends the middleware based architecture by introducing an access managing remote component. Gathering sensor data is moved to this so-called context server to facilitate concurrent multiple access. Besides the reuse of sensors, the usage of a context server has the advantage of relieving clients of resource intensive operations. As probably the majority of end devices used in context-aware systems are mobile gadgets with limitations in computation power, disk space etc., this is an important aspect. In return one has to consider about appropriate protocols, network performance, quality of service parameters etc., when designing a context-aware system based on client-server architecture.

Sensors can be classified in three groups (Indulska & Sutton, 2003): *Physical sensors* - The most frequently used type of sensors are physical sensors. Many hardware sensors are available nowadays which are capable of capturing almost any physical data. Table 1 shows some examples of physical sensors (Schmidt a&van Laerhoven, 2001). *Virtual sensors* - Virtual sensors source context data from software applications or services. For example, it is possible to determine an employee's location not only by using tracking systems (physical sensors) but also by a virtual sensor, e.g., by browsing an electronic calendar, a travel-booking system, emails etc., for location information. Other context attributes that can be sensed by virtual sensors include, e.g., the user's activity by checking for mouse-movement and keyboard input. *Logical sensors*- These sensors make use of a couple of information sources, and combine physical and virtual sensors with additional information from databases or various other sources in order to solve higher tasks. For example, a logical sensor can be constructed to detect an employee's current position by analysing logins at desktop PCs and a database mapping of devices to location information.

Context-Aware Applications

Popular context-aware systems include the stick-e-notes and post-it applications. Stick-e-notes enable the user to leave virtual notes around buildings, on objects etc. The stick-e-notes can then be accessed by other people in the environment. Some examples of stick-e-notes are GeoNotes, Active-Campus, CoolTown, InfoRadar, Place-Its, Mobile Bristol, or Semapedia. The post-it metaphor was first proposed by stick-e-notes project, which defined the infrastructure enabling the edition, discovery and navigation of virtual context-aware post-it notes. Everything (a location, am object or even a person) can be augmented with an XML document (stick-e-notes) which can later be discovered and matched, taking into consideration the contextual attributes associated to a tag. A key aspect on a mobile mass annotation systems as these is to address the tradeoff between creating an open and social information space while still enabling to navigate and find relevant information and services in the that space. The more contextual information used in the content matching process the better filtering results are obtained.

The Sentient Graffiti infrastructure presented in (López de Ipiña et al. 2007) also builds on the post-it metaphor but also combines in the Web 2.0 technology. Users tag their graffiti notes which they place in locations in order to make the graffiti notes searchable. To do this they include keywords with the graffities so other users can also search and locate certain locations which have attached graffites. The graffiti notes are tagged using XML. The graffiti notes can also bookmarked for easy access. The system also includes garbage collection where old graffiti notes are removed or archived. It associates graffities to objects tagged by a diverse range of technologies, TRIPP rincodes (enabling interaction by pointing) or RFID tag (enabling interaction by touching, perceiving location (GPS) and to Bluetooth coverage areas (proximity attributes) .

Dey and Abowd (Dey & Abowd, 2000) present *context-based reminders* application. Users define reminders and place a situation criteria where the reminder is triggered when the criteria conditions are met. The reminder is then delivered to the recipient at the time and location and the device which the user is using. This system works on the ContextToolkit infrastructure. There is not enough research in this area. Other systems which use time aware reminders is Lifestreams, this is a system which organising documents that is intended to replace conventional files and directory structures. Lifsetreams organises files temporally based on when they were created modified or received. The beginning of the stream contains the file which was created first and the end of the stream contains the file which was created last. ComMotion project uses both location and time information to deliver relevant messages. When a reminder is created a location is associated with it. Then when the intended recipient arrives at that location the intended reminder is delivered. Poem is a wearable computer-based system that supports profile-based cooperation. Wearers can writes simple rules that indicate their interest in other people. When another wearer has a profile similar to the wearer that person is alerted. MemoryGlasses is a wearable context aware reminder system. It uses time and location as a reminder. It focuses on user body-worn sensors (a camera and microphone) to determine what activity the wearer is engaged in, including walking downstairs or taking part in a conversation.

Other context-aware applications include collaborative context aware systems [Salkham et al 2006]. In (Salkham et al 2006) collaborative context aware systems are defined as "a system that comprises a group of entities, capable of sensing, inferring, and actuating to communicate in order to achieve a common goal". Collaboration among context-aware entities may not only be based on communicating contextual information but also sensed and fused data in addition to next actions to perform. (Salkham et al 2006) present a comprehensive overview of collaborative context-aware systems.

The WWW infrastructure and information retrieval techniques were the motivation for the development of the context-aware architecture presented in (Liu & Connnelly, 2006). The challenges that need to be addressed are: *scalability* - the infrastructure should support a large volume of context sources, where both the context source and the people are supported in a distributed environment; *fault tolerance*- the infrastructure should be tolerant to faults in the network; *heterogeneity*- the infrastructure must be able to handle heterogeneous context sources provided by different organizations and individual users. Quality and even availability of individual context sources cannot be guaranteed; *dynamicity*- context service may join and leave the system at any time. When a known context service is gone, user agents need to find alternative services, so as to accomplish their tasks. Automated discover. Context aware applications should be able to discover and process context sources without human intervention.

Oh et al (Oh et al 2007) present a context integrator architecture. Context fusion and reasoning is the central functionality provided by this system. In this work the so called 5W1H architecture is presented to express the contextual information in components with regard to Who, What, Where, When and Why. A user centric view of context is used which is required for the anticipated system. The architecture is as follows. The context object analyser collects the contexts periodically from various kinds of sensors which are placed in the same active area. The context repository stores and manages the history of the integrated contexts.

CONCLUSION AND FUTURE WORK

In this chapter we presented the techniques for adaptation which can be used to provide a means for providing innovative architectures and applications for mass customization. We presented a survey of adaptation techniques which have been successfully deployed in web based applications such as e-commerce. A way forward in this area of research is the integration of the user modelling and personalization techniques which have successfully been deployed in web-based systems with ubiquitous computing systems, in particular context-sensitive techniques. Successful integration of these techniques can bring about novel and innovative architectures to be deployed in mass customization.

REFERENCES

Bachem, B. (1999). *Personalisation in E-Commerce, Online Marketing.*

Baeza-Yates, R., & Ribeiro-Neto, B. (1999). *Modern Information Retrieval.* Reading, MA: Addison Wesley.

Balabanovic, M. (1998). *Learning to Surf: Multiagent Systems for Adaptive Web Page Recommendation.* PhD thesis, Department of Computer Science, Stanford University, Paolo Alto, CA.

Balabanovic, M., & Shoham, Y. (1997). Fab: Content-based, collaborative recommendation. *Communications of the ACM, 40*(3), 6672. doi:10.1145/245108.245124

Baldauf, M., & Dustdar, S. (2004). A survey on context-aware systems. *International Journal of Ad Hoc and Ubiquitous Computing.*

Blattberg, R., Getz, G., & Thomas, S. (2001). *Customer Equity n Building and Managing Relationships as Valuable Assets.* Boston: Harvard Business School Press.

Brown, J. (1996). The Stick-e Document a framework for developing context-aware applications. In *Proceedings of the Electronic Publishing*.

Bursilovsky, P., & Maybury, M. (2002). From Adaptive Hypermedia to the adaptive Web. *Communications of the ACM, 45*(5), 30–33.

Byun, H., & Cheverst, K. (2001). Exploiting User Models and Context-Awareness to Support Personal Daily Activities. In *Proc. of International Workshop on User Modelling for Context-Aware Applications*, Sonthofen, Germany.

Chen, L., & Sycara, K. (1998). Webmate: A personal agent for browsing and searching. In *2nd International Conference on Autonomous Agents*, Minneapolis, MN.

Chen, Y., & Wang, Y., & Wong, M. (2001). A Web-based fuzzy mass customization system. *Journal of Manufacturing Systems*.

Dey, A. (1998). Context-Aware Computing: The CyberDesk Project. In *Proceeding of AAAI Spring Symposium*.

Dey, A. K., & Abowd, G., D. (2000). CyberMinder: A Context-aware System for Supporting Reminders. In *Proceeding of CHI*.

Dey, A., & Abowed, G. (2000). Towards a better understanding of context and context-awareness. In *Proceedings of the Workshop on the What, Who, Where, when and How of Context Awareness*. New York: ACM Press.

Franke, N., & Piller, F. (2002). *Configuration toolkits for mass customization: setting a research agenda*. Technical report.

Harter, A., Steggles, P., Ward, A., & Webster, P. (1991). The Anatomy of a Context-Aware Application. In *Mobile Computing and Networking*, (pp. 59-68). New York: ACM Press.

Herlocker, J., Konstan, J., Borchers, A., & Reidl, J. (1999). An algorithmic framework for performing collaborative filtering. In *Proceedings of the Conference on Research and Development in Information Retrieval*.

Hof, R., Green, H., & Himmelstein, L. (1998). Now its your Web. *Business Week*, 68–75.

Hruschka, H. (1986). Market Definition and Segmentation Using Fuzzy Clustering Methods. *International Journal of Research in Marketing, 3*(2), 117–135. doi:10.1016/0167-8116(86)90015-7

Hsu, T. H. (2000). An Application of Fuzzy Clustering in Group-Positioning Analysis. In *Proceedings National Science Council of tile Republic of China, 10*(2), 157-167.

Hull, R. Neaves, N. & Bedford-Roberts, J. (1997). Towards Situated Computing. In *Proceedings of IEEE First International Symposium on Wearable Computers*, Cambridge, MA.

Jiao, X., & Tseng, M. (1999). A methodology of developing product family architecture for mass customization. *Journal of Intelligent Manufacturing, 10*, 3–20. doi:10.1023/A:1008926428533

Kaltz, J., Wolfgang, J., Ziegler, S., & Lohmann, L. (2005). Context-aware Web Engineering: Modeling and Applications. *RIA - Revue d'Intelligence Artificielle . Special Issue on Applying Context-Management, 19*(3), 439–458.

Kautz, H., Selman, B., & Shah, M. (1997). Referral web: Combining social networks and collaborative filtering. *Communications of the ACM, 40*(3), 6365. doi:10.1145/245108.245123

Kay, J. (2000). User Modelling for Adaptation. In C. Stephanidis, (Ed.), *User Interfaces for All: Human Factors Series,* (pp. 271-294). Mahwah, NJ: Lawrence Erlbaum.

Kay, J., Kummerfeld, B., & Lauder, P. (2003). *Managing private user models and shared personas*. Workshop on User Modelling for Ubiquitous Computing in conjunction with User modelling.

Knostan, J., Miller, B., Maltz, D., Herlocker, J., Gordon, L., & Riedl, J. (1997). Grouplens: Applying collaborative filtering to Usenet news. *Communications of the ACM, 40*(3), 7787.

Kobsa, A. (2001). Generic User Modeling Systems. *User Modeling and User-Adapted Interaction, 11*(1-2), 49–63. doi:10.1023/A:1011187500863

Kobsa, A., Koenemann, J., & Pohl, W. (2001). Personalized Hypermedia Presentation Techniaues for Improving Customer Relationships. *The Knowledge Engineering Review*.

Lang, K. (1995). Newsweeder: Learning to filter Netnews. In *12th International Conference on Machine Learning*.

Liberman, H. (1995). Letzia: An agent that assists in web browsing. In *Proceedings of International Joint Conference on Artificial Intelligence*, Montreal, Canada.

Liu, Y., & Connelly, K. (2006). Towards Wide Area Context-Aware Environments, In *the 4th IEEE International Conference on Pervasive Computer and Communications*, Pisa, Italy.

López de Ipiña, D., Ignacio Vázquez, J., & Abaitua, J. (2007). *A Web 2.0 Platform to Enable Context-Aware Mobile Mash-Ups,* (pp. 266-286).

Meier, A., & Werro, N. (2007). A Fuzzy classification model for on-line customers. *Informatica*.

Meier, A., Werro, N., Albrecht, M., & Sarakinos, M. (2005). Using a Fuzzy Classification Query Language for Customer Relationship Management. *Proceedings 31st International Conference on Very Large Data Bases (VLDB)*, Trondheim, Norway, (pp. 1089-1096).

Mladenic, D. (1996). *Personal WebWatcher: design and implementation*. Technical report, Department for Intelligent Systems, J. Stefan Institute, Ljubljana, Slovenia.

Mobasher, B. (2005). Web usage mining and Personalization. In M. P. Singh (ed.), *Practical Handbook of Internet Computing*. Boca Raton, FL: CRC Press.

Moon, A., Hyoungsun, K., Hyun, K., & Soowoo, L. (2007, April). Context-Aware Active Services. *Ubiquitous Computing Environments ETRI Journal, 29*(2), 169–178.

Moukas, A. (1996). Amalthaea: Information discovery and filtering using a multi-agent evolving ecosystem. In *Proc. 1st Intl. Conf. on the Practical Application of Intelligent Agents and Multi Agent Technology*, London.

Oard, D. (1997). The state of the art in text filtering. *User Modeling and User-Adapted Interaction, 7*.

Pazzani, M., & Billsus, D. (1997). Learning and revising user profiles: The identification of interesting web sites. *Machine Learning, 27*, 313–331. doi:10.1023/A:1007369909943

Peppers, D., & Rogers, M. (1993). *The One to One Future: Building Relationships One Customer at a Time*. New York: Currency Doubleday.

Peppers, D., & Rogers, M. (1997). *Enterprise One to One: Tools for Competing in the Interactive Age*. New York: Currency Doubleday.

Pignotti, E., & Edwards, P. (2004). *Context-Aware Personalised Service Delivery*. ECAI.

Pine, J. (1993). *Mass Customization - The New Frontier in Business Competition*. Boston: Harvard Business School Press.

Przybilski, M., Nurmi, P., & Floréen, P. (2005). A Framework for Context Reasoning Systems. In *Proc. IASTED International Conference on Software Engineering*.

Resnick, P., & Varian, H. (1997). Recommender systems. *Communications of the ACM, 40*(3), 5658. doi:10.1145/245108.245121

Rheingold, J. (2002). *Smart Mobs: The Next Social Revolution*. New York: Perseus Publishing.

Ryan, N., Pascoe, J., & Morse, D. (1997). Enhanced reality fieldwork: the context-aware archaeological assistant. In V. Gaffney, V. Leusen & S. Exxon (Eds.), *Computer Applications in Archaeology*.

Salkham, A., Cunningham, R., Senart, A., & Cahill, V. (2006). A Taxonomy of Collaborative Context-Aware Systems. In *Proceedings of the Workshop on Ubiquitous Mobile Information and Collaboration Systems (UMICS'06)*, CAiSE'06, (pp. 899-911), Luxembourg.

Schafer, J., Konstan, J., & Riedl, J. (1999). Recommender Systems in E-commerce. *ACM Conference on Electronic Commerce*.

Schilit, B., & Theimer, M. (1994). Disseminating active map information to mobile hosts. *IEEE Network*, 8.

Shehzad, A., Hung, Q., Ngo, K., & Sungyoung L. (2004). Formal Modeling in Context Aware Systems, *KI-Workshop Modeling and Retrieval of Context (MRC2004)*, Germany, (pp.13-24), September 23-27.

Terveen, L., Hill, W., Amento, B., McDonald, D., & Creter, J. (1997). Phoaks: A system for sharing recommendations. *Communications of the ACM, 40*(3), 5962. doi:10.1145/245108.245122

Tseng, M. M., & Jiao, J. (2001). Mass Customization. In *Handbook of Industrial Engineering, Technology and Operation Management* (3rd Ed.)

Varki, S., Cooil, B., & Rust, R. T. (2000). Modeling Fuzzy Data in Qualitative Marketing Research. *JMR, Journal of Marketing Research, 37*(November), 480–489. doi:10.1509/jmkr.37.4.480.18785

Want, R., Hopper, A., Falcao, V., & Gibbons, J. (1992). The active badge location system. *ACM Transactions on Information Systems, 10*(1), 91–102. doi:10.1145/128756.128759

Wedel, M., & Steenkamp, H.-B. E. M. (1991). A Clusterwise Regression Method for Simultaneous Fuzzy Market Structuring and Benefit Segmentation. *JMR, Journal of Marketing Research, 28*(November), 385–396. doi:10.2307/3172779

Weibelzahl, S. (2003). Evaluation of Adaptive Systems, PhD Thesis, University of Trier, Germany.

Weiser, M. (1991). Computers for the 21st Century. In *Scientific American*, (pp. 94-100).

Yoosoo, O., Schmidt, A., & Woontack, W. (2007, April). *Designing, Developing, and Evaluating Context-Aware Systems Multimedia and Ubiquitous Engineering, International Conference*, (pp. 1158 – 1163).

Zarikas, V., Papatzanis, G., & Stephanidis, C. (2001). *An architecture for a Self-Adapting Information System for Tourists Workshop on multiple user interface over the internet: Engineering and application trends in conjunction with HCI IMH*.

Chapter 9

Personalizing the TV Experience:
Vocomedia – A Case Study from Interactive TV

Regina Bernhaupt
ruwido, User Experience Research, Austria

David Wilfinger
ruwido, User Experience Research, Austria

Thomas Mirlacher
ruwido, User Experience Research, Austria

ABSTRACT

Personalized services and products are only successful when the usage context is taken into consideration. For interactive TV services, where usage is typically taking place in a living room, the question on how to develop an interaction technique to enable personalization is central. Based on an extensive literature review a set of requirements for personalized iTV services was developed. Following these requirements, a case study from interactive TV, called vocomedia, shows the development of an interaction concept for interactive TV supporting personalization by using a fingerprint recognition.

INTRODUCTION

Interactive TV (iTV) is currently one of the fastest changing media in terms of personalization. In the last 40 years TV was seen as a medium typically addressing the masses. But this mass medium is changing. New (digital) TV offers start to change the media landscape enabling users to experience new forms of interactivity in front of the TV. The traditional viewing behavior is starting to change: watching TV is no longer a passive activity, but TV becomes an active medium, offering consumers new ways of interacting with the content by enabling more interactivity (Eronen, 2003). Interactive TV therefore provides people with a bundle of new services that can be personalized for the household.

Interactivity allows users to actively engage in front of the TV by selecting information from teletext style services, by enjoying enhanced TV shows or by engaging in live interactive TV games.

DOI: 10.4018/978-1-60566-260-2.ch009

Interactivity in iTV can simply be defined as anything that takes the user beyond the passive experience of watching and that lets the user make choices and take actions (Gawlinski, 2003). The level of interactivity in iTV applications is limited by the potential of the technology used, but it is not determined by it. It is the user who makes a program interactive, given that the technology allows an interactive use. The user decides how much interactivity she wishes to employ in a specific situation (Vorderer, 2000).

Previous research in Human-Computer Interaction (HCI) on interactive TV was mainly focused on the design of the electronic program guide (EPG), and rarely considered the enhancement of the TV content. In particular, previous research approached iTV from a technological perspective, and did not consider the iTV user as a TV viewer (Chorianopoulos and Spinellis, 2003). In addition to that research on iTV cannot be addressed without a clear understanding of the context of use (Hughes, 2000). It has to look at the background issues such as how the home differs from other environments, what motivates people to use domestic technologies, and how patterns of use differ between users. The home exposes us to the demands of new user groups, including the elderly, which has to be considered in the design (Crabtree, 2004)."

With the introduction of the return-channel households can use "real" interactive TV, including the ability to identify usage on household level. The identification on a household level offers the ability to personalize TV content, information and to even tailor advertisements to the members of the household. But how can we address individual users in front of the TV? How can we enable users to personalize their iTV services to the same extend as they experience personalization in internet-based services?

The goal of this chapter is to develop an interaction technique that supports all the typical requirements for personalization in the context of interactive TV. Goal is to show, how personaliza-tion of services is affected by going beyond the typical PC-based/Internet usage context towards another usage context, like the home.

The next section is going to present an overview on related work in the area of interactive TV and presents (based on a literature review) all requirements for personalized interactive TV. The case study called vocomedia shows how the selected interaction technique is offering solutions for all the requirements for the personalization of interactive TV. Finally we present our lessons learned and some conclusion on how this interaction technique might be used in other products and services.

Personalization in the Area of Interactive TV

Personalization of services depends on context. Context can be broadly referred to as "information about who is involved in the interaction and what they are trying to accomplish" (Karat, Karat, Bro-edie, 2003, p. 7). When applying personalization for products and services related to interactive TV, the usage context is different from web-applications. People watch TV typically in their living rooms, but also in the kitchen or sleeping room. Interactive TV can be used in groups and alone. Interactive TV services are influenced from the general TV watching behaviour that include TV usage to get informed, distracted or entertained. Customers of iTV thus are not trying to fulfill the typical need when using e-customer services on the web, but expect to be entertained by the service. Thus mechanisms from personalizing web-applications might not be applicable in the iTV context.

Related Work

TV viewers today have to face an enormous amount of information. The simple action of selecting a TV channel is becoming difficult when users have to choose from a set of 500+ channels.

If you do some channel surfing or channel hopping, the selection of a TV channel might take quite a long time when 500+ TV channels are provided. Assuming you will take 10 seconds to change from one program to the other it will take 83 minutes to select your program (Ehrmantraut et al., 1996, p. 243). Relying on a printed program guide might be even more time consuming as you will have a (presumably very expensive) book of several hundred pages in front of you (10 channels per double page, makes 350 pages for a weeks program). The introduction of personal electronic program guides (EPG) should help overcome these usage problems. Personal EPGs can display all the information of all channels, by reducing the amount of displayed information through personalization, based on the users' preferences. But in general, personalized TV today is most often understood as simply using pieces of hardware enabling time-shift of TV (Jensen, 2003).

We use the *term personalization* to describe the objective of delivery of personalized information, meaning to *deliver information that is relevant to an individual or a group of individuals*, where the content is in the format and layout and in time intervals specified by the individual or group of users.

Looking at the personalization of TV, various systems and possible concepts have been proposed to personalize electronic programming guides (EPGs), TV programs and even broadcast news (Ardisonno, 2004). Personalization of TV primarily focused on supporting households, with some exceptions taking also into account the possible group of users in front of the TV (Ardisonno, 2004). From the technological perspective Björkman et al. (2006) presented a design and middleware implementation of a personalized home media center. They used a detailed model within the system to be able to personalize content, and customize user interface and settings for various user needs. Among others Blanco-Fernandez et al. (2006) use ontologies to make the system flexible for personalization needs. The technical

infrastructure for the personalization of media entertainment centers is thus "ready for use".

Requirements for Personalization

Given the heterogeneity of TV users, personalized TV services and products must provide solutions for the following fundamental challenges (Ardissono, 2004): viewer modeling, viewer identification, program processing, program representation and reasoning, presentation generation and tailoring, interaction management and evaluation. These fundamental challenges are discussed from an HCI perspective, defining a set of requirements for a user-friendly interaction technique supporting personalization.

Viewer Modeling

The viewer modeling describes the modeling of the user (user profile) to represent her preferences, needs and habits. Viewer modeling thus includes models of both individual viewers and groups of viewers (Ardissono, 2004). Today viewer modeling is realized with various technical solutions, but can be classified from a user-oriented perspective in automatically and user generated profiles, sometimes called implicit and explicit rating (Nichols, 1997).

First, profiles can be generated automatically, based on the viewing habits of a household. Content then is selected and presented based on the automatically generated profile. The TIVO system uses this kind of technique to select content that might be interesting for the household members by recording the relevant content automatically (Ali, 2004). When user preferences are generated automatically we are facing the following problems: the system needs some time to learn the user habits and preferences, it thus can not be used immediately after installation in the household but needs two to three weeks to learn the profile. If the system starts to recommend content, not reasonable for the profile, the user can not actively change the

151

profile to correct the "wrong" recommendations. Automatic personalization might provide the user with a wrong selection of content, so users might not want to use the system anymore. In the worst case, the automatic personalization might hinder the user to access some content not displayed due to the personalization, as users might not notice that their content was filtered based on an profile, not reflecting their needs appropriately (Zaslow, 2002).

The second way of generating user profiles actively involves the user in the profile generation. Users can choose their preferences, by making the user profile editable or customizable providing a user interface on the TV screen. An active involvement of the user can help to correct profiles and can help to make personalization of the content more accurate. But on the downside there are several reasons why users are not willing to fill out user profiles: the amount of work to fill in the profile (maybe repeatedly), security and privacy issues like fearing that the profile might be accessible beyond the home, and experiences with recommendations or personalization of content not matching the user profile.

From a user-oriented perspective an interaction technique should support both approaches, automatic and user generated profiles. To enable a positive user experience it is required to automatically select content and services but still give the user the possibility to actively change the profiles if needed. The interaction technique thus should allow to easily change the profile used.

Viewer Identification

Identification of users in front of the TV is typically realized using automatic profile generation of the whole household. Currently there are some interactive TV systems under development that enable the identification of the viewer (and viewers). Systems available on the market include identification by a simple key on the remote control (NDS, 2005), identification by (security) codes (Premiere, 2008) or identification by biometric measurements (ruwido, 2008).

From a user-oriented perspective individual viewer identification is becoming a necessary component of an interactive TV system, to enable each user of the system to access her personal information or profiles. Users must be identified to use their personalized ordering of TV channels, to enable security for miss-use of the system (e.g. children buying pay-TV content without authorization), to enable family friendly TV selection strategies (child safety, by omitting special TV channels or shows, limited TV usage etc.), and to enable social TV services, like the individual participation in polls, user-generated content or social communication. Finally viewer identification helps to increase the user experience for example by making recommendations more accurate for each individual user but also for groups of users.

Program Processing

From the service provider side personalization of iTV services must be supported by enabling automatic identification, indexing, segmentation, summarization and visualization of television programs. This is especially true for new forms of interactive TV services, like enhanced TV shows including personalized advertising.

From the user-oriented view, the program processing must support the identification of new, additional information and material related to all kinds of iTV services. For example, adding of new TV channels, new video on demand content or the availability of personalized interactive advertising must be (visually) represented in the user interface of the iTV system.

Program Representation and Reasoning

Program representation deals with the ability of the system to represent the general characteristics and specific content of programs and shows. It also allows to connect parts of the programs with interactive advertising or to enrich programs with additional content. Reasoning about similarity or dissimilarity of programs can be achieved with a range of techniques. To ensure that the right kind of people are receiving the right kind of similar content, content-based filtering or collaborative filtering are most commonly used. The success of content-based filtering lies in the ability to recommend new items that still fit the user profile. The technical solutions for content-based filtering are difficult to realize, as they rely on the accuracy of the user profile and the labeling of the content.

From a user-oriented perspective the ability of social recommendations can help to overcome the shortcomings of a content-based recommendation system. In general recommendation systems should take into account the following aspects during system development (Bernhaupt, Wilfinger, Weiss, Tscheligi, 2008):

- reflect the social aspect or indicate clearly from which authority the recommendation is coming from,

- balance carefully the number of novelties compared to the number of recommendations that are within the user profile,

- design the recommendations in a way to limit the so called "mirror effect". Recommendations typically reflect the users habits and preferences, giving the user the possibility to reflect on their usage. The recommendations should allow deleting recommendations or enable to change settings, so unwanted recommendations or preferences can be avoided.

- Help users access the (automatically recorded) recommendations by guiding them to novel recommendations

- clearly communicate the intended user group (or individual user),

- and inform users in time about current recommendations.

Presentation Generation and Tailoring

Depending on the viewer's preferences, usage of TV programs and services, and user identification, the interactive TV platform or product must select, organize and customize the related material. To fit users' needs it is also necessary that a customization of the user interface (e.g. how to display content, what font size, what kind of feedback, what kind ordering of channels) is possible. Customization of the interface must not be confused with the personalization of the iTV related material. Personalization includes a selection of material, that is presented based on the user profiles, while customization allows the user to change the basic settings of the user interfaces and iTV services preferably for every (individual) user of the system.

Interaction Management and Evaluation

The challenge is to design usable interfaces for interactive TV that fulfill high standards, in terms of efficiency, effectiveness and user satisfaction, but also in terms of the entertaining user experience that an interactive TV services and product must offer. Usability studies in the area of iTV have shown various concepts and ideas how to improve the interaction techniques and user interface design in the living rooms of tomorrow (Chorianopoulous, Lekakos, Spinellis, 2003; Lekakos et al., 2001) ranging from PC and desktop oriented EPG designs (van Barneveld, 2004) to 3D representations on the TV screen (Ardissono, 2004). The current trend in user interface design for interactive TV services is "back to simplicity" (Bernhaupt et al., 2007). Especially the interaction technique (input device and user interface) has become a focus of attention. Standard remote controls are having less buttons, with some added complexity in the user interface. New modalities are tested to increase the bandwidth of the input device, like gestures-based approaches (Topolsky, 2007), speech (Harmony, 2008) and rotational input (ruwido, 2007).

Figure 1. Vocomedia system including remote control with fingerprint recognition

We have to take into account that interactive TV will only be utilized, when offering the user an intuitive and easy-to-use interface (van Barneveld & van Stetten, 2004). The development of any form of interaction management for interactive TV must take the needs, wants and wishes of the users into account. Thus an iterative development with user-centered evaluations is the only way to develop this kind of interaction management (van Barneveld, 2004) to make personalized TV a success.

CASE STUDY: VOCOMEDIA

The vocomedia case study is part of the iTV4ALL project on new forms of interaction techniques in the living room. Goal of the project was to investigate how an interaction technique should be set up to enable personalized interactive TV. Based on a series of ethnographic studies current trends in the living room were investigated (Bernhaupt et al, 2006, Bernhaupt, et al., 2007; Bernhaupt, Obrist, Weiss, Beck, Tscheligi, 2008; Obrist, Bernhaupt, Tscheligi, 2007). It was found that users prefer easy-to-use, safe, bio-metrical measurements, to unsafe technologies, like codes or key combinations. Based on these studies a remote control including fingerprint recognition was developed (see Figure 1). To show that an input device including fingerprint recognition

(and only 6 navigation keys) allows to interact with all types of interactive TV services, a concept prototype called vocomedia was designed. The following section presents how the input device combined with the interaction technique fulfills the requirements of a personalized interactive TV service (presented in the previous section).

Viewer Identification

Studies on TV usage in households revealed that TV systems are still used by several people, even in single households (Bernhaupt et. al, 2007; Bernhaupt, Obrist, Bernhaupt, Tscheligi, 2008). Usage by various persons in a household leads to the need of personalization, especially regarding default settings or children safety restrictions.

Most systems today use PINs to guarantee that only the person who knows the PIN is allowed to use certain functionalities. Unfortunately these PINs only provide a limited degree of security and increase the mental effort for the user when using such a system. This is caused by people having difficulties remembering codes and so they either use easy to remember or guessable numbers, or they write them down somewhere which lowers the security or they have to train the PIN hard and to invest effort every time it is needed to remember the number again.

To overcome these problems and to additionally offer functions that fulfill both the need of

Figure 2. left: User logging in after pressing the fingerprint and a positive recognition; right: Personalized menu for user called "Ferdinand".

security and personalization, the interaction technique uses an additional key that allows fingerprint recognition on the remote control. This has several advantages. Firstly the fingerprint is relatively save compared to a PIN, secondly the only thing users have to remember when they identify themselves via fingerprint is which finger they use to press the fingerprint scanner. In terms of identification the fingerprint recognition enables the system to identify unique users, which can be associated with the individual user modeling.

At any time users can log in and out of this system, which is immediately acknowledged by a notification as well as a status icon for the logged in user. The only action required by the user is a brief press of the fingerprint scanner. If no user is logged in, the system provides default functionality of the user with the fewest right (Figure 2: log-in to the system).

Groups of Users and Viewer Modeling

To make the fingerprint concept work, the users of the system are divided into three groups:

Administrator: The administrator has the right to use all functions and to change all settings. The administrator can add and remove users and give/take usage rights. The administrator normally is the head of the family and the household, mother and/or father.

Standard User: The Standard User is allowed to use all functions but cannot change settings of other users or give/take rights. The typical standard user is an adult, who is not interested in configuring the system but wants to use most of the functions.

Restricted User: The restricted users are only allowed to use a limited functionality. They are not allowed to change any settings and filters, that are described later and that can be applied by the administrator, who is able to restrict their usage of the system.

To make usage of the system easier, and to decrease the visual load of the menu, the system hides menu items, which are not accessible for single users (i.e. Channels, Profiles or Filters). This has the advantage that these users are not disturbed and irritated by menu items they cannot use.

The implemented system can be used with several underlying technical concepts. In the current prototypical version each user is assigned to one user group (administrator, standard or restricted user). The administrator user can add new users to the system and then develop different profiles for each user, like for example a child is a standard user, but the number of channels and the daily TV watching time are limited. The child is allowed to buy some video on demand content in the children area of the VoD offer, and it is allowed to spend maximum 2€ per week on

Figure 3. Filters that can be applied to single users like children by an adult

games. The viewer modeling includes some basic demographic data of the user, their set preferences and some filters that can be applied (preferences for TV areas and channels, restrictions). Viewer modeling also includes the individually stored communication features (id, name, buddy-list), a list of last visited videotext pages, bought video-on-demand content, uploaded videos, photos and music. The system is offering also favorites for each individual user.

Related to the discussion about individual profiles and groups of users in front of the TV, our current research in an ongoing ethnographic study shows, that if several users are in front of the TV, the user having an administrator status is typically logged-in the system. The need for a group-log-in was not expressed explicitly. When a group of people is watching TV, typically the default TV profile is used, and the one with administrator rights is used when buying a movie (controlling the sensitive areas). The system would allow the setup of groups of users, by simply adding different profiles. But a group of users typically argued to have the standard user as a common group, and to use the individual profiles for special content (with information that should not be shared, like the buddy/friends list on the social communication channels).

Tailoring

Tailoring the system to the users, includes selecting and applying several filter and preferences items,

so the system can be adjusted to mach each users needs. Filters are mostly restrictions for protecting children against inappropriate content (see Figure 3). These filter include:

- Channel filters: Single Channels can be blocked.
- Duration filter: The daily TV usage of the profile owner can be limited to a certain amount.
- Age filters: Dependent on the age of the profile owner and the law situation in the country where the system is used, TV program with a special rating can be blocked.
- Time filters: Time filters allow the limitation of the TV usage to a timeframe.
- Money filters: Limit the maximum amount of money spent on games or VideoOnDemand offers.

Program Representation and Reasoning, Generation

For recommender systems or the possibility to store personal data like images or music, the system requires to the ability to distinguish between several users due to privacy and personalization issues. Besides that, modern technology offers functionality like TV shopping or Video on Demand (VoD) that can cause financial damage if not used properly.

Besides security issues the fingerprint concept makes several aspects of personalization possible

Figure 4. Sequence of purchasing a movie; User has to identify with the fingerprint, after positive identification the movie can be seen.

(see Figure 4: for buying a movie). As living room entertainment systems are mostly used by several persons, the system gives these persons the possibility to configure the system according to their needs without the problem of changed settings when another user had used the system before and changed settings. Relevant features and functions for the personalization are:

- Channel sequence (Channels in EPG)
- Sound adjustments
- Picture adjustments
- Menu Design and feel (Color, speed of scrolling, etc.)
- Private files like photos, videos or music
- Language settings
- Contacts (for video and audio communications)
- Recommendations
- Favorites
- social communication: video conferencing or voice communication via interactive TV, buddy lists, user identification by video and photo
- direct storage of photos (via USB connection directly on the set top box)

Lessons Learned and Recommendations

To enable individual users in front of the TV to benefit from personalized services it is necessary to develop a new form of interaction technique. Personalization is typically closely connected to privacy, security and trust, therefore an interaction technique supporting these aspects might be beneficial.

What we learned within the iTV4all project is that the home environment is a usage context that implies other contextual factors to personalization than web-application oriented services, or even mobile services. Any system for personalization of iTV services must take today's services and usages into account. New personalized services like social TV ask for a simple user identification that is quick, easy-to-use and easy to remember. The secure identification of users can help solve security problems that are related to personalization issues like secure payment or access limitation.

For the development of personalized services for iTV contextual factors have to be taken into account. The evaluation of the development with respect to the contextual factors is a difficult undertaking. Studies in the lab do not typically reflect the real usage situation and do not allow investigation of long term usage. Thus evaluation has to be adopted to reasonably reflect the usage context. The field of mobile HCI has developed variations of (usability) evaluation methods, to improve evaluation for mobile interaction. Evaluation of personalized interactive TV services must take into account gained knowledge from that field, as well as consider the specific aspects of personalization (Kramer, Noronha and Vergo, 2000).

SUMMARY AND OUTLOOK

Interactive TV is a rapidly changing media. New forms of personalized services demand higher attention from the users in front of the TV, as most of the user interfaces are badly designed and do not help the majority of users to really beneficially use the available content and services. To enhance the experience in front of the TV we investigated the requirements of personalized services in the home and developed an interaction technique to support personalized services. How fingerprint recognition helps in a typical interactive TV offer was demonstrated in a case-study called vocomedia, presenting solutions for the typical requirements for personalized TV services. Additionally the interaction technique supports key elements like security and trust, allowing users to secure their individual content or to limit access for their children.

For all forms of personalized services in the home context we can generalized that it is necessary to have a clear understanding of the user, the usage context and the technical solutions available in that area. Viewer identification is frequently used in new forms of interactive TV offers but we learned that the identification must be easy to use, fast and robust (in terms of security). Any form of automatic processing or content must be clearly displayed in the user interface, allowing the user to actively engage in the selection process. Selection of the content is still part of the entertainment experience of the user, and can not be fully automatic, but well presented automatic

content selection can be perceived as "taking care" of the user. Reasoning mechanisms should allow to include social annotations or social filtering to enhance the user experience, while still using automatic content-based recommendations to support user groups that are not interested in social interaction on iTV. In general the presentation generation, tailoring of content and the interaction management are the most important aspects of any form of personalized service. Users must have an easy-to-user interface, to be able to relax in front of the TV, still enjoying all the additional functionality interactive TV currently is providing. The system vocomedia shows several solutions to the named challenges, providing an easy-to-use interaction with fast and quick user identification.

Future work should be focusing on the new services offered by interactive TV: social TV and communication should be solved, supporting individual and group usage. As interactive TV is a rapid changing field, ethnographic studies have to be conducted, to investigate adoption of interactive TV and help to discover new opportunities of services that will be really beneficial for all kinds of users.

REFERENCES

Ali, K., & van Stam, W. (2004). TiVo: making show recommendations using a distributed collaborative filtering architecture. In *Proceedings of the Tenth ACM SIGKDD international Conference on Knowledge Discovery and Data Mining (KDD '04)* (pp. 394-401). New York: ACM Press.

Ardissono, L., Kosa, A., & Maybury, M. (2004). *Personalized digital Television: Targeting Programs to Individual Viewers*. Boston: Kluwer Academic Publishers.

Bernhaupt, R. Obrist. M., Weiss, A., Beck, E. & Tscheligi, M. (2007). Trends in the Living Room and Beyond. In: P. Cesar, K. Chorianopoulos, J. F. Jensen, (Ed.), *Interactive TV: A shared Experience, 5th European Conference, EuroITV 2007*, (pp. 146-155). Heidelberg: Springer.

Bernhaupt, R., Obrist. M., Weiss, A., Beck, E. & Tscheligi, M. (2008). Trends in the Living Room and Beyond. *Computers in Entertainment, 6*(1), online.

Bernhaupt, R., Obrist, M., & Tscheligi, M. (2006). Usability and Usage of iTV Services: Lessons learned in an Austrian Field Trial. In [Heidelberg: Springer.]. *Proceedings of EuroiTV, 2006*, 234–241.

Bernhaupt, R., Wilfinger, D., Weiss, A., & Tscheligi, M. (2008) An Ethnographic Study on Recommendations in the Living Room: Implications for Design of iTV Recommender Systems. In M. Tscheligi, M. Obrist, & A. Lugmair, (Ed.) *Proceedings of EuroiTV 2008* (LNCS Vol. 5066, pp. 92-101). Heidelberg: Springer.

Björkman, M., Aroyo, L., Bellekens, P., Dekker, T., Loef, E., & Pulles, R. (2006). Personalised Home Media Centre Using Semantically Enriched TV-Anytime Content. In [Heidelberg: Springer.]. *Proceedings of EuroiTV, 2006*, 165–173.

Blanco-Fernandez, Y., Pazos-Arias, J. J., & Gil-Solla, A. Ramos-Cabrer-M., & Lopez-Nores, M. (2006). Bringing together Content-based methods, Collaborative Filtering and Semantic Inference to Improve Personalized TV. In *Proceedings of EuroiTV 2006*, (pp. 174—182). Heidelberg: Springer.

Chorianopoulos, K., Lekakos, G., & Spinellis, D. (2003) Intelligent User Interfaces in the Living Room: Usability Design for Personalized Television Applications. In *Proceedings of IUI 2003* (pp. 230 – 232). New York: ACM Press.

Chorianopoulos, K., & Spinellis, D. (2003). Usability Design for the Home Media Station. In *Proceedings of the 10th HCI International 2003 Conference* (pp. 439-443).

Crabtree, A., & Rodden, T. (2004). Domestic Routines and Design for the Home. *Journal of Collaborative Computing, 13*(2), 191–220. doi:10.1023/B:COSU.0000045712.26840.a4

Ehrmantraut, M., & Härder, T. Wittig, H., & Steinmetz, R. (1996) The Personal Electronic Program Guide – Towards the Pre-selection of Individual TV Programs. *Proceedings of CIKM 1996*, (pp. 243 – 250).

Eronen, L. (2003). User Centered Research for Interactive Television. In J. Masthoff, R. Griffiths, & L. Pemberton, (Ed.), *From viewers to actors? Proceedings of the European Conference on Interactive Television (EuroITV '03)* (pp. 5-12), Brighton, UK.

Gawlinski, M. (2003). *Interactive Television Production*. Oxford, UK: Focal Press.

Harmony (2008). *Harmony Remotes To Include Speech Recognition*. Retrieved May 5, 2008, from http://www.physorg.com/news97575605.html

Hughes, J., O'Brien, J., Rodden, T., Rouncefield, M., & Viller, S. (2000). Patterns of Home Life: Informing Design for Domestic Environments. *Journal of Personal Technologies Special Issue on Domestic, 4*(1), 25–38.

Jensen, J. F. (2003). Interactive Television: New Genres, New Format, New Content. In *Proceedings of the 2nd Australasian conference on Interactive Entertainment* (pp. 89–96).

Karat, J., Karat, C.-M., & Broedie, C. (2003). Personalizing Interaction. In C.-M. Karat, J. O. Blom, & J. Karat, (Eds.) *Designing Personalized User Experiences in eCommerce* (pp. 7 – 14). Dordrecht: Kluwer Academic Publishers.

Kramer, J., Noronha, S., & Vergo, J. (2000). A user-centered design approach to personalization. *Communications of the ACM, 43*(8), 44–48. doi:10.1145/345124.345139

Lekakos, G., & Chorianopoulos, K. Spinellis, D. (2001) Information Systems in the Living Room: A Case Study of Personalized Interactive TV Design. In *Proceedings of the 9th European Conference on Information Systems* (pp. 319-329), Bled, Slovenia.

NDS. (2005). Retrieved from www.nds.com

Nichols, D. (1997). Implicit Rating and filtering. In *Proceedings of the 5th DELOS Workshop on Filtering and Collaborative Filtering* (pp. 31 – 35).

Obrist, M., Bernhaupt, R., & Tscheligi, M. (2008). Interactive TV for the Home: An ethnographic study on users' requirements and experiences. *International Journal of Human-Computer Interaction, 24*(2), 174–196. doi:10.1080/10447310701821541

Premiere (2008). Retrieved from www.premiere. de ruwido (2008). vocomedia. Retrieved online April 3, 2008 from http://www.ruwido.com/ products/voco-media/1/

ruwido (2007). Vexo. Retrieved online April 3, 2008 from http://vexo.ruwido.com

Topolsky, J. (2007). *Gesture-based remote control developed*. Retrieved online May 5, 2008 from http://www.engadget.com/2007/07/15/gesture-based-television-control-developed/

van Barneveld, J., & van Stetten, M. (2004). Desiging Usable Interfaces for TV Recommender Systems. In L. Ardissono, (Ed.) *Personalized Digital Television* (pp. 259 – 285). London: Springer.

Vorderer, P. (2000). Interactive Entertainment and Beyond. In D. Zillmann, & P. Vorderer, (Ed.), *Media Entertainment. The Psychology of its Appeal* (pp. 21-36). Mahwah, NJ: Erlbaum.

Zaslow, J. (2002). If TiVo Thinks You Are Gay, Here's How To Set It Straight -- Amazon.com Knows You, Too, Based on What You Buy; Why All the Cartoons? *The Wall Street Journal*, November 26, A, p. 1

KEY TERMS AND DEFINITIONS

Interactive TV: Interactive TV describes the ability of a user to interact with the TV set, for example selecting a video on demand, to interact with the TV-program (currently only rarely available) and to interact with TV-program related content (like advertising).

Context: Context can be broadly defined as information about who is involved in the interaction and what they are trying to accomplish. The home context can be divided into physical context, time context, social context.

Personalization in iTV: Several techniques allowing to tailor content according to a household profile.

Interaction Technique: An interaction technique is the fusion of input and output, consisting of all software and hardware elements, that provides a way for the user to accomplish a task.

Section 3
Innovative Applications and Services with Customized Adaptive Behaviour

Chapter 10
Affective Human Factors Design with Ambient Intelligence for Product Ecosystems

Roger J. Jiao
Georgia Institute of Technology, USA

Qianli Xu
Nanyang Technological University, Singapore

ABSTRACT

The fulfillment of affective customers needs may award the producer extra premium in gaining a competitive edge. This entails a number of technical challenges to be addressed, such as, the elicitation, evaluation, and fulfillment of affective needs, as well as the evaluation of capability of producers to launch the planned products. To tackle these issues, this research proposes an affective human factor design framework to facilitate decision-making in designing product ecosystems. In particular, ambient intelligence techniques are applied to elicit affective customer needs. An analytical model is proposed to support affective design analysis. Utility measure and conjoint analysis are employed to quantify users' affective satisfaction, while the producers' capability to fulfill the respective customer needs is evaluated using a capacity index. Association rule mining techniques are applied to model the mapping of affective needs to design elements. Configuration design of product ecosystems is optimized with a heuristic genetic algorithm. A case study of designing the living room ecosystem is reported with dual considerations of customers' satisfaction and producer's capacities. It is demonstrated that the affective human factors design framework can effectively manage the elicitation, analysis, and fulfillment of affective customer needs.

INTRODUCTION

Among the spectrum of customer needs, affective needs, which focus on customers' emotional response and aspirations, are arousing more and more attention in comparison to the functional needs which focus on the product performance and usability factors (Jordan, 2000; Khalid, 2001). As an extension of traditional human factors and ergonomics, which have concerned with cause and effect relations between products and human performance, affective design emphasizes the emotional

DOI: 10.4018/978-1-60566-260-2.ch010

relations between them (Talbot, 2005). Affect is a basis for the formation of human values and human judgment. For this reason, it might be argued that models of product design that do not consider affect are essentially weakened (Helander and Tham, 2003). This is especially true for consumer products, where a broad spectrum of similar products is available, with minor differences in functionality (Stanton, 1998). Therefore, it is essential for manufacturers to incorporate the affective human factors in their product offerings in order to gain competitive advantages. However, until recently, the affective aspects of product development have been substantially absent from formal design theories (Helander and Tham, 2003).

Affective customer needs basically imply an issue of addressing the customer perceptions with context-awareness. In this regard, the environment or ambience is an important determinant of customer perceptions. Hence, the performance of a product is human-centred and could only be tackled through the study of human-product-ambient interactions. At the same time, rapid response to diversified customer needs at affordable cost presents a constant challenge to manufacturers. Traditional mass production paradigm is inadequate to meet this challenge because the actual production volume usually cannot defray the huge investments in product development, equipment, tooling, maintenance and training. Mass customization lends itself to be a paradigm shift for manufacturing industries to provide products that best serve individual customer needs while maintaining near mass production efficiency (Tseng and Jiao, 1996). At the front-end, it caters to the requirements of individual customers or customer groups by developing product families that cover a spectrum of product performance requirements. At the back-end, production efficiency is ensured by developing product platforms that leverage upon commonality, standardization, and modularity across different products, along with process platforms that accommodate flexibility and reusability of the production systems (Meyer and Lehnerd, 1997).

This research proposes an analytical model for product design with consideration of fulfilling customer's affective needs and the mass customization rationale. The aim is to develop a decision framework that incorporates various technologies to fulfil affective customer needs in product planning and development. In this chapter, Section 2 presents the background research related to affective design. The major challenges and key research issues are formulated in Section 3. In section 4, a decision framework is proposed to address the major research issues. The implementation of the framework to facilitate affective design of the living room is presented in Section 5. The merits and limitations of the research are discussed in Section 6, and conclusions are drawn in Section 7.

RELATED WORK

From a business perspective, product development aims at maximizing of the overlap of the producers' capabilities with the window of customers' needs in the marketplace. This can be achieved either through expanding producers' capabilities by developing the company's portfolio, including products, services, equipments, and skills that market demands, or through channelling customers to the total capacity of the company so that customers are better served. The former strategy is largely the research focus of product planning and platform-based product development, where strategic development of product and process platforms gives the producer an advantage of improved resource utilization (Meyer, 1997; Sanderson, 1991). The latter strategy advocates directing market needs to the capacity of a producer, where a clear understanding of customer needs and subsequent fulfilment of the customer needs with the appropriate design elements suggest themselves to be critical issues.

A major difficulty for affective design is the elicitation of customer needs. In most cases, it is difficult to capture the affective customer needs due to their linguistic origins. Therefore, the elicitation of customer needs emphasizes the transformation of customer verbatim constructs, which are often tacit and subjective, into an explicit and objective statement of customer needs. Appropriate elicitation techniques that are able to offer a compromised solution between the extensiveness of expertise and the genuineness of the Voice of Customer (VoC) are necessary for effective acquisition of customer needs (Yan et al., 2002).

A wide range of research has been geared toward investigating the means by which the needs of customers can be captured more effectively (Stauffer and Morris, 1992). Customer needs may originate from diverse customer groups in various market segments through different channels, such as, interviews, questionnaires, feedback from sales agents and retailers, customer comments and complaints, as well as field maintenance reports. Kano et al. (1984) distinguish between three types of requirements which affect customer satisfaction in different ways, including must-be requirements, one-dimensional requirements, and attractive requirements. Such a differentiation of customer satisfaction helps the designer identify the customers' expected, high-impact, low-impact or hidden requirements, and thus guides through their fulfilment process. Other approaches for customer needs elicitation include psychology-based approaches (Nagamachi, 1989; Burchill and Fine, 1997), artificial intelligence-based approaches (Turksen and Willson, 1992; Jenkins, 1995; Hauge and Stauffer, 1993), and knowledge recovery approaches (Tseng and Jiao, 1998; Chen et al., 2002; Du et al., 2003). Despite these efforts, the consideration of ambience where the behaviours of customers are contextualized is generally lacking during the elicitation process. To achieve reliable and efficient customer needs elicitation, it is desirable to render the customers

with the actual product ambience and study their response in an unobtrusive way.

Mapping the customer needs to design elements constitutes another important research topic. Quality Function Deployment (QFD) has been widely adopted to translate customer requirements to technical design requirements (Akao, 1990). A key component of QFD is the customer requirement framework to aid the designer's view in defining product specifications (Clausing, 1994). While QFD excels in converting customer information to design requirements, it is limited as a means of discovering the VoC (Hauge and Stauffer 1993). To empower QFD with market aspects, Fung et al. (1998) propose to pre-process the customer needs prior to their being entered as customer attributes into the House of Quality (HoQ). Fung et al. (2002) extend the QFD-based customer requirement analysis method to a non-linear fuzzy inference model. McAdams et al. (1999) propose a matrix approach to identify relationships between customer needs and product functions. Kansei engineering has been well recognized as a technique of translating consumers' psychological feelings about a product into perceptual design elements (JSKE, 2003). Nagamachi (1996) proposes six technical styles of Kansei engineering methods with applications to the automobile industry, cosmetics, house design, and sketch diagnosis. Nadia (2001) adopts Kansei modeling to reduce the uncertainty and complexity involved in the mapping between visual expressions and impressive words used to convey them. Sedgwick et al. (2003) adopt semantic differential techniques to inform the customers of the surface's physical characteristics for their packaging to enhance their emotional engagement with the products. Matsubara and Nagamachi (1997) propose to develop hybrid expert systems for Kansei design support.

While the aforementioned methods are useful from various perspectives, a designer must be aware that prospective customers may respond in a survey what they like to buy, but regret and decline the purchase at the time of the sale. There is a long mental step between intention and behaviour (Fishbein and Ajzen, 1972). Hence, the information on customer needs may be sketchy, and designers may proceed by ignoring customer needs and estimate functional requirements as much as they can. The mapping from the affective customer domain to the design domain will have to be inferred based on incomplete information.

Fulfilment of affective customer needs is mainly concerned with product portfolio planning considering both producer's capacity and the customer-perceived value. An optimal product portfolio has to account for both the consumer surplus (i.e., the amount that customers benefit by being able to purchase a product for a price that is less than that they would be willing to pay) and the producer surplus (i.e., the amount that producers benefit by selling at a market price that is higher than that they would be willing to sell for) (Jiao and Zhang, 2005b).

Product portfolio planning has been traditionally dealt with in the management and marketing fields focusing on portfolio optimization based on customer preferences. The objective is to maximize profit, share of choices, or sales (Urban and Hauser, 1993). Typically, customer preference has been investigated using market analysis techniques, such as, conjoint analysis (Green and DeSarbo, 1978; Tseng and Du, 1998), discrete choice experiments (Green and DeSarbo, 1978), fuzzy systems (Turksen and Willson, 1992), etc. However, the effectiveness of these methods in affect evaluation is limited because the interpretation of the customer needs and derivation of quantitative customer satisfaction is always absent.

On the other hand, cost commitment at the production stage constitutes the major concern of the producer surplus. Estimation of an absolute figure of production costs is deemed to be very difficult, if not impossible (Dobson and Kalish, 1993; Jiao and Tseng, 1999). Accordingly, a general consensus is that design and manufacturing admit resources (and thus the related costs) to be

shared among multiple products in a reconfigurable fashion, as well as per-product fixed costs (Moore et al., 1999). As a matter of fact, of critical importance is to justify the optimal product offerings in terms of their relative magnitudes of the deviations from existing product and process platforms due to design changes and process variations in relation to the product variety. Towards this end, various indices have been introduced to measure or indicate the cost effects. Collier (1981) proposes the Degree of Commonality Index (DCI) as a metrics of commonality underlying a product architecture based on the company's Bill-of-Materials (BOM). Wacker and Treleven (1986) extend the DCI and develop the Total Constant Commonality Index (TCCI) which distinguishes commonalities within a product from those between products. Furthermore, Treleven and Wacker (1987) explore the process commonality based on set-up time, flexibility in sequencing, and flexibility in expediting decisions. Jiao and Tseng (2000) develop the commonality index which incorporates component commonality and process commonality into a unified formulation. Kota et al. (2000) establish a product line commonality index to assess the commonality levels of a product family based on various manufacturing factors, such as, size, shape, material, processes, assembly, etc. Siddique (2000) proposes two measures, namely, component commonality and connection commonality and applied them to modularity analysis of automobile under bodies. Jiao and Tseng (2004) propose to model the cost consequences of providing variety by varying the impacts on process capabilities. The process capability index has been extended to be an instrument for handling the sunk costs that are related to the product families and shared resources.

PROBLEM FORMULATION

Affective customer needs involve not only the customers' interactions with the product, but

Figure 1. Affective needs and product ecosystem

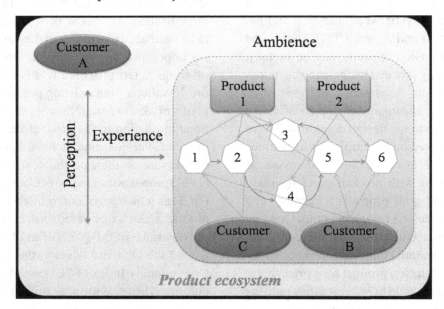

also with the environment where the product is operating, referred to as the ambience. The consideration of human-product-ambience interactions is consistent with the wisdom of 'product ecosystems', which essentially entail a scenario of affective design of the entire system with customer perception and experience in the loop, as shown in Figure 1. The affective feelings of the customer (customer A) are formed along two perspectives: (1) perception, which is a static, temporary feeling that the customer has when interacting with products or other customers (e.g., customer B and C); and (2) experience, which involves the process of product usage or customer activities to fulfil a specific task. Thus, the products and humans with which the customer interacts comprise the ambience of the respective customer. Accordingly, all customers and products, in combination with the task fulfilment process constitute the product ecosystem. The aim of affective design is to address human's emotional responses and aspirations, and to achieve aesthetic appreciation and pleasurable experience through human-product-ambience interactions.

Figure 2 shows an affective design process transforming affective customer needs into configurations of product ecosystems. This process is represented in the form of mapping relationships between the customer domain and the design domain. In general, the process involves three technical issues as elaborated next.

(1) *Acquisition of customer needs.* Acquisition of affective needs is deemed to be the starting point of affective design. At this stage, it is important to establish a set of qualitative and quantitative affective descriptors that are of interest to describe customer perceptions. Rather than describing individual customers needs, the affective needs should be representative for customer groups with respect to market segments.

(2) *Analysis of customer needs.* An analytical model should be developed to explicitly signify the capacity of the producer, and to channel the customer needs to the producer capacity based on certain mapping schemes. In particular, the following issues have to be

Figure 2. General process of affective design

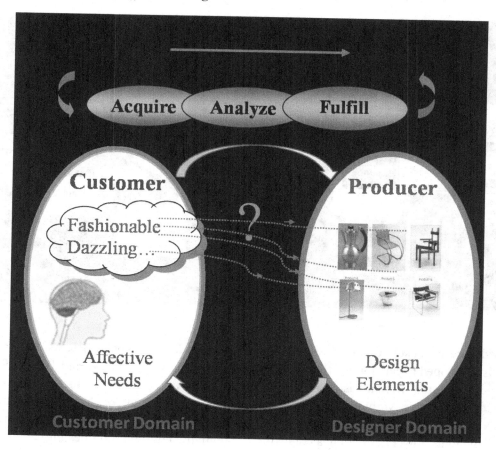

addressed: (a) Identify the design elements that constitute the configuration of the product ecosystem; (b) Identify the mapping relationship between affective needs and the corresponding design elements; (c) Quantify customer satisfaction with respect to the affective needs; and (d) Quantify the producer capacity in terms of production costs.

(3) *Fulfilment of customer needs.* This is achieved by determining optimal product ecosystem configurations for given customer affective needs. The configuration of the product ecosystem involves combinations of different design elements to achieve the desired affective expectation as quantified in the previous stage. The major concerns include (a) Define objective functions that leverage both the consumer surplus and the producer surplus; and (b) Develop efficient solution algorithms to deal with the large search space of the configuration design problem.

METHODOLOGY

Figure 3 shows a framework of affective design. It is consistent with the general process of mapping the affective needs to specific configurations of the product ecosystem. There are five major steps involved in this model, as elaborated next.

(1) Affective needs elicitation defines the process of extracting the affective descriptors that

Figure 3. An analytical model of affective design

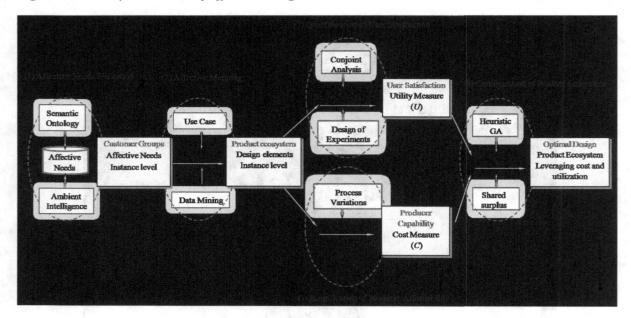

can be used to define customer groups. Semantic ontology is developed to categorize affective descriptors according to different customer groups and market segments. Ambient intelligence techniques are adopted to facilitate the elicitation process owing to its power of creating a context-aware environment.

(2) Affective mapping is concerned with the identification of design elements and the mapping relationship from affective needs to design elements. This is enabled by analyzing historical data using data mining techniques. In this research, association rule mining techniques are employed to discover the patterns of mapping mechanisms (Jiao and Zhang, 2005a).

(3) User satisfaction is quantified based on a part-worth model, for which conjoint analysis is used to establish the relationship between individual affective descriptors and the cohort impression/satisfaction of a particular customer on a specific configuration of the product ecosystem.

(4) For a specific planned set (configuration) of design elements, the producer capacity is measured according to their consequence on existing design

and production capabilities. As such, a capacity index is introduced (Jiao and Tseng, 1999).

(5) An optimal product configuration is generated through an optimization process with the shared-surplus as the objective function. Essentially, configuration design entails a combinatorial optimization problem. In this research, a heuristic genetic algorithm (GA) is developed for this purpose.

Affective Needs Elicitation with Ambient Intelligence

Affective needs are difficult to capture due to its qualitative and intangible nature. To tackle such a problem, this research proposes to apply ambient intelligence techniques to explore customer needs and to develop semantic ontology to describe and categorize the affective needs explicitly.

(1)   *Ambient intelligence.* Ambient intelligence suggests itself to be a new paradigm of information and communication technologies, taking the integration provided by ubiquitous

and pervasive computing one step further to realize context-aware environments that are sensitive and responsive to the presence of people (Ducatel, et al., 2001). The strength of an ambient intelligence is to support affective design with context-aware adaptive applications. In particular, it can facilitate the elicitation of affective needs from two perspectives. Firstly, ambient intelligence can generate an environment that simulates the actual scenario of the respective product ecosystems. Technology advancements in hardware and software have made it possible to place a customer in a virtual reality (VR) or augmented reality (AR) environment that closely match the actual environment of customers' experience with product ambience. In addition, an ambient intelligence-enabled environment can be easily reconfigured to reduce costs of imitating a real environment. Secondly, with ambient intelligence embedded in the product ecosystem, the behaviors and reactions of the customers can be captured in real time without interrupting the customers' normal activities. Unlike traditional survey approaches, where customers have to follow predefined procedures and express their feelings depending on their own reflection and imagination, customers enjoy more freedom in interacting with the product ecosystem and expressing their feelings spontaneously. Moreover, the surveillance system embedded in the ambience intelligence environment can capture customer responses throughout the investigation process for offline analysis afterwards.

This research proposes to apply VR technologies to construct an ambient intelligence-enabled environment. In a VR environment, various digital product models are built, which consist of a number of customizable product features. The advantages of a VR environment include lower costs and

simpler operations for reconfiguring product ecosystems. Moreover, surveys are carried out such that each customer is situated in the environment and is guided through a series of interaction with the product, while changing the configuration of products. The feedback of the customers, including voices, expressions, and behaviours are recorded throughout the survey process. The preliminary set of affective customer needs is extracted from the descriptive words that the customers have used during the survey.

(2) *Semantic ontology.* The purpose of semantic ontology is to describe and categorize the affective needs that are communicable among customers and designers from different sectors using a limited number of terminology that is as small as possible yet comprehensive enough to cover the major aspects of affective design. Each type of product ecosystems is supported by a set of affective terminology and taxonomy based on different customer requirements with respect to the particular product systems (e.g., automobile, living room, shopping mall, etc.). The development of semantics starts with the customer survey. Next, semantic scales can be constructed for affect evaluation, which involves the collection of a large number of descriptive words for the product ecosystem, and the clustering of the words that are similar in meaning into categories according to diverse customer groups (Karlsson et al., 2003). From each category, one or several words are chosen to represent the category along with the associated semantic scales in order to characterize the market segment-level affective assessment on the product ecosystem. Finally, the assessment semantic scales can be interpreted by domain experts to delineate the usage of the terminology.

Based on the semantic ontology, all customer affective needs can be described using a set of affective descriptors, represented as $\overline{X} = \left\{ x_m \right\}_M$ where $x_m \equiv \left\{ x_{mi}^* \right\}_I$ denotes each affective descriptor along with its scale instances, M is the total number of affective descriptors, and I is the number of scale instances related to a particular affective descriptor. Assume that there are multiple market segments, $\left\{ \Lambda_s \right\}_S$, each containing homogeneous customers. The respective affective needs category can be represented as $\left\{ \left\{ x_{mis}^* \right\}_{M \times I} \right\}_S$, where $M \times I$ is the total number of affective words (i.e., instances of affective descriptors) used for representing the *s-th* customer group. The set of scale instances of affective needs related to a particular customer group is denoted as $\overline{X_s^*} = \left\{ x_{mis}^* \right\}_{M \times I}$.

Analytical Model of Affective Satisfaction

(1) Translation of affective needs into design elements. Product ecosystem design yields many design alternatives that are desired by different customers. Each design entails a set of design elements, $\overline{Y} = \left\{ y_n \right\}_N$, where $y_n = \left\{ y_{nj}^* \right\}_J$ stands for a design element and its individual specifications, N is the total number of design elements, and J is the number of individual specifications related to a particular design element. Organized based on the rationale of product family design, these design elements are customizable features that facilitate the fulfillment of respective affective needs. Typically, these features are determined by engineers based on domain knowledge of the elements and the ease with which these elements can be changed. Typically, the specification of a design element includes such attributes as dimension, color, material, auxiliary components, etc.

Given that affective needs are fulfilled by a certain set of design elements, the set of design elements used to address the affective needs belonging to the sth customer group can be denoted as $\overline{Y_s^*} = \left\{ y_{njs}^* \right\}_{N \times J}$. Differentiation between the affective needs and design elements is consistent

with the fact that customers' affective impressions are associated with the gestalt design, rather than individual elements. The customers do not know what their affective needs mean by mapping to specific design elements. This is a typical 'data-rich yet knowledge-sparse' decision making problem. Kansei engineering and data mining techniques have been adopted to deal with this type of problems (Jiao and Zhang, 2005b; Jiao et al., 2006). A prerequisite for carrying our data mining is that a set of sales records is available which contains information of the affective customer needs and the actual selection of design elements that characterize the product variants delivered to the customers.

In this research, an association rule mining mechanism is developed to reveal the mapping from various affective needs to different product and ambience parameters (referred to as design elements of the product ecosystem), i.e., $\overline{X_s^*} \Rightarrow \overline{Y_s^*}$, where an association rule, '$\Rightarrow$', indicates an inference from the precedent ($\overline{X_s^*}$) to the consequence ($\overline{Y_s^*}$). The association rules are extracted from transaction data that contain order information corresponding to the customers and products. Each set of transaction data indicates a particular mapping relationship from the customer needs to the design elements. Such transaction data is available from the company's sales records and product documentation, usually constituting a large data set.

The general form of an association rule in association rule mining is given as:

$$\begin{aligned} &\alpha_1 \wedge \alpha_2 \cdots \wedge \alpha_k \cdots \wedge \alpha_K \Rightarrow \\ &\beta_1 \wedge \beta_2 \cdots \wedge \beta_l \cdots \wedge \beta_L \end{aligned} \quad \left[Support = p\%; \ Confidence = c\% \right]$$

$$(1)$$

where $\alpha_k = exist\left(x_{mis}^* \right), \forall k = 1, \cdots, K \leq M$ $\beta_l = exist\left(y_{njs}^* \right), \forall l = 1, \cdots, L \leq N$, and $p\%$ and $c\%$ refer to the support and confidence levels for this rule, respectively. Equation (1) states that whenever a set of customer needs exist, a particular set of design elements must be available to accommodate these needs. The confidence denotes the strength of an association, and the support indicates the frequency of the occurring patterns contained in the rule.

(2) Quantification of affect satisfaction. It is important to discern the cohort customer satisfaction (U) on the entire product ecosystem from the customer satisfaction on individual design elements ($\overline{Y_s^*}$). This essentially implies a mapping between two domains, i.e., $U = f\left(\overline{Y_s^*}\right)$. Obviously, this process is highly subjective and intangible. The affect satisfaction does not mean the summation (e.g., a weighted sum) of individual assessments at the design element level per se. But rather, it is a holistic impression on the cohort of all the design elements involved in a product ecosystem, namely, an overall consequence of individual measures regarding $\overline{Y_s^*}$.

To derive such a conjoint effect on the overall satisfaction (U) by a number of customer impressions on individual design elements ($\overline{Y_s^*}$), this research applies conjoint analysis techniques that are widely used in marketing research (Jiao et al., 2006). Conjoint analysis starts with the construction of product profiles. Due to the numerous product configurations that can be constructed based on the design elements, the Design of Experiment (DOE) (Nair et al., 1995) technique is useful to compose orthogonal testing profiles in order to minimize the collection of response data and the effort in setting up focus groups for interviewing with respondents. Customers' satisfaction levels with respect to each product configuration are collected from the experiment. For example, a respondent is asked to evaluate a product configuration and give a mark based on a 9-point scale, where '9' means the maximum satisfaction level, and '1' means the minimum satisfaction level.

Because different groups of customers may exhibit quite diverse expectations of product ecosystem design, the above satisfaction measure must be related to different market niches. In addition to demographic data, a number of other dimensions should be taken into account in relation to particular customer profiles. A set of market segmentation models based on fuzzy clustering techniques has been reported in consumer electronics products (Jiao and Zhang, 2005b). This can be readily extended to explore customer experience regarding affects.

Following the part-worth model, the utility of the sth segment for the dth design, U_{sd}, is assumed to be a linear function of the part-worth preferences (utilities) of the design elements of dth design, i.e.,

$$U_{sd} = a_d + \sum_{n=1}^{N} u_{sn} y_{dn}, \qquad \forall s \in \left\{1, \cdots, S\right\}, \qquad \forall d \in \left\{1, \cdots, D\right\} \tag{2}$$

where u_{sn} is the part-worth utility of sth segment for the nth design element, D denotes the total number of design alternatives, a_d is a constant associated with the derivation of a composite utility from part-worth utilities with respect to d^{th} design, and y_{dn} is a binary variable such that $y_{dn} = 1$ if the nth design element is contained in d^{th} design and $y_{dn} = 0$ otherwise.

(3) Quantification of producer capacity. To circumvent the difficulties inherent in estimating the actual cost figure of launching the product variants, this research adopts a capacity index to indirectly evaluate the cost of producing the design elements. The capacity index is a measure of the economic latitude of production process variations due to product customization (Jiao and Tseng, 1999). It is formulated based on the legacy process capability which is an instrument for handling the sunk costs that are related to the product families and shared resources. In particular, the expected cycle time can be used as a performance indicator of variations in process capabilities (Jiao and Tseng, 1999). The characteristic for the cycle time

is of 'the smaller the better' type. The cycle time demonstrates the distinctions between variables that differ as a result of random error and are often well described by a normal distribution. Hence, the one-side specification limit capacity index (C^{IN}) can be formulated as:

$$C^{IN} = \frac{\mu^T - LST^T}{3\sigma^T} \quad (3)$$

where LST^T, μ^T, and σ^T are the lower specification limit, the mean, and the standard deviation of the estimated cycle time, respectively. Variations in the cycle time are characterized by μ^T, and σ^T, reflecting the compound effect of multiple products on production in terms of process variations. The LST^T can be determined ex ante based on the best case analysis of a given process platform, in which standard routings can be reconfigured to accommodate various products derived from the corresponding product platform (Jiao et al., 2005).

Based on the capacity index, the cost of launching a product variant (the dth design) is estimated as:

$$C_d = \lambda \exp\left(\frac{1}{C_d^{IN}}\right) \quad (4)$$

where λ is a constant indicating the average dollar cost per variation of process capabilities. The meaning of λ is consistent with that of the dollar loss per deviation constant widely used in Taguchi's loss functions (Taguchi, 1986). It can be determined ex ante based on the analysis of existing product and process platforms. Such a cost function produces a relative measure, instead of actual dollar figures, for evaluating the extent of overall process variations among multiple products.

Product Ecosystem Configuration Design

The design of optimal product ecosystem must accommodate the consideration of both the cost of product ecosystem development and the corresponding customers' affective satisfaction, a shared-surplus model is proposed, where the objective function is formulated as the ratio of the customer-perceived utility (U_{sd}) and the costs (C_d) to produce the respective product, i.e.,

$$\max E[V] = \sum_{s=1}^{S} \sum_{d=1}^{D} \frac{U_{sd}}{C_d} P_{isd} Q_s y_d \quad (5)$$

where $E[V]$ denotes the expected value of the shared-surplus (V). It is defined as the utility (U_{sd}) per cost (C_d), modified by the probabilistic choice model, $\{P_{sd}\}_{S \times D}$, and the market size, $\{Q_s\}_S$. y_d is a binary variable such that:

$$y_d = \begin{cases} 1 & \text{if the manufacturer decides to offer product } d, \\ 0 & \text{otherwise} \end{cases}$$

The underpinning principle of the shared-surplus coincides with the implications of customer values in marketing, i.e., the customer's expectations of product quality in relation to the actual amount paid for it. This is different from the consumer surplus which is usually defined as a function of utility minus price (Green and Krieger, 1985). It is also different from the producer surplus which is defined as a function of price minus cost (Dobson and Kalish, 1993). In essence, the customer-perceived utility (U_{sd}) indicates the customers' willingness to buy the product, and the costs (C_d) reflects the capacity of producers to launch the product.

The conjoint-based search for an optimal product ecosystem always results in combinatorial optimization problems because typically discrete parameters are used in conjoint analysis (Zeithaml,

1988). Nearly all of these problems are known to be mathematically intractable or NP-hard, and thus mainly heuristic solution procedures have been proposed for the various problem types (Kaul and Rao, 1995). Comparing with traditional calculus-based or approximation optimization techniques, GAs have been proven to excel in solving combinatorial optimization problems. In this regard, a heuristic GA is adopted to solve such a combinatorial optimization problem (Jiao and Zhang, 2005b).

5. A CASE STUDY

The proposed affective design model has been applied to design the living room environment (Figure 4). In particular, the interior environment of the living room is designed toward fulfilling affective customer needs (e.g., comfort, quiet, convenient, etc.).

5.1 Affective Needs Elicitation

To ensure that the affective descriptors reflect the actual needs of the users, surveys have been carried out in a VR environment, where behaviours and conversations of customer are recorded in a usability laboratory (Figure 5). A number of pre-defined digital design elements are available for selection which constitute the living environment. Using the VR interface, the user can easily select and modify the living room features according to his/her preferences, and see right away how they look like in such an ambience intelligence-enabled environment. In addition, surveillance cameras are mounted into the system to inspect the users' responses in real time, which are analyzed offline afterwards. The voice of customers and their perceptions on experiencing with the living room configurations are recorded during the investigation process.

Based on the survey and experiments, a number of affective needs are extracted. These affective needs are categorized into different groups, forming the semantic ontology. For purpose of illustration, 10 affective descriptors are shown in **Table 1** for describing affect information as perceived by different users. The major design elements that influence the affective needs are identified by senior design engineers from the respondents' reactions during the survey and experiment. A total of 18 design elements are recognized as the ambience parameters that characterize a living room ecosystem, as shown in Table 2.

5.2 Affective Mapping

Based on the identified affective needs and design elements, 85 sales orders are organized into transactional database, where each transaction record denotes the presence of a set of affective needs and the corresponding customers' selection of design elements. In this case, the transactional data is organized in two segments, which are identified based on established market research of the company. A data mining tool, Magnum Opus (Version 2.0) (www.rulequest.com), is employed to find the mapping relationships between affective needs and design elements. The mining process terminates with a set of rules containing 66 association rules, as shown in Table 3.

5.3 Quantification of User Satisfaction and Producer Capacity

Conjoint analysis is applied for evaluating the part-worth utility of the design elements. Given all design elements as shown in Table 2, a total number of $3 \times 2 \times 2 \times 3 \times 3 \times 2 \times 3 = 648$ combinations may be constructed, representing 648 possible product configurations. To overcome such an explosion of configurations by enumeration, orthogonal product profiles are generated based on the principle of DOE (Nair et al., 1995). Using the Taguchi orthogonal array selector provided by SPSS software (www.spss.com), a total number of 16 orthogonal product profiles are generated,

Figure 4. The living room ecosystem © 2009 Roger Jianxin Jiao. Used with Permission.

as shown in Table 4. In the table, the columns under 'Conjoint Test' indicate the specification of offerings that are involved in the profiles, and the 'Satisfaction Scale' column collects the satisfaction level given by the respondents.

Another group of 20 customers were invited to act as the respondents for conjoint analysis. The same ambience intelligence-enabled environment used for affective needs elicitation is reconfigured to simulate the living room ambience according to diverse choices of design elements. Each re-spondent is asked to evaluate all 16 profiles one by one and give a mark based on a 9-point scale, where '9' means the user prefers a product most and '1' least. This results in 20×16 groups of data. For each respondent, 16 regression equations are obtained by interpreting his original choice data as a binary instance of each part-worth utility. With these 16 equations, the part-worth utilities for this respondent are derived. By averaging the part-worth utility results of all respondents belonging to the same market niche, a segment-

Figure 5. Usability laboratory for customer needs survey

Table 1. Affective descriptors for living rooms

Descriptor	Code	Descriptor	Code
Comfortable	X1	Bright	X6
Complicated	X2	Spacious	X7
Advanced	X3	Entertaining	X8
Secured	X4	Luxurious	X9
Clean	X5	Accessible	X10

level utility is constructed for each design element. Columns 2 and 5 in Table 5 show the part-worth utilities of two segments with respect to every design element.

Table 5 also shows the capacity indices for design elements based on empirical studies. The company fulfills customer orders through assembly-to-order production while importing all components and parts via global sourcing. With assembly-to-order production, the company has identified and established standard routings as basic constructs of its process platform. The capacity index of each design element is established based on time and motion studies of the related assembly and testing operations.

Optimal Living Room Configuration

Based on the established living room semantic ontology, a customer order is interpreted as a set of affective needs {comfort, clean, quiet, spacious, secured}. Based on the affective mapping rules in Table 3, the corresponding design elements are identified as Y1, Y4, Y9, Y13, Y15, and Y17. To determine an optimal living room ecosystem configuration for this customer, the heuristic GA procedure is applied to search for a maximum of expected shared-surplus among all possible combinations of these design elements (Jiao and Zhang, 2005b). In the GA, a chromosome string consists of 18 genes, each represented as a bit that denotes the presence of a design element. A gene may assume a value '1', indicating that a design element is selected in the product configuration; otherwise, a bit with a value '0' indicates that the design element is not selected. For each generation, the population size is set to be 30, meaning that only the top 30 fit product configurations are kept for reproduction. The GA solver returns the best configuration as shown in Table 6, which

Table 2. Living room affective design elements

Code	Description	Figure	Code	Description	Figure	Code	Description	Figure
Y1	Sofa royal		Y7	Curtain color-white		Y13	Book shelf color_brown	
Y2	Sofa soft		Y8	Lamp tall		Y14	Art piece nature	
Y3	Sofa leather		Y9	Lamp short		Y15	Art piece ancient	
Y4	Rug style_ancient		Y10	Lamp thin		Y16	Wall texture A	
Y5	Rug style_modern		Y11	Book shelf color_coper		Y17	Wall texture B	
Y6	Curtain color-blue		Y12	Book shelf color_white		Y18	Wall texture C	

Table 3. Identified association rules of affective mapping

Rule No	Inference Relationship	Support	Confidence
1	X1 ⟹ Y2	0.230	0.128
2	X2 ⟹ Y4	0.211	0.333
3	X3 ⟹ Y10 & Y12	0.170	0.450
4	X4 ⟹ Y6	0.122	0.137
5	X6 ⟹ Y7 & Y10	0.235	0.432
6	X8 ⟹ Y9 & Y14	0.323	0.270
7	X9 ⟹ Y1 & Y4 & Y15	0.262	1.020
8	X10 ⟹ Y9	0.424	0.277
...			
60	X1 & X3 ⟹ Y4 & Y7	0.214	0.775
61	X3 & X4 & X8 ⟹ Y12 & Y13 & Y17	0.296	0.843
62	X1 & X10 ⟹ Y15	0.193	0.385
63	X5 & X6 & X9 ⟹ Y3 & Y8	0.220	0.823
64	X5 & X9 & X10 ⟹ Y2 & Y5 & Y8 & Y12	0.402	0.228
65	X2 & X8 ⟹ Y4 & Y16	0.222	0.876
66	X3 & X5 ⟹ Y5 & Y12 & Y18	0.319	0.612

achieves an expected shared-surplus of 36.2. The shared surplus value is a performance indicator that leverages the customer satisfaction and producer capacity. It should be noted the absolute value of the share surplus is not significant. But rather, it suggests the relative superiority of a product configuration.

DISCUSSIONS

The difficulty in affective needs elicitation could be effectively alleviated with the support of an ambient intelligence environment. Previously surveys have been carried out to tackle affective needs using paper- or electronic-based question-naires, where the design elements are presented separately in pictures or sample objects. However, this method is both inefficient and ineffective. The

Table 4. Response surface experiment design

Conjoint Test															Satisfaction Scale
Choice	V1	V2	V3	V4	V5	V6	V7	V8	V9	V10	V11	...	V17	V18	
1	1	0	0	1	0	1	0	1	0	0	0	...	1	0	4
2	0	0	1	1	0	0	1	0	0	1	1	...	0	1	7
3	1	0	0	0	1	0	1	0	1	0	1	...	1	0	8
...	...	...	...	...	...	...	...	...	...	...	...	...	...	...	...
14	1	0	0	1	0	1	0	1	0	0	0	...	0	0	5
15	0	0	1	0	1	0	1	0	0	1	1	...	1	0	3
16	0	1	0	1	0	0	1	0	0	1	1	...	0	1	9

Table 5. Part-worth utilities

Code	Part-worth Utility	Capacity index
Y1	0.31	201
Y2	0.35	121
Y3	0.13	215
Y4	0.81	102
Y5	1.40	54.6
Y6	1.23	19.7
Y7	0.49	32
Y8	1.45	172
Y9	0.32	9
Y10	0.90	6.6
Y11	0.11	20.8
Y12	0.22	102
Y13	1.01	126
Y14	1.12	64.8
Y15	1.99	68.7
Y16	0.45	45.6
Y17	0.59	88
Y18	1.08	102

respondents are slow in response because it usually involves a long mental process for the customer to correlate the design elements with their ambiences. Moreover, the respondents suffer a general difficulty of expressing their feelings using linguistic words because they may be easily misled by the way the questions are presented. Within an ambient intelligence environment, design elements are rendered in its entirety such that a respondent can easily evaluate a design element in relation to the ambience. The customer behaviors recorded during the probing process can be further analyzed to extract useful affect information. One drawback of the current application of ambient intelligence is that it involves additional costs of setting up the environment with an initial investment on hardware and software. However, with more and more third party vendors providing low cost VR solutions, such an investment becomes affordable. Moreover, the investment can be compensated by the savings in carrying out the survey because the VR environment can be easily reconfigured to present diversified design alternatives.

The analytical model is an important tool for understanding the affective design process with consideration of the producer's capacity. A mapping scheme between affective needs and design elements can be represented as a set of mutually compatible association rules. It involves a bottom-up process of discovering possible patterns and then applying these patterns to facilitate decision-making in the future. This is advantageous over those methods that depend solely on the designer's experience. On the other hand, a few precautions for using the data mining method have been identified. Firstly, the original data for rule mining must be up-to-date; otherwise the rules could not reflect the current market trend and technology advancement. Secondly, the data mining tools themselves cannot determine whether the rules are valid and

Table 6. The best living room design for the given customer order

Design element	Parameter value
Y1: Sofa	Royal
Y4: Rug style	Ancient
Y9: Lamp	Short
Y13: Book shelf	Brown
Y15: Art piece	Ancient
Y17: Wall texture	B
Expected Shared-Surplus	**36.2**

useful. Sometime, it requires additional effort to interpret the outcome and to judge the validity of the outcome by domain experts. The post-process of discovered patterns is deemed to be important and cannot be overlooked.

The configuration of product ecosystems must be optimized in terms of both customer satisfaction and producer capacity. It is expected that the shared-surplus formulation is important for the manufacturer's interest, because customer perceived utility alone cannot ensure the manufacturer's business success. Ultimately, the manufacturer has to launch the product at an affordable cost so as to gain a profit margin. The proposed system does not require a huge investment that extends the manufacturer's production capacity. Instead, it focuses on directing the customers' needs to the existing capacity of the manufacturer. Such a practice is more practicable for a company because a huge investment or a radical change of company's structure will inevitably meet managerial barriers.

CONCLUSION

From a business perspective, the fulfilment of affective needs is an important enabler of product added value. However, a few major challenges have to be addressed, such as, the acquisition and understanding of the affective customer needs, and the fulfilment of affective needs at afford-able costs. The proposed framework of affective design presents an effort to enhance customer satisfaction based on the manufacturer's existing capabilities. Within this framework, ambient intelligence provides an effective means to elicit affective customer needs by incorporating ambience factors into the customer experiences. It is advantageous over traditional customer survey methods because it facilitates the study of customer behaviours through exploring extensive interactions between the customer, the product, and the ambience. Moreover, this research extends affective design analysis and modeling techniques to the downstream product design and production stages. To map affective needs to design elements, this research adopts the association rule mining technique, which features a bottom-up process of finding possible patterns, and then applying these patterns to facilitate decision-making in the future. A shared-surplus model is proposed based on an analysis of user satisfaction and producer capacity. Accordingly, the configuration of product ecosystems is optimized according to the manufacturer's capacity to fulfil the affective needs. The affective design method with analytical affect modeling and evaluation sheds light on answering such questions as (1) how to measure an affective design with respect to different customers' preferences; (2) how to incorporate the ambience in evaluating customer affective perceptions; and (3) how to predict affective design in terms of customer perceived utility and producer capacity.

REFERENCES

Akao, Y. (1990). *Quality function deployment: integrating customer requirements into product design*. Cambridge, MA: Productivity Press.

Burchill, G., & Fine, C. H. (1997). Time versus market orientation in product concept development: Empirically-based theory generation. *Management Science, 43*(4), 465–478. doi:10.1287/mnsc.43.4.465

Chen, C.-H., Khoo, L. P., & Yan, W. (2002). A strategy for acquiring customer requirement patterns using laddering technique and ART2 neural network. *Advanced Engineering Informatics, 16*(3), 229–240. doi:10.1016/S1474-0346(03)00003-X

Clausing, D. (1994). *Total quality development: a step-by-step guide to world class concurrent engineering*. New York: ASME Press.

Collier, D. A. (1981). The Measurement and Operating Benefits of Component Part Commonality. *Decision Sciences, 12*(1), 85–96. doi:10.1111/j.1540-5915.1981.tb00063.x

Dobson, G., & Kalish, S. (1993). Heuristics for pricing and positioning a product-line using conjoint and cost data. *Management Science, 39*(2), 160–175. doi:10.1287/mnsc.39.2.160

Du, X., Jiao, J., & Tseng, M. M. (2003). Identifying customer need patterns for customization and personalization. *Integrated Manufacturing Systems, 14*(5), 387–396. doi:10.1108/09576060310477799

Ducatel, K., Bogdanowicz, M., Scapolo, F., Leijten, J., & Burgelman, J.-C. (2001). *Scenarios for ambient intelligence in 2010*, ISTAG Report, European Commission.

Fishbein, M., & Ajzen, L. (1972). Attitudes and opinions. *Annual Review of Psychology, 23*, 487–554. doi:10.1146/annurev.ps.23.020172.002415

Fung, R. Y. K., Popplewell, K., & Xie, J. (1998). An intelligent hybrid system for customer requirements analysis and product attribute targets determination. *International Journal of Production Research, 36*(1), 13–34. doi:10.1080/002075498193912

Fung, R. Y. K., Tang, J., Tu, Y., & Wang, D. (2002). Product design resources optimization using a non-linear fuzzy quality function deployment model. *International Journal of Production Research, 40*(3), 585–599. doi:10.1080/00207540110061634

Green, P. E., & DeSarbo, W. S. (1978). Additive decomposition of perceptions data via conjoint analysis. *The Journal of Consumer Research, 5*(1), 58–65. doi:10.1086/208714

Green, P. E., & Krieger, A. M. (1985). Models and heuristics for product line selection. *Marketing Science, 4*(1), 1–19. doi:10.1287/mksc.4.1.1

Hauge, P.L. & Stauffer, L.A. (1993). ELK: A method for eliciting knowledge from customers. *Design and methodology, 53*, 73-81.

Helander, M. G., & Tham, M. P. (2003). Hedonomics-affective human factors design. *Ergonomics, 46*(13/14), 1269–1272. doi:10.1080/00140130310001610810

Jenkins, S. (1995). Modeling a perfect profile. *Marketing, 6*(July 13).

Jiao, J., & Tseng, M. M. (1999). A pragmatic approach to product costing based on standard time estimation. *International Journal of Operations & Production Management, 19*(7), 738–755. doi:10.1108/01443579910271692

Jiao, J., & Tseng, M. M. (2000). Understanding product family for mass customization by developing commonality indices. *Journal of Engineering Design, 11*(3), 225–243. doi:10.1080/095448200750021003

Jiao, J., & Tseng, M. M. (2004). Customizability analysis in design for mass customization. *Computer Aided Design, 36*(8), 745–757. doi:10.1016/j.cad.2003.09.012

Jiao, J., Zhang, L., & Pokharel, S. (2003). Process platform planning for mass customization. In *Proceedings of the 2nd Interdisciplinary World Congress on Mass Customization and Personalization,* Technical University, Munich [CD-ROM].

Jiao, J., Zhang, L., & Pokharel, S. (2005). Coordinating product and process variety for mass customized order fulfillment. *Production Planning and Control, 16*(6), 608–620. doi:10.1080/09537280500112181

Jiao, J., & Zhang, Y. (2005a). Product portfolio identification based on association rule mining. *Computer Aided Design, 37*(2), 149–172. doi:10.1016/j.cad.2004.05.006

Jiao, J., & Zhang, Y. (2005b). Product portfolio planning with customer-engineering interaction. *IIE Transactions, 37*(9), 801–814. doi:10.1080/07408170590917011

Jiao, J., Zhang, Y., & Helander, M. G. (2006). A Kansei mining system for affective design. *Expert Systems with Applications, 30*(4), 658–673. doi:10.1016/j.eswa.2005.07.020

Jordan, P. W. (2000). The four pleasures-A framework for pleasures in design, In P. W. Jordan (Ed.), *Proceedings of Conference on Pleasure Based Human Factors Design.* Groningen, The Netherlands: Philips Design.

JSKE. (2003). *Japan Society of Kansei engineering.* Available at http://www.jske.org/

Kano, N., Seraku, N., Takahashi, F., & Tsuji, S. (1984). Attractive quality and must-be quality, Hinshitsu. *The Japan Society for Quality Control, 14*(2), 39–48.

Karlsson, B., Aronsson, N., & Svensson, K. (2003). Using semantic environment description as a tool to evaluate car interiors. *Ergonomics, 46*(13/14), 1408–1422. doi:10.1080/0014013031 0001624905

Kaul, A., & Rao, V. R. (1995). Research for product positioning and design decisions: an integrative review. *International Journal of Research in Marketing, 12*, 293–320. doi:10.1016/0167-8116(94)00018-2

Khalid, H. M. (2001). Towards affective collaborative design. In M. J.Smith, G. Salvendy, D. Harris, & R. J.Koubek, *Usability Evaluation and Interface Design, Proceedings of HCI International 2001* (Vol. 1). Mahwah, NJ: Lawrence Erlbaum.

Kota, S., Sethuraman, K., & Miller, R. (2000). A metric for evaluating design commonality in product families. *ASME Journal of Mechanical Design, 122*(4), 403–410. doi:10.1115/1.1320820

Matsubara, Y., & Nagamachi, M. (1997). Hybrid Kansei engineering system and design support. *International Journal of Industrial Ergonomics, 19*(2), 81–92. doi:10.1016/S0169-8141(96)00005-4

McAdams, D. A., Stone, R. B., & Wood, K. L. (1999). Functional interdependence and product similarity based on customer needs. *Research in Engineering Design, 11*(1), 1–19. doi:10.1007/s001630050001

Meyer, M. H. (1997). Revitalize your product lines through continuous platform renewal. *Research Technology Management, 40*(2), 17–28.

Meyer, M. H., & Lehnerd, A. P. (1997). *The power of product platforms- building value and cost leadership.* New York: The Free Press.

Moore, W. L., Louviere, J. J., & Verma, R. (1999). Using conjoint analysis to help design product platforms. *Journal of Product Innovation Management, 16*(1), 27–39. doi:10.1016/S0737-6782(98)00034-4

Nadia, B.-B. (2001). Kansei mining: Identifying visual impressions as patterns in images. In *Proceedings of International Conference IFSA/NAFIPS*, Vancouver.

Nagamachi, M. (1989). *Kansei engineering*. Tokyo: Kaibundo Publisher.

Nagamachi, M. (1996). *Introduction of Kansei engineering*. Tokyo: Japan Standard Association.

Nair, S. K., Thakur, L. S., & Wen, K. (1995). Near optimal solutions for product line design and selection: beam search heuristics. *Management Science*, *41*, 767–785. doi:10.1287/mnsc.41.5.767

Sanderson, S. W. (1991). Cost models for evaluating virtual design strategies in multicycle product families. *Journal of Engineering and Technology Management*, *8*(3-4), 339–358. doi:10.1016/0923-4748(91)90017-L

Sedgwick, J., Henson, B., & Barnes, C. (2003). Designing pleasurable products and interfaces, In *Proceedings of the 2003 International conference on designing pleasurable products and interfaces*, Pittsburgh, 2003.

Siddique, Z. (2000). Common platform development: design for product variety, Ph.D. Dissertation, Georgia Institute of Technology, Atlanta, GA.

Stanton, N. (1998). *Human factors in consumer products*. London: Routledge.

Stauffer, L., & Morris, L. (1992). *A new program to enhance the development of product requirements*. Presented at NSF Design and Manufacturing Systems Conference, Atlanta, Georgia.

Taguchi, G. (1986). *Introduction to quality engineering: designing quality into products and processes*. Tokyo: Asian Productivity Organization.

Treleven, M., & Wacker, J. G. (1987). The sources, measurements, and managerial implications of process commonality. *Journal of Operations Management*, *7*, 11–25. doi:10.1016/0272-6963(87)90003-9

Tseng, M. M., & Du, X. H. (1998). Design by customers for mass customization products. *Annals of the CIRP*, *47*(1), 103–106. doi:10.1016/S0007-8506(07)62795-4

Tseng, M. M., & Jiao, J. (1996). Design for mass customization. *Annals of the CIRP*, *45*(1), 153–156. doi:10.1016/S0007-8506(07)63036-4

Tseng, M. M., & Jiao, J. (1998). Computer-aided requirement management for product definition: A methodology and implementation. *Concurrent Engineering: Research and Application*, *6*(2), 145–160. doi:10.1177/1063293X9800600205

Turksen, I. B., & Willson, I. A. (1992). Customer preferences models: fuzzy theory approach. In *Proceedings of the SPIE - International Society for Optical Engineering*, (pp.203-211), Boston, MA.

Urban, G. L., & Hauser, J. R. (1993). *Design and marketing of new products*. Englewood Cliffs, NJ: Prentice-Hall.

Wacker, J. G., & Treleven, M. (1986). Component part standardization: an analysis of commonality sources and indices. *Journal of Operations Management*, *6*, 219–244. doi:10.1016/0272-6963(86)90026-4

Yan, W., Chen, C.-H., & Khoo, L. P. (2002). An integrated approach to the elicitation of customer requirements for engineering design using picture sorts and fuzzy evaluation. *AIEDAM*, *16*(2), 59–71. doi:10.1017/S0890060402020061

Zeithaml, V. A. (1988). Consumer perceptions of price, quality, and value: a means-end model and synthesis of evidence. *Journal of Marketing*, *52*, 2–22. doi:10.2307/1251446

Chapter 11

Technological and Psychological Fundamentals of Psychological Customization Systems:
An Example of Emotionally Adapted Games

Timo Saari
Temple University, USA; Helsinki Institute for Information Technology, Finland; Helsinki School of Economics, Finland

Marko Turpeinen
The Royal Institute for Technology, Sweden; Helsinki Institute for Information Technology, Finland

Niklas Ravaja
Helsinki School of Economics, Finland

ABSTRACT

Psychological Customization systems can customize the experiences of users of various information technology-based products and services. In this context customization entails the intelligent automatic or semi-automatic adaptation of information per user profile, which may systematically manipulate transient psychological states of the user such as emotion or cognition. The chapter presents the psychological and technological fundamentals of Psychological Customization and discusses an example of an application area in emotionally adapted games.

INTRODUCTION

Mass Customization takes place when a product is designed to meet the needs of a particular customer (Duray et al, 2000). Typically the customer is involved in specifying the product for the provider. Such customization can be called *collaborative customization* (Pine, 1992).

Cosmetic customization refers to a product that is presented differently to different customers. This approach to customization is functional when customers use the product in similar ways and there is a need for the presentation to differ. The standard package of the product is then altered and packaged differently for each customer or customer segment. (Pine, 1992)

Transparent customization is an approach where a company provides unique products and services to

DOI: 10.4018/978-1-60566-260-2.ch011

a customer without explicitly telling them about such customization. This approach is useful when the customers preferences and needs are specific and easy to predict, or when customers can not or do not wish to state their needs repeatedly. In a way transparent customization is about observing the behavior of customers, inferring the customization needs and then providing the customized product to the customer. (Pine, 1992)

Adaptive customization implies that users can alter the product themselves based on one standard, but customizable product. This type of customization may be important when the customer wishes a product to perform in different ways in different circumstances or contexts. The customer interacts with a customizable product directly to mold and modify its properties, rather than interacting with the provider of the product. (Pine, 1992)

Adaptive customization is similar to *Adjustable Customization* (see Anderson, 2002). It is a reversible way to customize a product by electrical or mechanical modifications and adjustments. The possibilities for adjustments of the product can be defined by the customer or the provider of product or service. Adjustments can be realized in the form of configurations or discrete adjustments or they could be infinitely variable. For adjustment one can use for instance software-controlled configurations, or electronic switches and jumpers. (Anderson, 2002)

The rise of the experience economy (see Gilmore and Pine, 1997) has created a drive towards customized products and services that are characterized by unique and differentiated experiences. Assets in designing products that facilitate such experiences are not only the traditional utility, convenience, pricing and superior technologies but rather quality, feelings, values, meaning, identity and aesthetics for consumers (Nielsen, 2004).

It is experience, then, that is at the center of many customized and segmented experience-intensive products and services, such as video games, mobile services, rock concerts and tourist destinations. However, there has been little psychological research into the experiential aspects of customized products and services.

In this chapter we will discuss customization of products and services delivered via media- and communication technologies – *Psychological Customization*. Our approach to customization is adaptive, adjustable and partly transparent. We will present a system which allows the user to configure and adjust the product or service. Additionally, the product or service can be customized in a transparent manner without explicitly asking the user for continuous feedback for adjustment information. Our system is based on the customization of the *experiences* of users with various products and services when using media- and communication technologies.

The chapter first discusses the conceptual basis of Psychological Customization. Secondly, the chapter presents some empirical evidence for the feasibility of the concept of customizing experiences with products and services. We focus on emotion as a fundamental type of experience. Then a basic system design is presented for Psychological Customization systems. Finally, we will discuss emotionally adapted games as one promising application area of Psychological Customization along with an example of a psychophysiologically adapted game.

PSYCHOLOGICAL CUSTOMIZATION

Basic Concept

Our concept of technology is that of Media- and communication technology. It refers to information technology used to transmit and receive information. It takes into account the "media" aspects of information (such as TV, radio, newspapers, web pages, blogs, social networking sites) implying that people will process the information, learn from it, have experiences and that the information could have been designed as "media" in the

Table 1. Key variables in media and communications technologies influencing psychological effects. Adapted and modified fromSaari (2001).

Layer of technology	Factors influencing psychological effects
1. Hardware Type of hardware	-Display, interaction devices, peripheral devices -Large or small vs. human scale (including the visual screen) -Mobile or immobile -Close or far from body (intimate-personal-social distance)
2. Software (logical) Ways of interaction Via user interface	-Dialogical (lots of user control, lots of adaptive computer response, active exploration) -Narrative (lots of user control, little adaptive computer response, active exploration) -Multimodal interaction
Visual and functional form of user interface	-Way of presenting controls in an interface visually and functionally -Blended with the form of symbolical information
3. Content **A. Substance**	-The essence of the event described -Type of substance (factual/imaginary; genre, other) -Ways of emphasizing explicit, literal meanings to describe events by authors -Ways of emphasizing less explicit meanings, such as symbols or archetypes or aesthetic devices such as narrative techniques to describe events by authors
B. Form Modalities	-Text, video, audio, graphics, animation, etc.
Visual layout	-Ways of presenting various shapes, colors, font types, groupings and other relationships or expressive properties of visual representations -Ways of integrating modalities into the user interface
Structure	-Ways of presenting modalities, visual layout and other elements of form and their relationships over time -Linear and/or non-linear structure (sequential vs. parallel; narrative techniques, hypertextuality)

first place by the producers of the information. Communication technology refers to the fact that people interact with technologies and each other, surfing the web, navigating web pages, playing interactive videogames, writing text messages, taking and sharing pictures with mobile phones, and chatting in real-time messaging systems.

Media- and communication technologies may be considered as consisting of three layers (Benkler, 2000). At the bottom is a *physical* layer that includes the physical technological device and the connection channel that is used to transmit communication signals. In the middle is a *logical* layer that consists of the protocols and software that make the physical layer run. At the top is a *content* layer that consists of multimodal information. The content layer includes both the substance and the form of multimedia content (Benkler, 2000; Saari, 2001). Substance refers to the core message of the information. Form implies aesthetic and expressive ways of organizing the

substance, such as using different modalities and structures of information (Saari, 2001). These layers create a possibility to deconstruct different levels of possible triggers or stimuli in a product or service that may influence transient experiences, even though the layers may also interact with each other in producing the experiences. These layers are summarized in Table 1.

The three layers of technology and their subsets can be considered as "stimuli" to have a psychological impact on a user when using media- and communication technology. For instance, the substance (or core) of a message can impact the user to create interest, emotion, flow and learning. One can then customize the substance of information to produce experiential effects. However, in this chapter we focus more on the form of information and the software layer and their effects on user experience.

The reason for this focus is that the design space for customizing the form of information and the software layer is much larger than that of customizing the substance of information. It would also be difficult in real-life to think of producing a vast number of different messages or information to facilitate systematic experiential effects. Such labor would also have to be manual, stories made by humans, which would make it costly. By concentrating on the selected aspects of customization, we are able to suggest automatic or semi-automatic designs and formats for the same or different substance of information which could be applied widely in various application areas for different products and services.

It should be noted that it is very difficult to separate substance and form of information as they are both integral parts of what is being communicated via a media- and communication technology. We have taken the approach of isolating as much as possible the psychological influences of the form of information and the software layer in our experiments. Indeed, it has been shown that several aspects of form of information do produce psychological effects in interaction with a certain type of substance of information. Hence, it is possible to a degree separate these different layers of technology from each other at least from the point of view of user experience, or transient psychological effects. We are now able to define the basic concept of Psychological Customization.

Psychological Customization entails the customization of *transient* (i.e. short-term) *user experiences* (i.e. psychological effects) when interacting with media- and communication technologies. Experience-based customization means the automatic or semi-automatic adaptation of information per user, task and context in an intelligent way with information technology.

A subset of Psychological Customization is to vary the form of information (modality for instance) per user profile, task and context, which may systematically manipulate (approach, avoid, modify intensity, frequency and duration, create combinations, create links to behavior) different

psychological effects. Psychological effects can be considered transient states, such as emotion, mood, types of cognition, learning, flow, presence, involvement and enjoyment. (e.g. Saari, 2003a; Saari, 2003b; Saari and Turpeinen, 2004; Saari et al, 2004; Saari et al, 2005)

Different psychological states can be present in consciousness simultaneously, creating different types of combinations and interactions of experiences (e.g. positive emotion and efficient information processing, joy and anger). The interactions of experiences can also be sequential, as previous experiences (e.g. emotional state) can prime and influence following experiences (e.g. cognition, other emotions). Customizing experiences may also influence behavior as some psychological states carry rather direct motivational and action tendencies (e.g. emotion and behavior).

Psychological Customization works on the principle of target experiences which can be set by using the system either by providers of a service or by users. Target experiences are different types of transient psychological states that have varying durations, frequencies, intensities, combinations, and motivational and action tendencies as well as a linked stimulus class which facilitates a particular state. The system is set up to either approach or avoid a certain target experience within the other parameters of customization such as altering the intensity, duration or frequency of a certain effect or creating simultaneous combinations or links to probable behavior of different target experiences.

Psychological Customization can infer customer needs via user models and various feedback loops observing customer behavior and responses. Psychological Customization also provides different adaptations of presenting information to different customers based on the customer interacting with the configuration settings of the product or service.

The basic functioning of the system is based on a classic control theory model, the biocybernetic loop. It defines two kinds of control loops in complex and adaptive systems that can be established: negative (avoid an undesirable standard) and positive (approach a desirable standard) loops of feedback (e.g. Pope et al, 1995; Wiener, 1948). Target experiences are then controlled by this type of reasoning in the system based on real-time feedback from user responses and/or based on ready-made design-rule databases.

Psychological Customization can be used in various application areas such as Augmentation Systems (augmented and contextualized financial news), Notification Systems (alerts that mobilize a suitable amount of attention per task or context of use), Affective Computing (emotionally adapted games), Collaborative Filtering (group-focused information presentation), Persuasive Technology (advertising for persuasion, e-commerce persuasion), Computer Mediated Social Interaction Systems (collaborative work, social content creation templates), Context sensitive computing (adaptation of information per context and situation), and Messaging Systems (emotionally adapted mobile multimedia messaging and email). (Saari and Turpeinen, 2004; Saari et al, 2005)

There is also an application area for using Psychological Customization in game-like technology for enhanced learning (TEL) environments. Such learning environments are created on the basis of continuous psychophysiological recordings which infer emotional, motivational, and cognitive processes of the end-user, thereby enabling real-time adaptation of the design of the game. That is, the design of the learning game will be adapted to fit the emotional, motivational, and cognitive state of the user, thereby creating an optimal situation for learning.

In online advertising banners on a webpage are already changed in real-time per user profile when a web page loads. One could build systems that enable the creation of various emotional states that are suspect to driving up persuasiveness, recall and recognition of an ad (for a review of the use of Psychological Customization in online advertising and product information presentation, see Saari et al, 2004).

Emotional search is yet another possible application area of Psychological Customization. Using our system one could identify and measure the emotional search criteria people would most likely use or respond to. A Psychological Customization system running on top of a search system could also be beneficial in customizing the search results in a way which would be cognitively optimal or functional or even emotionally shaded in a desired manner. There may be a strong interaction with using Psychological Customization with search engines as they are the dominant customized advertising medium in the web currently.

Another promising area are mission-critical applications, such as remote operators of machinery, remote tactical operators in the military, or making of critical decisions, such as financial decision making. In these application areas the necessary hardware and software could be available more easily than in mainstream consumer applications. Also, the users would be more likely to accept invasive psychophysiological measurement in return for higher safety margins for the use of the system. A useful example is a Psychological Customization system that based on tracking the user gives out a warning notification that the user is about to make a critical decision in a very unfavorable emotional state, and that there is an increased risk that the decision being made is wrong.

Empirical Evidence

To make Psychological Customization functional the key is to be able to model and capture the systematic relationships of technology, user and psychological effects. If these relationships can be captured, measured, modeled and quantified to a sufficient degree, one may claim that it is possible to build various types of technologies that are based on the probable and systematic control (e.g. avoid or approach, fill parameters) of various target experiences.

There are several complexities, however, in this process, beyond the general difficulty of accessing the state of consciousness of a given person in the first place with suitable methods. For instance, psychological effects can be extremely transient or then rather persistent, ranging from milliseconds to tens of minutes. One solution is choosing a suitable temporal resolution of the particular psychological effect that the system responds to, such as a longer-lasting psychological effect like mood. Another complexity is that there may be any number of various psychological effects present in the user's consciousness at any given time. One may for instance be in a good mood, persuaded to buy a product, learning new information based on browsing product information. The solution here could be to focus on one "channel" of experience only as the dominant target area of the system, such as mood. Hence, a Psychological Customization system would not try to facilitate overly complex psychological states, rather it would concentrate on providing and guiding desired types of "streams" of user experiences and psychological effects. The other way around, if the customization system was capable enough, it could manage several simultaneous combinations of psychological states.

Obviously it is a highly challenging task to model and capture user's psychological effects, such as efficiency of cognition, emotional states and moods or depth of presence or involvement and even more difficult to do so in real-time. As the task of capturing and predicting user's psychological state in real time is highly complex, one possible realization for capturing user's psychological state is to have the user linked to a sufficient number of measurement channels of various i) psychophysiological signals (electroencephalography [EEG], facial electromyography [EMG], electro dermal activity [EDA], cardiovascular activity, other), ii) eye-based measures (eye blinks, pupil dilation, eye movements), iii) behavioral measures (response speed, response quality, voice pitch analysis etc.) and iv) identification of the facial expressions and emotional state of the user from a video image (a nonintrusive method). An index based on these signals then would verify to the system whether a desired psychological effect has been realized.

Another approach would be to conduct a large number of user studies on certain tasks and contexts with certain user groups, psychological profiles and content-form variations and measure various psychological effects as objectively as possible. Here, both subjective methods (questionnaires and interviews) and objective measures (psychophysiological measures, behavioral methods or eye-based methods) may be used as well interviews (for a review on the use of psychophysiological methods in media research, see Ravaja, 2004b). This would constitute a database of design-rules for automatic adaptations of information per user profile to create similar effects in highly similar situations with real-life applications. Naturally, a hybrid approach would combine all these methods for capturing and facilitating the user's likely psychological state.

Capturing context and short-term user behavior is a challenge. Computational approach to modeling context utilizes a mass of sensors that detect various signals in an environment. Intelligent software then massively computes from the signal flow significant events either directly or with the help of some simplifying rules and algorithms. Capturing user behavior in context is easier if the user is using an internet browser to buy an item, for instance. In this case behavior can be captured by the system as the user clicks his mouse to buy an item, navigates with certain patterns, and spends a certain amount of time on different web pages. To capture behavior in the physical context is more difficult. If the user is wandering around in a supermarket with a mobile phone that presented an advertising message to buy the items on sale on aisle number seven it may be difficult to verify this other than cross-reference his checkout bill with the displayed adverts inside the store. Naturally, video-based surveillance and positioning systems could also be used to infer user movement and action. However, using multiple tracking systems easily creates ethical problems with the privacy of the users.

Naturally, to claim that Psychological customization systems could exist in the first place requires explicit empirical proof beyond the general concept. Our focus here is to present evidence regarding the psychological impact of the form of information and the software layer as presented in Table 1.

Empirical, but indirect evidence found in literature supports the feasibility and validity of our idea: i) there are individual differences in cognitive processes such as attention, memory and language abilities and this has a considerable effect on computer-based performance (e.g. Egan, 1988); ii) individual differences in memory capacity have an effect on people's behavior in many types of activities (Vecchi et al, 2001); iii) different modalities, such as visual and auditory, may lead to different kinds of psychological influences and the valence of a preceding subliminal stimulus influences the subsequent evaluation of a person evaluated (Cuperfain and Clarke, 1985; Krosnick et al, 1992); iv) different ways of processing information influence learning and emotion of stimuli with certain modality (Riding and Rayner, 1998); v) emotional information increases the user's self-reported emotion (Lang et al, 1996); attention (physiological and self-reported) (Lang et al, 1995) and memory for mediated messages, particularly arousing messages (Lang, 1990; Lang et al, 1995; Lang et al, 1996) and vi) recognition and memory can be influenced or even enhanced by previous exposure to subliminal visual or auditory images of which the subjects are not consciously aware (Kihlström et al, 1992). Some of these effects are produced in interaction with individual differences, such as cognitive style, personality, age and gender.

More direct evidence of Psychological Customization comes from our own research. We have studied the influence of form factors of informa-tion presented on color screen PDA´s and mobile phones (such as news, games, messaging content and entertainment content) on psychological effects and have produced many interesting results. Typical experiments we have conducted on the influence of form of information on psychological effects have included such manipulations as animation and movement (for orienting response), fonts of text, layout of text, skin texture, background colors of text, user interface navigation element shapes (round vs. sharp), user interface layout directions, adding background music to reading text, use of subliminal affective priming in the user interface (emotionally loaded faces) and use of different modalities of information, for instance. We have used various methods, such as i) psychophysi-ological signals, ii) eye-based measures (eye blinks, pupil dilation, eye movements) and iii) behavioral measures (response speed, response quality, voice pitch analysis etc.).

In sum, the results from our own research to support the feasibility of Psychological Customi-zation from the point of view of the influence of form of information are the following: i) subliminal exposure to happy affective primes in connection with video messages presented on a small screen has several putatively positive influences (i.e., increased pleasure, perceived message trustworthiness, and memory) (Ravaja et al, 2004); ii) media messages can be modified in terms of audio characteristics (Kallinen and Ravaja, 2004; Ravaja and Kallinen, 2004) and the presence of image motion (Ravaja, 2004a) to meet the personality (as defined in terms of dispositional behavioral activation system sen-sitivity) of the user, thereby enhancing his or her attentional engagement, information processing, and enjoyment; iii) there are personality-related differences in people's aesthetic and emotional evaluations of different aspects (e.g., color, skin texture) of visual design (Laarni, 2003; Laarni et al, 2004 a; Laarni et al, 2004) and iv) user-changeable covers of mobile devices may also influence the emerging psychological effects (e.g. Laarni and Kojo, 2001).

While our results are not comprehensive nor cover the whole range of Psychological Customization we feel that the progress has been significant and that at least some possibilities of experience-based customization have been verified in our experiments. This suggests that the design-space exists and could be extended with more empirical research into this area.

Emotion and Mood as Target Experiences

There are many experiences that can be labeled "psychological effects" which can be present in consciousness at any given time when processing information and interacting with media- and communication technologies. Rather than listing all the possible candidates for the content of experience, we focus on emotion and mood as target experiences for Psychological Customization. This choice is made to reduce complexity and base our further discussions of "customizing experience" on a more concrete basis, as emotional responses to media- and communication technologies have been researched rather extensively. It should be noted that even though several emotions (as well as other types of psychological states) can co-exist at any given moment in consciousness we now focus our efforts on the single, "dominant" emotional states rather than their combinations with each other and other psychological states or their links to probable behavior to further reduce complexity.

Although various definitions of emotions have been proposed, the most general definition is that emotions are biologically based action dispositions that have an important role in the determination of behavior (e.g., Lang, 1995). It is generally agreed that emotions comprise three components: subjective experience (e.g., feeling joyous), expressive behavior (e.g., smiling), and physiological activation (e.g., sympathetic arousal; Scherer, 1993).

Motivational state or action tendency and cognitive processing have also been regarded as important constituents or determinants of emo-

tions. According to the motivational model of emotional organization, the different forms of emotional expression are driven by two separate but interactive motivational systems: (a) the behavioral inhibition system (BIS; or aversive system), prototypically expressed by behavioral escape, avoidance, and withdrawal and (b) the behavioral activation system (BAS; or appetitive system), prototypically expressed by behavioral approach and activation (Gray, 1991; Lang, 1995). The BIS and BAS underlie the experience of negative emotions and positive emotions, respectively (Gray, 1991), negative emotions including behavioral components of withdrawal and positive emotions a tendency to approach the source of the stimulus (Frijda, 1994).

There are two main competing views of emotions. Proponents of the basic distinct emotions argue that emotions, such as anger, fear, sadness, happiness, disgust, and surprise, are present from birth, have distinct adaptive value, and differ in important aspects, such as appraisal, antecedent events, behavioral response, physiology, etc. (e.g., Ekman, 1992). In contrast, according to a dimensional theory of emotion, emotions are fundamentally similar in most respects, differing only in terms of one or more dimensions. Proponents of the dimensional view have suggested that all emotions can be located in a two-dimensional space, as coordinates of valence and arousal (or bodily activation; e.g., Lang, 1995; Larsen & Diener, 1992). The valence dimension reflects the degree to which an affective experience is negative (unpleasant) or positive (pleasant). The arousal dimension indicates the level of activation associated with the emotional experience, and ranges from very excited or energized at one extreme to very calm or sleepy at the other.

Other theorists have, however, suggested that the two main, orthogonal dimensions of emotional experience are negative activation (NA) and positive activation (PA) that represent a 45° rotation of the valence and arousal axes (Watson & Tellegen, 1985; Watson et al, 1999). The NA axis extends from highly arousing negative emotion (e.g., fear) on one end to low-arousal positive emotion (e.g., pleasant relaxation) on the other, while the PA axis extends from highly arousing positive emotion (e.g., joy) to low-arousal negative emotion (e.g., depressed affect). The self-report NA and PA dimensions have been suggested to represent the subjective components of the BIS and BAS, respectively (e.g., Watson et al., 1999; see also Gray, 1991).

We adopt the latter definition of emotion. On the NA axis we call the high arousal negative emotion anxiety and stress while the low arousal emotion can be termed as pleasant relaxation. On the PA axis we see the high arousal emotion as joy and the low arousal emotion as depression.

We further differentiate between three types of categories of affective responses, as emotions, moods and sentiments (see Brave and Nass, 2003). Emotions are reactions to events, typically short-lived and directed at a specific target object. They carry specific motivational action tendencies such as the need to "fight or flee". Moods last longer and act as lenses or filters through which events and objects are appraised. They carry more vague motivational action tendencies. (Brave and Nass, 2003)

Moods are low intensity, diffuse feeling states, that usually do not have a clear antecedent (Forgas, 1992), and can be characterized as relatively unstable short-term intra-individual changes (Tellegen, 1985). As described by Lazarus (1991), a mood "is a transient reaction to specific encounters with the environment, one that comes and goes depending on particular conditions" (p. 47). Sentiments are more persistent, if not permanent attitudes of people they hold towards a certain class of objects (Brave and Nass, 2003). Emotions, moods and sentiments share similar attributes though and can be placed in the valence-arousal space according to the dimensional model of emotion.

Emotions are very dynamic as they are transient responses to various stimuli. The time dynamics of emotion mean that emotions can constantly change

with certain decay times and that there may be several different emotions in the consciousness at any given time if the amount of stimuli is high. This means that the measurement of emotion would best be based on a continuous, real-time measurement, such as psychophysiological methods.

Moods, on the other hand are combinatory indexes of several emotions that last longer (minutes to tens of minutes or even hours). Moods are more stable than emotions and are not dependent on continuously changing psychological "micro-stimuli" processed by the user. Mood may then be a more fruitful concept than emotion in guiding the research in real-life settings. However, depending on the case both can be used to describe, capture and conceptualize the content of an emotional experience.

In our studies we have successfully used both psychophysiological measurements and self-report to index emotional processes, also when playing computer games. In computer games, there is a dynamic flow of events and action, games potentially eliciting a multitude of different emotions varying across time. A serious limitation of prior game studies is that they have used tonic, rather than phasic, psychophysiological measures. Tonic measures (e.g., the mean physiological value during the game minus pre-game baseline) do not enable the examination of the varying emotions elicited by different instantaneous game events. Given that psychophysiological measurements can be performed continuously with a high temporal resolution, it is possible to quantify phasic responses to instantaneous game events (e.g., by comparing the local pre-event baseline to physiological activity immediately following event onset). (Ravaja et al, 2005)

It is then evident that psychophysiological measurement of emotional states when playing a computer game is both feasible and fruitful in providing an account of some aspects of the moment-to-moment experience of the user. Naturally, psychophysiology could be extended to function as a feedback loop into the gaming engine making real-time adaptation of the game relative to the emotional state or mood of the user a possibility.

PSYCHOLOGICAL CUSTOMIZATION SYSTEM DESIGN

System Architecture for Psychological Customization

It can be hypothesized that the selection and manipulation of substance of information takes place through the technologies of the various application areas of Psychological Customization. Underlying the application areas is a basic technology layer for customizing design. This implies for instance that within some limits one may automatically vary the form of information per a certain category of substance of information. The design space for Psychological Customization is formed in the interaction of a particular application area and the possibilities of the technical implementation of automated design variation.

One can also have various sensors to extract the state of the environment and users. Technologies such as eye-tracking, video capture of situations and contexts, microphones and psychophysiological recording can be used. Naturally, if these signals can be captured in a non-intrusive manner it would be optimal. Various data analysis and machine learning techniques can be used to construct the necessary models used in our system, such as regression analysis, Bayesian classifiers, nearest neighbor, decision trees and support vector machines (e.g. Carberry and de Rosis, 2008).

A general architecture for a Psychological Customization System is depicted in Figure 1. The *user* is engaged with media and communication technology, where the media stimuli are customized to the individual. The user profile data is collected, either at individual or group level, augmented by contextual profile information, by the *profiler* component. The profile information

is made available to the *adaptation controller* component. Individual's psychophysiological and behavioral responses as well as contextual information (e.g. behavior, situational factors, physical and social context) can be measured by various sensor devices and collected, combined and interpreted with the *analyzer* component. For example, the analyzer can, based on psychophysiological and contextual information inputs, interpret that the user is bored or joyful and alone at home. The analyzer transforms psychophysiological data into meaningful information of user's state and the results are fed to the adaptation controller. The media stimuli for the user is created by selecting content elements or reacting to user input in the *media and communication technology system*, which can be, for example, a Web content system, a messaging system or a game. The adaptation controller receives as input the profile data, the user state and the media and communication technology system state, based on which it transmits customization commands to impact the next state of the media and communication technology system. There is a feedback loop in the overall system as the user state impacts adaptations and media content stimuli in a real-time fashion. Another feedback loop exists between the adaptation controller and the media and communication technology system.

A more specific example of a Web-based Psychological Customization System is described in Figure 2. In this example, the real-time psychophysiological information or contextual information feed, and the associated analyzer component are not included. To achieve efficient customization, a database of design rules is needed to define the desired cognitive, emotional or other types of psychological effects for different types of profiles. Once these components are in place, customer relationship management and content management components can be extended to cover variations of form and substance of information on a web page based on profiles and design rules to create the desired psychological effects. This can be considered as an additional layer in a

Figure 1. General System Architecture for a Psychological Customization System

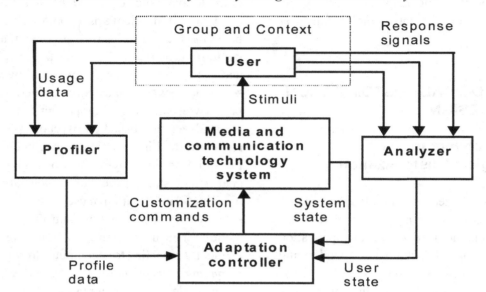

Web content system architecture. (e.g. Saari and Turpeinen, 2004)

The system architecture consists of databases, application servers, and presentation servers and three middleware layers: content management layer, customer relationship management layer, and Psychological Customization layer. The profiles of the users and the communities are available in the profile repository. The content management system is used to define and manage the content repositories. This is typically based on metadata descriptions of the content assets. The metadata of the content repositories is matched against the user and community profiles by the customer relationship management system. (Turpeinen and Saari, 2004)

The web-based Psychological Customization System acts as transformation middleware between the application servers, web service components, and databases. It provides an interface for designing desired psychological effects and target experiences for individual users or user groups. The Psychological Customization system performs the optimization of the form of

the content (or the software layer) as selected by the customer relationship management layer. This functionality can be implemented with content transformation rules that based on the design rules, produce the content presentation variation according to the profile of the user. After this optimization, the content is passed to the presentation layer. (Turpeinen and Saari, 2004)

To illustrate the functionality of this system we use online advertising as an example. When entering a webpage in a mood of pleasant relaxation, the user is displayed a certain type of advertising banner that increases the probability of recall and recognition of the product advertised perhaps also resulting in higher click-through rates for the ad. Hence, online advertising could be made more efficient by the profiling and modeling features of our system, such as the constant user modeling based on previous use of the system which could produce indirect predictions of the emotional state of the user at any given moment when using a website. The provider of the service could set the following Psychological Customization rule "for all people in a state of pleasant relaxation who

Figure 2. Web-based Psychological Customization System. Adapted and modified from Turpeinen and Saari, 2004.

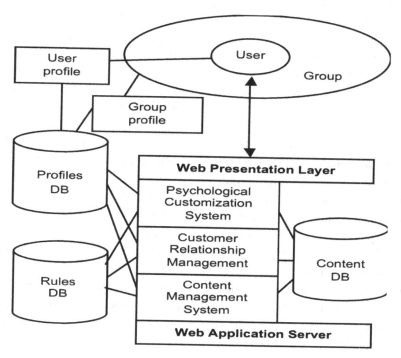

are about to enter webpage x, display advertising banner n", hence driving up the efficiency of the ad, perhaps also being able to price the ads differently based on the higher probability of impact on the users. (see Saari et al, 2004)

Naturally the critical issue with Psychological Customization is being able to adapt various layers and elements of media- and communication technologies (as presented in Table 1) to reliably manage various psychological effects. This is based on the ability to use the design rules to control the desired effects with the adaptation controller.

To build such a database would initially require a large enough population to be systematically tested with high-resolution research methods to infer how psychological effects are realized by various stimuli (a selected application area) in interaction with individual, situational and contextual differences. Once such a prototype database has been produced, it can be applied to a similar user population as a base of customization of similar stimuli. The stimulus-response relationships moderated by individual, situational and contextual differences are turned into various types of metadata structures to describe, abstract and compute these relationships.

However, such initial rules database probably requires much fine-tuning in real-life circumstances. For this purpose our system has components to follow the user's behavior and other type of feedback such as psychophysiological data and fine-tune the user profile accordingly using various types of machine learning techniques. This analyzer component tracks the responses of the user to using the system and infers the probability that a certain stimuli in the system has produced or avoided a certain psychological effect with certain parameters. Of course, multiple calculations of the probability of the origin of the effect can be conducted, including some external situation or circumstance that the system is not aware of, but also including something not initially present in the design rules database as stimuli. Hence, it would be possible to create "new" stimulus-response relationships and perhaps filter out erroneous ones when comparing a possible effect to the stimulus-response relationships in the original rules database. Such an approach also creates a richer metadata structure for the relationships in the rules database.

This constant updating of the design rules per user profile as the user uses a Psychological Customization system is the basis of achieving better hit-rates for the adaptations done with the system. It also creates the possibility for "emergent design-rules" for the system that have not necessarily been realized from the original database resulting from user tests. Such new rules could be any meaningful patterns or connections that seem to elicit specific types of experiences and behavior from the user. In this case our system really turns into a "user experience and behavior mining tool" and evolves beyond its original limits of the design rules database. The system could be used for tracking and modeling users at multiple levels when they are using various products and services.

Setting and Inferring Target Experiences

Psychological Customization systems naturally require explicit information on the type of target experience required for different users. These target experiences can in principle be anything from joy, pleasure, enjoyment and flow to ease of information processing. As some of these effects interact with various individual, contextual and situational differences, such factors are incorporated in our user model.

When using the system for the first time the user ideally goes through a brief questionnaire-based and behavioral testing phase which determines relevant individual differences, such as personality, cognitive style and temperament

but also task, context and other relevant factors. These are stored in the initial user profile that can be iterated as the user uses the system based on various feedback loops implemented in the system. Similarly, contextual and situational variables could be incorporated as models in the system via various types of environmental sensors or direct user feedback.

The experiential targets for a certain unit of analysis in a product or service (such as a webpage, a whole website, an advertisement or a gaming episode) can be set and modified by either the provider of the service or by the user. In the case of the provider of the service setting the target experience, our system includes a visualization and effect-setting tool. This tool enables the service provider to visualize and target various types of users and segments of users based on their user profiles. One can for instance pick out users that have a high threshold for stimuli (sensation seekers) and provide them with "busier" web pages in a website with more graphical elements, colors and movement available in the design. The provider basically selects the user populations and creates a rule "*when this population uses a certain element of information, always use these graphical elements in the background to create an effect of energetic enthusiasm*". The provider could also browse or search the possibilities of the system from the point of view of available experiential target effects. The query could go: "*show me the all users and all information in my databases with which I could set the experiential effect of the information to pleasant relaxation*". The system would then show possibilities of available user populations and parts or segments of a product or service where this effect could be realized and managed.

The user could also set desired experiential targets for the use of our system. For instance, the system could provide an "experience-knob" that would serve as a way for the user to input desired experiential states with accompanying parameters. To set such an experience-knob to a position for instance in emotional desired states, such as pleasant relaxation, the system would adapt the information to be consumed accordingly where possible. Alternatively, the user input could be used as query into the available information and services based on experiential criteria, much like in the case of the provider of the service setting the effect. The user could query all the "highly arousing" materials available on a website and get a list of possible web pages to visit to realize this effect. This type of approach would then constitute an "emotional search" into a content database that produces hits congruent with the user's desired target experience. The user can then plan and direct his consumption of information accordingly, perhaps when sad, seeking out for uplifting and comforting information (e.g. conducting mood management).

It should be noted that the Psychological Customization operates in a predictive manner, i.e. it predicts a given effect for a given user profile, stimuli, application area, task and context. Hence, our system is able to operate "before" real-time responses coming through our tracking program (e.g. analyzer component) enter the system to index whether a predicted psychological effect that has been set by the provider of the service or by the user has been realized.

Our system is then not strictly based on a real-time closed feedback loop that it responds to make the adaptations. This makes our system to a degree more independent from real-time feedback signals from the user's psychological states to infer adaptations, and also makes it more applicable in real-life where it would be inconvenient if an undesired psychological state signal enters the system and the system responds with some delay to the event. However, the system naturally works better with high-resolution real-time feedback loops that index the moment-to-moment experience of the user. The tracking programs can use this information to build the individual user profile to be more robust over time.

Figure 3 summarizes the key components and functionalities of a Psychological Customization

system in more detail. The Rules and scenarios database is the base for setting desired target experiences and their parameters by providers of the service or by users themselves. The database includes the systematized multidimensional relationships of user profile, stimulus (content), external factors (task, context, application area, other) and various psychological effects. A user profile is constantly updated based on feedback loops from the responses to the use of a Psychological Customization system. The content database includes the available content repository for the system, including the modularized layers of technology presented in Table 1. This modularized content database acts as stimuli to provide responses from the users. The Effect Tracker- program (embodiment of our analyzer component) follows the management of psychological effects by tracking the responses of the users via several feedback loops, such as psychophysiological indexes. The Effect Tracker software also gathers information on the external factors present in the moment of receiving and responding to stimuli, such as context, task, presence of other people, or other similar factors. The Effect Tracker integrates all levels of potential stimuli (the stimulus, external factors) to infer which of these may have produced the given psychological effect to which degree. This reasoning is stored in the new and adapted user model. If there are changes in the user model, this may also change the relationship of the elements in the Rules and scenarios database.

Figure 3 is a process model of how the setting and inferring of psychological effects takes place. When a user or a provider of service sets a desired psychological effect (Set Effect 1) at the time t0, this effect is based on the target experience setting- tool consulting with the Rules and scenarios database to seek for user profiles and content which could be matched to facilitate the desired psychological effect in a certain manner. The target experience set- tool then returns a possible cluster of users and content in available databases that realize the given target experience

Figure 3. Setting and inferring psychological effects with a Psychological Customization system

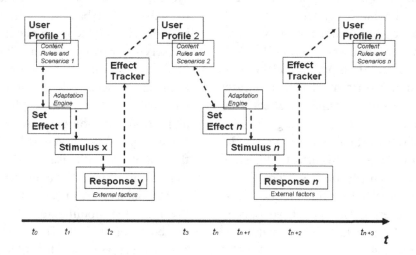

set with a high degree of probability. The effect set- tool bases its output on User Profile 1 and Rules and scenarios database 1.

At the time t1 a user is using the Psychological Customization system and is about to enter for instance a webpage where a psychological effect has been set (Set Effect 1) previously. The Adaptation Engine- software (an embodiment of our adaptation controller component) then parses a webpage with all the necessary layers of stimuli from the Content database. This creates Stimulus *x*. After the presentation of Stimulus *x* there is a Response *y* from the user at time t2. This response is captured by the Effect Tracker- program together with potential other sources of the target experience arising from external factors.

At time t3 the Effect Tracker creates a new User Profile 2 which may change the Rules and scenarios database, creating new relationships amongst elements, resulting in Rules and scenarios database 2. At time tn there is another target experience set for the same user of a Psychological Customization system (Set Effect *n*). When setting this effect, the new User profile 2 and Rules and scenarios 2 database are consulted. The Adapta-

tion Engine then creates a new Stimulus *n* at time tn+1. This creates Response *n* at time tn+2. The response is captured by the Effect Tracker- software which may change the user profile, resulting in User Profile n at time tn+3. There may also be changes resulting in a new Rules and scenarios database *n*. These are then the basis of setting new target experiences in a Psychological Customization system.

From the point of view of cost-and-benefit analysis of the management of target experiences, the hit-rate of success should be rather high. This means for instance that if the target experience for a certain webpage that is being consumed by a user is pleasant relaxation it should be realized with a high degree of probability. However, as our approach to the system is partly about transparent customization (where the customer is not at all times aware that the product or service is being customized), it may be possible that the cost of errors, such as producing a neutral state instead of pleasant relaxation, is not terribly high. It may be that in many cases the user does not even realize that an effect and its parameters have not been filled. This could significantly lessen the risk of errors. However, in the case of the user setting the dial of an "emotion knob" to excitement and then being bored may be different. Unfortunately, at this point we have not researched the psychological impact of the suggestion made by the user dialing in a target experience to the expectations and actual experiences resulting from using a particular media- and communication technology.

Yet another critical aspect of our system is the availability of ready-made or modular and easily configurable content repositories. Here we have focused on the form of information, or modalities, structures and layouts that could be modified without much changing the substance of information. Web pages and websites are one possible product category that could be customized using our system. For instance, the same "information" for a news story could be available as text, video or audio in the database and these could be varied. Similarly, there could be several types of skins or layout modifications with background patterns and colors for a single website to be adapted to different users with the same information. Different types of adaptation engines could be built for these purposes using our system.

Emotionally Adapted Games

Gaming Templates and Emotion

Emotionally adapted games are one promising application area of Psychological Customization. We aim to sketch an approach to automatically adapt the game based on the principles of Psychological Customization and preset experiential targets. Hence, game developers would not craft the storylines or gaming events by hand for a specific emotional target experience. Rather, the game AI engine would use a set of design rules to establish modifications of gaming structures with existing elements of the game that would fill the target experience and its parameters. In terms of economics of game development there would not necessarily be a dramatic expense in

integrating our system into the process of game design beyond the initial investment into our system and its integration with existing gaming engines and platforms.

There are several applications one can think of in the single-player game market for our system. It is feasible to think that at least driving games, first person shooters, action-adventure games and level-playing games could benefit from the use of a Psychological Customization system. In multiplayer games our system would also be valuable in several ways but we focus only on single player games within this article.

Consequently, we will now present emotionally adapted gaming more in depth to illuminate the possible uses of our system. First, we discuss the role of emotions in games. Then we present the idea of gaming templates which are episodic, short, narrative structures within the game. After this, the potential design space for emotional adaptation regards emotions is discussed. We will then define emotionally adapted games more explicitly and present a system design for such games. Finally, an example of a psychophysiologically adapted game is presented.

Apparently, emotions or emotion-related variables (e.g., competitiveness) play a critical role also in gaming behavior (Grodal, 2000; Vorderer et al, 2003). People seek, and are eager to pay for, games that elicit positive emotional experiences and enjoyment; however, an enjoyable game may not elicit only positive emotions but possibly also negative ones (e.g., anger, fear). Thus, one of the major goals for video game designers is to elicit optimal emotional responses or response patterns. Prior psychological game studies have focused on negatively valenced emotions elicited by video games in trying to unravel their potential adverse effects. Ballard and Weist (1996) and Anderson and Dill (2000) found that a violent video game elicited hostile affect, while three other studies showed virtually no effect (Nelson & Carlson, 1985; Calvert & Tan, 1994).

How then to link emotions in games and basic

elements of games? One obvious answer is to look at the narrative element in games in which the other possible emotionally significant elements of games reside. In fact, games have often been researched from the point of view of narrative, consisting of a dramaturgical structure focused on crisis and the resolution (Meyer, 1995). However, it may be that gaming is not easily understood as a linear narrative. For instance, a gamer may be more interested in collecting points and more powers for his character inside the game and mere survival between different levels of the game than in moving along a story line coherently towards a climax (Lankoski, 2003).

Similarly, it has been argued that the participatory aspect of gaming is the key to the experience of gaming (Darley, 2000). It may be stated that the algorithm of the game is another key source of experiencing a game (Manovich, 2001). This implies that as the player learns the hidden rules and logic behind the game and is therefore successful in playing it, a state of satisfaction may arise. Further, it is evident that the skills of the gamer vs. the challenges presented in the game should be in balance (Järvinen et al, 2002). If a game is too difficult or too easy to play, it may not be involving, but rather frustrating or boring. Another difference between narrative and games is that the tensions in narrative are dependent on the irreversibility of the consequences of the events of the narrative (Poole, 2000).

Despite the differences between traditional narratives and games, many similarities exist. One way to look at this is to observe the narrative schema as a basic way of organizing memories (see Mandler, 1984). A narrative schema in storytelling may have the following structure: i) introduction of a setting and key characters, ii) explanation of the current state of affairs or the situation at hand, iii) initiating event leading to a motivation to act or change the state of affairs, iv) emotional response of the protagonist and a goal for acting or changing the state of affairs, v) the difficulty experienced by the protagonist while perform-

ing actions to change the state of affairs and vi) the outcome of the action of the protagonist, i.e. success or failure in changing the state of affairs (Branigan, 1992).

This implies that i) the role of the characters in the game is of key importance, including the role and point of view of the player and his character or role and ii) it is possible to create emotional reactions and motivation in the player to act in a desired manner by introducing events in a certain manner, or by offering a chance to succeed in attaining a goal. Hence, from the point of view of emotions, manipulating the events within a particular sequence of the game as well as introducing the situation and creating basic tensions and motivations as a basis for the task of the user in the game are important. (e.g. Saari et al, 2005)

Outside narrative elements of a game, also the factors related to the presentation of the substance of the game or the form of the game, such as visual representations of the gaming events, amount and pace of image motion, audio effects and background music, and the level of interactivity offered to the player, are important from the point of view of emotion. (Saari et al, 2005)

A basic approach to an element to be adapted inside a game is a psychologically validated template that is embedded inside the game to create a particular psychological effect. A broad view of templates may be that the whole game consists of a database of psychologically validated templates that are dynamically presented by the gaming engine in sequences during gameplay. A limited view entails that a smaller collection of templates is used. The element of psychological evaluation means that the selected psychological influence (such an emotional response) of the template on a particular type of user is sufficiently well predictable. These psychologically evaluated templates may consist of i) manipulating the substance of a game, such as story line (initiating events, new characters etc.) and manipulating the situations specifically related to the character of the player (such as putting the character into sudden and

Table 2. Technological possibilities of Psychological Customization in emotionally adapted gaming. Adapted and modified from Saari et al, 2005

Layer of Technology	Emotionally Adapted Gaming Templates
1. Physical	-Mobile device: user changeable covers in colors and shapes that facilitate desired emotion -PC, console, display, peripherals: colors and shapes that facilitate desired emotions
2. Software (logical)	-The user interface elements (color, forms, shapes, directions of navigation buttons etc.) may be varied in real-time per user to create various emotions and ease of perceptual processing -Emotion visualization, i.e. making player's emotional state transparent for example through the avatar, which can usable for example in social online gaming. -Audio channel may be used to create emotional effects (using audio input/output sound, varying pitch, tone, background music, audio effects etc.) -Interaction modalities may be adapted to suit the nature of the task
3. Content A. Substance	-The genre of the game or type of game should be taken into account (first person shooter, simulation game, level playing game, other) -Emotionally engaging story lines and episodes and events may be used to facilitate certain emotions -The role of the user in the story can be varied to create emotional reactions -Adding subliminal extra content to create desired emotions while playing
B. Form Modality	-Modality may be matched to cognitive style or pre-existing mood of the receiver to create ease of processing -Background music, audio effects or ringing tones may be used as a separate modality to facilitate desired emotions and moods
Visual presentation	-Emotionally evaluated and positioned layout designs and templates for (colors, shapes and textures) may be utilized per type of user segment
Structure -linear/non-linear	-Using emotionally evaluated and positioned narrative templates and gaming episode structures for creating emotionally engaging story structures and varying sub-elements of the narrative and form within the template to create different emotional emphasis of the events unfolding (related to substance of content) -Game-world mechanics, such as gravitation and lighting, can be adapted, also in real-time -Using different temporal resolutions, such as fast or slow pace of events that may influence arousal

dangerous situations inside the game) and ii) manipulating the form or way of presentation of the game (such as visual elements, shapes, colors, types of objects, sound effects, background music, level of interactivity and feedback etc.). The difficulty level of the game may also be continuously automatically be adjusted, thereby keeping the skills and challenges in balance, which results in a maintenance of an optimal emotional experience and possibly also a flow-state. (Saari et al, 2005)

The possibilities for manipulating the form of the game inside a gaming episode or a meta-narrative are presented in Table 2.

Emotional Adaptation Space for Games

Why and when then to adapt emotion in gaming on the basis of avoiding or approaching a specific emotional state? First, there are the transient basic emotional effects of games that are dependent of the phase of the game or some specific events. These are emotions such as happiness, satisfaction, sadness, dissatisfaction, anger, aggression, fear and anxiousness. These emotions are the basis of narrative experiences, i.e. being afraid of the enemy in a shooting game, feeling aggression and wishing to destroy the enemy and feeling satisfaction, even happiness, when the enemy has been destroyed. Emotional regulation systems in these instances most naturally may focus on manipulating the event structures, such as characters, their roles, events that take place and other features of the narrative gaming experience. (Saari et al, 2005)

Second, there are possibilities for emotional management, especially in the case of managing arousal, alertness and excitation. Also, one may wish to manage negative emotions, such as sadness, dissatisfaction, disappointment, anger, aggression, fear and anxiousness. The case for managing these emotions is twofold. On the one hand, one may see that these emotions could be eliminated altogether in the gaming experience. This can happen via either eliminating, if possible, the emergence of such an emotion in the game. For example, one can make a deliberately happy game with level-playing monkeys in a far away island throwing barrels at obstacles and gathering points. This would include minimum negative emotions. Or, in a game where negative emotion is a basic part of the game, one may wish to limit the intensity, duration or frequency of the emotions via manipulating gaming events and gaming elements so that sadness or fear are at their minimum levels, or that gaming events do not lead to sadness at all. (Saari et al, 2005)

Similarly, managing level of arousal or the intensity, duration and frequency of select negative emotions may be quite feasible in the case of children as a form of parental control. On the other hand, one may wish to maximize arousal, alertness and excitation, perhaps even anger, fear and aggression for hardcore gamers.

Third, there are possibilities related to the avoidance of certain types of emotions that are typically indicative of a poor gaming experience. Inactivity, idleness, passivity, tiredness, boredom, dullness, helplessness as well as a totally neutral experience may be indicating that there is some fundamental problem in the user-game interaction. This could be due to poor gaming skills of the user vs. the difficult challenges of the game or some other factors, such as the user is stuck in an adventure game for too long and can not proceed without finding a magic key to enter the next level or so. When a gaming engine detects these emo-

tions in the user, it may adapt its behavior to offer the user more choices of selecting the difficulty level of the game or offer the user some clues as to how to go forward in the game. The game can also adapt its level of difficulty to the player's skill level. (e.g. Saari et al, 2005)

Fourth, it is also possible to create different combinations of emotional states (satisfied and angry) or emotional states and other psychological states (pleasant relaxation and efficient information processing) or emotional states and behavior (using specific motivational and action tendencies).

All of these possibilities may be relevant. However, the elimination or minimization of certain emotions may be specifically feasible in the case of indicated overly poor gaming experience in which the game may adapt its behavior to assist the user. It should be noted that events in games may change quickly and produce complex situations and hence complex emotions that may change rapidly. Consequently, one should better integrate these approaches into the genre or type of the game, such as driving simulator, first person shooter, sports game such as golf, or an adventure game, or a level-playing game for children. (Saari et al, 2005)

In Table 3 the three first possibilities of emotional regulation and adaptation in games are summarized. The fourth possibility of combinations of different states and behavior is left out to reduce complexity. The possibilities are listed per cell. A plus indicates possibilities to approach a given emotional state whereas a minus indicates possibilities to avoid or eliminate a given emotional state from the gameplay experience. Of course, Table 3 and the possibilities are relative to a game genre, gameplay task, circumstance or situation within a given game. The table should then be taken as a generic example of the possibilities of adapting emotions within gameplay at the more general level.

A brief example of meaningful emotional adaptations can be thought of when playing a driving

Table 3. A dimensional approach to emotionally adapted gaming. Adapted and modified from Saari et al, 2005.

	Low arousal	Neutral arousal	High arousal
Positive Valence	*Pleasant relaxation, calmness* +Useful in relaxation and concentration games with peaceful atmosphere +Short break in an adventure game, after having achieved a goal, a "break to breathe" and experience some reward -Little use in aggressive games, could then perhaps be avoided in such games	*Happiness, satisfaction* +When reaching a goal in a game this is elementary and can be motivating to play the game further -Perhaps not feasible to avoid altogether	*Energetic, peppy, joyfulness, enthusiasm* +Important in many games, related to success in the game or one's gaming skills, a motivating factor to play further +Can indicate a successful gaming session -Perhaps not feasible to avoid altogether
Neutral valence	*Inactivity, idleness, passivity* +Perhaps not feasible to set as an approachable state, unless the goal of the game is too passivate the person -Perhaps should be avoided in most games	*Neutral experience* +Not very feasible to approach -Perhaps feasible to avoid this state as it may indicate disinterest in the game	*Arousal, alertness, excitation* +In many games the gaming challenge and events could lead to this state +One could also maximize arousal in driving games, adventures or violent games if one wishes +Arousal management could be feasible without taking into account the valence dimension
Negative valence	*Tiredness, boredom, dullness, helplessness, depression* +Perhaps not feasible to set as an approachable state -Perhaps should be avoided in most games as these may be indicators of poor gaming skills vs. the challenge of the game, a boring game or some other fundamentally distracting factors to the gaming experience	*Sadness, dissatisfaction, disappointment* +These are basic elements of experience in many games, for instance, when not succeeding to reach a goal -May also indicate poor gaming skills and hence could be avoided	*Anger, aggression, fear, anxiousness, stress* +In many games this state is a basic element of experience in the game +One could also maximize aggression in a game -Totally avoiding or controlling aggression in a game, for instance for children or those wishing to have a less aggressive gaming experience

simulator game. The game is set to be arousing and exciting for the player. If the Psychological Customization system detects inactivity or boredom it may choose to investigate whether this is due to an overly easy or overly difficult situation for the player based on previous patterns of gameplay of the user. Once this is completed the game AI can adopt accordingly, for instance making the game more challenging by adding obstacles to the driving course or by reducing traction of the tires or by changing the background music or visuals of the game to be more arousing and exciting. This would result in increased arousal of the player which would be verified by the Psychological Customization system.

In an adventure fantasy game one can think of an emotionally more complex situation where the player is detected to be angry and anxious even though the game does not explicitly facilitate these states in the situation the player is in. The game AI, with the help of a Psychological Customization system, could adopt a next scenario of the task of the player, whose character is a knight, to lessen this stage of anxiousness within the framework story of the game. The knight is approached by another character who asks for his help in defending a village nearby from dragons. The game could alter the character asking the favor to be a small child instead of an adult warrior, leading to more compassion towards the character's needs. The whole scenario of the knight defending the village could be made just a little bit less challenging that it could be (but not to the point of being overly easy and boring). Then it would be a little easier for the knight (e.g. player's character) to save the village. The game AI could also add a scene where, after having defeated the dragons successfully, the knight is surrounded by many families with children from the village who all want to thank the knight for saving them. The player would then experience compassion for the villagers, a moderate level of arousal when fighting off the dragons and a joy after having defeated the dragons added by satisfaction or happiness when receiving thanks from the villagers. These experiences could counter the initial angry and anxious states of the user.

Naturally, our examples are limited but they offer a brief peek into what kind of adaptations are possible using existing game engines with a Psychological Customization system for emotional adaptation purposes. In both examples the game AI and our system are trying to manage a certain fine balance between what they reason (based on preprogrammed data on target experiences and user profiles and different algorithms) are optimal psychological states relative to the task of the user. Several components of the game can be adopted to manage target experiences in meaningful ways and the Psychological Customization system can also create emergent design-rules for such management tactics for the game AI based on the feedback loops constantly enriching the player's user profile.

System Design for Emotionally Adapted Games

We will now present a basic system schematic of an emotionally adapted game in Figure 4. The process of a typical gaming engine is depicted on the left-hand side of the diagram. The engine continuously monitors user input, which is typically collected using a keyboard, a joystick, or other game controllers. This input data is then processed and transferred to the layer that handles the game's internal logical state, and the user input may influence the game state. After the logical state of the

game is defined the system alters the actions of the synthetic agents in the game world. For example, these include the actions of computer-controlled non-player characters. The complexity of this AI layer varies greatly depending on the game. Based on the game state and the determined actions of the synthetic agents, the physics engine determines the kinetic movements of different objects within the world. Finally, the game world is synthesized for the player by rendering the graphical elements and producing and controlling the audio elements within the game. (see Saari et al, 2005)

The proposed emotional regulation can be implemented as a middleware system that runs parallel to the actual game engine. The input processing layer of the game engine can receive a data flow of captured and pre-processed sensor data. The real-time signal processing may consist of different forms of amplifying, filtering and feature selection on the psychophysiological signals. This data flow may directly influence the state of the game world, or it can be used by the emotional regulation sub-module of the emotion feedback engine. This module consists of the rules of emotional balancing for different player profile types and gamer-related explicitly set preferences controlled by the "emotion knob". In addition, it contains a collection of design rules for narrative constructions and game object presentation within the game world. The emotional regulation module also receives input from the game engine's logical layer to make selections related to desired emotional balance and narrative structures within the game. (Saari et al, 2005)

The outputs of emotional regulation engine may then be applied to various different levels of the actions of the game engine: i) the logical state of the world may be re-directed, ii) the actions of the synthetic agents may be controlled, iii) the kinetics of the game may be altered and iv) the rendering of the game world may be changed. First two options are more relevant to high-level and story-related structures of the game, whereas the last two are more directly related to the selec-

Figure 4. Emotional adaptation system design for games. Adapted from Saari et al, 2005.

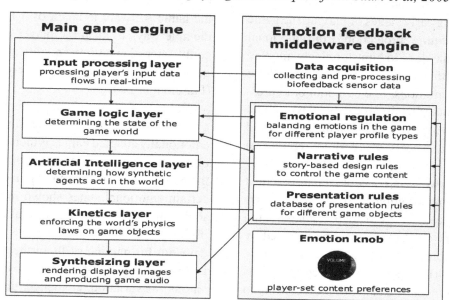

tion of presentation of objects within the virtual environment. (e.g. Saari et al, 2005)

The system in Figure 4 follows the logic of Figure 3 of the process model of Psychological Customization. With our system design for games it is possible for the game designer as well for the user to set desired emotional targets to be approached or avoided. The system uses both positive and negative feedback loops to determine the ideal adaptations case-by-case for gameplay for various emotional effects to be realized and managed.

The question arises, what type of automated reasoning needs to take place within a Psychological Customization system for emotionally adapted gaming? To answer this we take examples from biofeedback gaming where various biosignals (in essence psychophysiological signals discussed above) are used as an input to both infer the psychological state of the user and influence gaming events and gaming controls (e.g. Kuikkaniemi et al., 2008; Fairclough, 2007). The focus of biofeedback games is to create a psychophysiological representation of the user and use this

model as a means to adopt the game. The model also contains the idea of desirable and undesirable zones related to gameplay. That is, some zones of the model need to be avoided while others can be maximized. (e.g. Fairclough, 2007)

The biocybernetic loop can be used for reasoning inside the game engine to determine the adaptations of the game. The negative control loop may provide more stability in the system, such as a psychophysiologically adapted computer game. In previous research it has been shown that this control loop allows the user to avoid the undesirable emotional effects of game playing (see Freeman, 1999). This type of adaptation of the game avoids emotional states associated with sudden transition and instability. However, one wonders how fruitful this type of adaptation really is, as gameplay is also about surprising events one must react to, a constant struggle between what one is capable of and the challenges in the game.

The positive control loop leans towards instability as the player-game adaptation develops towards higher levels of desirable performance. However, both types of control loops could be incorporated in emotionally adapted gaming. For instance, during early stages of playing the game a novice may require "protection" from emotional states which may lead to him stopping gameplay altogether. In this sense it would be sensible to avoid certain emotions, like boredom or depression. On the other hand, an expert player could prefer a positive control loop that maximizes and stretches some aspects of "desired" emotional states, such as joy, excitation or relaxation.

There is however a conceptual and practical caveat in playing a computer game that uses psychophysiological signals to adapt gameplay: the emotional state has to occur and be detected by the system before the system can react to the emotional state with negative or positive control loops or some other means of adaptation. According to Fairclough (2007) one solution to this would be to acquire large amounts of psychophysiological data per user included in the user model and then use this data in a predictive sense. This would enable the game to respond to probable future events rather than past events.

To give an example of such a psychophysiologically adapted game in real-life one can imagine a player who has played a game for long enough to evolve from a novice to an expert. As a novice the player noticed and was aware of how the game adapted to his psychophysiological signals with a negative control loop. When the player started performing better in the game and turned into an expert the game software had to switch between negative and positive control loops to provide challenge for the more experienced player. The player then has to adapt his behavior accordingly as the game has also changed, partly based on his psychophysiological user model and input. In this sense the player and the game software may enter a co-evolving spiral where they are mutually interdependent on each other's behavior (see Kelly, 1994).

If one follows the example and evaluates the "value" of a psychophysiologically adapted game it may be stated that the value is determined by

the co-evolutionary potential, or the capacity of the game software to adapt over time in unpredictable ways to keep the player engaged. This could determine both the quality and quantity of game play experience for a player of such a game. (Fairclough, 2007)

Based on the example of psychophysiological gaming the key of making sensible and usable emotionally adapted games is then in the richness of the co-evolutionary potential of the player and the game. It may not be enough merely to avoid certain emotional states shown in Table 3 as it soon will become boring or too easy for an expert player. Once the player turns into an expert and develops his gaming skills further the challenge is then in the area of how to create a sufficient amount of variation, challenge, unpredictability and instability for the expert player via a feedback loop from the user's emotional states to the game adoption engine.

One may think of at least two sources of such emotional adaptation for the expert player. First source are the intentions or pre-set effects of the game designer. These are the psychological effects set by the designer of the game for different player profiles, similarly to setting psychological effects explained in Figure 3. These effects could be set to function based both on the negative and positive feedback loops. The designer of the game could set the positive feedback loops based on multiple levels of demonstrated expertise found in the player's user profile. Of course, depending on how many effects the game designer is able or wishes to set, these may act as a source of richness and variation of gameplay and the co-evolution of the player and the game.

Second source of variation and richness is the player himself. By providing a control-knob for the player to select desired target emotion states (see Table 3) and set their intensities (high-low), frequencies (often-seldom), or combinations (joy-anger) may create unexpected and surprising gameplay sessions as the game software handles and processes these inputs and sets them as targets for the game based on both the negative and positive control loops.

Additionally, the control-knob may be used for other selections regarding the game not strictly on emotional basis. The control knob could offer the possibility of more or less of "sex and violence", for instance. Or it could offer any other meaningful category of the "style" or even genre of the game to be changed, such as combining humorous story lines or characters with a die-hard first person shooter game to create interesting mixes of gameplay. Naturally, the system could capture the emotional effects of these selections and turn them into emergent design-rules based on how a user responds to the new created stimuli collections. These stimuli collections could then in turn be labeled more systematically to respond to categories of emotional states by the software. The re-categorizations of various aspects of stimuli can then even be incorporated back into possible classes of objects/events or emotional states the user could select with a control knob as an input into the gaming system.

In many games there are already sliders and controls for the amount of graphic violence and enemy AI intelligence level. Some of these controls indirectly infer emotional tones such as less violence indicating less arousal or more enemy AI indicating more arousal via more challenging gameplay. Our emotion knob could be used in conjunction with widely used types of game adaptation sliders set by users. The knob does not literally have to be a knob but could be visualized and implemented in the sliders in various ways to make it intuitive and integrated within typical gaming preference input tools. The advantage of the emotion control knob as we have discussed it is that it is based on an explicit relationship of the settings of the knob, the stimuli and adaptations presented in the game and emotional responses. Hence, many indirectly emotional existing sliders such as the amount of graphic violence could perhaps be grouped under the more explicit emotional tuning category using the concept of

the emotion control knob. Of course, empirically founded design-rules for integrating existing sliders in games for this purpose need to be created. Such rules can also be created "on the fly" using our approach to generate emergent design-rules with our system.

Based on our suggestions, an emotionally adapted game could provide more extended possibilities for the co-evolution of the game and the player and hence provide more value in terms of the experiential quality as well as frequency and duration of gameplay, than a game adapting to the player with a real-time psychophysiological signal only.

Psychophysiologically Adaptive First-Person Shooter Game

We are now able to explicitly define an emotionally adaptive game after our elaborations. An emotionally adaptive game is a game built based on a Psychological Customization system. Such a game includes a set of target experiences, such as emotional states or moods, as well as other relevant psychological states (e.g. learning, flow, presence), set by the designer of the game to be realized with select gaming templates consisting of for instance various events, circumstances, storylines, characters and objects relative to the user profile of the player. Target emotional and other psychological states can also be set by the player by using specially made emotion-control knobs that enable the manipulation of types, intensities, frequencies, durations, combinations and other relevant parameters of emotional and other psychological states the player wishes to emphasize during a gameplay session.

An emotionally adaptive game tracks the user's emotional and other relevant psychological responses (or the realization of the parameters of set psychological states) with different methods of measurement, such as psychophysiological signals and gaming behavior modeling (joystick movements, type of gameplay, amount of use of controls, amount of movement, performance, for example). The game is emotionally adaptive in the sense that it aims to realize previously set emotional state targets and their parameters with maximum probability. The emotional state targets can be realized with both negative (avoid a certain emotional state) and positive (approach a certain emotional state) feedback loops, or by using other methods of optimization.

The adaptations in the game may take place at all three levels of media- and communication technology and their subcomponents: hardware layer, software/logical layer (user interface, way of interaction) and the information layer (substance of information, form of information: modality, visual layout, structure). An adaptation is a (meaningful) change in the state of the game which acts as a trigger or stimuli for an emotional response from the player. Preset rules of what type of object or event likely causes a certain emotional state in a certain user can also emerge from the use of the system. These emergent design-rules can be based on machine learning techniques that mine the user's behavior in the game and find patterns that are emotionally significant as evident from the psychophysiological or other signals of the user. Such emergent design-rules can be input back into the system as new classes of potential stimuli to elicit emotional responses to be explicitly selected by the user for manipulation with a control-knob. Emergent design-rules can also function as important information of game design success and give ideas for new directions of design to the designers of the game in the case that the company behind the game could access a user's profile and game log. An emotionally adaptive game evolves over time as it learns more from the player and is able to provide more challenging, varied and rich gameplay experiences over longer periods of time than a traditional computer game.

An emotionally adaptive game can also be a psychophysiologically adaptive game that merely responds to a real-time psychophysiological signal to influence gameplay.

Indeed, to implement and evaluate some of the ideas presented, we have explored novel technical solutions and tested different kinds of psychophysiological adaptations that can be implemented. EMOShooter is a prototype platform for psychophysiologically adaptive 3D first-person shooter (FPS) gaming. It is built on top of open-source graphics engine (OGRE 3D) and physics engine (ODE). In this experimental platform we have the possibility to modify practically any game world element, player avatar, avatar outlook, or control parameter.

EMOShooter is a simple psychophysiologically adaptive game and hence a part of our emotionally adapted games definition. The system uses psychophysiological signals to influence the ease of use of the controls of the game hence affecting gameplay difficulty and gameplay experience. The system does not have target experiences systematically implemented at this moment nor does it have an emotion knob to tune the system. However, the EMOShooter game is a valuable example of one type of emotionally adapted games in demonstrating one feasible link between real-time emotional state measurement with psychophysiology and the gameplay.

The goal of the EMOShooter game is to kill cube-like enemies either with sniper or machine gun. We have been testing various adaptation patterns with EMOShooter by primarily EDA and respiration as psychophysiological signals in our adaptive feedback system regards how these signals can be meaningfully connected to the actual gameplay via adapting game controls.

Adaptation of game controls includes changes in rate of fire, recoil, movement speed and shaking. If a player is aroused this will be reflected in EDA and respiration signals which in turn will make rate of fire and movement slower and will make the aim shaky. Hence, for a highly aroused player the game becomes more difficult. For a mildly aroused or calm player the controls become more efficient and easy to use hence facilitating performance at gameplay. Game events are mostly arousing. The amount of cubes to shoot, their approach and firing on the user, the amount of health left after being hit and the sound effects all are geared to drive up arousal in the game. The players task is to be calm as indexed by psychophysiological signals to be able to operate the controls more efficiently.

In our tests of the game we have collected also EMG data to infer the valence dimension of emotion during gameplay. In addition to the psychophysiological signals we have collected data from the players using behavioral game logging, video capture, interviews and questionnaires. During our tests we noticed that proper calibration and base lining of the psychophysiological signals is very important for the adaptations to work. We also noticed that having robust stimuli in the game is crucial for the adaptations to work because in many cases the stimulus functioned as a trigger in adaptation. The psychophysiological signals used are calibrated by using dynamic range (basically a variation of dynamic signal normalization algorithm), which has a memory buffer of a few seconds (depending on signal). Dynamic range is easy to use and effective calibration mechanism, and relative change seems to be more practical than absolute values in this kind of gaming.

According to our early analysis, there are three key issues in designing psychophysiologically adaptive games i) understanding the meaningful emotionally adaptive gaming patterns, ii) implementation of adaptation algorithms and signal processing, and iii) purposeful use of sensors in the game context (Kuikkaniemi et al., 2008).

The design patterns used in emotionally adaptive gaming must be meaningful and enjoyable for the player, and the utilization of signals must also obey the overall goal of the game. In order to achieve the goal player should find the right rhythm or balance of playing the game and control of psychophysiological responses and signals.

Signals should be analyzed as close to real-time as possible in psychophysiologically adaptive gaming in order to keep the feedback loop in pace with the game adaptations and game events. We have used time-series analysis with short sample windows. In practice, ECG, EEG and EMG always require extensive data processing, but EDA and respiration can be almost used as such to create the adaptation signal. This implies that not all psychophysiological signals are equally open to be used as real-time inputs into an adaptive game at least in this stage of signal processing hardware and software development.

Usability of psychophysiological recording devices remains quite poor. Respiration, HR [heart rate] and EDA are probably the easiest to implement. Also in case of emotional adaptation the design of the game may include the physical design of the sensors, e.g. "Detective hat" for EEG sensors or "Sniper-gloves" for EDA sensors. Hence, the sensors could be designed as part of the game story rather than presented as cumbersome and invasive laboratory-originated equipment.

In future versions of EMOShooter we may also employ the system design of emotionally adapted games including setting of explicit experiential targets and their parameters for gaming sessions and the emotion control knob.

DISCUSSION

There are several challenges for Psychological Customization systems. We see four main areas which are critical: i) measurement of experience, ii) quality of reasoning in an adaptive system, iii) finding successful commercial application areas and iv) acceptability by users.

The measurement of experience in the first place is a key challenge. However, we have presented an approach to concentrate on those aspects of experience, such as emotion, which are perhaps better defined than experiential states in general. Despite this focus, there is still disagreement in theorizing, operationalizing and measuring emotions.

Another problem is the stimulus that produces a given emotional state. How to reliably capture these responses in a way which could be generalized over similar, but not exactly the same stimuli? While we have no final answers to these challenges, we have some solution paths to consider.

First, measurement of emotion and emotional responses to stimuli within a Psychological Customization system when producing the initial Rules and scenarios database is of course important. However, a Psychological Customization system is designed to evolve over time with feedback loops enabling the building of emergent design-rules which can produce better hit-rates for the system for psychological effects. In a way, if one envisions a Psychological Customization system a user has used in several application areas over longer periods of time, there are likely "new" design rules which have emerged and fine-tuned the system's capacity regarding that particular user or other users with a similar user profile. In a way, with a solid enough starting point a Psychological Customization system could over time produce a much better functioning system without the explicit need for a final theory of emotion. Naturally, to prove this case is an empiric question of real-life use of various applications based on the Psychological Customization design principles.

Second, when producing these emergent design-rules with massive amounts of data from various sensors and other sources such as psychophysiological data it may be possible to capture high-resolution indexes of the responses of a user to set of stimuli by combining direct and indirect measurement of experience and behavior from multiple angles. Hence, the amount of data, the multiplicity of sources of data and the resolution of user tracking could ideally produce high-quality design rules. Of course, they could also act as sources of noise. It is likely then that a massively computational approach to user modeling, or modeling of the realization of psychological effects needs some mediating medium-level concepts and constructs based on which the meaningful patterns

of responses could be mined from a continuous, multiple data streams tracking the user.

The quality of reasoning in an adaptive system is often a bottle-neck in performance. If a closed system is produced with fixed design-rules it would inevitably encounter situations, stimuli and users which would challenge the systems fixed rules and produce errors in adaptations. While there are several deep and sophisticated technical and mathematical approaches to this problem including different ways of machine learning and reasoning (which are beyond the scope of this article), we propose a higher-level solution possibility. Again, our answer is to rely on the co-evolutionary potential of our system design with changing user models and emergent design-rules. Of course, this approach needs working algorithms and techniques to form the necessary metadata and other data structures to be processed by the system.

To find commercially feasible application areas for Psychological Customization is naturally a challenge in transferring research results from the academic world to real-life products and services. It is our view that a Psychological Customization system can be an important middle-ware layer of various types of systems, working as a separate component with Customer Relationship Management systems, for instance.

A Psychological Customization system can add the possibility of adaptation and target experience realization and management for even simple systems of content and service delivery to consumers. It should be noted that the system could in principle operate without an explicit feedback loop from the experiences and behavior of the users in real-time. Such a system would operate based on the Rules and scenarios database adaptations only. It may also be possible to build indirect ways of inferring the realization probability of given target experiences with lighter methods than invasive psychophysiological measurement.

Further, one can use a Psychological Customization system "off-line" in the form of a user-testing tool for product development purposes. One could for instance conduct user research on a population of users of a to-be-launched product or existing service being redesigned. The designs and solutions and their functionality (relative to the goals of the designers, brand image, usability, emotionality, or other experiential factors) could be validated with a representative sample of test users. The results could then indicate problems areas or successful aspects of the design and provide valuable, quantified data to help the design of a product or service.

Gaming, as we have presented it in this chapter is perhaps one of the most promising application areas of Psychological Customization. We see that both casual and hardcore gamers could benefit from the use of our system and entirely new types of games can be created. Psychological Customization would enable game designers to use our tools both when developing the game and testing it with users in a rapid manner as well as part of the final product. From the user's point of view, using various types of control knobs of emotion or other experiences enables them to customize and have more control over their gaming experiences.

Good games are composed of delicate synthesis of the components creating a pleasant game balance and challenge for players. Introducing emotional adaptation increases the complexity of game design tasks involved. However, regards the economics of game development our system would not induce a dramatic cost. The system automatically establishes gaming patterns and structures which would fill a target experience and its parameters. Our system could be a modular toolset that can be adapted to various types of gaming platforms and gaming engines. The emotional tuning knob could be integrated into existing game controls including sliders for level of graphic violence in the game, for instance. Of course, development work is needed to create an easy-to-use game adaptation interface for users to set their preferences for gameplay.

Even if there are promising commercial applications of Psychological Customization systems there is still the question of user acceptance. The question here without doubt is whether users will tolerate some loss of their privacy in return for a fully functioning and value-providing Psychological Customization system in a particular application area. It may be easy to convince an expert-user such as a remote operator of an industrial machine that using for instance psychophysiological sensors reduces the possibility of error in the operation of the system. However, even semi-invasive psychophysiological sensors beyond their application in games may be problematic to accept by many users. Hardcore gamers may be more suspect to accept new peripheral devices linking them to game than gaming novices or casual gamers. However, the culture of connecting one's body to a game is already evolving. Think of Wii as an example with a controller tied to one's wrist, constantly touching the skin. It would not be unimaginable to think of psychophysiological sensors embedded in similar controls as people are more used to "semi-invasive" gaming controls beyond the use of a mouse and keyboard. The solution here could be to design sensors as embedded into essential existing or new types of gaming peripherals. A driving wheel with EDA and ECG sensors or driving gloves with similar sensors with added blood pressure, muscle tension and finger movement sensors could be used as easily acceptable controls of a driving simulator, for example.

In general, the problem lies with giving unprecedented access to one's experiential states to outside parties, let alone commercial parties. There is really no direct solution to the question of user acceptance. However, we call for better user anonymization techniques as well as better indirect and direct ways of measuring experiential states and behavior of users. The question still remains of trust: whether the user trusts the system or the provider of a product or service enough to give them access to his emotional states in real-time.

Perhaps this could be partly mediated by keeping the transmission of such private data between the computer and the user, and either encrypting or anonymizing the data to be sent over networks to Psychological Customization servers. Of course, for the user, the benefits of using a Psychological Customization system need to outweigh the risks or inconveniences. Perhaps letting users dial in their desired experiential states and have more control over the customization of various products and services, while keeping the vital feedback loops of measurement of their experiences, and perhaps even their user profiles, to themselves.

One aspect to be dealt with is related to the social status brought about by gaming achievement. If a game adapts differently to different users would this erode the status position of high scores among peers playing the game? Our response is that emotional adaptation is not necessarily heavily linked with gaming difficulty. Gaming difficulty typically increases using various algorithms from the beginning until the completion of a game. However, people can already set the "enemy" intelligence levels for the game AI engine from less to more intelligent to tune the level of challenge in the game. We have not heard of discussions related to high scores and their social status based on these settings. We expect that emotional adaptation of personal gaming preferences would then not influence the social nature of high scores or gaming achievement.

We briefly conclude that our proposal for emotionally adapted games is based on Psychological Customization which we have shown to be grounded on empirical evidence as proof of concept. We have presented a system design, and emotional adaptation space for games and an example of a psychophysiologically adapted game. In our tests of the psychophysiologically adaptive game as a first prototype of emotionally adapted games we have been able to produce meaningful gaming patterns and game adaptations. We argue that our approach to emotionally adapted games is novel and creates new opportunities for design-

ing games. We feel that our approach may result in a new type of enabling technological platform focused on the customization of gaming experiences. This new enabling technology platform can facilitate the development new types of games but can also be used with existing types of games and gaming platforms.

REFERENCES

Anderson, C. A., & Dill, K. E. (2000). Video games and aggressive thoughts, feelings, and behavior in the laboratory and in life. *Journal of Personality and Social Psychology*, *78*, 772–790. doi:10.1037/0022-3514.78.4.772

Anderson, D. M. (2002). *Build-to-Order & Mass Customization*. Cambria, CA: CIM Press.

Ballard, M. E., & Weist, J. R. (1996). Mortal Kombat: The effects of violent video game play on males' hostility and cardiovascular responding. *Journal of Applied Social Psychology*, *26*, 717–730. doi:10.1111/j.1559-1816.1996.tb02740.x

Benkler, Y. (2000). From Consumers to Users: Shifting the Deeper Structures of Regulation. *Federal Communications Law Journal*, *52*, 561–563.

Branigan, E. (1992). *Narrative comprehension and film*, (4th Ed.). London: Routledge.

Brave, S., & Nass, C. (2003). Emotion in human-computer interaction. In J. A. Jacko & A. Sears (Ed.), *The Human-Computer Interaction Handbook. Fundamentals, Evolving Technologies and Emerging Applications*, (pp. 81-96). London: Lawrence Erlbaum Associates.

Calvert, S. L., & Tan, S. (1994). Impact of virtual reality on young adults' physiological arousal and aggressive thoughts: Interaction versus observation. *Journal of Applied Developmental Psychology*, *15*, 125–139. doi:10.1016/0193-3973(94)90009-4

Carberry, S., & de Rosis, F. (2008). Introduction to special issue on "Affective modeling and adaptation.". *User Modeling and User-Adapted Interaction, 18*, 1–9. doi:10.1007/s11257-007-9044-7

Cuperfain, R., & Clarke, T. K. (1985). A new perspective on subliminal perception. *Journal of Advertising, 14*, 36–41.

Darley, A. (2000). *Visual digital culture: Surface play and spectacle in new media genres.* London: Routledge.

Duray, R., & Ward, P., T., Milligan, G. W. & Berry, W. L. (2000). Approaches to mass customization: Configurations and empirical validation. *Journal of Operations Management, 18*(6), 605–625. doi:10.1016/S0272-6963(00)00043-7

Egan, D. E. (1988). Individual differences in human-computer interaction. In M. Helander (Ed.), *Handbook of Human-Computer Interaction*, (p. 543 – 568). Elsevier: New York.

Ekman, P. (1992). An argument for basic emotions. *Cognition and Emotion, 6*, 169–200. doi:10.1080/02699939208411068

Fairclough, S. H. (2007). Psychophysiological inference and physiological computer games. In A. Nijholt & D. Tan (Ed.), *BRAINPLAY 07: brain-computer interfaces and games workshop at ACE (Advances in computer entertainment) 2007,* Salzburg, Austria.

Forgas, J. P. (1992). Affect in social judgments and decisions: A multiprocess model. *Advances in Experimental Social Psychology, 25*, 227–275. doi:10.1016/S0065-2601(08)60285-3

Freeman, F. G. (1999). Evaluation of an adaptive automation system using three EEG indices with a visual tracking task. *Biological Psychology, 50*, 61–76. doi:10.1016/S0301-0511(99)00002-2

Frijda, N. H. (1994). Varieties of affect: Emotions and episodes, moods, and sentiments. In P. Ekman & R. J. Davidson (Ed.), *The Nature Emotion: Fundamental Questions* (pp. 59-67). Oxford, UK: Oxford University Press.

Gilmore, J. H., & Pine, B. J., II. (1997). The four faces of mass customization. In J. H. Gilmore, & B. J. Pine II (Ed.), *Markets of One*, (pp. 115-132). Boston: President and Fellows of Harvard College.

Gray, J. A. (1991). The neuropsychology of temperament. In J. Strelau & A. Angleitner (Ed.), *Explorations in temperament: International perspectives on theory and measurement* (pp. 105-128). New York: Plenum Press.

Grodal, T. (2000). Video games and the pleasures of control. In D. Zillmann & P. Vorderer (Ed.), *Media entertainment: The psychology of its appeal* (pp. 197-212). Mahwah, NJ: Lawrence Erlbaum Associates.

Järvinen, A., Heliö, S., & Mäyrä, F. (2002). *Communication and community in digital entertainment services: Prestudy research report.* Hypermedialaboratorion verkkojulkaisuja 2, Tampere. Retrieved from http://tampub.uta.fi/tup/951-44-5432-4.pdf

Kallinen, K., & Ravaja, N. (2004). Emotion-related effects of speech rate and rising vs. falling background music melody during audio news: The moderating influence of personality. *Personality and Individual Differences, 37*, 275–288. doi:10.1016/j.paid.2003.09.002

Kelly, K. (1994). *Out of control: The new biology of machines, social systems and the economic world.* Reading, MA: Addison Wesley.

Kihlström, J. F., Barnhardt, T. M., & Tataryn, D. J. (1992). Implicit perception. In R. F. Bornstein & T.S. Pittmann (eds.) *Perception without awareness. Cognitive, clinical and social perspectives*, (pp. 17-54). New York: Guilford.

Krosnick, J. A., Betz, A. L., Jussim, J. L., & Lynn, A. R. (1992). Subliminal conditioning of attitudes. *Personality and Social Psychology Bulletin, 18,* 152–162. doi:10.1177/0146167292182006

Kuikkaniemi, K., Laitinen, T., & Kosunen, I. (2008). *Designing emotionally adaptive gaming.* Proceedings of EHTI08: The First Finnish Symposium on Emotions and Human-Technology Interaction (pp. 13 – 17), University of Tampere, Tampere, Finland

Laarni, J. (2003). Effects of color, font type and font style on user preferences. In C. Stephanidis (Ed.) *Adjunct Proceedings of HCI International 2003* (pp. 31-32). Heraklion, Greece: Crete University Press.

Laarni, J., & Kojo, I. (2001). Reading financial news from PDA and laptop displays. In M. J. Smith & G. Salvendy (Ed.) *Proceedings of HCI International, Systems, Social and Internationalization Design Aspects of Human-Computer Interaction* (Vol. 2, pp. 109 – 113). Hillsdale, NJ: Lawrence Erlbaum.

Laarni, J., Ravaja, N., & Saari, T. (2005). Aesthetic and emotional evaluations of computer interfaces. In C. Stephanidis (Ed.) *Proceedings of HCI International 2005.* Mahwah, NJ: Lawrence Erlbaum Associates

Laarni, J., Ravaja, N., Saari, T., & Liukkonen, S. (2004). Effects of color and texture on emotional evaluations. In J. P.Frois, P. Andrade & J. F. Marques (Eds.) *Art and Science: Proceedings IAEA 2004 XVIII Congress.* Lisbon:IAEA.

Lang, A. (1990). Involuntary attention and physiological arousal evoked by structural features and mild emotion in TV commercials. *Communication Research, 17*(3), 275–299. doi:10.1177/009365090017003001

Lang, A., Dhillon, P., & Dong, Q. (1995). Arousal, emotion and memory for television messages. *Journal of Broadcasting & Electronic Media, 38,* 1–15.

Lang, A., Newhagen, J., & Reeves, B. (1996). Negative video as structure: Emotion, attention, capacity and memory. *Journal of Broadcasting & Electronic Media, 40,* 460–477.

Lang, P. J. (1995). The emotion probe. Studies of motivation and attention. *The American Psychologist, 50,* 372–385. doi:10.1037/0003-066X.50.5.372

Lankoski, P. (2003). *Vallan jäljet. Lähtökohtia pelin ja draamallisen tv-sarjan yhdistämiseen.* Hypermedialaboratorion verkkojulkaisuja 4, Tampere. Retrieved from http://tampub.uta.fi/tup/951-44-5705-6.pdf

Larsen, R. J., & Diener, E. (1992). Promises and problems with the circumplex model of emotion. In M. Clark (Ed.), *Review of personality and social psychology* (Vol. 13, pp.25-59). Newbury Park, CA: Sage.

Lazarus, R. S. (1991). *Emotion and Adaptation.* New York: Oxford University Press.

Mandler, J. M. (1984). *Stories, scripts and scenes: Aspects of schema theory.* Mahwah, NJ: Lawrence Erlbaum.

Manovich, L. (2001). *The language of new media.* Cambridge, MA: The MIT Press.

Meyer, K. (1995). Dramatic narrative in virtual reality. In F. Biocca & M. Levy (Ed.) *Communication in the age of virtual reality.* Hillsdale, NJ: Lawrence Erlbaum.

Nelson, T. M., & Carlson, D. R. (1985). Determining factors in choice of arcade games and their consequences upon young male players. *Journal of Applied Social Psychology, 15,* 124–139. doi:10.1111/j.1559-1816.1985.tb02339.x

Nielsen, L. B. (2004). Post Disney experience paradigm? Some implications for the development of content to mobile tourist services. In *Proceedings of ICEC'04, Sixth International Conference on Electronic Commerce*, Delft, The Netherlands.

Pine, J., II. (1992). *Mass Customization: The New Frontier in Business Competition*. Cambridge, MA: Harvard Business School Press

Poole, S. (2000). *Trigger happy: The inner life of video games*. London: Fourth Estate.

Pope, A. T., Bogart, E. H., & Bartolome, D. S. (1995). Biocybernetic system evaluates indices of operator engagement in automated task. *Biological Psychology, 40*, 187–195. doi:10.1016/0301-0511(95)05116-3

Ravaja, N. (2004a). Effects of a small talking facial image on autonomic activity: The moderating influence of dispositional BIS and BAS sensitivities and emotions. *Biological Psychology, 65*, 163–183. doi:10.1016/S0301-0511(03)00078-4

Ravaja, N. (2004b). Contributions of psychophysiology to media research: Review and recommendations. *Media Psychology, 6*, 193–235. doi:10.1207/s1532785xmep0602_4

Ravaja, N., & Kallinen, K. (2004). Emotional effects of startling background music during reading news reports: The moderating influence of dispositional BIS and BAS sensitivities. *Scandinavian Journal of Psychology, 45*, 231–238. doi:10.1111/j.1467-9450.2004.00399.x

Ravaja, N., Kallinen, K., Saari, T., & Keltikangas-Järvinen, L. (2004). Suboptimal exposure to facial expressions when viewing video messages from a small screen: Effects on emotion, attention, and memory. *Journal of Experimental Psychology. Applied, 10*, 120–131. doi:10.1037/1076-898X.10.2.120

Ravaja, N., Laarni, J., Saari, T., Kallinen, K., & Salminen, M. (2005). Phasic Psychophysiological Responses to Video Game Events: New Criterion Variables for Game Design. In C. Stephanidis (Ed.) *Proceedings of HCI International 2005*. Mahwah, NJ: Lawrence Erlbaum Associates

Riding, R. J., & Rayner, S. (1998). *Cognitive styles and learning strategies. Understanding style differences in learning and behavior*. London: David Fulton Publishers.

Saari, T. (2001). *Mind-Based Media and Communications Technologies. How the Form of Information Influences Felt Meaning*. Acta Universitatis Tamperensis 834. Tampere, Finland: Tampere University Press.

Saari, T. (2003a). Designing for Psychological Effects. Towards Mind-Based Media and Communications Technologies. In Harris, D., Duffy, V., Smith, M. & Stephanidis, C. (eds.) *Human-Centred Computing: Cognitive, Social and Ergonomic Aspects. Volume 3 of the Proceedings of HCI International 2003*, (pp. 557-561). Heraklion, Greece: Crete University Press.

Saari, T. (2003b). Mind-Based Media and Communications Technologies. A Framework for producing personalized psychological effects. In *Proceedings of the Human Factors and Ergonomics Society 47th Annual Meeting*.

Saari, T., Ravaja, N., Turpeinen, M., & Kallinen, K. (2005). Emotional Regulation System for Emotionally Adapted Games. In *Proceedings of FuturePlay 2005 conference*, 13.-15.10. Michigan State University, Lansing, MI.

Saari, T., & Turpeinen, M. (2004). Towards Psychological Customization of Information for Individuals and Social Groups. In J. Karat, J. Blom & M.-C. Karat (Ed.), *Personalization of User Experiences for eCommerce*. New York: Kluwer.

Saari, T., Turpeinen, M., Laarni, J., Ravaja, N., & Kallinen, K. (2004). Psychologically targeted persuasive advertising and product information presentation in eCommerce. In *Proceedings of ICEC 2004, 3rd international conference for entertainment computing.* 1.-3.9. 2004, Eindhoven, The Netherlands (LNCS Vol. 3166, 476-486). Berlin: Springer.

Scherer, K. R. (1993). Neuroscience projections to current debates in emotion psychology. *Cognition and Emotion, 7,* 1–41. doi:10.1080/02699939308409174

Tellegen, A. (1985). Structure of mood and personality and their relevance to assessing anxiety, with an emphasis on self-report. In A. H. Tuma & J. D. Maser (Ed.), *Anxiety and the Anxiety Disorders* (pp. 681-706). Hillsdale, NJ: Lawrence Erlbaum.

Turpeinen, M., & Saari, T. (2004) System Architecture for Psychological Customization of Information. *37th Hawaii International International Conference on Systems Science (HICSS-37 2004), Proceedings,* 5-8 January 2004, Waikoloa, Big Island, HI. Washington. DC: IEEE Computer Society.

Vecchi, T., Phillips, L. H., & Cornoldi, C. (2001). Individual differences in visuo-spatial working memory. In M. Denis, R. H. Logie, C. Cornoldi, M. de Vega, & J. Engelkamp (Ed.), *Imagery, language, and visuo-spatial thinking.* Hove, UK: Psychology Press.

Vorderer, P., Hartmann, T., & Klimmt, C. (2003). Explaining the enjoyment of playing video games: The role of competition. In D. Marinelli (Ed.), *Proceedings of the 2nd International Conference on Entertainment Computing (ICEC 2003),* Pittsburgh (pp. 1-8). New York: ACM.

Watson, D., & Tellegen, A. (1985). Toward a consensual structure of mood. *Psychological Bulletin, 98,* 219–235. doi:10.1037/0033-2909.98.2.219

Watson, D., Wiese, D., Vaidya, J., & Tellegen, A. (1999). The two general activation systems of affect: Structural findings, evolutionary considerations, and psychobiological evidence. *Journal of Personality and Social Psychology, 76,* 820–838. doi:10.1037/0022-3514.76.5.820

Wiener, N. (1948). *Cybernetics: Control and communication in the animal and the machine.* 2nd edition. Cambridge, MA, MIT Press.

Section 4
Case Studies and Evaluations of Mass Customization

Chapter 12
Expected and Realized Costs and Benefits from Implementing Product Configuration Systems

Kasper Edwards
Technical University of Denmark, Denmark

ABSTRACT

Product configuration systems (PCS) are a technology well suited for mass customization and support the task of configuring the product to the individual customer's needs. PCS are at the same time complex software systems that may be tailored to solve a variety of problems for a firm, e.g. supporting the quotation process or validating the structure of a product. This chapter reports findings from a study of 12 Danish firms, which at the time of the study have implemented or are in the process of implementing product configuration systems. 12 costs and 12 benefits are identified in literature, and using radar diagrams as a tool for data collection the relative difference are identified. While several of the firms are mass customizers it is not the primary driver for implementing PCS. The analysis reveals that expected and realized benefits are consistent: 1) Improved quality in specifications, 2) Using less resources, and 3) Lower turnaround time. Interestingly, the realized benefits are all higher than the expected benefits. The expected benefits highlight the motivation, and this has implications for human factors as they point in the direction of significant changes to come in the adopting organization. It is observed that product configuration projects are treated as simple technical projects although they should be regarded as organizational change projects.

INTRODUCTION

Customers have become accustomed to the price of mass produced goods and are increasingly demanding that products are customized to their personal needs. But, unlike previously, customers do not wish to pay a premium for customized goods, which are now becoming a commodity rather than a special case. This is referred to as mass customization (Davis, 1987) and has indeed become an important issue for many firms.

DOI: 10.4018/978-1-60566-260-2.ch012

A means for firms to achieve mass customization is the use of product configuration systems. A product configuration system consists of a computer model of a product, which contains information about the relationship between the individual components of the product and any noteworthy restrictions, which one component imposes on another. For instance, a product model of a bicycle would have information regarding the frame, wheel, tube, tires, saddle, color and style of the different components etc. Restrictions in the model define what size of wheel fits with a given frame – no use in mounting a 26" wheel on a 12" frame.

The purpose of this paper is to identify the expected and realized costs and benefits from implementing product configuration systems. The paper draws on empirical evidence from a study of twelve Danish firms, which have implemented or at the time of data collection were in the process of implementing product configuration systems. The data used in this paper was collected ultimo 2003 through primo 2004. The main thrust of the chapter is to identify costs and benefits. The identified benefits are then used to understand the organizational implications – which essentially are organizational changes rather than a mere technical project.

The chapter is structured as follows: The next section explain what a product configuration system is. This is followed by a section briefly describing the project, study and methodology, which again is followed by a description of the involved firms and the results. The results are presented, and the implications for human factors discussed.

Product Configuration Systems

In order to appreciate product configuration systems these must be placed within a context of mass customization. The definition of mass customization is by itself a subject of controversy; Gilmore and Pine (1997), Duray et al. (2000),

Tseng and Jiao (2001), Piller (2004) give a number of different definitions. This is not unexpected, as the field of mass customization attracts scholars from diverse fields such as computer science, engineering, strategy and marketing, see Silveira et al. (2001) for a literature review. In this paper the definition by Duray et al. (2000) is used as it has both a engineering and a cost perspective, which is in agreement with the views of this paper. In this definition mass customization is defined by two dimensions: 1) The basic nature of customization, and 2) The means for achieving customization at or near mass production costs.

The basic nature of customization refers to the observation that variety in itself does not constitute customization, and the customer must be involved in the specification of the product. The means to achieve mass customization at or near mass production costs are essentially economics of scale as a consequence of the modularity of the product. By modularizing a product and reusing as many modules as possible in all product variations it is possible for these modules to be produced at or near mass production prices.

Product configuration systems are enablers in both dimensions. A product configuration system allows the customer or sales person to easily configure a product to their specific needs. The product configuration system keeps track of the possible combinations of product properties that are allowed. A product configuration system also influences costs, as the costs of configuring a "standard" product are the same as a custom product. The costs of making product specification are the same for all product configurations.

A product configuration system is basically a model of a product, describing the relationship between individual parts. This makes it possible to interactively design a product by specifying which parts should be used in the final product. Product configuration systems can be categorized based on the type of knowledge (performance/ structure) and number of decision variables (few/many) (Ladeby, Edwards, & Haug, 2007).

However, for this purpose two extremes can be identified: 1) Quotation configuration systems and 2) Production configuration systems. A quotation configuration system is a product configuration system with high level knowledge and few decision variable. Such a system is well suited in the preliminary sales and configuration phase e.g. for making quotes. This implies that the product configuration system only needs to possess knowledge regarding larger elements, which have a significant impact on the total price. Quotation configuration systems are often used in heavy engineering, where the rough price of the elements is known, whereas precise information about price of material etc. is unknown. Producing quotes in heavy engineering projects, e.g. a large production plant, is in itself very costly, and a quotation configuration system can significantly lower the cost of producing a quote. One of the interviewed firms documented a reduction from 2.650 man/hrs to 130 man/hrs for making a detailed first quote (Interview with firm B, 28th Oct 2003). Quotation configuration systems are sometimes referred to as meta configuration systems (Forza & Salvador, 2007), however, in this context the key term is quotation.

In the opposite end of the spectrum we find production configuration systems, which are product configuration systems capable of generating a complete production-ready product specification. Production configuration systems are most often linked to or integrated in an ERP system offering further advantages for automating production- and materials planning. Thus, when the desired configuration has been created, the system has complete knowledge of the product to be produced. The configuration is used by the EPR system to create routing, bill of material, inventory etc. Production configuration systems find use in situations, where the product can be completely configured by using the product configuration system. Standard cars, bicycles etc. would be examples of products, which lend themselves to this kind of configuration. It must be stressed that

we make a distinction between product, production, and quotation configuration systems, where the latter two are subsets of the first.

Product configuration systems are a means of achieving customization, however, product configuration systems are not per se a means for achieving customization at or near mass production costs. As Pine (1999) notes: "The best method for achieving mass customization – minimising costs while maximising individual customization - is to create modular components that can be configured into a wide variety of end products and services", which is also recognised by Duray et al. (2000). While it is easy to design a product configuration system around a fully modular product, it is not a necessity, and it is possible to design a product configuration system for a non-modular product. The latter product will not see the cost advantages of modularisation, and the process of creating the configuration system will also be more complex due to idiosyncrasies in the individual product variants. Naturally, this is recognised by other scholars, and Riis (2003) strongly encourages the use of strict product reviews before creating a product configuration system.

Product configuration systems exist in many forms and are based on a variety of underlying technologies. The knowledge base in these systems can be either rule-, model- or case-based (Blecker, Abdelkafi, Kreutler, & Friedrich, 2004; Bei Yu & Skovgaard, 1998). In this paper only rule-based configuration systems is encountered. Configuration systems are also found in some ERP suits with SAP's R/3 being one such example (Haag, 1998). The advantage of the ERP approach is the integration with existing data, and that ERP systems focus on the business process as opposed to stand-alone configuration, both of which has their place. The Baan SalesPLUS product configuration system (Bei Yu et al., 1998) is an example of a stand-alone configuration system which may integrate with existing databases.

Project Description and Methodology

This research was conducted in the "The Product Models, Economy, Technology, and Organisation" project (PETO), which was formed with the intention of studying the process and effects of implementing product configuration systems. Most of the literature on product configuration systems deals with technical issues, and only a few recent papers have taken economic and organizational issues (Forza & Salvador, 2001; Forza & Salvador, 2002) into consideration. It is evident from several implementation projects (Riis, 2003; Hansen, 2003) that there are significant costs associated with implementation and realizing benefits. This research tries to measure costs and benefits associated with implementing product configuration systems in a number of Danish firms.

Given the fact that no other interdisciplinary studies of product configuration systems, to our knowledge, have been conducted, a qualitative and yet hypothetically deductive approach was selected.

Based on earlier research and experience within the project group, a number of possible costs and benefits were deduced. A questionnaire was developed with the intention of capturing expectations and results from product configuration systems as well as the actual implementation process. The questionnaire was populated with questions directed at: 1) The specification process before and after implementing product configuration systems, this is the foundation for understanding the changes induced by implementing a product configuration system; 2) Technical issues of the implemented product configuration system; 3) Economic issues and 4) Organizational issues. It goes far beyond the limits of this paper to describe all questions and aspects of the questionnaire, and we shall limit ourselves to focus on the costs and benefits related to the use of product configuration systems. The questionnaire consists of 196 questions of which 47 were directed at economic

issues, 33 at technical issues, 97 at organizational issues, and 19 regarded the specification process. The specification processes before and after implementing product configuration systems were drawn in two different process diagrams allowing for easy comparison. The questions were designed to be both closed and open ended questions, in the latter case leading respondents to elaborate and explain certain positions (Jacobsen, 1997). The open ended questions were used deliberately to allow some degree of exploration in the interview process, and respondents were allowed to pursue their line of thought before being interrupted and directed towards the question. Concluding questions were used to confirm and summarize the meaning of open ended questions.

20 firms were selected, from a larger pool of 43 firms with affiliation to the Danish Association of Product Modelling*, these firms had known experience in product configuration systems. The firms were contacted by letter explaining the research project and ensuring anonymity. Shortly after the invitation letter, the firms were contacted by telephone where the project was explained to them and they were told why they were invited. Of the 20 invited firms, 14 firms agreed to participate in the study. Two firms later withdrew from the study, one citing lack of time and the other firm abandoned their product configuration system. The remaining 12 firms participated in the study.

Firms were asked to provide interview subjects in the following categories: 1) Project sponsor, 2) Technician/programmer, 3) User, and 4) Project manager. These four roles were chosen, as they represent several organizational levels of a product configuration project as well as both users and developers of the system. This also ensures a broad understanding of the impact of the product configuration system in the respective organisations

The interviews intended to be conducted with a single respondent at a time, allowing for a detailed interview with personal opinion expressed. To gain a relation of trust, respondents were provided with a written and signed statement expressing that the information would remain anonymous and certainly not shared with their colleagues.

However, in some cases it was not possible to conduct individual interviews, and a group interview was the only option for having the particular firm participate in the study. It must be expected that these interviews to some degree fail to uncover interpersonal problems with effect on the configuration system and its implementation. Group interviews have a tendency to express consensus among the respondents.

The actual measurement of costs and benefits was done using what we refer to as radar diagrams, which are explained in detail in the following section. This is essentially Liker scale type questions (Clason & Dormody, 1994) presented on a radar. This has the effect that the respondent becomes aware of the relative differences in his answers. It is our opinion that the ranking of costs and benefits becomes more precise.

In all interviews multiple investigators (Eisenhardt, 1989) were used to ensure complementary opinions and insights and to enhance confidence in the findings. During all interviews two investigators were present, and on some occasions even three and four investigators found their time to participate in the interviews. The combination of multiple investigators and open ended questions is very powerful, if investigators deliberately keep silent to pressure respondents into answering. On many occasions this was the deciding factor for getting a meaningful answer.

The interviews were taped and subsequently transcribed and then followed by a condensing procedure for extracting the meaning of the interviews (Kvale, 1997).

Radar Diagrams

Costs and benefits from implementing product configuration were uncovered in two stages: 1) The questionnaire and 2) Radar diagrams. A radar diagram is an intuitive graphical representation

of a number of variables. Two Radar diagrams were used to explicitly gain information about costs and benefits from implementing a product configuration system, see Figure 1 for an example of the radar diagram for measuring benefits. The radar diagrams constitute a hypothesis regarding what could be considered costs and benefits of implementing product configuration systems (explained in the following section).

In the actual interview respondents were first shown the radar diagram for benefits, and upon completion the radar diagram for costs were shown. The meaning of each cost and benefit was explained to the respondents, and they were asked to give points for both expected and realized costs and benefits. Respondents were asked to rate the most important realized or expected benefit with the highest score of five points, and the remaining expected and realized costs should be compared to this.

This allows us to compare expected and realized benefits to the highest scoring element. There are some problems related to this approach: Benefits, whether expected or realized, are intangible, and respondents only have a qualitative impression of the expected benefits, e.g. the time to produce a quote is too long and must be cut down. While respondents know the current time consumption of a process, it is unclear how much it should be reduced. Still, this approach allows us to gain insight as to what firms expect from product configuration systems, and what they gain.

Costs are more straight forward to measure, and respondents are also more aware of costs. The cost of a system is often estimated before proceeding with the project. Respondents were asked to pick the highest expected or realized costs and assign five points. Other expected or realized costs were compared to this. For instance, if a software package was the most expensive element, costing 100.000 EURO, this would be given five points. Other elements would be compared to this, and if hardware costs amounted to 60.000 EURO, it would be given three points. This approach was

Figure 1. Radar diagram for rating benefits, one axis left open for respondents to add.

Benefits

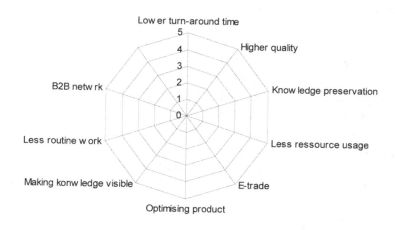

chosen because we did not expect companies to reveal the actual costs of their product configuration system. We did, however, expect to reveal the cost structure of the product configuration system using the rating system.

Investigating expected costs and benefits allowed us to gain an insight into the incentives for implementing a product configuration system and compare it to the realized benefits. While the chosen companies are not easily compared, this method allows for some degree of comparability. Given the varying size and scope of the investigated product configuration systems, actual monetary costs and benefits are interesting but not comparable. We did, however, expect to observe a similar distribution of costs across companies.

When the first interviews were conducted, the list of costs and benefits were somewhat shorter, and this highlights a known problem of explorative research: Is it legitimate to add items during a study? In this research we emphasize the explorative element and we did indeed find it legitimate to do so. Adding items allows the investigators to explore new hypotheses and follow new lines of thinking during the study (Eisenhardt, 1989).

Since we measure costs and benefits by using

a Likert scale (Clason et al., 1994), it is not possible to use standard statistics, which assume the answers to follow a normal distribution. Rather, the use of a Likert scale in combination with a radar diagram will emphasize the relative difference between the individual costs and benefits.

1.1 Benefits

Benefits were deduced from literature (Forza et al., 2001; Forza et al., 2002; Riis, 2003; Hansen, 2003; Hvam, 1999) by scanning said authors for claims of costs and benefits. A list of nine distinct benefits were compiled from literature: 1) Lower turn-around time, i.e. the time from order confirmation to delivery, 2) Improved quality, i.e. the quality of product specifications, 3) Preserved knowledge, i.e. knowledge is preserved in the configuration system, 4) Using less resources, i.e. fewer resources are used for specifying a product, 5) E-trade, i.e. e-trade is made possible by interfacing with the product configuration system, 6) Optimizing products, i.e. the product configuration system makes it possible to optimize with regard to price, performance, etc., 7) Making knowledge visible, i.e. knowledge contained in the system is easily available and presented to users, 8) Less routine work, i.e. trivial tasks are performed by the system, 9) B2B networks i.e., the product configuration system allows other companies to interface directly with the product configuration system.

Three additional benefits were suggested by respondents during the first few interviews: 10) Improved certainty of delivery, i.e. detailed knowledge about specifications lead to detailed knowledge about what and when to produce, 11) Focus on standard goods, i.e. a product configuration system can only handle standard goods, in which case everything else is non-standard, and 12) Job training made easier, i.e. examples of different types of product configurations can be illustrated by using the product configuration system. These benefits were added to the questionnaire.

1.2 Costs

The literature is sparse on possible costs arising from the use of product configuration systems. However, Hvam (1999) and Riis (2003) present a procedure for implementing product configuration systems, which can be broken into a number of cost elements. To this list one significant cost was added: "Increased cost of innovation", which is based on the hypothesis that firms innovate when customer demand new features or modifications to existing products.

Product configuration systems may easily cause a lock-in effect (Arthur, 1989) where customers and employees favour standard products. This is because employees as well as customers will face a significant time penalty if they do not use the configuration system. The time penalty may also result in a price penalty which, depending on company policy, may be placed on the customer. The consequence of this may be loss of input for innovation and new product development.

With this cost we try to capture a long term potential negative effect of using product con-

figuration systems. The compiled list of costs was not altered during the study and consists of the following elements: 1) Specifying the product model, i.e. the task of defining what should be part of a product model. 2) Choosing software, i.e. while off-the-shelf software is available, not all is equally suited for all tasks. 3) Coding, i.e. the task of programming the product configuration system. 4) Integrating with existing systems, i.e. the task of integrating necessary elements of existing information systems in the product configuration system. 5) Implementation, i.e. the cost of teaching employees to use the system including related costs of bringing the system from completed development to production use. 6) Maintenance, i.e. the cost of maintaining the system. 7) Increased cost of innovation, i.e. costs associated with not getting information feedback from regular sales channels. 8) Project management, i.e. the cost of managing the project from start up to production. 9) Documentation, i.e. the cost of documenting the implemented system. 10) Consultants, i.e. the cost of using consultants. 11) Software, i.e. license costs related to a fully functioning system. 12) Hardware, i.e. costs related to server investments.

DATA

12 firms participated in the study with 30 interviews, covering 39 individuals, resulting in more than 45 hours of taped interviews. What follows is a brief description of the participating firms, which is made anonymous at the request of the participating firms. The firms are grouped after company type, before they introduced product configuration, and the categories are: Heavy engineering, Mass producers, Batch producers, or One of a kind producers. This division is chosen because it reflects the production processes and the type of products produced. Heavy engineering firms have no continuous production and

essentially make one of a kind, although based on proven concepts. Firms are anonymous and referred to as A, B, C... etc.

Firm A and B are heavy engineering firms producing large production plants, where orders typically ranged from 27 million to 100 million Euros. The main problem in these firms was the cost of producing a quote, which, in the worst case, could cost up to 4,500 engineering hours, thus putting a significant strain on the organisation. Firms A experienced total costs for developing and implementing their product configuration systems of approximately 1.6 million Euros, and the project lasted about three years. It should be noted that at the time of interview the firm A was in the process of implementing a product configuration system. Firm B is also engaged in heavy engineering and experienced problems producing quotes at the rate required by the market. In 2003 their product configuration system processed quotes worth 4.4 billion Euros.

Firms C, D, E, F, G have traditionally been mass producers with turnovers ranging from 12.5 million Euros to 600 million Euros and 166 to 3,765 employees. All are well positioned in their market and some are market leaders.

Firms H, I, J are batch producing, the firm I sometimes modifying their products to such a degree that one-of-a-kind production might also be a suitable description. Turnover in this group was from 550 million Euro and 801 employees to 22 million Euro and 166 employees.

The firm G was the only firm where the listed expected benefits did not match at all. Firm G implemented product configuration with the sole intent of improving inter-company sale, and their second cited reason was to gain complete insight into their production plants across Europe. Firm G had observed that in some cases a customer would demands product which could not be produced in the local company, in which case a sister company in another country was approached by the local company. As the inter-firm profit is lower than regular sales, such requests were frequently de-

layed to the point, where the customer would take his order and placed it elsewhere. The solution was a product configuration system to be used in all sister firms across Europe. The system provides a configuration system which is not tied to the local production system, and a sales person in Austria may configure and allocate production resources in Denmark. This benefit was not observed in other firms and not added to the list of items in the belief that this is a special case.

ANALYSIS AND RESULTS

In this section we analyse firstly the correlation between expected and realized benefits and secondly the correlation between expected and realized costs. Expected and realized benefits are illustrated in figure 2 and realized costs are illustrated in figure 3, raw data can be found in appendix 1. As we are interested in the effects of product configuration systems, it is the correlation between expected and realized costs within the individual firms that will be analysed. A simple ranking of benefits can not be made, as the total aggregated score of benefits provide little insight into the effect of a product configuration system, as one firm might have had expectations and another accidentally realized that same benefit. The collected data was gathered using a qualitative approach as explained in section 3 and represent the respondents' interpretation of expected and realized costs and benefits in the interview situation. For this reason it makes little sense to use and present a rigid statistical analysis, which would only dilute the reader as to the confidence that one might place in the data. However, the qualitative insight is indeed interesting.

1.3 Benefits

12 firms have participated, all of which have answered the radar diagrams for both expected and realized benefits. The benefits are grouped

Figure 2. Expected and realized benefits, aggregated, max score=60, all firms.

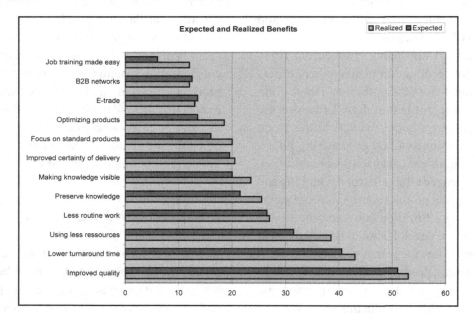

in three categories: High importance representing four or five points, medium representing two and three points and low representing zero or one point. Firms that awarded high importance to a benefit had the feeling that this was an incentive for implementing PCS and important for the success. Medium importance was given to benefits that were reported to be interesting but not critical

Figure 3. Realized costs listed in aggregared stacks, 11 of 12 firms.

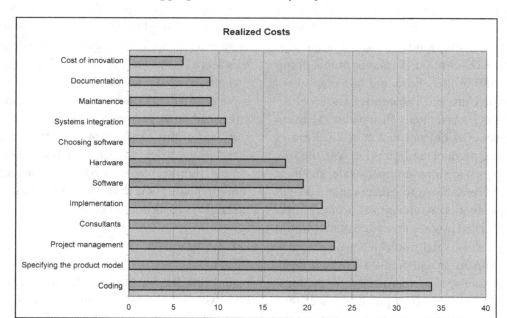

and not used as a core argument for implementing PCS. Benefits who received low importance were unimportant to the project and were never mentioned as an incentive, but none the less nice to have, if realized.

Firm G holds a special position in this analysis, as the driving incentive for implementing PCS was to improve inter-company coordination.

Lower turnaround time was an important expected benefit to 8 of 12 firms, medium important to two firms and unimportant to two firms. All of the firms, which found this benefit important, experienced that customers were lost because of the turnaround time for delivering quotes. The two firms I and J that found this unimportant had particular reasons for this. Firm I had just implemented a new ERP system, which also focused on reducing turnaround time. Firm J had a specific problem with the quality of their product specifications, but the time to produce the specifications was not a problem. Only two firms, E and H met their expectations..

Improved quality was an important expected benefit to all but one firm (firm G). The importance of improved quality is explained by the consequences of poor product specification quality. Product specifications that are not correct, and the required correction will be increasingly costly to fix, as the product passes through the production process. Firm F reported that incorrect product specifications could lead to a complete production halt on night shifts, when the engineers are off duty. Implementing a production configuration system, in this case, raised the rate of correct specifications from 60% to 100%, and no production stops had been reported since. All but two firms achieved their expectations, and these two were just marginally below (one point).

Using less resources was an important expected benefit to 4 firms, of medium importance to 4 firms and unimportant to the last four firms. The firms that found this issue important were experiencing that producing a quote was a significant cost driver and had to be reduced. In particular

firms B and L experienced that the quote/order ratio had been declining over the past 15 years, and this was becoming a problem. Using less resources was found to be linked to the turnaround time in the sense that if less resources (different staff) were involved, the turnaround time would drop, simply because of the reduction of the number of times a quote would have to wait for staff.

Preserve knowledge was an important expected benefit to 3 firms (A, C and D) and of medium importance to 3 firms and unimportant to 7 firms. Interestingly enough, firms A, C, and D did so for different reasons. Firm A needed to preserve knowledge because of a generation gap in the organisation and foresaw the upcoming pension of a major part of their key engineers. This potential problem had to be countered by using an information system, which became the configuration system. Firm C needed to allow sales staff to easily access knowledge of the different product variants. Firm D sells high quality, expensive, durable goods, where individual products can be linked together to form a system. Over time customers buy additional products and link into the existing system. Firm D then uses the product configuration system to keep track of valid historic configurations allowing sales staff to quickly answer questions about integrating a new product into an existing system of older products. As new products offer new and improved features, the sales staff must be able to identify what features integrate seamlessly and what not thus allowing customers to make an informed decision. All but one firm had their expectations met.

E-trade was an important expected benefit to 3 firms (C, E and L) and unimportant to the remaining 9 firms. Firm C expected to make their configuration system available on the internet, but later decided against it and thus they did not achieve their expectations at all. Firm E achieved their goal and felt this was important due to their sales organisation. Firm E had an autonomous sales organisation dispersed with offices in many countries over the world that had their own IT systems for configuring and ordering. The configuration system was to bypass some of the local IT systems and allow for a common interface for configuration and also allowing the firm E to control the sales process. Firm L envisioned from the beginning that their production configuration system was to be available on the internet and hoped to reduce the load on their sales staff by allowing customers to configure and order the products without intervention by sales staff. All of the other firms did not want to allow customers to access their product configuration system and used it as an internal tool. Firm H based their business on e-trade, but already had this capability and therefore rated it as unimportant in relation to their product configuration system.

Optimizing products was an important expected benefit to 3 firms (E, H and L), 2 firms found it to be of medium importance, and the remaining 7 said it was unimportant. Firms E and L have their configuration systems available on the internet, and therefore it is important that customers can use the configuration system as a means of optimizing their product choice. Firm H makes their product configuration system available to their sales offices, and it is important to use the product configuration system to guide the sales staff to the right product for the particular situation.

Making knowledge visible was an important expected benefit to 2 firms (A and L), 2 firms found this to be of medium importance, and the remaining 8 found it unimportant. Firm A was the heavy engineering firm focused on preserving knowledge. However, preservation was not enough, and their knowledge should be easily available to all employees. To leverage this, their product structure was organised by using Lotus Notes. This allows employees to view a particular product, identify parts and their relation to other parts as well as key staff with knowledge about the particular part. Firm L produces a complex product with many rules for its composition, and these rules have been integrated in the product

model. Customers and staff should be able to access these rules when configuring a product of which the configuration conflicted with one or more rules and offer a reason and a possible solution. Both had their expectations met.

Less routine work was an important expected benefit to 4 firms (A, B, D, and L), 3 firms found this to be of medium importance, and the remaining 5 found it unimportant. The four firms thtat found this important experienced a large amount of repetitive work in the process of producing a quote. Firms A, B, and D achieved the expected benefit, but not firm L. While the product configuration system is functional in firm L and is used by customers, the sales staff has not experienced the hoped-for reduction in routine work. This is mainly because the sales staff does not use the product configuration system and keeps working in their old ERP system. Two factors seem to be causing this: 1) A large part of the routine work is producing urgent quotes. A customer calls and asks to have a product delivered within three days, and since there is little or no spare production capacity, the sales person has to negotiate overtime work and further negotiate a suitable price with the customer. This may appear expensive, but in fact it is a very profitable price parameter: quick delivery = high price.

B2B networks constituted an important expected benefit to 4 firms (A, C, E, and L), all the other firms found it unimportant. Firms A and E achieved it and allowed other companies to access their configuration system and order products. Firm C abandoned all access to their configuration system from outside agents. Firm L envisioned several companies with access to their configuration system, but ended up with a strategic alliance with only one firm. Other firms were in general weary of exposing too much information and knowledge to other firms, be it partners or competitors.

Improved certainty of delivery was an important expected benefit to 3 firms (F, H, and I). Firms F and H reached their goal, and firm I did not. Firm I implemented a new ERP system, which the configuration system was part of. However, the required organisational discipline was not strictly enforced, and staff did not always report status changes to the system, which lead to problems. Although the situation had improved compared to before system implementation, there was a clear awareness of the problem of data discipline. Interestingly enough, firm C and G realized this to full effect although not expected. When firm C upgraded their ERP system, the new system contained a new and improved materials planning algorithm, which is the sole reason for achieving this benefit.

Focus on standard products was an important expected benefit to 2 firms (H and I), 2 firms found it of medium importance, and the remaining 8 found it to be unimportant. Both firm H and I realized this, and it had special impact on firm I, which is manufacturing products in which a 40-60 m tower is a central component. It so happens that a tower which is 2 meters higher that a standard tower may cost more than 100% more to produce due to changes in the structural dynamics as well as the cost of additional engineering resources to make the required additional calculations. Before implementing the product configuration system, this knowledge was not immediately visible to sales staff that accommodated customers to the highest tower. (A higher tower produces a higher benefit to the customer). With the new immediate access to real prices, sales staff can communicate this to customers, who find it difficult to justify a 100% cost increase in the light of a 4% increase in production capacity.

Job training made easy was a medium important expected benefit to just two firms (H and J), and the rest of the firms found this unimportant. The two firms expected to use the configuration systems as part of the company training system.

1.4 Costs

The task of analysing costs is hampered by the fact that of the 11 firms that reported realized costs only 5 of these reported expected costs. This is by it self interesting as it indicate that 50% of the firms did not accurately calculate or predict costs before beginning to implement their configuration system.

Specifying the product revealed that firms are actually good at predicting the cost of specifying the product. In some cases (firm F and I) this can be time consuming and very expensive. Firm F estimated that 8 person years had gone into specifying their product. For firm I this was also a painful task, as the firm was used to a very fluid understanding of their product, thus documenting that the product and related processes turned out to be very consuming.

Choosing software is interesting, as some of the firms did not realize the importance hereof. Firm E in particular set out to use the Baan configurator (a specific brand name), but found, after a few month of work, that integration to their ERP system was difficult, and they decided to use the configuration system integrated in their ERP system.

Coding is high ranking in both realized and expected costs. What is interesting is the systematic misjudgement of the required resources to code. Firm C expected this to be fairly cheap, but found that the bulk of costs were in fact related to coding. The lesson learned is to be aware of the cost of coding, like the complexity of software projects is high, and attention to detail is paramount, which makes it difficult to predict. This is not unlike software projects in general, which exhibit cost and time overruns.

Integration to existing systems is straight forward, in particular when using a configuration system, which is part of the company ERP system. Because the interfaces are often specified, it is possible to predict the amount of coding necessary to integrate with existing systems. However, as illustrated by "Choosing Software", there may be prohibitive difficulties when integrating to other systems.

Implementation, i.e. the cost of training, can also be a surprise to some firms. In particular firms with users in different countries (Firms C, D, G, H) realize high costs. This is related to different organisational setups, different computer systems and to some extent different cultures.

Maintenance costs are in general low. Some firms rated maintenance costs to zero, which is disturbing, as a product configuration system must be maintained to be useful. Follow-up questions revealed that the true cost of maintenance was present, but too low to be significant compared to other costs.

Cost of innovation was only given a rating by two firms. The remaining firms gave this rating zero points. These two firms recognised that they had to use resources to obtain information about the market, because of the changed specification process. However, most of the responding firms are new to configuration, and this may have an impact on their answers.

Project management was underestimated in three out of four firms.

Documentation was the highest expected costs. Interestingly, this is also one of the lowest realized costs. All but one firm expected this to be fairly costly, but decided to not document it because of a pressing schedule and lack of resources. It is expected that firms not documenting their system will have a potential maintenance problem if key employees leave the firm.

Consultants are, not surprisingly, expensive. Two firms (C and D) miscalculated the need for consultants, although the two situations are very different. Firm C needed to meet a target deadline and did not have the required in-house resources, which lead to use of expensive consultants. Firm D did not specify clearly what jobs the consultants should do and more importantly not do, in which case the consultants kept working on the system.

Software costs are also very low, which was not expected. This is related to the fact that many of the interviewed firms use the configuration system present in their ERP system. This provides the firms with a configuration system at no additional cost.

Hardware was only rated high in one case, and others rated it low compared to other costs. Four firms found the hardware costs to be negligent.

IMPLICATIONS FOR HUMAN FACTORS

The expected benefits reveal the firms' motivation for implementing product configuration systems. Examining the three main expected benefits: 1) Improved quality of specifications, 2) Using less resources, and 3) Lower turnaround time, it becomes apparent that they are all productivity drivers. Improved quality of specifications may initially appear not to be a direct productivity driver, but faulty specifications – if discovered before being shipped to the customer – will result in rework.

Being productivity drivers has implications for the employees in the affected jobs, as they are to become more efficient. In this study the general observation was that employees became more specialized and would work at a higher pace. But the work also changed qualitatively from having almost complete freedom to create a product configuration which would perfectly match the customer, to being confined to the closed solution space of the product configuration system. The specification process also changed from being adapted to the specific customer and configuration, to a predetermined process i.e. the configuration process followed a defined sequence of steps.

The employees attitudes towards this change can be divided into two extreme cases: 1) engineers and 2) sales staff.

Engineers generally did not appreciate this change, as the configuration system would leave them with less influence on the design of the customers' solution. In firm A, one engineer had already developed counter strategies based on selecting configurations that were not part of the system's solution space. This allowed the engineer to revert back to the specification process from before implementing the configuration system. The engineer was the only person with detailed knowledge of what customers wanted and was thus in a position to argue why a non-standard configuration (not part of the configuration system) should be used.

Engineers represent one end of the spectrum, as they have the capability to modify the products and on their own present solutions without using a configuration system. Engineers will naturally perceive configuration systems as a threat to their domain of expertise. In the other end of the spectrum we find sales staff with little technical knowledge. This group of users are very fond of configuration systems, as they support their job function.

Sales staff in firm I was very happy to get configuration systems, as they became able to service customers without always having to consult engineers. In this case, the configuration system was able to map from functional requirements to structure and for all practical purposes come up with a complete product specification. The sales staff felt empowered, as the configuration system clearly showed the possible solutions to a customer, who would normally pressure the sales staff into a configuration to their advantage. Experience, however, showed that the firm often lost money because what appeared to be harmless changes e.g. making the product a couple of percent higher would result in significant structural changes and costly re-engineering.

Product configuration systems can have severe consequences for the employees, but firms are not aware of this prior to implementation. The uncovered expected or realized costs do not mention organizational change or negative impact on job satisfaction as a cost. Respondents mention implementation, however, only in the sense of costs related to educating employees in using the configuration system. This is a very mechanistic perception of how new technology is implemented which essentially assume that the plan is followed. The problem is that the plan also assume that employees will participate in a process that might have a negative impact on their work situation. While they may not loose their job, it will certainly change.

Firms must realized that product configuration systems change the processes and roles of employees within their organization. Product configuration systems cannot be implemented as simple technical systems with no organizational impact, they must be handled as organizational change projects.

ACKNOWLEDGMENT

This research has been funded by The Danish Technical Research Council, STVF (Statens Teknisk Videnskabelige Forskningsråd) http://www.forsk.dk/eng/stvf/index.htm.

We would also like to acknowledge the help from our fellow researchers participating in the project (listed alphabetically): Assistant professor Benjamin Loer Hansen, associate professor PhD Lars Hvam, a, PhD. Martin Mails, research assistant Morten Møldrup, associate professor Niels Møller, associate professor Jørgen Lindgaard Pedersen and PhD Jesper Riis. Without the help of these fine individuals this paper would not have been the same, however, we are responsible for any remaining vulnerabilities.

REFERENCE

Arthur, W. B. (1989). Competing technologies and lock-in by historical events. *The Economic Journal, 99*, 116–131. doi:10.2307/2234208

Bei, Yu., & Skovgaard, H. J. (1998). A configuration tool to increase product competitiveness. *IEEE Intelligent Systems*, *13*, 34–41. doi:10.1109/5254.708431

Blecker, T., Abdelkafi, N., Kreutler, G., & Friedrich, G. (2004). Product Configuration Systems: State of the Art, Conceptualization and Extensions. *Munic Personal RePEe Archive*.

Clason, D. L. & Dormody, T. J. (1994). Analyzing Data Measured by Individual Likert-Type Items. *Journal of Agricultural Education 35*.

Davis, S. (1987). *Future Perfect*. Reading, MA: Addison-Wesley.

Duray, R., Ward, P. T., Miligan, G. W., & Berry, W. L. (2000). Approaches to mass customization: configurations and empirical validation. *Journal of Operations Management*, *18*, 605–625. doi:10.1016/S0272-6963(00)00043-7

Eisenhardt, K. M. (1989). Building Theories from Case Study Research. *Academy of Management Review*, *14*, 532–550. doi:10.2307/258557

Forza, C., & Salvador, F. (2001). Managing for variety in the order acquisition and fulfilment process: The contribution of product configuration systems. *International Journal of Production Economics*, *76*, 98.

Forza, C., & Salvador, F. (2002). Product configuration and inter-firm co-ordination: an innovative solution from a small manufacturing enterprise. *Computers in Industry*, *49*, 37–46. doi:10.1016/S0166-3615(02)00057-X

Forza, S., & Salvador, F. (2007). *Product Information Management for Mass Customization*, (1 Ed.). New York: Palgrave Macmillan.

Gilmore, J., & Pine, B. J. (1997). The Four Faces of Mass Customization. *Harvard Business Review*, *75*, 91–101.

Haag, A. (1998). Sales configuration in business processes. *IEEE Intelligent Systems*, *13*, 78–85. doi:10.1109/5254.708436

Hansen, B. L. (2003). *Development of Industrial Variant Specification Systems*. Department of Manufacturing Engineering and Management, Technical University of Denmark.

Hvam, L. (1999). A procedure for building product models. *Robotics and Computer-integrated Manufacturing*, *15*, 77–87. doi:10.1016/S0736-5845(98)00030-1

Jacobsen, J. K. (1997). *Interview – Kunsten at lytte og spørge*. Copenhagen: Hans Reitzels Forlag.

Kvale, S. (1997). *InterView*. Copenhagen: Hans Reitzels Forlag.

Ladeby, K. R., Edwards, K., & Haug, A. (2007). *Typology of Product Configuration Systems*. In T. Blecker, K. Edwards, G. Friedrich, L. Hvam, & F. Salvadore (Eds.), *IMCM'07 & PETO'07* (pp. 175-184), GITO.

Piller, F. (2004). Mass Customization: Reflections on the State of the Concept. *International Journal of Flexible Manufacturing Systems*, *16*, 313–334. doi:10.1007/s10696-005-5170-x

Pine, B. J. I. (1999). *Mass customization – The New Frontier in Business Competition*. Cambridge, MA: Harvard Business School Press.

Riis, J. (2003). *Fremgangsmåde for Opbygning, implementering og vedligeholdelse af produktmodeller*. Ph.D. Department of Manufacturing Engineering and Management, Technical University of Denmark.

Silveira, G. D., Borenstein, D., & Foglitto, F. S. (2001). Mass customization: Litterature review and research directions. *International Journal of Production Economics*, *72*, 1–13. doi:10.1016/S0925-5273(00)00079-7

Tseng, M., & Jiao, J. (2001). Mass Customization. In G. Salvendy (Ed.), *Handbook of Industrial Engineering* (3rd ed., pp. 684-709). New York: Wiley.

APPENDIX 1

Expected Benefits	A	B	C	D	E	F	G	H	I	J	K	L
Lower turnaround time	2	5	4	5	5	4	0	5	0	1	5	5
Improved quality	5	4	4	4	5	5	0	5	5	5	5	4
Preserve knowledge	5	1	4	5	0	3	0	2	0	2	0	0
Using less resources	2	5	4	5	4	3	0	2	0	3	0	4
E-trade	0	0	4	0	5	0	0	0	0	0	0	5
Optimizing products	3	2	0	0	5	0	0	5	0	0	0	5
Making knowledge visible	4	1	0	0	0	3	0	1	3	0	0	4
Less routine work	5	4	1	5	3	3	0	2	0	0	0	4
B2B networks	4	0	5	0	5	1	0	0	0	0	0	5
Improved certainty of delivery	0	0	0	0	0	4	0	4	4	0	0	1
Focus on standard products	0	2	0	0	0	0	0	5	4	0	0	3
Job training made easy	0	0	0	0	0	0	0	3	0	3	0	0

Chapter 13
Usability and User Experience Evaluation Methods

Regina Bernhaupt
ruwido, User Experience Research, Austria

ABSTRACT

Usability and user experience are two important factors in the development of mass-customizable personalized products. A broad range of evaluation methods is available to improve products during an user-centered development process. This chapter gives an overview on these methods and how to apply them to achieve easy-to-use, efficient and effective personalized products that are additionally fun to use. A case study on the development of a new interaction technique for interactive TV helps to understand how to set up a mix of evaluation methods to cope with some of the limitations of current usability and user experience evaluation methods. The chapter concludes with some guidelines of how to change organizations to focus on usability and user experience.

INTRODUCTION

Mass customization has become a buzz word relating to the ability to provide customized products or services through flexible processes in high volumes at reasonable costs (Da Silveira, Borenstein and Fogliatto, 2001). Customization can be found in almost all areas of daily life ranging from T-shirts with personalized messages, shoes with personalized color concepts to the personalization of IT and ICT products, like cell phones with new forms of ring-

tones, to new forms of entertainment like interactive TV, allowing users to personalize and individualize their content (Riemer and Totz, 2001). Following these examples we use the term mass customization describing "a system that uses information technology, flexible process, and organizational structures to deliver a wide range of products and services that meet specific needs of individual customers" (Da Silveira et al., 2001, p. 2).

Mass customization can exist on varying levels and several factors contribute to the success of a mass customization system. From the organizational and market-related perspective the customer

DOI: 10.4018/978-1-60566-260-2.ch013

demand for variety and customization must exist, market conditions must be appropriate, the value chain should be ready, the technology must be available, the products should be customizable and the knowledge about the process must be shared (Da Silveira et al., 2001). Usability and user experience evaluation method contribute to these success factors, taking additionally into account that the final product or service should be usable and have a positive user experience. When developing a product that can be mass customized, a user-centered development perspective (UCD) helps to understand who is using when, what, how often, in what kind of context and how to improve usability and user experience (Kramer, Noronha & Vergo, 2000).

Usability evaluation methods have been developed in the field of human-computer interaction (HCI) during the last 25 years, offering a wide range of applicable methods for all stages in the development cycle. User experience (UX) in contrast is a relatively new focus point in HCI. There is a still on-going development of methods and approaches to understand, investigate, and evaluate UX.

This chapter is going to present an overview on usability and UX evaluation methods. Goal of this chapter is to explain from the perspective of human-computer interaction the importance of usability and UX evaluation within the development cycle of mass-customizable personalized products. Describing some of the most commonly used evaluation methods we show how these methods can be applied within a user-centered development process, and when application of standard usability evaluation methods is limited. Additionally methods are presented that are not typical for the industrial context, but which can help to understand how to make mass-customizable personalized products and services usable and how to develop products that have a positive user experience.

Using a case study we describe how to set up a methodological mix, to (in our opinion)

successfully support the development of a mass-customizable personalized product. The chapter concludes giving practical implications for managers on how to take usability and UX into account from an organizational perspective.

USABILITY EVALUATION METHODS

Usability evaluation is a set of methods used in the area of human-computer interaction to increase the efficiency, effectiveness and user satisfaction when interacting with any form of computer or more general any form of information and communication technologies. The document ISO 9241-11 18 Guidance on Usability (ISO, 2008) specifies usability as: "The extent to which a product can be used by specified users to achieve specified goals with effectiveness, efficiency and satisfaction in a specified context of use." A major issue for products and services being mass customized is the overall utility of such systems or products. The area of usability evaluation today can be summarized as all forms of methods that can help to understand how to improve the usability of a system, to investigate usability problems in all kinds of usage contexts, or even to understand the long-term usage of a product in the field to inform new generations of the product.

From the perspective of human-computer interaction the development of a usable product can only be achieved following an iterative development process. Goal of a user-centered design process (ISO 13407) is to develop a usable product typically in various iterative phases. A typical product development could start with investigating new ideas for a product in the field, followed by a user and task analysis and a simple paper prototype. Usability evaluation is conducted continuously during the whole development to understand how to improve the product or service in terms of usability. At each stage during the development different methods can be used to improve usability aspects of the product. Usability evaluation methods can be categorized in four different groups (Bernhaupt, Palanque, Winkler, Navarre, 2007):

- Inquiry oriented methods: questionnaires, probing, interviews, …
- User studies and testing: usability tests, field studies, …
- Inspection or expert oriented methods: heuristic evaluation, cognitive walkthrough, …
- Analytical modeling: task model analysis, performance models, …

Following we briefly describe some of the most commonly used methods and their application during a user-centered design process.

Usability Evaluation during User-Centered Development

When starting to develop a new product, during the *idea generation phase*, various methods can help to understand users needs and desires. Most commonly used are methods from social sciences like *interviews*, *questionnaires* or *focus group* to evaluate first design ideas. But especially when looking at how to improve a current product, usage of the existing product in the field should be taken into account. Commonly used is customer feedback from internet sites or hot-lines.

Mass customized personalized products today are used anytime, anywhere, alone or with others: in a rock concert with thousands of people, alone in your car or in the living room together with your family. To investigate product usage in all kinds of context ethnographic studies (see e.g. Fetterman, 1998) are used in the area of human-computer interaction. To limit the typical problems of ethnographic studies of researchers taking part in the field study and to enable the investigation of daily life without researchers' participation *cultural probes* (Gaver et al. 1999)

were invented as a methodological variation of ethnographic studies (Atkinson, 2003). Developed in the tradition of artists and designers and not based on typical engineering approaches, cultural probing is purposefully designed to inspire, reveal and capture the forces that shape an individual and his/her life, at home, at work or on the move (Harper, 2003). It is a method for understanding participant's experiences and behavior in situ. Probes are mainly used to gather insights on the users' context in order to better inform the design process in an early stage (Gaver et al. 1999; Jääskö and Mattelmäki, 2003).

For *early development stages*, especially when a first (paper) prototype is available *expert or inspection oriented methods* can be applied. Evaluation based on inspection methods assumes that human factors experts rely on ergonomic knowledge provided by guideline recommendations or on their own experience to identify usability problems while inspecting the user interface. Methods belonging to this category include *cognitive walkthrough* (Wharton, Rieman, Lewis & Pohlsen, 1994) and *heuristic evaluation* (Nielsen & Mack, 1994).

Analytical modeling like *task model analysis* and *performance model* can help to understand if personalization is really useful for the user. If you are able to adopt your running shoes to any kind of ground – this might be a reasonable personalization. But if it might mean that the user has to stop running, bend down to his shoes, change a setting, go up again, inspect if he is comfortable with the setting – or start the process again – this kind of personalization might fail in terms of usability. Same holds true for the (often cumbersome) mass customization of new information and communication technologies – upload of a ring tone might be done only once, but lots of user groups will never succeed to do so – as their knowledge of the interaction with a mobile phone is limited. Especially the usage of task model analysis and performance models can help to understand how difficult the customization of the product will be, and if this increased effort outweighs the perceived benefits for the user.

Once a prototype is available user testing can help to reveal typical usage problems. *Usability tests* are performed asking users to perform selected tasks. Observation of the user can be performed by the so called test-leader, or is done using cameras. The results of the user performance (time to solve the task, number of errors, the user's solution of the task) help to understand possible usability problems. The usability problems can be related to several principles related to the concept of usability, like learnability, flexibility or the robustness of the system.

But a usability test only shows the usability problems and does not offer solutions. Asking participants performing a task how they would improve the interaction to make the task easier to perform is one possibility. Typically the improvement of the user interaction in terms of usability is a long process, having designers, usability specialists and engineers working close together.

During later development stages performing *user studies in the lab and in the field* can help to understand how the users are customizing their products, how they use the technical infrastructure to personalize and individualize their content and what kind of usability problems might arise.

The application of usability evaluation methods always has to take into account the product currently under development. Especially when developing products that will be mass-customizable and personalized we have to keep in mind the limitations and shortcomings of some methods. Table 1 gives an overview on advantages and limitations of usability evaluation methods, once applied to products that allow the user to customize and personalize. For further information on expert oriented methods like heuristic evaluation, cognitive walkthrough or pluralistic walkthrough we refer to (Nielsen and Mack, 1993), for conducting usability studies, tests or experiments see Dix, Finlay, Abowd and Beale (2004), for evalua-

tion methods in mobile settings see Marsden and Jones (2006).

The listing in Table 1 shows typical benefits and shortcomings of the various usability evaluation methods, once applied for mass-customized products. But usability is only one aspect that contributes to the overall success of a product. There are several other factors – today discussed in human-computer interaction using the term user experience – that have an impact on the overall success of the product or service. How user experience is defined in the area of HCI and how to evaluate this concept is explained in the next section.

User Experience Evaluation Methods

When customizing products not only usability aspects have to be evaluated, but more general the attitudes, feelings and emotions before, during and after product usage have to be taken into account. The term user experience is best introduced using a simple example. Assume you are playing a game. To play the game you simply have to click a button. And then you reach the goal of the game: YOU WIN! This is a perfectly usable game – but unfortunately it is not what a game is about (Huinziga, 1950). Playing a game is not only about being usable – but about mastering the game play. It is about having fun, experiencing emotions, having a great time, perceiving a state which is called flow – forgetting about the real world and just living for the moment.

The term user experience has his roots as one additional dimension of usability, referred to as fun (Lewis, 1988). Currently there are three different perspectives in literature: a perspective going beyond the instrumental, looking at factors like hedonic quality, beauty or aesthetics, an emotional perspective including affect, mood and emotions and an experiential perspective looking at the situated, temporarily bound, dynamic, unique, and complex aspects of user experience (Hassenzahl and Tractinsky, 2006).

Table 1. Advantages and Shortcomings for typical usability evaluation methods when evaluating customization and personalization.

Method	Key Facts	Advantage(s)	Shortcoming(s)
Idea generation phase			
Interviews, Questionnaires	Investigating ideas based on (telephone) interviews or questionnaires	Time: Quick, Budget: low	Findings: difficult for people to envision how they really would personalize and adopt their products
Focus Group	Idea generation or first feedback on product ideas	Time: Quick, Budget: low	Findings: Group results can be biased by the participants in the group, by the artifact used to present the ideas, real usage of a final product typically differs
Cultural Probes	Using probing material to support the self-observation of participants in an ethnographic study	Findings: Detailed insight in daily habits, user needs and desires and real usage	Time: Results are typically qualitative thus analysis of data is time consuming, Budget: high
Early development phase			
Cognitive Walkthrough	Investigate the learnability of the product	Findings: Focuses on one of the most prominent aspects of personalization: how people can learn to do so Time: quick, Budget: low,	Availability of experts with HCI and domain knowledge sometimes difficult
Heuristic Evaluation	Investigate usability aspects of the product	Time: quick, Budget: low	Availability of heuristics and guidelines for personalization is limited
Analytical modeling	Understand the user interaction	Helps understand new forms of interaction technique (e.g. multimodal interfaces, non-standard input and output)	Time: intensive, Budget: high
Late(r) development phase			
- Usability Testing	Users are performing typical tasks, which are observed in a lab environment	Standardized environment allowing repetitive testing of similar situations, technical infrastructure can be easily influenced	No long term usage, no insights on how personalization develops over time, how mental models are changing.
- Field user studies (Field trials)	Evaluating the technology in the field	Insights into real usage of the system, typically revealing usability problems that can not be found during lab testing	Budget: high, Time: high

How user experience shall be evaluated is still focus of a scientific discourse. But several methods exist, helping to understand user experiences and the user needs and desires that form the basis for any user experience. To investigate user experience from a research perspective methods from social science are applied. To understand aspects of user needs and wants, their motivations and experiences ethnographic studies can be used.

Table 2 gives an overview on evaluating user experience in terms of the three existing research perspectives, describing briefly advantages and limitations. Following a brief description of these methods and some of their methodological variations is given.

Ethnographic studies including methods like *cultural probing* can help to understand the user and the usage context. While quantitative research

Table 2. *User Experience Evaluation Methods*

Evaluation Methods for UX	Key Facts	Advantage(s)	Shortcoming(s)
Ethnographic Studies/ Various Probing Approaches	Qualitative insights on people's daily live	Gives insight on people daily life on a qualitative basis, can be used before a product is developed	Probing material has to be carefully designed
Experience Sampling Method	Insight in people's daily live	ESM can be used throughout the design life cycle	Technological based ESM can be time and resource intensive and personalization and individualization are difficult to be logged
AttrakDiff	Questionnaire to evaluate the dimensions of hedonic and pragmatic quality	Easy to use, fast	Measures only a short term perspective of one factor that contributes to user experience
SAM/Emocards	Questionnaire oriented self-assessment of emotions	Easy, fast, cheap	Typically used after interacting with the product, so effects like the recency effect can influence the judgment and people might not remember well their emotions during the interaction.
Bio-metrical measurements	Using heart rate, skin conductance or facial expression changes to investigate emotions	Detailed insight on minimal physiological changes	Interpretation of bio-metrical measurements is still unclear, set-up is expensive and resource intensive

can tell us what kind of products are used in the home, how many hours they are used, qualitative, ethnographic research tells us how and why people use products and services. New forms of mass customization are addressing products which are mostly used in the context of home. Studies (e.g. Venkatesh, 1996, Venkatesh, Kruse and Chuan-Fong Shih, 2003, Haddon, 2006) agree that studying the home is a difficult endeavor, as the home contains many areas of human life.

To explore the ways in which households use communication, information and other domestic technologies, Crabtree, Hemmings, Rodden, Cheverst, Clarke, Dewsbury, Hughes and Rouncefield (2004) used ethnographically oriented methods. They visited household and investigated daily routines and interactions, ownership of space and how household members manage interactions. Findings were reported using ethno-methodologically informed ethnographic descriptions based on Garfinkel (1967). Hindus, Mainwaring, Leduc, Hagsrom and Bayley (2001) investigated how media space concepts could be incorporated into households and family life. They

used ethnographically inspired field studies and in-depth interviews to evaluate early prototypes for home communication in real world settings.

In the early development phase usage of *cultural probing* can help to understand the users in terms of experiences they make. When looking at how people want to individualize and personalize their IT products and services, adoption of these methods can help to gain further insights on possible contributing factors influencing a positive long term experience of a product (Bernhaupt, Obrist, Weiss, Beck and Tscheligi, 2008).

When conducting a study using cultural probing a so called probe package is provided to study participants. The probe package normally consists of diaries, cameras, post cards, sometimes maps of the explored environments, and several other means to obtain as much insight as possible from the participants live style, usage patterns and behaviors. Participants are free to control time and means of capture. Gaver et al. (1999) reported that return rates of materials can vary significantly in different settings and populations. This possible disadvantage of low return rates was alleviated in studies conducted (Bernhaupt, Weiss, Obrist, Tscheligi, 2007; Obrist, Bernhaupt, Tscheligi, 2006) by combining the collection of probing material with a final interview conducted in all households.

Today a set of methodological variations of cultural probes is available to investigate usability and user experience issues in all kinds of contexts, areas and situation: Hutchinson et al. (2003) developed technology probes, Crabtree et al. (2004) adapted cultural probes to inform design in sensitive settings, and Hulkko, Keinonen, Mattelmäki, Virtanen (2004) extended the method to cope with mobile settings.

Apart from several methodological variations for different settings and purposes, there is another trend trying to increase active and creative user involvement. To explore certain aspects of the home context two methodological variations called creative cultural probing and playful probing were developed (Bernhaupt, Weiss et al., 2007; Obrist et al., 2006).

Playful probing "uses the standard set-up of cultural probing, taking for example post-cards or post-its as probing material to gather insights on people's habits and usage. The playful probing approach differs from the traditional approach as it uses games that are specially designed for the study. In playful probing the games are designed focusing on the research area addressed within the study. The development for the game itself depends on the study set-up. Depending on the topic to be investigated, variations of existing games can be used or even new games are developed." (Bernhaupt, Weiss et al., 2007, p. 609). Main advantages of playful probing is the ability to focus on the research topic in a playful way, to include children in the in-situ research process within the household and to increase the frequency participants work on the research topic. Playful probing of course needs careful preparation, well designed games, focusing on the research topic and the method should be combined with other

forms of material, like creative cultural probing, technology probes.

Focus of the evaluation of UX can be to understand the emotional attachment of the user related to the product, feelings of the user while interacting with the product, as well as satisfaction, fun and other related concepts like acceptance of the product. Research in that area typically must be supported by research in marketing to find out if products are representing the current life-style and if the individualization of the product is perceived as useful by the users.

When investigating the user experience of mass customization a method called *experience sampling method (ESM)* can be used. Originally introduced by Csikszentmihalyi (see Hektner, Schmidt and Csikszentmihaly, 2006), the method asks the user to protocol his feelings and emotions before, during or after usage of a product. Computer-supported forms of the ESM today help to investigate everyday life. ESM is conducted in-situ, involves many participants, and takes place over time, and collects quantitative and qualitative data. When using experience sampling for usability evaluation the specific research interests as well as the measurement method, which are suitable to gain the desired information, must be carefully considered. The main qualities of experience sampling are that usability and user experience factors can be studied within a natural setting, in real time, on repeated time occasions, and by request. Computerized experience sampling on mobile devices has recently gained a lot of attention, especially since people are used to carrying mobile devices with them most of the time (Bernhaupt, Mihalic, Obrist, 2008).

Hedonic quality is evaluated using questionnaires like the *AttrakDiff* (www.attrakdiff.de). Focusing on emotions as an important part of user experience various forms of questionnaires have been used. *Emocards* (Desmet, Overbeeke & Dax, 2001) uses 16 faces representing eight emotions on the two dimensions arousal and pleasantness.

Other questionnaires measuring emotion have been developed in psychology, e.g. the *Self-Assessment-Manikin (SAM)* or usage of semantic differentials (Bradley and Lang, 1994). Especially in the area of games emotions have been evaluated using *bio-metrical measurements* (Mandryk, Atkin & Inkpen, 2006). The experimental perspective dealing with the nature of experience has been mainly investigated from a research perspective (Forlizzi and Battarbee, 2004).

CASE STUDY: DEVELOPING PERSONALIZED ITV

When developing a product that enables customers to personalize their content the selection of usability and user experience evaluation methods has to be done carefully. This case study reports the evaluation methods used during the development of a new form of interaction technique that supports users in personalizing interactive TV content. Goal of this project (called vocomedia) is to develop new forms of interaction techniques for the living room, to support personalization of interactive TV services.

Step one in the development of vocomedia was to investigate how people personalize their content. We investigated how the usage context of the final product looks like, how it influences the usage of the product and what peoples' needs, desires and experiences are. To investigate the home context, ethnographic studies have been extensively used in the field of human-computer interaction. As direct observation in households is limited, a probing approach was selected. To improve some shortcoming of certain probing methods we created a variation of the cultural probing approach called playful probing and combined it with a more creative form of cultural probing. Goal was to understand people's daily habits related to recommendations.

The method could help to understand how people perceive recommendations, to what level people want to have new recommendations, how many recommendations should include programs that are already watched (to increase trust), and that personalization of services is always working on a thin line: from what users want to become personalized/recommended and what they perceive as not relevant recommendation (Bernhaupt, Wilfinger, Weiss & Tscheligi, 2008).

Probing methods thus help to informally explore insights, to generate qualitative data, but also to understand behaviors and needs. Based on the findings in several other ethnographic studies a first prototype was developed. To allow users to secure their content, respect privacy concerns and to increase trust in the system, we developed a remote control including fingerprint recognition. The ethnographic studies showed that people would prefer a reduced number of keys on the remote control. We thus started to investigate usability issues of remote controls and compared three types of remote controls and corresponding interface designs.

To compare the three design prototypes we first conducted a heuristic evaluation. As the number of possible usability problems was high for all the three design prototypes we started to develop a flexible prototype allowing us to use all three different types of user interaction, based on the same data and functionality. To decide which user interface supports best users in terms of usability and user experience, we conducted a comparative usability study. The comparative usability study included measurements like task completion, errors and user satisfaction, but additionally used the AttrakDiff questionnaire to investigate hedonic quality. Users were also asked to work out their own design idea on how to order the keys on the remote control.

To investigate the concept further, we extended the prototype including functionalities like recommendations, video-on-demand, management of photos and music. We also included several forms of personalization. Based on the (identified) user, the user interface displays different orderings of the

TV channels, shows selected recommendations or allows social communication with other users. If personalization is usable was evaluated in a series of user studies, including various user groups. Especially during the testing of personalized systems various aspects of trust and security have been taken into account. This is especially true for the home environment. People, even living in the same households fear, that their private viewing habits do not stay private once recommendations (for the whole household) are based on them. Users mentioned that for example recommendations for late night shows or recommendations for movies with adult content should not be seen by the children living in the same household. The problem of testing personalized content is well known in the literature, especially when asking personal questions to select data. Kramer, Noronha and Vergo (2000) state that "users must clearly understand why the question is being asked and how fits in with their goals". They state that it is necessary to measure how well users understand the benefits of the personalized service.

Combining a set of methods during the development process helps to improve the overall usability of the system and to influence the product to convey a positive user experience. The example of vocomedia shows, how the usage of comparative usability testing helps to choose the best alternative for the user, by additionally improving the system with an heuristic evaluation. Additionally the focus on the user at early stages of the development helps to focus on the real needs for personalization of the user.

Organizational Implications

Features classified as "personalization" are wide-ranging, from simple display of the end-user's name on a Web page, to complex catalog navigation and product customization based on deep models of users' needs and behaviors. The role of personalization in the design of any form of service or product is increasing. From a managerial perspective user-centered design is a successful strategy allowing to focus on personalized products that are easy to use, fast to learn and effective. At the same time user-centered development helps to improve the overall positive user experience.

Kramer et al. (2000) have been proposing a six-step user-centered design approach to personalization, arguing to take participatory design as central means for the development of a product. Additionally various forms of evaluation methods can help to improve usability and user experience of the final product. User-centered design is typically a multidisciplinary design approach, involving typically one usability specialist within a project team of ten members (Mao, Vredenburg, Smith and Carey, 2005). Mao et al. (2005) also report that typically 10% of the budget of a project is devoted to usability and user experience. Effectiveness of the user centered design process are typically measured in terms of external (customer) satisfaction, enhances ease of use, impact on sales, reduced number of help desk calls or user feedback based on pre-releases. These measures might help to understand if the user-centered design used improved the development of the product.

CONCLUSION

Usability evaluation of systems and products enabling personalization can be conducted with a wide range of existing methods from the area of human-computer interaction. When evaluating user experience the range of methods is smaller. Depending on the research question user experience of personalized systems can be evaluated with a methodological mix of established usability evaluation methods e.g. in-situ evaluation and user-oriented design methods.

Still open is the question on what kind of methodological mix best respects the research topic on personalization, but in general – as personalization is depending on habits and usages of products and is influenced by various contextual factors - the multi-dimensionality of the research question can only be answered by a combination of methods.

We are currently looking at various combinations of usability and user experience evaluation methods that were used in different fields like interactive TV, human-robot interaction, multimodal interfaces for space operations and mobile interaction. An extensive meta-analysis of all these data should show on how to fruitfully combine methods to explore usability and user experience. Up to then, we will have to rely on case studies, describing methodological benefits and pitfalls to choose the right kind of method mix.

REFERENCES

Atkinson, P., Coffey, A., Delamond, S., Lofland, J., & Lofland, I. (2001). *Handbook of Ethnography*. London: Sage.

Bernhaupt, R., Obrist. M., Weiss, A., Beck, E. & Tscheligi, M. (2008). Trends in the Living Room and Beyond. *Computers in Entertainment, 6*(1), online.

Bernhaupt, R., Mihalic, K., & Obrist, M. (2008). Methods for Usability Evaluation of Mobile Applications. J. Lumsden, (Eds.) *Handbook of Research on User Interface Design and Evaluation for Mobile Technology*, (pp. 742-755). Hershey, PA: IGI Global.

Bernhaupt, R., Palanque, P., Winkler, M., & Navarre, D. (2007). Supporting Usability Evaluation of Multimodal Safety Critical Interactive Applications using Dialogue and Interaction Models. In E. Law, et al. (Eds.) *Maturing Usability: Quality in Software, Interaction and Value* (pp. 95-127). London: Springer.

Bernhaupt, R., Weiss, A., Obrist, M., & Tscheligi, M. (2007). Playful Probing: Making Probing more Fun. In [Heidelberg: Springer.]. *Proceedings of Interact, 2007*, 606–619.

Bernhaupt, R., Wilfinger, D., Weiss, A., & Tscheligi, M. (2008) An Ethnographic Study on Recommendations in the Living Room: Implications for Design of iTV Recommender Systems. In M. Tscheligi, M. Obrist, & A. Lugmair, (Ed.) *Proceedings of EuroiTV 2008* (LNCS Vol. 5066, pp. 92-101). Berlin: Springer.

Bradley, M. M., & Lang, P. J. (1994). Measuring emotion: the self-assessment manikin and the semantic differential. *Journal of Behavior Therapy and Experimental Psychiatry, 25*(1), 49–59. doi:10.1016/0005-7916(94)90063-9

Crabtree, A., Hemmings, T., Rodden, T., Cheverst, K., Clarke, K., Dewsbury, G., et al. (2003). Designing with care: adapting Cultural Probes to Inform Design in Sensitive Settings. In *Proceedings of OzCHI'03: New Directions in Interaction, information environments, media and technology*.

Crabtree, A., & Rodden, T. (2004). Domestic Routines and Design for the Home. *Computer Supported Cooperative Work, 13*(2), 191–220. doi:10.1023/B:COSU.0000045712.26840.a4

Da Silveira, G., Borenstein, D., & Fogliatto, F. S. (2001). Mass customization: Literature review and research directions. *Journal of Production Economics, 72*, 1–13. doi:10.1016/S0925-5273(00)00079-7

Desmet, P. M. A., Overbeeke, C. J., & Tax, S. J. E. T. (2001). Designing products with added emotional value: development and application of an approach for research through design. *The Design Journal, 4*(1), 32–47. doi:10.2752/146069201789378496

Dix, A., Finlay, J., Abowd, G., & Bealer, R. (2004) *Human-Computer Interaction*. London: Prentice Hall.

Fetterman, D. M. (1998). *Ethnography: step by step*. (2nd Ed.). Thousand Oaks, CA: Sage Publications.

Forlizzi, J., & Battarbee, K. (2004). Understanding experience in interactive systems. In *Proceedings of the 5th Conference on Designing interactive Systems: Processes, Practices, Methods, and Techniques* (pp. 261-268). New York: ACM.

Garfinkel, H. (1967). *Studies in ethnomethodology*. Englewood Cliffs, NJ: Prentice Hall.

Gaver, B., Dunne, T., & Pacenti, E. (1999). Design: Cultural Probes. *Interaction, 6*(1), 21–29. doi:10.1145/291224.291235

Haddon, L. (2006). The Contribution of Domestication Research to In-Home Computing and Media Consumption. *The Information Society Journal, 22*, 195–203. doi:10.1080/01972240600791325

Harper, R. (2003). *Inside the Smart Home*. London: Springer.

Hassenzahl, M., & Tractinsky, N. (2006). User experience – a research agenda. *Behaviour & Information Technology, 25*(2), 91–97. doi:10.1080/01449290500330331

Hektner, J. M., Schmidt, J. A., & Csikszentmihaly, M. (2006) *Experience Sampling Method – Measuring the Quality of Everyday Life*. Thousand Oaks, CA: Sage Publications.

Hindus, D., Mainwaring, S. D., Leduc, N., Hagstrom, N. L., & Bayley, O. (2001) Casablanca: Designing Social Communication Devices for the Home. In *Proceedings of the Conference on Human Factors in Computing Systems (CHI 2001)* (pp. 325-332). New York: ACM Press.

Huizinga, J. (1950). *Homo Ludens: A Study of the Play-Element in Culture*. Boston: Beacon Press.

Hulkko, S., Keinonen, T., Mattelmäki, T., & Virtanen, K. (2004). Mobile Probes. In . *Proceedings of NordiCHI, 2004*, 43–51. doi:10.1145/1028014.1028020

Hutchinson, H., Mackay, W., Westerlund, B., Bederson, B. B., Druin, A., Plaisant, C., et al. (2003). Technology Probes: Inspiring Design for and with Families. In *Proceedings of Conference on Human Factors in Computing Systems (CHI 2003)*, (pp. 17-24). New York: ACM Press.

ISO. (2008). ISO 16883. Retrieved October 12, 2008 from http://www.iso.org/iso/iso_catalogue/catalogue_tc/catalogue_detail.htm?csnumber=16883

ISO 13407 (2008). ISO 13407. Retrieved October 10, 2008 from http://www.iso.org

Jääskö, V., & Mattelmäki, T. (2003) Observing and Probing. In *Proceedings of the International Conference on Designing Pleasurable Products and Interfaces (DPPI'03)* (pp. 126-131). ACM Press.

Kramer, J., Noronha, S., & Vergo, J. (2000). A user-centered design approach to personalization. *Communications of the ACM, 43*(8), 44–48. doi:10.1145/345124.345139

Mandryk, R. L., Atkins, M. S., & Inkpen, K. M. (2006). A continuous and objective evaluation of emotional experience with interactive play environments. In *Proceedings of the SIGCHI Conference on Human Factors in Computing Systems*.

Mao, J., Vredenburg, K., Smith, P. W., & Carey, T. (2005). The state of user-centered design practice. *Communications of the ACM, 48*(3), 105–109. doi:10.1145/1047671.1047677

Marsden, G., & Jones, M. (2006). *Mobile Interaction Design*. London: Wiley.

Nielsen, J., & Mack, R. L. (Eds.). (1994). *Usability inspection methods*. New York, NY: John Wiley & Sons.

Obrist, M., Bernhaupt, R., & Tscheligi, M. (2006). Interactive Television for the Home: An ethnographic study on users requirements and experiences. *Proceedings of EuroiTV, 2006*, 349–358.

Riemer, K., & Totz, Ch. (2001). The many faces of personalization - an integrative economic overview of mass customization and personalization. In Tseng, M. & Piller, F. (Ed.), *Proceedings of the 2001 World conference on mass customization and personalization*, Hong Kong, October 1-2.

Venkatesh, A. (1996). Computers and other interactive technologies for the home. *Communications of the ACM, 39*(12), 47–54. doi:10.1145/240483.240491

Venkatesh, A., Kruse, E., & Chuan-Fong Shih, E. (2003). The networked home: an analysis of current developments and future trends. *Cognition Technology and Work Journal, 5*(1), 23–32.

Wharton, C., Rieman, J., Lewis, C., & Polson, P. (1994). The cognitive walkthrough method: a practitioner's guide. In Nielsen, J. & Mack, R. L. *Usability inspection Methods*, (pp. 105-140). New York: John Wiley & Sons.

KEY TERMS AND DEFINITIONS

Usability Evaluation Methods (UEMs): A set of methods used to evaluate a system, mock-up, or prototype in terms of usability.

Usability Test: Performance measurements of users to determine whether usability goals have been achieved.

Inspection-Oriented UEMs: Set of methods used by experts and most commonly based on guidelines to investigate possible usability problems.

In-Situ Evaluation Methods: Set of methods used to evaluate a system or prototype in its real usage context.

Context: Mobile services and devices can be used in various places and situations, by a single user or involving others. These circumstances are described as context of use or usage context.

Experience Sampling Method (ESM): An in-situ method especially suitable for collecting quantitative and qualitative data with mobile and ubiquitous systems. ESM studies user experience factors in a natural setting, in real time, and over a longer period of time.

Chapter 14
Effective Product Customization on the Web:
An Information Systems Success Approach

Pratyush Bharati
University of Massachusetts, USA

Abhijit Chaudhury
Bryant College, USA

ABSTRACT

Product customization is an important facility that e-commerce offers to its users. On the Web, choiceboard systems have become quite prevalent as the means by which users are able to customize their products. These systems allow customers to configure products and services by choosing from a menu of attributes, components, delivery options, and prices. In the context of a choiceboard environment, this research examines the impact of system and information quality and information presentation on interface satisfaction and decision satisfaction. Further, it examines the impact of the latter two satisfaction factors on overall user satisfaction and intention to use. The research reveals that improved system quality, vis-à-vis choiceboards, leads to better information and decision satisfaction on the part of the users. This in turn leads to higher overall satisfaction and intention to use. The research uses an experiment for data collection and examines these relationships using the structural equation modeling (SEM) approach.

INTRODUCTION

E-commerce continues to grow, and its iconic companies, such as Amazon, Yahoo, and Google, are now all billon-dollar firms employing thousands of people. The total impact of e-commerce, however, cannot be expressed in simple sales figures; rather, it lies in changing consumer behavior. Increasingly, consumers visit the Web site of a company to familiarize themselves with the firm's offerings and prices before deciding to buy. A Web site is becoming the gateway to a firm's brand, even in the case of off-line firms. Companies that realize the importance of their Web sites use technologies such as e-mail, FAQ, online customer support, bulletin boards, and search engines to assist customers in the buying decision process and, obviously, to persuade a purchase of their product.

The choiceboard is a recent addition to this repertoire of technologies, aiding consumers in the decision-making process (Andal-Ancion, Cartwright, & Yip, 2003; Bharati & Chaudhury, 2004a; Collins & Butler, 2003; Liechty, Ramaswamy, & Cohen, 2001; Slywotzky, 2000). A choiceboard is a system that allows customers to design their own products by choosing from a menu of attributes, components, prices, and delivery options (Slywotzky, 2000). For example, in the automobile industry (http://buyatoyota.com), users can "build" or customize a Toyota and then follow up with a local dealer. In the construction industry (http://kitchens.com), users can get help to design a kitchen and actually place an order. In the apparel industry (http://acustomtshirt4u.com), users can select color, fabric, and a suitable logo and lettering. In the entertainment industry (http://www.apple.com/itunes), customers at the iTunes music store can build customized CDs by selecting individual tracks from existing CDs. Finally, in information technology, the Web sites of most computer firms (e.g., http://www.ibm.com), present individuals with a basic configura-

tion defined by a processor and then "flesh out" the full configuration with choiceboards offering hard-drive size, memory, and add-ons such as CD/DVD drive, monitors, and printers.

Although choiceboard technology is being widely used to enhance the customer's experience, very little is known about the actual impact of this technology on overall user satisfaction or the intention to use the choiceboard. Similar concerns have been expressed for Web-based decision support systems (Bharati & Chaudhury, 2004b). In particular, it remains unclear how the provision of more information, facilitation of decision making through what-if analysis, and choice comparisons through the use of choiceboard technology affects user satisfaction and the intention to use.

In this research, the relationships are developed and operationalized between system-level factors (such as quality of the system and information in choiceboards, and presentation of information) and user's decision-making and interface satisfaction. Furthermore, the analysis investigates the relationship between information and decision-making satisfaction, with overall satisfaction and intention to use. The statistical analysis consists of path analysis, assessing a pattern of predictive relationships among the measured variables. This research employs the structural equation modeling (SEM) technique to analyze the data and then assess the pattern of predictive relationships.

The research views information systems' success in the new domain of e-commerce; and, in particular, in the context of choiceboard systems. It attempts to understand how choiceboards facilitate user decision making in the Web-based environment. It then develops a conceptual model that relates system-level factors, user satisfaction factors, and use factors. Specifically, it investigates interrelationships between components of user satisfaction–interface satisfaction, decision satisfaction, and overall satisfaction–and their combined impact on intention to use.

Literature Review

The research is related to multiple theories such as the consumer decision-making model (Mowen, 1995), consumer information-processing model (Bettman, 1979), cognitive decision-making model (Simon 1955), and information systems (IS) success model (Delone & McLean, 1992, 2002). According to Mowen (1995), a consumer transits through several phases (Figure 1) such as problem recognition, a search for alternatives, and an evaluation of alternatives before making a choice; that is, there is an information-processing phase and then a decision making one. In this process, a consumer tries to minimize cognitive effort required to make a decision and yet maximize the quality of the decision reached (Bettman, 1990). Furthermore, Bettman (1990) suggests that because of bounded rationality constraint (Simon, 1955), consumers actually will trade off decision quality for a reduction in information processing effort.

Consumers employ decision aids, such as calculators, spreadsheets, consumer guides, and Web-based comparison pricing, in order to lessen the impact of bounded rationality constraints on decision quality. E-commerce retailers are incorporating choiceboards on their Web sites to assist customers in several phases of the decision-making process (Bharati & Chaudhury, 2004a; Bharati & Chaudhury, 2004b). The information search phase, for example, is facilitated by easy revelation of product alternatives; and the decision-making phase of alternatives evaluation is made easier by price and feature comparison.

IS Success Model

Web sites have been extensively studied from different perspectives, emphasizing different aspects of Web-site quality. Timeliness aspects have been studied by Choudrie et al. (Choudrie, Ghinea, & Weerakkody, 2004), relevance has been studied by Barnes and Vidgen (2002), and accuracy aspects by Cao and Zhang (2002). Design aspects of a Web site, in terms of its attractiveness and appropriateness, have been studied by Cao and Zhang (2002). Diniz et al. (2005) and Yoo and Jin (2004) have researched into usability and reliability aspects of Web sites.

There has been, however, a gap in literature in terms of studies related to how Web sites have helped users make better decisions. The focus of Web site usability studies has not focused on studying a Web site as a decision tool. The IS success model (Delone & McLean, 1992, 2003), with its focus on issues relating to information processing and decision making and its previous research on Web-based DSS (Bharati & Chaudhury, 2004b), is useful in investigating the role of choiceboards in assisting users make appropriate choices. In the recent literature, this model has served as the basis for investigating similar research areas such as IS and service quality (Bharati & Berg, 2003). Delone and Mclean (2003) refer to about 285 research papers published in refereed journals that use their framework. The model has been empirically validated by Rai et al. (2002) and by Seddon and Kiew (1994)

The research on quality of information systems services (Jiang, Klein, & Carr, 2002; Jiang, Klein, & Crampton, 2000; Kettinger & Lee,

Figure 1. Customer decision process model (Mowen, 1995)

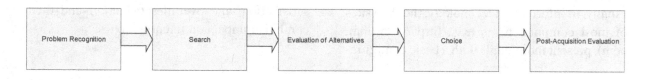

1997; Kettinger & Lee, 1999; Pitt, Watson, & Kavan, 1995; Pitt, Watson, & Kavan, 1997; Van Dyke, Kappelman, & Prybutok, 1997; Van Dyke, Prybutok, & Kappelman, 1999; Watson, Pitt, & Kavan, 1998), and WebQual (Loiacono, Chen, & Goodhue, 2002) has also attempted to investigate this topic in a slightly different way.

Communications theory (Shannon & Weaver, 1949) was illustrated and modified in Mason's work (1978) to show that classes of information output are at the technical level, semantic level, and influence level. The IS success model (Delone & McLean, 1992, 2002) expanded the concept of levels of output to illustrate stages within those levels. Information is communicated to a recipient who is either influenced or not; he/she then impacts organizational performance. In other words, the information flows from its production to influence the individual and then the organization.

System quality and information quality, both singularly and jointly, impact use and user satisfaction. This research model is based on the IS success model and employs some of the constructs of that model, specifically at the technical level of system quality and information quality, in the context of choiceboards, and in their impact on dif-

ferent components of user satisfaction (interface satisfaction, decision-making satisfaction, and resultant overall satisfaction). User satisfaction then influences the intention to use. The next section explains the research model and hypotheses.

RESEARCH MODEL AND HYPOTHESES

The research model (Figure 2 and Table 3) shows that system and information quality, and information presentation, impact the different components of user satisfaction; and then, intention to use. The various constructs and the resulting hypotheses of the model are explained in this section.

System Quality

System quality is the individual perception of a system's overall performance, which is itself a manifestation of system hardware and software. Ease of use (Belardo, Karwan, & Wallace, 1982), convenience of access (Bailey & Pearson, 1983), and system reliability and flexibility (Srinivasan,

Figure 2. Conceptual model

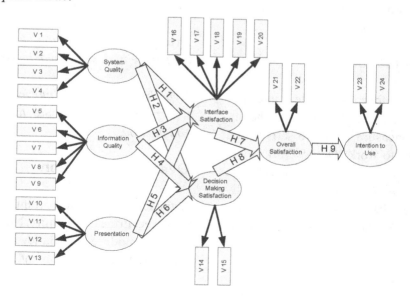

1985) are measures employed for the service quality construct.

Information Quality

The user estimates the value of an information system after evaluating the quality of information it provides (Gallagher, 1974). Information accuracy (Bailey & Pearson, 1983; Mahmood, 1987; Miller & Doyle, 1987; Srinivasan, 1985), completeness (Bailey & Pearson, 1983; Miller & Doyle, 1987), relevance (Bailey & Pearson, 1983; King & Epstein, 1983; Miller & Doyle, 1987; Srinivasan, 1985), content needs (Doll & Torkzadeh, 1988), and timeliness (Bailey & Pearson, 1983; King & Epstein, 1983; Mahmood, 1987; Miller & Doyle, 1987; Srinivasan, 1985) are the measures employed in the information quality construct.

Information Presentation

In information presentation, the display of information based on formats, colors, and graphs vs. tables is examined (Vessey, 1994). The interface evaluation has included presentation, format, and processing efficiency characteristics of the interface (Swanson, 1985). The measures used for information presentation construct are graphics, color, presentation style, and navigational efficiency (Swanson, 1985).

Interface Satisfaction

The quality of the information system interface is measured in interface satisfaction. The indicators used to measure interface satisfaction construct are easy to work (Doll & Torkzadeh, 1988; Goodhue, 1990), useful format (Doll & Torkzadeh, 1988; Goodhue, 1990), user friendly (Doll & Torkzadeh, 1988; Goodhue, 1990), does what I want it to do (Davis, 1989; Goodhue,

1990), and clear and understandable (Davis, 1989; Goodhue, 1990).

Hypothesis 1: System quality will positively contribute to interface satisfaction.

Hypothesis 3: Information quality will positively contribute to interface satisfaction.

Hypothesis 5: Good Information presentation will positively contribute to interface satisfaction.

Decision-Making Satisfaction

Decision-making satisfaction is the systems' ability to support the user's decision-making and problem-solving activities. The systems' support to the individual in recognizing problems, structuring problems, and making decisions related to the goal of controlling a business process are part of the construct (Garrity & Sanders, 1998). The construct measures the decision-making satisfaction using decision effectiveness (Chervany, Dickson, & Kozar, 1972) and decision confidence (Goslar, Green, & Hughes, 1986; Guental, Surprenant, & Bubeck, 1984; Zmud, Blocher, & Moffie, 1983).

Hypothesis 2: System quality will positively contribute to decision-making satisfaction.

Hypothesis 4: Information quality will positively contribute to decision-making satisfaction.

Hypothesis 6: Good Information presentation will positively contribute to decision-making satisfaction.

Overall Satisfaction

Satisfaction is an important and widely used construct in the IS literature. Numerous researchers have modified the Bailey and Pearson (1983) user-satisfaction instrument. The construct of overall satisfaction, a result of interface and decision-making satisfaction, was measured using extremely useful system (Sanders, 1984) and satisfactory in meeting user needs (Alavi & Henderson, 1981; Sanders & Courtney, 1985).

Hypothesis 7: Interface satisfaction will positively contribute to overall satisfaction.

Hypothesis 8: Decision-making satisfaction will positively contribute to overall satisfaction.

Intention to Use

Intention to use a system has often been employed as an important measure of IS success (Chang & Cheung, 2001; DeLone & McLean, 1992; Lucas, 1978; Van der Heijden, 2004; Welke & Konsynski, 1980). Possible to use and intend to use (DeSanctis, 1982) have been employed to measure the intention of user to use the system construct.

Hypothesis 9: Overall satisfaction will positively contribute to intention to use.

RESEARCH METHODOLOGY

The instrument (Appendix A) was constructed based on prior research; most indicator items were adapted or borrowed from previously validated instruments. The survey was first pre-tested with a smaller sample and then subsequently refined. The survey was administered to subjects who were undergraduate and graduate students at two different Universities. They were selected as subjects because they were users of, or familiar with, choiceboard systems. The experiment was conducted in a laboratory setting, with PCs running on the Windows operating system. The researchers, in conducting the experiment, adopted the following procedure.

First, the experimental procedure was explained to the subjects. Then, each subject was randomly assigned a Web site that employed a choiceboard that allowed the user to configure a product. The choiceboard sites were of a very similar nature, despite being owned by different firms. After configuring a product on the Web site, each subject completed a survey questionnaire. The total sample for the experiment was 192 subjects.

Structural equation modeling (SEM) was used to analyze the data. SEM subscribes to a causal indicator model, with the operational indicators reflective of the unobserved theoretical construct. It allows the specification of measurement errors within a broader context of assessing measurement properties. Confirmatory factor analysis, content validity, unidimensionality analysis, reliability analysis, convergent validity, and criterion-related validity tests were conducted to evaluate the model and constructs (Anderson & Gerbing, 1988; Bollen, 1989; Chin, 1998).

DATA ANALYSIS

Confirmatory Factor Analysis

The measurement properties of the survey instrument were assessed with confirmatory factor analysis. A measurement model comprising of a weighted linear combination of the items in the scale was analyzed. In confirmatory factor analysis, each theoretical construct is specified and analyzed to assess the fit of the data with the measurement model (Ahire, Golhar, & Waller, 1996; Ravichandran & Rai, 1999; Venkatraman, 1989). For constructs with four or more indicators, these guidelines were followed. As some constructs have fewer than three indicators, these constructs were pooled with constructs having four or more indicators. This was done to ensure adequate degrees of freedom for estimation of the model.

Table 1. Tests for unidimensionality, reliability, and convergent validity

No.	Construct	No. of Indicators	Unidimensionality: Goodness of Fit Index (GFI)	Reliability: Cronbach's α	Convergent Validity: Bentler Bonnet Λ
1.	System Quality	4	.99	.72	.97
2.	Information Quality	5	.97	.84	.95
3.	Information Presentation	4	.91	.82	.89
4.	Interface Satisfaction	5	.94	.87	.94
5.	Decision-making satisfaction* - System Quality - Information Quality - Information presentation	2	.95 .96 .91	.83	.92 .95 .90
6.	Overall Satisfaction* - Interface Satisfaction and Intention to Use	2	.91	.89	.93
7.	Intention to Use - Overall Satisfaction and Interface Satisfaction	2	.91	.74	.93
* A combined model was used for this construct.					

Content Validity

Content validity is ensured when the constructs are defined using the literature. The construct should adequately represent and measure the domain of meaning that it is supposed to represent (Bohrnstedt, 1983). If all the items grouped together for each construct reflect the underlying meaning, then content validity exists (Dunn, Seaker, & Waller, 1994). Since there is no rigorous way to assess content validity, in order to ensure thoroughness, multiple items were used to measure the construct (Bohrnstedt, 1983; Churchill, 1979). The instrument employed in the research used several indicators for each construct that was derived from an in-depth literature review; and thus content validity was ensured (Bohrnstedt, 1983).

Unidimensionality Analysis

A multidimensional construct helps with content validity and is acceptable as long as the scales are unidimensional. A scale has to be unidimensional in order to have both reliability and construct validity (Gerbing, & Anderson, 1988). The condition for a unidimensional scale is that the items of a scale estimate one factor. The goodness of fit index (GFI) measures a good fit of the measurement model, as it indicates that all items load significantly on one underlying latent variable. There is no evidence of lack of unidimensionality when GFI is 0.90 or higher for the model. The GFI indices for all the scales are summarized in Table 1, and the results suggest that all the scales are unidimensional.

Table 2. Test for criterion-related validity

No.	Construct	Interface Satisfaction	Decision-making Satisfaction	Overall Satisfaction	Intention to Use
1	System Quality	0.66**	0.65**	-	-
2	Information Quality	0.54**	0.69**	-	-
3	Information Presentation	0.50**	0.44**	-	-
4	Interface Satisfaction	-	-	0.49**	-
5	Decision-Making Satisfaction	-	-	0.51**	-
6	Overall Satisfaction	-	-	-	0.56**
** p<0.01					

Reliability

Reliability of a scale is ensured if the scale is dependable, consistent, or stable (Gatewood, & Field, 1990). Cronbach's alpha coefficient was used to measure reliability, as the items of a scale explain the majority of the variation in the construct vis-à-vis measurement error (Cronbach, 1951). The results indicate that the scale is reliable because the alpha coefficient is greater than .70 (Table 1).

Convergent Validity

Considering each item in the scale as a different approach to measure the construct usually assesses convergent validity. This was measured using the Bentler-Bonett coefficient (Δ) (Bentler and Bonett, 1980). The Bentler-Bonett coefficient (Δ) value of .9 or above means high convergent validity. All the scales had a Bentler-Bonett coefficient (Δ) of greater than .9 (Table 1).

Criterion-Related Validity

Criterion-related validity tests the degree to which the outcome is predicted by the constructs (Ahire et al., 1996; Venkatraman, 1989). Using SEM, the constructs are correlated with outcome constructs. As the correlation of the various constructs are positive and statistically significant (Table 2), criterion-related validity exists for these constructs.

SEM produces parameter estimates of links between the latent variables, and so, is also called latent variable analysis, or causal modeling. AMOS 4.0 and SPSS 10.1 (Arbuckle & Wothke, 1999) were employed for the SEM analysis.

RESULTS AND DISCUSSION

In summary, this research examined the impact of systems' quality, information quality, and information presentation on user satisfaction and intention to use in the context of choiceboard systems. The IS success model was used as the basis of the research model. The model was based on Shannon and Weaver's communication theory (1949), Mason's theory (1978), and the Delone and McLean (1992) model. The research model employed the constructs at the technical level, viz., systems' quality and information quality, in the context of choiceboards, and finally, its impact on different components of user satisfaction, such as interface satisfaction, decision-making satisfaction, and resultant overall satisfaction. The path coefficients calculated for the estimated model

Table 3. Survey constructs and indicators

Construct Name	Item No.	Item Measured
System Quality	V 1	System reliability
	V 2	Convenient to access
	V 3	System ease of use
	V 4	System flexibility
Information Quality	V 5	Information accuracy
	V 6	Information completeness
	V 7	Information relevance
	V 8	Information content needs
	V 9	Information timeliness
Information Presentation	V 10	Presentation graphics
	V 11	Presentation color
	V 12	Presentation style
	V 13	Navigationally efficient
Decision Making Satisfaction	V 14	Decision confidence
	V 15	Decision effectiveness
Interface Satisfaction	V 16	Easy to work
	V 17	Useful format
	V 18	User friendly
	V 19	Does what I want it to do
	V 20	Clear and understandable
Overall Satisfaction	V 21	Extremely useful system
	V 22	Satisfactory in meeting user needs
Intention to Use	V 23	Possible to use
	V 24	Intend to use

support the hypothesized relationships in both direction and magnitude with few exceptions. Overall, the statistical conclusions support the research model (Figure 3).

System quality is directly and positively correlated to interface satisfaction (H-1); so an increase in the quality of the system leads to an increase in satisfaction in using the interface. Information quality is directly and positively correlated to interface satisfaction (H-3); so an increase in the quality of the information leads to an increase in satisfaction in using the interface. Information presentation is not directly and positively correlated to interface satisfaction; (H-5) therefore, this hypothesis is not validated.

The path coefficients calculated for the estimated model also support the hypothesized rela-tionships in both direction and magnitude in the case of decision-making satisfaction. Most of the hypotheses in the area of decision-making satisfaction have been validated using the data. System quality is directly and positively correlated to decision-making satisfaction (H-2); so an increase in the quality of the system leads to an increase in decision-making satisfaction. Information quality is directly and positively correlated to decision-making satisfaction (H-3); so an increase in the quality of the information leads to an increase in decision-making. Presentation is not directly and positively correlated to decision-making satisfaction (H-6); as this hypothesis is not validated.

System quality includes system ease of use, convenience of access, and system reliability. Thus, a net positive effect from these factors will

Figure 3. Model with results

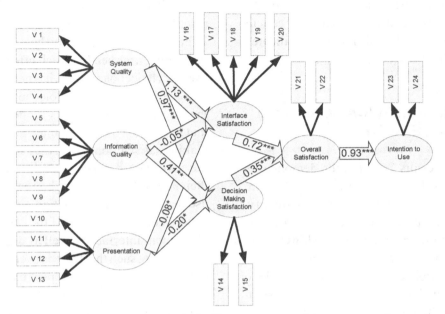

*** p<.01; ** p<.1; * Statistically insignificant

result in a positive effect on interface satisfaction and decision-making satisfaction. In choiceboards, as in other systems, the ease of use of the system, convenience of access, and system reliability are important considerations for the user. Information relevance, accuracy, completeness, and timeliness constitute the construct information quality. Thus, a net positive effect from these factors will result in a positive effect on decision-making satisfaction. Choiceboard systems should provide relevant, accurate, complete, and timely information for better decision-making satisfaction.

Graphics, color, presentation style, and navigational efficiency measures information presentation. Therefore, information presentation measures how information is displayed. It was hypothesized that a net-positive effect from graphics, color, presentation style, and navigational efficiency would result in a positive effect on interface satisfaction and decision-making satisfaction. The data did not support this hypothesis.

The statistical conclusions support the hypotheses on user satisfaction. Interface satisfaction is directly and positively correlated to overall satisfaction (H-7); so an increase in interface satisfaction leads to an increase in overall satisfaction. Similarly, decision-making satisfaction is directly and positively correlated to overall satisfaction (H-8); so an increase in decision-making satisfaction leads to an increase in overall satisfaction. Overall satisfaction is also found to be directly and positively correlated to intention to use (H-9); so an increase in overall satisfaction leads to an increase in intention to use. The results from the research model also demonstrate the relative weight of system quality compared to information quality. Interestingly, decision-making satisfaction of end-users, the quality of the system is more important than the quality of the information.

As with all regression and structural equation modeling techniques, correlation does not prove the causality of the relation. Since, however, these causal relationships are based on an established literature, and the theoretical grounding of the causality is adequate, it is reasonable to concur with the causality, where it has been validated (Gefen, Straub, & Boudreau, 2000).

MANAGERIAL IMPLICATIONS AND FUTURE RESEARCH

The research results empirically demonstrate the relationships between interface satisfaction, decision-making satisfaction, system quality, information quality, and information presentation. It also demonstrates the relationships among variables such as interface satisfaction, decision-making satisfaction, overall satisfaction, and the intention to use. These relationships are useful in influencing the intention to use among users of choiceboard systems. IS professionals need to understand these relationships to help their firms design choiceboard systems that are effective. This research provides an understanding of those interrelationships.

In the context of choiceboards, the quality of information influences decision-making satisfaction. So, for example, for a choiceboard system that allows users to develop their own holiday itinerary, the research suggests that users would value complete, accurate, and relevant information about holiday sites, weather, local costs, flights, rentals, and hotels. Similarly, users will have better decision-making satisfaction with timely, accurate, and complete information as they develop alternative scenarios for their holidays.

The research suggests that ease of use, convenience of access, and system reliability also influence the decision-making satisfaction of users. A choiceboard, other than just being available and accessible, should also be easy to use. A user should not feel overwhelmed by available choices. The research also suggests that ease of use, convenience of access, and system reliability and flexibility influences interface satisfaction.

The quality of the choiceboard system makes an impact if it is user friendly, clear, and understandable. Interface and decision-making satisfaction influences if the choiceboard has been satisfactory in meeting user needs, which effects intention to use. For choiceboard users, it is not only important that the quality of the choiceboard system and the information it provides is adequate, but also that it provides them with interface and decision-making satisfaction. Thus, they will intend to use the choiceboard if they find it useful and it meets their needs. This research shows that choiceboard users are deriving satisfaction with the system in a more complex fashion. If the choiceboard provides them interface as well as decision-making satisfaction, such that there is overall satisfaction, only then will they be a repeat user.

The empirical data suggest that the presentation of information is not important to the user in decision making. The users are not particularly impressed by color, graphics, and presentation style, but are more interested in the pertinent information being provided to them via the system. This is an interesting result because in the recent past, there has been an increase in color and graphics on Web sites, but this presentation is of limited use if these Web sites are not able to provide the desired quality of information.

This research has examined the perceptions of users relative to their intention to use, and how that perception is affected by overall satisfaction, which, in turn, depends on decision-making satisfaction and interface satisfaction. Much of the model has been validated by the data. Even the hypotheses that were not validated provided interesting insights. Studies should be conducted using other Web-based systems to test if the results of the present study can be extended to other situations. Qualitative studies can also be conducted to study choiceboard systems. These studies have the possibility of providing insight about choiceboard system users. These studies will help build a wider body of research, which is needed for designing effective choiceboard systems.

REFERENCES

Ahire, S. L., Golhar, D. Y., & Waller, A. M. (1996). Development and validation of TQM implementation constructs. *Decision Science, 27*(1), 23-56.

Alavi, M., & Henderson, J. C. (1981). An evolutionary strategy for implementing a decision support systems. *Management Science, 27*(11), 1309-1322.

Andal-Ancion, A., Cartwright, P. A., & Yip, G. S. (2003). The digital transformation of traditional businesses. *MIT Sloan Management Review.*

Anderson, J. C., & Gerbing, D. W. (1988). Structural equation modeling in practice: A review and recommended two-step approach. *Psychological Bulletin, 103*(3), 411-433.

Arbuckle, J. L., & Wothke, W. (1999). *AMOS 4.0 User's Guide.* Chicago: Small Waters Corporation.

Bailey, J., & Pearson, S. (1983). Development of a toll for measuring and analyzing user satisfaction. *Management Science, 29*(5), 530-545.

Barnes, S., & Vidgen, R. (2002). An integrative approach to the assessment of e-commerce quality. *Journal of Electronic Commerce Research, 3(3),* 114-127.

Belardo, S., Karwan, K. R., & Wallace, W. A. (1982). DSS Component Design through Field Experimentation: An Application to Emergency Management. In *Proceedings of the Third International Conference on Information Systems* (pp. 93-108).

Bentler, P. M., & Bonett, D. G. (1980). Significance tests and goodness of fit in the analysis of covariance structure. *Psychological Bulletin, 88,* 588-606.

Bettman, J. R. (1979). *An information processing theory of consumer choice.* Reading, MA: Addison-Wesley Publishing Company.

Bettman, J. R., Johnson, E. J., & Payne, J. W. (1990). A componential analysis of cognitive effort in choice. *Organizational Behavior and Human Decision Processes, 45*(1), 111-139.

Bharati, P., & D. Berg (2003). Managing information technology for service quality: A study from the other side. *IT and People, 16*(2), 183-202.

Bharati, P., & Chaudhury, A. (2004a). Using choice-boards to create business value. *Communications of the ACM, 47*(12), 77-81.

Bharati, P., & Chaudhury, A. (2004b). An empirical investigation of decision-making satisfaction in Web-based decision support systems, *Decision Support Systems, 37*(2), 187-197.

Bohrnstedt, G. (1983). *Measurement: Handbook of survey research.* In P. Rossi, J. Wright, & A. Anderson (Eds.). San Diego: Academic Press.

Bollen, K. A. (1989). *Structural equations with latent variables.* New York: John Wiley.

Cao, M., & Zhang, Q. (2002). Evaluating e-commerce web site design: A customer's perspective. In *Proceedings of the Decision Science Institute 2002 Annual Meeting* (pp. 1186-1191).

Chang, M. K., & Cheung, W. (2001). Determinants of the intention to use internet/ WWW at work: A confirmatory study. *Information and Management, 39*(1), 1-14.

Chervany, N. L., Dickson, G. W., & Kozar, K. (1972). *An experimental gaming framework for investigating the influence of management information systems on decision effectiveness.* MISRC Working Paper No. 71-12, Management Information Systems Research Center, University of Minnesota, Minneapolis, MN.

Chin, W. W. (1998). Issues and opinion on structural equation modeling. *MIS Quarterly, 22*(1), 7-16.

Choudrie, J. Ghinea, G., & Weerakkody, V. (2004). Evluating global e-government sites: A view using web diagnostic tools. *Electronic Journal of E-Government, 2*(2), 105-114.

Churchill, G. (1979). A paradigm for developing better measures of marketing constructs. *Journal of Marketing Research, 16*, 64-73.

Collins, N., & Butler, P. (2003). When marketing models clash with democracy. *Journal of Public Affairs, 3*(1), 52-62.

Cronbach, L. J. (1951). Coefficient alpha and internal structure of tests. *Psychometrica, 16*, 297-334.

DeLone, W. H., & McLean, E. R. (1992). Information systems success: The quest for the dependent variable. *Information Systems Research, 3*(1), 60-95.

DeLone, W. H., & McLean, E. R. (2002). Information systems success revisited. In *Proceedings of the 35th Annual Hawaii International Conference on Systems Sciences*. Sciences, IEEE Computer Society Press, Los Alamitos, CA.

DeLone, W. H., & McLean, E. R. (2003). The De-Lone and McLean Model of information systems success: A ten-year update. *Journal of Management Information Systems, 19*(4), 9-30.

DeSanctis, G. (1982). An examination of an expectancy theory model of decision support systems use. In *Proceedings of the Third International Conference of Information Systems* (pp. 121-135).

Diniz, E., Porto, M. R., & Adachi, T. (2005). Internet banking in Brazil: Evaluation of functionality, reliability, and usability. *The Electronic Journal of Information Systems Evaluation, 8*(1), 41-50.

Doll, W. J., & Torkzadeh, G. (1988). The measurement of end-user computing satisfaction. *MIS Quarterly, 12*(2), 259-274.

Dunn, S. C., Seaker, R. F., & Waller, M. A. (1994). Latent variables in business logistics research: Scale development and validation. *Journal of Business Logistics, 15*(2), 145-172.

Gallagher, C. A. (1974). Perceptions of the value of a management information system. *Academy of Management Journal, 17*(1), 46-55.

Garrity, E. J., & Sanders, G. L. (1998). Dimensions of information systems success. In E. J. Garrity & G. L. Sanders (Eds.), *Information systems success measurement*. Hershey, PA: Idea Group Publishing.

Gatewood, R. D., & Field, H. S. (1990). *Human resource selection*. Chicago: The Dryden Press.

Gefen, D., Straub, D. W., & Boudreau, M. C. (2000). Structural equation modeling and regression: Guidelines for research practice. *Communications of the Association for Information Systems, 4*(7), 1-57.

Gerbing, D., & Anderson, J. (1988). An updated paradigm for scale development incorporating unidimensionality and its assessment. *Journal of Marketing Research, 25*, 186-192.

Goodhue, D. (1990). *Developing a theory-based measure of user satisfaction: The task-systems fit questionnaire*. Working Paper, Information and Decision Science, University of Minnesota, June 28.

Goslar, M. D., Green, G. I., & Hughes, T. H. (1986). Decision support systems: An empirical assessment for decision making. *Decision Sciences, 17*(1), 79-91.

Guental, H. G., Surprenant, N., & Bubeck, K. (1984). Effectively utilizing computer-aided design technology: The role of individual difference variables. In *Proceedings of the Fifth International Conference on Information Systems* (pp. 21-30).

Jiang, J. J., Klein, G., & Carr, C. L. Measuring information systems service quality: SERVQUAL from the other side. *MIS Quarterly, 26*(2), 145-166.

Jiang, J. J., Klein, G., & Crampton, S. M. A note on SERVQUAL reliability and validity in information systems service quality measurement. *Decision Sciences, 31*(3), 725-744.

Kettinger, W. J., & Lee, C. C. (1997).Pragmatic perspectives on the measurement of information systems service quality. *MIS Quarterly*, 223-240.

Kettinger, W. J., & Lee, C. C. (1999). Replication of measures of information systems research: The case of IS SERVQUAL. *Decision Sciences, 30*(3), 893-899.

Khalifa, M., & Liu, V. (2003). Determinants of satisfaction at different adoption stages of Internet-based services. *Journal of the Association for Information Systems, 4*(5), 206-232.

King, W. R., & Epstein, B. J. (1983). Assessing information system value. *Decision Sciences, 14*(1), 34-45.

Liechty, J., Ramaswamy, V., & Cohen, S. H. (2001). Choice menus for mass customization: An experimental approach for analyzing customer demand with an application to a web-based information service. *Journal of Marketing Research*, (38), 183-196.

Loiacono, E., Chen, D., & Goodhue, D. (2002). *WebQual™ revisited: Predicting the intent to reuse a Web site.* Americas Conference on Information Systems (AMCIS), Dallas, Texas, August.

Lucas, H. C. (1978). Empirical model for a descriptive model of implementation. *MIS Quarterly, 2*(2), 27-41.

Mahmood, M. A. (1987). Systems development methods—A comparative investigation. *MIS Quarterly, 11*(3), 293-311.

Markillie, P. (2004). A perfect market. *The Economist,* May 13.

Mason, R. O. (1978). Measuring information output: A communication systems approach. *Information and Management, 1*(5), 219-234.

Miller, J., & Doyle, B. A. (1987). Measuring effectiveness of computer based information systems in the financial services sector. *MIS Quarterly, 11*(1), 107- 124.

Mowen, J. (1995). *Consumer behavior* (4th ed.). Englewoods Cliffs, NJ: Prentice Hall.

Pitt, L. F., Watson, R. T., & Kavan, C. B. (1995). Service quality: A measure of information systems effectiveness. *MIS Quarterly*, 173-185.

Pitt, L. F., Watson, R. T., & Kavan, C. B. (1997). Measuring information systems service quality: Concerns for a complete canvas. *MIS Quarterly*, 209-221.

Rai, A., Lang, S. S., & Welker, R. B. (2002). Assessing the validity of IS success models: An emperical test and theoretical analysis. *Information Systems Research, 13*(1), 50-69.

Ravichandran, T., & Rai, A. (1999). Total quality management in information systems development: Key constructs and relationships. *Journal of Management Information Systems, 16*(3), 124-155.

Sanders, G. L. (1984). MIS/DSS success measure. *Systems, Objectives, Solutions,* (4), 29-34.

Sanders, G. L., & Courtney, J. F. (1985). A field study of organizational factors affecting DSS success. *MIS Quarterly, 9*(9), 77-89.

Seddon, P.B. (1997). A Re-specification and extension of the DeLone and McLean model of IS success. *Information Systems Research, 8*(3), 240-253.

Seddon, P. B., & Kiew, M.-Y (1994). A partial test and development of DeLone and McLean model of IS Success. In J. I. DeGross, S. L. Huff, & M. C. Munro (Eds.), *Proceedings of the International Conference on Information Systems* (pp. 99-110). Atlanta, GA: Association of Information Systems.

Seddon, P.B., Staples, D.S., Patnayakuni, R., & Bowtell, M. (1999) Dimensions of IS success. *Communications of the AIS, 20*(2).

Shannon, C. E., & Weaver, W. (1949). *The mathematical theory of communication.* Urbana, IL: University of Illinois Press.

Shim, J. P., & Shin, Y. B. (2002). Retailer Web site influence on customer shopping: An exploratory study on key factors of customer satisfaction. *Journal of the Association for Information Systems, 3*, 53-76.

Shin, B. (2003). An exploratory investigation of system success factors in data warehousing. *Journal of the Association for Information Systems, 4*, 141-170.

Simon, H. A. (1955). A behavioral model of rational choice. *Quarterly Journal of Economics,* (69), 99-118.

Slywotzky, A. (2000). The age of the choiceboard. *Harvard Business Review,* (78), 40-41.

Srinivasan, A. (1985). Alternative measures of system effectiveness: Associations and implications. *MIS Quarterly, 9*(3), 243- 253.

Swanson, E. B. (1985). A note of informatics. *Journal of Management Information Systems, 2*(3), 86-91.

Syre, S. (2004). A revolution grows up. *The Boston Globe,* November 30.

Te'eni, D., & Feldman, R. (2001). Performance and satisfaction in adaptive Websites: An experiment on searches within task adapted Websites. *Journal of the Association for Information Systems, 2*(3), 1-30.

Yoo, S., & Jin, J. (2004). Evaluation of the home pages of the top 100 university web sites. *Academy of Information Management, 8*(2), 57-69.

Van Dyke, T. P., Kappelman, L. A., & Prybutok, V. R. (1997). Measuring information systems service quality: Concerns on the use of the SERVQUAL questionnaire. *MIS Quarterly,* 195-207.

Van Dyke, T. P., Prybutok, V. R., & Kappelman, L. A. (1999). Cautions on the use of the SERVQUAL measure to assess the quality of information systems services. *Decision Sciences, 30*(3), 877-891.

Van der Heijden. (2004). Hedonic information systems. *MIS Quarterly, 28*(4), 695-704.

Venkatraman, N. (1989). Strategic orientation of business enterprises: The construct, dimensionality, and measurement. *Management Science, 35*(8), 942-962.

Vessey, I. (1994). The effect of information presentation on decision making: A cost-benefit analysis. *Information and Management,* (27), 103-119.

Watson, R. T., Pitt, L. F., & Kavan, C. B. (1998). Measuring information systems service quality: Lessons from two longitudinal case studies. *MIS Quarterly, 22*(1), 61-79.

Welke, R. J., & Konsynski, B. R. (1980). An examination of the interaction between technology, methodology and information systems: A tripartite view. In *Proceedings of the First International Conference of Information Systems* (pp. 32-48).

Zmud, R., Blocher, E., & Moffie, R. P. (1983). The impact of color graphic report formats on decision performance and learning. In *Proceedings of the Fourth International Conference on Information Systems* (pp. 179-193).

This work was previously published in Innovative Technologies for Information Resources Management, edited by M. Khosrow-Pour, pp. 79-94, copyright 2008 by Information Science Reference (an imprint of IGI Global).

Compilation of References

aecXML (2006). Retrieved March 22, 2006, from http://www.iai-na.org/aecxml/mission.php

Afuah, A. (2000). How much do your co-opetitors' capabilities matter in the face of technological change? *Strategic Management Journal, 21,* 387–404. doi:10.1002/(SICI)1097-0266(200003)21:3<397::AID-SMJ88>3.0.CO;2-1

Agrawal, M., Kumaresh, T. V., & Mercer, G. A. (2001). The false promise of mass customization. *The McKinsey Quarterly, 3,* 62-71.

Ahire, S. L., Golhar, D. Y., & Waller, A. M. (1996). Development and validation of TQM implementation constructs. *Decision Science, 27*(1), 23-56.

Åhlström, P. & Westbrook, R. (1999). Implications of mass customization for operations management: An exploratory survey. *International Journal of Operations & Production Management, 19*(3), 262-274.

Akao, Y. (1990). *Quality function deployment: integrating customer requirements into product design.* Cambridge, MA: Productivity Press.

Alavi, M., & Henderson, J. C. (1981). An evolutionary strategy for implementing a decision support systems. *Management Science, 27*(11), 1309-1322.

Aldanondo, M., Rougé, S., & Vérnon, M. (2000). Expert configurator for concurrent engineering: Caméléon software and model. J*ournal of Intelligent Manufacturing, 11,* 127-134.

Aldanondo, M., Véron, M., & Fargier, H. (1999). Configuration in manufacturing industry, requirements, problems, and definitions.In *Proceedings of the IEEE International Conference on Systems, Man, and Cybernetics: Vol. 6* (pp. 1009-1014).

Ali, K., & van Stam, W. (2004). TiVo: making show recommendations using a distributed collaborative filtering architecture. In *Proceedings of the Tenth ACM SIGKDD international Conference on Knowledge Discovery and Data Mining (KDD '04)* (pp. 394-401). New York: ACM Press.

AlMellor (2004). *Introduction to model-driven architecture.* Addison-Wesley.

Andal-Ancion, A., Cartwright, P. A., & Yip, G. S. (2003). The digital transformation of traditional businesses. *MIT Sloan Management Review.*

Anderson, C. A., & Dill, K. E. (2000). Video games and aggressive thoughts, feelings, and behavior in the laboratory and in life. *Journal of Personality and Social Psychology, 78,* 772–790. doi:10.1037/0022-3514.78.4.772

Anderson, D. (2004). *Build-to-order and mass customization: The ultimate supply chain and lean manufacturing strategy for low-cost on-demand production without forecasts or inventory.* CIM Press.

Anderson, D. M., & Pine II, B. J. (1997). *Agile product development for mass customization.* Chicago: Irvin Publishers.

Anderson, J. C., & Gerbing, D. W. (1988). Structural equation modeling in practice: A review and recommended two-step approach. *Psychological Bulletin, 103*(3), 411-433.

Araujo, L., Dubois, A., & Gadde, L. E. (1999). Managing interfaces with suppliers. *Industrial Marketing Management, 28,* 497–506. doi:10.1016/S0019-8501(99)00077-2

Arbuckle, J. L., & Wothke, W. (1999). *AMOS 4.0 User's Guide.* Chicago: Small Waters Corporation.

Ardissono, L., Kosa, A., & Maybury, M. (2004). *Personalized digital Television: Targeting Programs to Individual Viewers*. Boston: Kluwer Academic Publishers.

Ariano, M., & Dagnino, A. (1996). An intelligent order entry and dynamic bill of materials system for manufacturing customized furniture. *Computers in Electrical Engineering, 22*(1), 45-60.

Arthur, W. B. (1989). Competing technologies and lock-in by historical events. *The Economic Journal, 99*, 116–131. doi:10.2307/2234208

Atkinson, P., Coffey, A., Delamond, S., Lofland, J., & Lofland, I. (2001). *Handbook of Ethnography*. London: Sage.

Ayersman, D. J., & Reed, W. M. (1998). Relationships among hypermedia-based mental models and hypermedia knowledge. *Journal of Research on Computing in Education, 30*(3), 222–238.

Bachem, B. (1999). *Personalisation in E-Commerce, Online Marketing*.

Baddeley, A. (1992). Working Memory. *Science, 255*, 556–559. doi:10.1126/science.1736359

Baeza-Yates, R., & Ribeiro-Neto, B. (1999). *Modern Information Retrieval*. Reading, MA: Addison Wesley.

Bailey, J., & Pearson, S. (1983). Development of a toll for measuring and analyzing user satisfaction. *Management Science, 29*(5), 530-545.

Bakos, J. Y. (1997). Reducing Buyer Search Costs: Implications for Electronic Marketplaces. *Management Science, 43*(12), 1676–1692. doi:10.1287/mnsc.43.12.1676

Balabanovic, M. (1998). *Learning to Surf: Multi-agent Systems for Adaptive Web Page Recommendation*. PhD thesis, Department of Computer Science, Stanford University, Paolo Alto, CA.

Balabanovic, M., & Shoham, Y. (1997). Fab: Content-based, collaborative recommendation. *Communications of the ACM, 40*(3), 6672. doi:10.1145/245108.245124

Balakrishman, A. Kumara, S., & Sundaresan, S. (1999). Manufacturing in the digital age: Exploiting information technologies for product realization. *Information Systems Frontiers, 1*, 25-50.

Baldauf, M., & Dustdar, S. (2004). A survey on context-aware systems. *International Journal of Ad Hoc and Ubiquitous Computing*.

Ballard, M. E., & Weist, J. R. (1996). Mortal Kombat: The effects of violent video game play on males' hostility and cardiovascular responding. *Journal of Applied Social Psychology, 26*, 717–730. doi:10.1111/j.1559-1816.1996.tb02740.x

Bardacki, A., & Whitelock, J. (2003). Mass-customisation in marketing: The consumer perspective. *Journal of Consumer Marketing, 20*(5), 463-479.

Bardakci, A., & Whitelock, J. (2004). How "ready" are customers for mass customisation? An exploratory study. *European Journal of Marketing, 38*(11/12), 1396–1416. doi:10.1108/03090560410560164

Barker, V. E., & O'Connor, D. E. (1989). Expert systems for configuration at Digital: XCON and beyond. *Communications of the ACM, 32*(3), 298-318.

Barnes, S., & Vidgen, R. (2002). An integrative approach to the assessment of e-commerce quality. *Journal of Electronic Commerce Research, 3(3)*, 114-127.

Barney, J. B. (1991). Firm resources and sustained competitive advantage. *Journal of Management, 17*(1), 99–120. doi:10.1177/014920639101700108

Bearden, W. O., & Etzel, M. J. (1982). Reference group influence on product and brand purchase decisions. *The Journal of Consumer Research, 9*(September), 183–194. doi:10.1086/208911

Beaty, R. T. (1996). Mass customisation. *IEE Manufacturing Engineer, 75*(5), 217-220.

Bei, Yu., & Skovgaard, H. J. (1998). A configuration tool to increase product competitiveness. *IEEE Intelligent Systems, 13*, 34–41. doi:10.1109/5254.708431

Belardo, S., Karwan, K. R., & Wallace, W. A. (1982). DSS Component Design through Field Experimentation: An Application to Emergency Management. In *Proceedings of the Third International Conference on Information Systems* (pp. 93-108).

Bendapudi, N., & Leone, R. P. (2003). Psychological implications of customer participation in co-production.

Journal of Marketing, 67(January), 14–28. doi:10.1509/jmkg.67.1.14.18592

Benkler, Y. (2000). From Consumers to Users: Shifting the Deeper Structures of Regulation. *Federal Communications Law Journal, 52,* 561–563.

Bentler, P. M., & Bonett, D. G. (1980). Significance tests and goodness of fit in the analysis of covariance structure. *Psychological Bulletin, 88,* 588-606.

Berger, C., Möslein, K., Piller, F. T., & Reichwald, R. (2005). Cooperation between Manufacturers, Retailers, and Customers for User Co-Design: Learning from Exploratory Research. *European Management Review, 1,* 70–87. doi:10.1057/palgrave.emr.1500030

Berman, B. (2002). Should your firm adopt a mass customization strategy? *Business Horizons, 45*(4), 51-60.

Bernhaupt, R. Obrist. M., Weiss, A., Beck, E. & Tscheligi, M. (2007). Trends in the Living Room and Beyond. In: P. Cesar, K. Chorianopoulos, J. F. Jensen, (Ed.), *Interactive TV: A shared Experience, 5th European Conference, EuroITV 2007,* (pp. 146-155). Heidelberg: Springer.

Bernhaupt, R., Mihalic, K., & Obrist, M. (2008). Methods for Usability Evaluation of Mobile Applications. J. Lumsden, (Eds.) *Handbook of Research on User Interface Design and Evaluation for Mobile Technology,* (pp. 742-755). Hershey, PA: IGI Global.

Bernhaupt, R., Obrist, M., & Tscheligi, M. (2006). Usability and Usage of iTV Services: Lessons learned in an Austrian Field Trial. In [Heidelberg: Springer.]. *Proceedings of EuroiTV, 2006,* 234–241.

Bernhaupt, R., Obrist. M., Weiss, A., Beck, E. & Tscheligi, M. (2008). Trends in the Living Room and Beyond. *Computers in Entertainment, 6*(1), online.

Bernhaupt, R., Palanque, P., Winkler, M., & Navarre, D. (2007). Supporting Usability Evaluation of Multimodal Safety Critical Interactive Applications using Dialogue and Interaction Models. In E. Law, et al. (Eds.) *Maturing Usability: Quality in Software, Interaction and Value* (pp. 95-127). London: Springer.

Bernhaupt, R., Weiss, A., Obrist, M., & Tscheligi, M. (2007). Playful Probing: Making Probing more Fun. In [Heidelberg: Springer.]. *Proceedings of Interact, 2007,* 606–619.

Bernhaupt, R., Wilfinger, D., Weiss, A., & Tscheligi, M. (2008) An Ethnographic Study on Recommendations in the Living Room: Implications for Design of iTV Recommender Systems. In M. Tscheligi, M. Obrist, & A. Lugmair, (Ed.) *Proceedings of EuroiTV 2008* (LNCS Vol. 5066, pp. 92-101). Berlin: Springer.

Berre, A. (2002). Overview of international standards on enterprise architecture. *SINTEF.*

Bettman, J. R. (1979). *An information processing theory of consumer choice.* Reading, MA: Addison-Wesley Publishing Company.

Bettman, J. R., Johnson, E. J., & Payne, J. W. (1990). A componential analysis of cognitive effort in choice. *Organizational Behavior and Human Decision Processes, 45*(1), 111–139. doi:10.1016/0749-5978(90)90007-V

Bharati, P., & Chaudhury, A. (2004). Using choice-boards to create business value. *Communications of the ACM, 47*(12), 77-81.

Bharati, P., & Chaudhury, A. (2004). An empirical investigation of decision-making satisfaction in Web-based decision support systems, *Decision Support Systems, 37*(2), 187-197.

Bharati, P., & D. Berg (2003). Managing information technology for service quality: A study from the other side. *IT and People, 16*(2), 183-202.

Björkman, M., Aroyo, L., Bellekens, P., Dekker, T., Loef, E., & Pulles, R. (2006). Personalised Home Media Centre Using Semantically Enriched TV-Anytime Content. In [Heidelberg: Springer.]. *Proceedings of EuroiTV, 2006,* 165–173.

Blanco-Fernandez, Y., Pazos-Arias, J. J., & Gil-Solla, A. Ramos-Cabrer-M., & Lopez-Nores, M. (2006). Bringing together Content-based methods, Collaborative Filtering and Semantic Inference to Improve Personalized TV. In *Proceedings of EuroiTV 2006,* (pp. 174—182). Heidelberg: Springer.

Blattberg, R., Getz, G., & Thomas, S. (2001). *Customer Equity n Building and Managing Relationships as Valuable Assets.* Boston: Harvard Business School Press.

Blecker, T., Abdelkafi, N., Kreutler, G., & Friedrich, G. (2004). Product configuration systems: State of the art, conceptualization, and extensions, In A. B. Hamadou, F. Gargouri, & M. Jmaiel (Eds.), *Proceedings of the Eighth Maghrebian Conference on Software Engineering and Artificial Intelligence (MCSEAI 2004)* (pp. 25-36).

Blecker, T., Friedrich, G., Kaluza, B., Abdelkafi, N., & Kreutler, G. (2005). *Information and management systems for product customization.* New York: Springer.

Blecker, T., Friedrich, G., Kaluza, B., Abdelkafi, N., & Kreutler, G. (2005). *Information and Management Systems for Product Customization.* New York: Springer Science Business Media Inc.

Bloch, P. H., Brunel, F. F., & Arnold, T. J. (2003). Individual differences in the centrality of visual product aesthetics: Concept and measurement. *The Journal of Consumer Research, 29*(March), 551–565. doi:10.1086/346250

Blom, J. (2000). *Personalization – A Taxonomy.* New York: ACM.

Blom, J. O., & Monk, A. F. (2003). Theory of personalization of appearance: Why users personalize their PCs and mobile phones. *Human-Computer Interaction, 18*, 193–228. doi:10.1207/S15327051HCI1803_1

Böhms, M. (2001). Building construction extensible markup language (bcXML) description: E-construct bcXML. *A Contribution to the CEN/ISSS eBES Workshop, Annex A, ISSS/WS-eBES/01/001.*

Bohrnstedt, G. (1983). *Measurement: Handbook of survey research.* In P. Rossi, J. Wright, & A. Anderson (Eds.). San Diego: Academic Press.

Boissier, R. (1995). Architecture solutions for integrating CAD, CAM and machining in small companies. In *Proceedings of the IEEE/ECLA/IFIP International Conference on Architectures and Design Methods for Balanced Automation Systems* (pp. 407-416). London: Chapman & Hall.

Bollen, K. A. (1989). *Structural equations with latent variables.* New York: John Wiley.

Bonehill, E., & Slee-Smith, P. (1998). Product configurator. *IEE Workshop on Responsiveness in Manufacturing (Digest No. 1998/213),* 9/1-9/4.

Bradley, M. M., & Lang, P. J. (1994). Measuring emotion: the self-assessment manikin and the semantic differential. *Journal of Behavior Therapy and Experimental Psychiatry, 25*(1), 49–59. doi:10.1016/0005-7916(94)90063-9

Bramham, J., & MacCarthy, B. (2004). The demand-driven chain. *IEE Manufacturing Engineer, 83*(3), 30-33.

Branigan, E. (1992). *Narrative comprehension and film*, (4th Ed.). London: Routledge.

Brave, S., & Nass, C. (2003). Emotion in human-computer interaction. In J. A. Jacko & A. Sears (Ed.), *The Human-Computer Interaction Handbook. Fundamentals, Evolving Technologies and Emerging Applications,* (pp. 81-96). London: Lawrence Erlbaum Associates.

Breton, E., & Bézivin, J. (2001). Using metamodel technologies to organize functionalities for active system schemes. In *Proceedings of the 5th International Conference on Autonomous Agents,* Canada.

Brockhoff, K. (1967). A Test for the Product Life Cycle. *Econometrica, 35*(3-4), 472–484. doi:10.2307/1905649

Broekhuizen, T. L. J., & Alsem, K. J. (2002). Success factors for mass customization: A conceptual model. *Journal of Market-Focused Management, 5*(4), 309-330.

Brown, D. (2004). *Wave goodbye to the era of one-size-fits all.*

Brown, J. (1996). The Stick-e Document a framework for developing context-aware applications. In *Proceedings of the Electronic Publishing.*

Brown, S., & Bessant, J. (2003). The manufacturing strategy-capabilities links in mass customization and agile manufacturing – an exploratory study. *International Journal of Operations & Production Management, 23*(7), 707–730. doi:10.1108/01443570310481522

Bruhn, M. (2003). *Relationship Marketing.* Harlow, UK: Pearson.

Bruhn, M., & Georgi, D. (2006): Services *Marketing. Managing The Service Values Chain,* Harlow, UK: Pearson.

Burchill, G., & Fine, C. H. (1997). Time versus market orientation in product concept development: Empirically-based theory generation. *Management Science, 43*(4), 465–478. doi:10.1287/mnsc.43.4.465

Burroughs, J. E., & Mick, D. G. (2004). Exploring antecedents and consequences of consumer creativity in a problem-solving context. *The Journal of Consumer Research, 31*(September), 402–411. doi:10.1086/422118

Bursilovsky, P., & Maybury, M. (2002). From Adaptive Hypermedia to the adaptive Web. *Communications of the ACM, 45*(5), 30–33.

Byun, H., & Cheverst, K. (2001). Exploiting User Models and Context-Awareness to Support Personal Daily Activities. In *Proc. of International Workshop on User Modelling for Context-Aware Applications*, Sonthofen, Germany.

Calvert, S. L., & Tan, S. (1994). Impact of virtual reality on young adults' physiological arousal and aggressive thoughts: Interaction versus observation. *Journal of Applied Developmental Psychology, 15*, 125–139. doi:10.1016/0193-3973(94)90009-4

Cao, M., & Zhang, Q. (2002). Evaluating e-commerce web site design: A customer's perspective. In *Proceedings of the Decision Science Institute 2002 Annual Meeting* (pp. 1186-1191).

Carberry, S., & de Rosis, F. (2008). Introduction to special issue on "Affective modeling and adaptation." . *User Modeling and User-Adapted Interaction, 18*, 1–9. doi:10.1007/s11257-007-9044-7

Cassady, J. C. (2004). The influence of cognitive test anxiety across the learning–testing cycle. *Learning and Instruction, 14*(6), 569–592. doi:10.1016/j.learninstruc.2004.09.002

Cassady, J. C., & Johnson, R. E. (2002). Cognitive Test Anxiety and Academic Performance. *Contemporary Educational Psychology, 27*(2), 270–295. doi:10.1006/ceps.2001.1094

Catry, B., & Chevalier, M. (1974). Market Share Strategy and the Product Life Cycle. *Journal of Marketing, 38*(4), 29–34. doi:10.2307/1250388

CEN/ISSS (2006). *European Committee for Standardisation - Information Society Standardization System*. Retrieved March 22, 2006, from http://www.cenorm.be/isss

Chandra, C., & Kamrani, A. K. (2003). Knowledge Management for Consumer-Focused Product Design. *Journal of Intelligent Manufacturing, 14*(6), 557–580. doi:10.1023/A:1027358721819

Chang, M. K., & Cheung, W. (2001). Determinants of the intention to use internet/ WWW at work: A confirmatory study. *Information and Management, 39*(1), 1-14.

Chen, C.-H., Khoo, L. P., & Yan, W. (2002). A strategy for acquiring customer requirement patterns using laddering technique and ART2 neural network. *Advanced Engineering Informatics, 16*(3), 229–240. doi:10.1016/S1474-0346(03)00003-X

Chen, L., & Sycara, K. (1998). Webmate: A personal agent for browsing and searching. In *2nd International Conference on Autonomous Agents*, Minneapolis, MN.

Chen, Y., & Wang, Y., & Wong, M. (2001). A Web-based fuzzy mass customization system. *Journal of Manufacturing Systems.*

Chervany, N. L., Dickson, G. W., & Kozar, K. (1972). *An experimental gaming framework for investigating the influence of management information systems on decision effectiveness.* MISRC Working Paper No. 71-12, Management Information Systems Research Center, University of Minnesota, Minneapolis, MN.

Chin, W. W. (1998). Issues and opinion on structural equation modeling. *MIS Quarterly, 22*(1), 7-16.

Chira, O., Chira, C., Roche, T., Tormey, D., & Brennan, A. (2006). An Agent-based Approach to Knowledge Management in Distributed Design. *Journal of Intelligent Manufacturing, 17*(6), 737–750. doi:10.1007/s10845-006-0042-0

Chorianopoulos, K., & Spinellis, D. (2003). Usability Design for the Home Media Station. In *Proceedings of the 10th HCI International 2003 Conference* (pp. 439-443).

Chorianopoulos, K., Lekakos, G., & Spinellis, D. (2003) Intelligent User Interfaces in the Living Room: Usability Design for Personalized Television Applications. In *Proceedings of IUI 2003* (pp. 230 – 232). New York: ACM Press.

Choudrie, J. Ghinea, G., & Weerakkody, V. (2004). Evluating global e-government sites: A view using web diagnostic tools. *Electronic Journal of E-Government, 2*(2), 105-114.

Churchill, G. (1979). A paradigm for developing better measures of marketing constructs. *Journal of Marketing Research, 16*, 64-73.

Cingil I., Dogac A., & Azgin A. (2000). A broader approach to personalization. *Communications of the ACM, 43*(8). cyLEDGE Media (2008). *Disentangling Web 2 and Mass Customization.*

Clason, D. L. & Dormody, T. J. (1994). Analyzing Data Measured by Individual Likert-Type Items. *Journal of Agricultural Education 35.*

Clausing, D. (1994). *Total quality development: a step-by-step guide to world class concurrent engineering.* New York: ASME Press.

Clements, P. (1997). Standard support for the virtual enterprise. In *Proceedings of the International Conference on Enterprise Integration Modeling Technology – ICEIMT '97, Torino, Italy.* Retrieved March 22, 2006, from http://www.mel.nist.gov/workshop/iceimt97/pap-cle2/stdspt2.htm

Clifford, D.K. (1965). Managing the Product Life Cycle. *Management Review, Tge McKinsey Quarterly,* Spring, 34-38.

Collier, D. A. (1981). The Measurement and Operating Benefits of Component Part Commonality. *Decision Sciences, 12*(1), 85–96. doi:10.1111/j.1540-5915.1981.tb00063.x

Collins, N., & Butler, P. (2003). When marketing models clash with democracy. *Journal of Public Affairs, 3*(1), 52-62.

Collis, D. J., & Montgomery, C. A. (2005). *Corporate Strategy: A Resource-Based Approach,* (2nd Ed.). Boston: McGraw-Hill/Irwin.

Comstock, M., Johansen, K., & Winroth, M. (2004). From mass production to mass customization: Enabling perspectives from the Swedish mobile telephone industry. *Production Planning & Control, 15*(4), 362-372.

Conner, K. R. (1991). A Historical Comparison of the Resource-Based Theory and Five Schools of Thought Within Industrial Organization Economics: Do We Have a New Theory of the Firm? *Journal of Management, 17*(1), 121–154. doi:10.1177/014920639101700109

Cox, W. E. (1967). Product Life Cycles as Marketing Models. *The Journal of Business, 40*(4), 375–384. doi:10.1086/295003

Crabtree, A., & Rodden, T. (2004). Domestic Routines and Design for the Home. *Journal of Collaborative Computing,* 13(2), 191–220. doi:10.1023/B:COSU.0000045712.26840.a4

Crabtree, A., Hemmings, T., Rodden, T., Cheverst, K., Clarke, K., Dewsbury, G., et al. (2003). Designing with care: adapting Cultural Probes to Inform Design in Sensitive Settings. In *Proceedings of OzCHI'03: New Directions in Interaction, information environments, media and technology.*

Crawford, C. M. (1992). Business Took the Wrong Life Cycle from Biology. *Journal of Product and Brand Management, 1*(1), 5–11. doi:10.1108/10610429210036690

Cronbach, L. J. (1951). Coefficient alpha and internal structure of tests. *Psychometrica, 16,* 297-334.

Csikszentmihalyi, M. (1996). *Creativity: Flow and the psychology of discovery and invention.* New York: HarperCollins Publishers.

Cuperfain, R., & Clarke, T. K. (1985). A new perspective on subliminal perception. *Journal of Advertising, 14,* 36–41.

Cusumano, M. A., & Nobeoka, K. (1998). *Thinking beyond lean.* New York: Free Press.

D'Souza, D., & Wills, A., (1998). *Objects, components, and frameworks with UML: The catalysis.* Addison-Wesley. Retrieved March 23, 2006, from http://www.catalysis.org

Da Silveira, G., Borenstein, D., & Fogliatto, F. S. (2001). Mass customization: Literature review and research directions. *Journal of Production Economics, 72,* 1–13. doi:10.1016/S0925-5273(00)00079-7

Darley, A. (2000). *Visual digital culture: Surface play and spectacle in new media genres.* London: Routledge.

Das, T. K., & Teng, B. S. (2000). A resource-based theory of strategic alliances. *Journal of Management, 26*(1), 31–61. doi:10.1016/S0149-2063(99)00037-9

Davis, S. (1987). *Future Perfect.* Reading, MA: Addison-Wesley.

Davis, T. R. V. (1999). *Different service firms, different core competencies.* Bloomington, IN: Business Horizons.

Day, G. S. (1981). The Product Life Cycle: Analysis and Application Issues. *Journal of Marketing, 45*(4), 60–67. doi:10.2307/1251472

Day, G. S. (1994). The Capabilities of Market-Driven Organizations. *Journal of Marketing, 58*(4), 37–52. doi:10.2307/1251915

De Bra, P., Aroyo, L., & Chepegin, V. (2004). The next big thing: Adaptive Web-based systems. *Journal of Digital Information, 5*(1), 247.

Dellaert, B. G. C., & Stremersch, S. (2005). Marketing mass-customized products: Striking a balance between utility and complexity. *Journal of Marketing Research, 42*(2), 219-227.

DeLone, W. H., & McLean, E. R. (2002). Information systems success revisited. In *Proceedings of the 35th Annual Hawaii International Conference on Systems Sciences*. Sciences, IEEE Computer Society Press, Los Alamitos, CA.

DeLone, W. H., & McLean, E. R. (1992). Information systems success: The quest for the dependent variable. *Information Systems Research, 3*(1), 60-95.

DeLone, W. H., & McLean, E. R. (2003). The DeLone and McLean Model of information systems success: A ten-year update. *Journal of Management Information Systems, 19*(4), 9-30.

Demetriou, A., Efklides, A., & Platsidou, M. (1993). The architecture and dynamics of developing mind: Experiential structuralism as a frame for unifying cognitive development theories. *Monographs of the Society for Research in Child Development, 58* (Serial No. 234), 5-6.

DeSanctis, G. (1982). An examination of an expectancy theory model of decision support systems use. In *Proceedings of the Third International Conference of Information Systems* (pp. 121-135).

Desmet, P. M. A., Overbeeke, C. J., & Tax, S. J. E. T. (2001). Designing products with added emotional value: development and application of an approach for research through design. *The Design Journal, 4*(1), 32–47. doi:10.2752/146069201789378496

Dey, A. (1998). Context-Aware Computing: The CyberDesk Project. In *Proceeding of AAAI Spring Symposium*.

Dey, A. K., & Abowd, G., D. (2000). CyberMinder: A Context-aware System for Supporting Reminders. In *Proceeding of CHI*.

Dey, A., & Abowed, G. (2000). Towards a better understanding of context and context-awareness. In *Proceedings of the Workshop on the What, Who, Where, when and How of Context Awareness*. New York: ACM Press.

Diniz, E., Porto, M. R., & Adachi, T. (2005). Internet banking in Brazil: Evaluation of functionality, reliability, and usability. *The Electronic Journal of Information Systems Evaluation, 8*(1), 41-50.

Dix, A., Finlay, J., Abowd, G., & Bealer, R. (2004) *Human-Computer Interaction*. London: Prentice Hall.

Dobson, G., & Kalish, S. (1993). Heuristics for pricing and positioning a product-line using conjoint and cost data. *Management Science, 39*(2), 160–175. doi:10.1287/mnsc.39.2.160

Dodge, H. R., & Fullerton, S. (1984). Copy Length Across the Product Life Cycle. *Current Issues and Research in Advertising, 7*(1), 149–158.

Doll, W. J., & Torkzadeh, G. (1988). The measurement of end-user computing satisfaction. *MIS Quarterly, 12*(2), 259-274.

DOM (Document Object Model) (2006). Retrieved March 23, 2006, from http://www.w3.org/TR/REC-DOM-Level-1

Du, X., Jiao, J., & Tseng, M. M. (2003). Identifying customer need patterns for customization and personalization. *Integrated Manufacturing Systems, 14*(5), 387–396. doi:10.1108/09576060310477799

Ducatel, K., Bogdanowicz, M., Scapolo, F., Leijten, J., & Burgelman, J.-C. (2001). *Scenarios for ambient intelligence in 2010*, ISTAG Report, European Commission.

Dunn, S. C., Seaker, R. F., & Waller, M. A. (1994). Latent variables in business logistics research: Scale development and validation. *Journal of Business Logistics, 15*(2), 145-172.

Duray, R. (2002). Mass customization origins: Mass or custom manufacturing? *International Journal of Operations & Production Management, 22*(3), 314-328.

Duray, R., & Ward, P., T., Milligan, G. W. & Berry, W. L. (2000). Approaches to mass customization: Configurations and empirical validation. *Journal of Operations Management, 18*(6), 605–625. doi:10.1016/S0272-6963(00)00043-

Dyer, J. H., & Singh, H. (1998). The Relational View: Cooperative Strategy and Sources of Interorganisational Competitive Advantage. *Academy of Management Review, 23*(4), 660–679. doi:10.2307/259056

Egan, D. E. (1988). Individual differences in human-computer interaction. In M. Helander (Ed.), *Handbook of Human-Computer Interaction*, (p. 543 – 568). Elsevier: New York.

Ehrmantraut, M., & Härder, T. Wittig, H., & Steinmetz, R. (1996) The Personal Electronic Program Guide – Towards the Pre-selection of Individual TV Programs. *Proceedings of CIKM 1996*, (pp. 243 – 250).

Eisenhardt, K. M. (1989). Building Theories from Case Study Research. *Academy of Management Review, 14*, 532–550. doi:10.2307/258557

Ekman, P. (1992). An argument for basic emotions. *Cognition and Emotion, 6*, 169–200. doi:10.1080/02699939208411068

empirica GmbH (2005). *The European e-Business Report: A portrait of e-business in 10 sectors of the EU economy, 2005 edition*. Retrieved March 23, 2006, from http://www.ebusiness-watch.org/resources/documents/Pocketbook-2005_001.pdf

ENV 13 550 (1995). *Enterprise Model Execution and Integration Services (EMEIS)*. Brussels, Belgium: CEN.

Eronen, L. (2003). User Centered Research for Interactive Television. In J. Masthoff, R. Griffiths, & L. Pemberton, (Ed.), *From viewers to actors? Proceedings of the European Conference on Interactive Television (EuroITV'03)* (pp. 5-12), Brighton, UK.

Ezzedine, H., Kolski, C., & Peninou, A. (2005). Agent-oriented design of human-computer interface: application to supervision of an urban transport network. *Engineering Applications of Artificial Intelligence, 18*(3), 255–270. doi:10.1016/j.engappai.2004.09.013

Fairclough, S. H. (2007). Psychophysiological inference and physiological computer games. In A. Nijholt & D. Tan (Ed.), *BRAINPLAY 07: brain-computer interfaces and games workshop at ACE (Advances in computer entertainment) 2007*, Salzburg, Austria.

Felder, R. M., & Silverman, L. K. (1988). Learning and Teaching Styles in Engineering Education. *English Education, 78*, 674–681.

Felfernig, A., Friedrich, G., Jannach, D., & Stumptner, M. (2004). Consistency-based diagnosis of configuration knowledge bases. *Artificial Intelligence, 152*(2), 213-234.

Fenves, S. J., Sriram, R. D., Choi, Y., & Robert, J. E. (2003). *Advanced Engineering Environments for Small Manufacturing Enterprises, 1*.

Fenves, S. J., Sriram, R. D., Choi, Y., Elm, J. P., & Robert, J. E. (2004). *Advanced Engineering Environments for Small Manufacturing Enterprises, 2*.

Fetterman, D. M. (1998). *Ethnography: step by step.* (2nd Ed.). Thousand Oaks, CA: Sage Publications.

Fiore, A. M., Lee, S.-E., & Kunz, G. (2004). Individual differences, motivations, and willingness to use a mass customization option for fashion products. *European Journal of Marketing, 38*(7), 835–849. doi:10.1108/03090560410539276

Fiore, A. M., Lee, S.-E., Kunz, G., & Campbell, J. R. (2001). Relationships between optimum stimulation level and willingness to use mass customisation options. *Journal of Fashion Marketing and Management, 5*(2), 99–107. doi:10.1108/EUM0000000007281

Fischer, G. (2002). Beyond 'couch potatoes': From consumers to designers and active contributors. *First Monday (Peer-Reviewed Journal on the Internet), available at* http://firstmonday.org/issues/issue7_12/fischer/.

Fishbein, M., & Ajzen, L. (1972). Attitudes and opinions. *Annual Review of Psychology, 23*, 487–554. doi:10.1146/annurev.ps.23.020172.002415

Fleischanderl, G., Friedrich, G., Haselböck, A., Schreiner, H., & Stumptner, M. (1998). Configuring large-scale systems with generative constraint satisfaction. *IEEE Intelligent System- Special issue on Configuration, 13* (7), 59-68.

Fohn, S. M., Liau, J. S., Greef, A. R., Young, R. E., & O'Grady, P. J. (1995). Configuring computer systems through constraint-based modeling and interactive constraint satisfaction. *Computers in Industry, 27*, 3-21.

Forgas, J. P. (1992). Affect in social judgments and decisions: A multiprocess model. *Advances in Experimental*

Social Psychology, 25, 227–275. doi:10.1016/S0065-2601(08)60285-3

Forlizzi, J., & Battarbee, K. (2004). Understanding experience in interactive systems. In *Proceedings of the 5th Conference on Designing interactive Systems: Processes, Practices, Methods, and Techniques* (pp. 261-268). New York: ACM.

Forza, C., & Salvador, F. (2002). Product configuration and inter-firm co-ordination: an innovative solution from a small manufacturing enterprise. *Computers in Industry, 49,* 37–46. doi:10.1016/S0166-3615(02)00057-X

Forza, C., & Salvador, F. (2002). Managing for variety in the order acquisition and fulfilment process: The contribution of product configuration systems. *International Journal of Production Economics, 76,* 87-98.

Forza, S., & Salvador, F. (2007). *Product Information Management for Mass Customization,* (1 Ed.). New York: Palgrave Macmillan.

Fowler, J. (2000). *Co-operative use of STEP and PLib.* Retrieved March 22, 2006, from http://www.nist.gov/sc4

Franke, N., & Piller, F. (2002). *Configuration toolkits for mass customization: setting a research agenda.* Technical report.

Franke, N., & Piller, F. T. (2003). Key research issues in user interaction with user toolkits in a mass customisation system. *International Journal of Technology Management, 26*(5/6), 578–599. doi:10.1504/IJTM.2003.003424

Franke, N., & Piller, F. T. (2004). Value creation by toolkits for user innovation and design: The case of the watch market. *Journal of Product Innovation Management, 21*(6), 401–415. doi:10.1111/j.0737-6782.2004.00094.x

Franke, N., & Schreier, M. (2008). Product uniqueness as a driver of customer utility in mass customization. *Marketing Letters, 19*(2), 93–107. doi:10.1007/s11002-007-9029-7

Franke, N., Keinz, P., & Schreier, M. (2008). Complementing mass customization toolkits with user communities: How peer input improves customer self-design. *Journal of Product Innovation Management, 25*(6), 546–559. doi:10.1111/j.1540-5885.2008.00321.x

Freeman, F. G. (1999). Evaluation of an adaptive automation system using three EEG indices with a visual tracking task. *Biological Psychology, 50,* 61–76. doi:10.1016/S0301-0511(99)00002-2

Frijda, N. H. (1994). Varieties of affect: Emotions and episodes, moods, and sentiments. In P. Ekman & R. J. Davidson (Ed.), *The Nature Emotion: Fundamental Questions* (pp. 59-67). Oxford, UK: Oxford University Press.

Füller, J., Bartl, M., Ernst, H., & Mühlbacher, H. (2006). Community based innovation: How to integrate members of virtual communities into new product development. *Electronic Commerce Research, 6*(January), 57–73. doi:10.1007/s10660-006-5988-7

Fung, R. Y. K., Popplewell, K., & Xie, J. (1998). An intelligent hybrid system for customer requirements analysis and product attribute targets determination. *International Journal of Production Research, 36*(1), 13–34. doi:10.1080/002075498193912

Fung, R. Y. K., Tang, J., Tu, Y., & Wang, D. (2002). Product design resources optimization using a non-linear fuzzy quality function deployment model. *International Journal of Production Research, 40*(3), 585–599. doi:10.1080/00207540110061634

Gallagher, C. A. (1974). Perceptions of the value of a management information system. *Academy of Management Journal, 17*(1), 46-55.

Gallaher, M. (2004). *Cost analysis of inadequate interoperability in the U.S. capital facilities industry* (NIST GCR 04-867). Washington, DC: National Institute of Standards and Technology, Department of Commerce.

Garfinkel, H. (1967). *Studies in ethnomethodology.* Englewood Cliffs, NJ: Prentice Hall.

Garrity, E. J., & Sanders, G. L. (1998). Dimensions of information systems success. In E. J. Garrity & G. L. Sanders (Eds.), *Information systems success measurement.* Hershey, PA: Idea Group Publishing.

Gatewood, R. D., & Field, H. S. (1990). *Human resource selection.* Chicago: The Dryden Press.

Gaver, B., Dunne, T., & Pacenti, E. (1999). Design: Cultural Probes. *Interaction, 6*(1), 21–29. doi:10.1145/291224.291235

Gawlinski, M. (2003). *Interactive Television Production.* Oxford, UK: Focal Press.

Gefen, D., Straub, D. W., & Boudreau, M. C. (2000). Structural equation modeling and regression: Guidelines for research practice. *Communications of the Association for Information Systems, 4*(7), 1-57.

Gerbing, D., & Anderson, J. (1988). An updated paradigm for scale development incorporating unidimensionality and its assessment. *Journal of Marketing Research, 25,* 186-192.

Germanakos, P., Mourlas, C., Isaia, C., & Samaras, G. (2005). An Optimized Review of Adaptive Hypermedia and Web Personalization - Sharing the Same Objective. In *Proceedings of the 1st International Workshop on Web Personalization, Recommender Systems and Intelligent User Interfaces (WPRSIUI 2005) of the 2nd International Conference on E-business and TElecommunications Networks (ICETE2005)*, Reading, October 3-8, (pp. 43-48).

Germanakos, P., Tsianos, N., Lekkas, Z., Mourlas, C., & Samaras, G. (2008). Realizing Comprehensive User Profiling as the Core Element of Adaptive and Personalized Communication Environments and Systems. *The Computer Journal, Special Issue on Profiling Expertise and Behaviour.* Retrieved from doi:10.1016/j.chb.2007.07.010

Germanakos, P., Tsianos, N., Lekkas, Z., Mourlas, C., Belk, M., & Samaras, G. (2007). A Semantic Approach of an Adaptive and Personalized Web-based Learning Content - The case of AdaptiveWeb. In *Proceedings of the 2nd International Workshop on Semantic Media Adaptation and Personalization (SMAP 2007)*, London, UK, December 17-18, (pp. 68-73). Washington, DC: IEEE Computer Society.

Germanakos, P., Tsianos, N., Lekkas, Z., Mourlas, C., Belk, M., & Samaras, G. (2008). Towards an Adaptive and Personalized Web Interaction using Human Factors. In M. Angelides (Ed.) *Advances in Semantic Media Adaptation and Personalization*, (Vol.2). San Francisco: Taylor & Francis Group, LLC.

Gilmore, J. H., & Pine II, B. J. (1997). The four faces of customization. *Harvard Business Review, 75*(1), 91-101.

Goldsmith, R. E., & Freiden, J. B. (2004). Have it your way: Consumer attitudes toward personalized marketing. *Marketing Intelligence & Planning, 22*(2), 228–239. doi:10.1108/02634500410525887

Goodhue, D. (1990). *Developing a theory-based measure of user satisfaction: The task-systems fit questionnaire.* Working Paper, Information and Decision Science, University of Minnesota, June 28.

Goslar, M. D., Green, G. I., & Hughes, T. H. (1986). Decision support systems: An empirical assessment for decision making. *Decision Sciences, 17*(1), 79-91.

Graber, D. A. (2000). *Processing Politics.* Chicago: The University of Chicago Press.

Grant, R. M. (1991). The Resource-Based Theory of Competitive Advantage: Implications for Strategy Formulation. *California Management Review, 33*(3), 114–135.

Grant, R.M., (1996). Toward a Knowledge-Based Theory of the Firm. *Strategic Management Journal* (17), Winter Special Issue, 109-122.

Gray, J. A. (1991). The neuropsychology of temperament. In J. Strelau & A. Angleitner (Ed.), *Explorations in temperament: International perspectives on theory and measurement* (pp. 105-128). New York: Plenum Press.

Green, P. E., & DeSarbo, W. S. (1978). Additive decomposition of perceptions data via conjoint analysis. *The Journal of Consumer Research, 5*(1), 58–65. doi:10.1086/208714

Green, P. E., & Krieger, A. M. (1985). Models and heuristics for product line selection. *Marketing Science, 4*(1), 1–19. doi:10.1287/mksc.4.1.1

Gregory, T. (1999). *Interoperability cost analysis of the U.S. automotive supply chain* (99-1 Planning Rep.). Washington, DC: National Institute of Standards and Technology, Department of Commerce.

Grilo, A., & Jardim-Goncalves, R., (2005). Analysis on the development of e-platforms in the AEC sector. *International Journal of Internet and Enterprise Management, 3*(2).

Grodal, T. (2000). Video games and the pleasures of control. In D. Zillmann & P. Vorderer (Ed.), *Media entertainment: The psychology of its appeal* (pp. 197-212). Mahwah, NJ: Lawrence Erlbaum Associates.

Grönroos, C. (2002). *Service Management and Marketing. A Customer Relationship Management Approach*, (2nd Ed.). West Sussex, UK: Wiley & Sons.

Guental, H. G., Surprenant, N., & Bubeck, K. (1984). Effectively utilizing computer-aided design technology: The role of individual difference variables. In *Proceedings of the Fifth International Conference on Information Systems* (pp. 21-30).

Günter, A. & Kühn, C. (1999). Knowledge-Based Configuration: Survey and future directions. *In XPS-99: Knowledge Based Systems, Proceedings of the 5th Biannual German Conference on Knowledge Based Systems. Springer Leture Notes in Artifical Intelligence 1570.*

Gummesson, E. (1987). Marketing – A Long Term Interactive Relationship. *Long Range Planning, 20*(4), 10–20. doi:10.1016/0024-6301(87)90151-8

Gummesson, E. (1994). Making Relationship Marketing Operational. *International Journal of Service Industry Management, 5*(5), 5–20. doi:10.1108/09564239410074349

Haag, A. (1998). Sales configuration in business processes. *IEEE Intelligent Systems, 13*, 78–85. doi:10.1109/5254.708436

Haag, A. (2005). "Dealing" with configurable products in the SAP business suite. *Workshop on Configuration, International Conference on Artificial Intelligence (IJCAI 2005), Edinburgh, Scotland* (pp. 68-71).

Haddon, L. (2006). The Contribution of Domestication Research to In-Home Computing and Media Consumption. *The Information Society Journal, 22*, 195–203. doi:10.1080/01972240600791325

Hansen, B. L. (2003). *Development of Industrial Variant Specification Systems.* Department of Manufacturing Engineering and Management, Technical University of Denmark.

Harmony (2008). *Harmony Remotes To Include Speech Recognition.* Retrieved May 5, 2008, from http://www.physorg.com/news97575605.html

Harper, R. (2003). *Inside the Smart Home.* London: Springer.

Hart, C. H. L. (1995). Mass customization: conceptual underpinnings, opportunities and limits. *International Journal of Service Industry Management, 6*(2), 36–45. doi:10.1108/09564239510084932

Harter, A., Steggles, P., Ward, A., & Webster, P. (1991). The Anatomy of a Context-Aware Application. In *Mobile Computing and Networking,* (pp. 59-68). New York: ACM Press.

Hassenzahl, M., & Tractinsky, N. (2006). User experience – a research agenda. *Behaviour & Information Technology, 25*(2), 91–97. doi:10.1080/01449290500330331

Hauge, P.L. & Stauffer, L.A. (1993). ELK: A method for eliciting knowledge from customers. *Design and methodology, 53*, 73-81.

Heatley, J., Agraval, R., & Tanniru, M. (1995). An evaluation of an innovative information technology - The case of carrier EXPERT. *Journal of Strategic Information Systems, 4*(3), 255-277.

Hegge, H. M., & Wortmann, J. C. (1991). Generic bill-of-material: A new product model. *International Journal of Production Economics, 23*.

Heiskala, M., Anderson, A., Huhtinen, V., Tiihonen, J., & Martio, A. (2003). A tool for comparing configurable products. *Workshop on Configuration, International Conference on Artificial Intelligence (IJCAI 2005), Acapulco, Mexico* (pp. 64-69).

Hektner, J. M., Schmidt, J. A., & Csikszentmihaly, M. (2006) *Experience Sampling Method – Measuring the Quality of Everyday Life.* Thousand Oaks, CA: Sage Publications.

Helander, M. G., & Tham, M. P. (2003). Hedonomics-affective human factors design. *Ergonomics, 46*(13/14), 1269–1272. doi:10.1080/00140130310001610810

Hennig-Thurau, T., & Hansen, U. (Eds.). (2000). *Relationship Marketing. Gaining Competitive Advantage Through Customer Satisfaction and Customer Retention.* Berlin: Springer.

Herlocker, J., Konstan, J., Borchers, A., & Reidl, J. (1999). An algorithmic framework for performing collaborative filtering. In *Proceedings of the Conference on Research and Development in Information Retrieval.*

Heskett, J. L., Sasser, W. E., & Schlesinger, L. A. (1997). *The Service Profit Chain. How leading Companies Link Profit and Growth to Loyalty, Satisfaction, and Value.* New York: Free Press.

Hindus, D., Mainwaring, S. D., Leduc, N., Hagstrom, N. L., & Bayley, O. (2001) Casablanca: Designing Social Communication Devices for the Home. In *Proceedings of the Conference on Human Factors in Computing Systems (CHI 2001)* (pp. 325-332). New York: ACM Press.

Hof, R., Green, H., & Himmelstein, L. (1998). Now its your Web. *Business Week*, 68–75.

Hollensen, S. (2003). *Marketing Management: A Relationship Approach.* Prentice Hall: Harlow.

Hruschka, H. (1986). Market Definition and Segmentation Using Fuzzy Clustering Methods. *International Journal of Research in Marketing, 3*(2), 117–135. doi:10.1016/0167-8116(86)90015-7

Hsu, T. H. (2000). An Application of Fuzzy Clustering in Group-Positioning Analysis. In *Proceedings National Science Council of tile Republic of China, 10*(2), 157-167.

Huang, G. Q., Zhang, X. Y., & Lo, V. H. (2005). Optimal supply chain configuration for platform products: Impacts of commonality, demand variability, and quantity discount. *International Journal of Mass Customization, 1*(1).

Huffman, C., & Kahn, B. E. (1998). Variety for sale: Mass customization or mass confusion. *Journal of Retailing, 74*(4), 491–513. doi:10.1016/S0022-4359(99)80105-5

Hughes, J., O'Brien, J., Rodden, T., Rouncefield, M., & Viller, S. (2000). Patterns of Home Life: Informing Design for Domestic Environments. *Journal of Personal Technologies Special Issue on Domestic, 4*(1), 25–38.

Huizinga, J. (1950). *Homo Ludens: A Study of the Play-Element in Culture.* Boston: Beacon Press.

Hulkko, S., Keinonen, T., Mattelmäki, T., & Virtanen, K. (2004). Mobile Probes. In. *Proceedings of NordiCHI, 2004*, 43–51. doi:10.1145/1028014.1028020

Hull, R. Neaves, N. & Bedford-Roberts, J. (1997). Towards Situated Computing. In *Proceedings of IEEE First International Symposium on Wearable Computers,* Cambridge, MA.

Hutchinson, H., Mackay, W., Westerlund, B., Bederson, B. B., Druin, A., Plaisant, C., et al. (2003). Technology Probes: Inspiring Design for and with Families. In *Proceedings of*

Conference on Human Factors in Computing Systems (CHI 2003), (pp. 17-24). New York: ACM Press.

Hvam, L. (1999). A procedure for building product models. *Robotics and Computer-integrated Manufacturing, 15,* 77–87. doi:10.1016/S0736-5845(98)00030-1

Hvam, L., Malis, M., Hansen, B., & Riis, J. (2004). Reengineering of the quotation process: Application of knowledge-based systems. *Business Process Management Journal, 10*(2), 200-213.

IAI/IFC (1997). *IFC End User Guide. International Foundation Classes Release 1.5. IAI.*

IDEAS Project (2003). Ontology state of the art - Final report.

ISO 13407 (2008). ISO 13407. Retrieved October 10, 2008 from http://www.iso.org

ISO TC184/SC4 Standards (2006). Retrieved March 23, 2006, from http://www.tc184-sc4.org

ISO. (2008). ISO 16883. Retrieved October 12, 2008 from http://www.iso.org/iso/iso_catalogue/catalogue_tc/catalogue_detail.htm?csnumber=16883

ISO1030-1 (1994). ISO 10303 - Standard for the exchange of product data, Part 1, Overview and fundamentals principles. *International Organization for Standardization.*

ISO10303-11 (1998). ISO 10303 Standard for the exchange of product data (STEP), Part 11, Description methods, The EXPRESS language reference manual. *International Organization for Standardization.*

ISO10303-22 (2001). ISO 10303 Standard for the exchange of product data (STEP), Part 22. *International Organization for Standardization.*

Jääskö, V., & Mattelmäki, T. (2003) Observing and Probing. In *Proceedings of the International Conference on Designing Pleasurable Products and Interfaces (DPPI'03)* (pp. 126-131). ACM Press.

Jacobsen, J. K. (1997). *Interview – Kunsten at lytte og spørge.* Copenhagen: Hans Reitzels Forlag.

Jardim-Goncalves, R. (2004). Ontology-based framework for enhanced interoperability in networked industrial environments. In *Proceedings of the 11ᵗʰ IFAC Symposium on Information Control Problems in Manufacturing, IN-COM2004.* Salvador, Brazil.

Jardim-Goncalves, R., & Steiger, A. (2002). Integration and adoptabilidade of APs – The role of ISO TC184/SC4 standards. *Special issue: Applications in Industry of Product and Process Modelling Using Standards International Journal of Computer Applications in Technology.*

Jardim-Goncalves, R., & Steiger-Garcão, A. (2001). Supporting interoperability in standard-based environments - Towards reliable integrated systems. Advances in Concurrent Engineering. In *Proceedings of the 8ᵗʰ ISPE International Conference on Concurrent Engineering (CE2001),* Anaheim, CA.

Jardim-Goncalves, R., & Steiger-Garcão, A. (2002a). Implicit hierarchic metamodeling - In search of adaptable interoperability for manufacturing and business systems. In *Proceedings of the 5ᵗʰ IEEE/IFIP BASYS2002,* Mexico.

Jardim-Goncalves, R., & Steiger-Garcão, A. (2002b). Implicit multi-level modeling to support integration and interoperability in flexible business environments. *Communications of ACM, Special Issue on Enterprise Components, Services, and Business Rules,* 53-57.

Järvinen, A., Heliö, S., & Mäyrä, F. (2002). *Communication and community in digital entertainment services: Prestudy research report.* Hypermedialaboratorion verkkojulkaisuja 2, Tampere. Retrieved from http://tampub.uta.fi/tup/951-44-5432-4.pdf

Jenkins, S. (1995). Modeling a perfect profile. *Marketing, 6*(July 13).

Jensen, J. F. (2003). Interactive Television: New Genres, New Format, New Content. In *Proceedings of the 2nd Australasian conference on Interactive Entertainment* (pp. 89–96).

Jeppesen, L. B. (2005). User toolkits for innovation: Consumers support each other. *Journal of Product Innovation Management, 22*(4), 347–362. doi:10.1111/j.0737-6782.2005.00131.x

Jia, H. Z., Ong, S. K., Fuh, J. Y. H., Zhang, Y. F., & Nee, A. Y. C. (2004). An adaptive and upgradeable agent-based system for coordinated product development and manufac-

ture. *Robotics and Computer-integrated Manufacturing, 20*(2), 79–90. doi:10.1016/j.rcim.2003.08.001

Jiang, J. J., Klein, G., & Carr, C. L. Measuring information systems service quality: SERVQUAL from the other side. *MIS Quarterly, 26*(2), 145-166.

Jiang, J. J., Klein, G., & Crampton, S. M. A note on SERVQUAL reliability and validity in information systems service quality measurement. *Decision Sciences, 31*(3), 725-744.

Jiao, J., & Tseng, M. M. (1999). A pragmatic approach to product costing based on standard time estimation. *International Journal of Operations & Production Management, 19*(7), 738–755. doi:10.1108/01443579910271692

Jiao, J., & Tseng, M. M. (2000). Understanding product family for mass customization by developing commonality indices. *Journal of Engineering Design, 11*(3), 225–243. doi:10.1080/095448200750021003

Jiao, J., & Tseng, M. M. (2004). Customizability analysis in design for mass customization. *Computer Aided Design, 36*(8), 745–757. doi:10.1016/j.cad.2003.09.012

Jiao, J., & Zhang, Y. (2005). Product portfolio identification based on association rule mining. *Computer Aided Design, 37*(2), 149–172. doi:10.1016/j.cad.2004.05.006

Jiao, J., & Zhang, Y. (2005). Product portfolio planning with customer-engineering interaction. *IIE Transactions, 37*(9), 801–814. doi:10.1080/07408170590917011

Jiao, J., Zhang, L., & Pokharel, S. (2003). Process platform planning for mass customization. In *Proceedings of the 2nd Interdisciplinary World Congress on Mass Customization and Personalization,* Technical University, Munich [CD-ROM].

Jiao, J., Zhang, L., & Pokharel, S. (2005). Coordinating product and process variety for mass customized order fulfillment. *Production Planning and Control, 16*(6), 608–620. doi:10.1080/09537280500112181

Jiao, J., Zhang, Y., & Helander, M. G. (2006). A Kansei mining system for affective design. *Expert Systems with Applications, 30*(4), 658–673. doi:10.1016/j.eswa.2005.07.020

Jiao, X., & Tseng, M. (1999). A methodology of developing product family architecture for mass customization. *Journal of Intelligent Manufacturing, 10,* 3–20. doi:10.1023/A:1008926428533

Jordan, P. W. (2000). The four pleasures-A framework for pleasures in design, In P. W. Jordan (Ed.), *Proceedings of Conference on Pleasure Based Human Factors Design.* Groningen, The Netherlands: Philips Design.

JSKE. (2003). *Japan Society of Kansei engineering.* Available at http://www.jske.org/

JTC 1/SC 7/WG 17 (2006). *ISO - International Organization for Standardization.*

Kakati, M. (2002). Mass customization - Needs to go beyond technology. *Human Systems Management, 21,* 85-93.

Kallinen, K., & Ravaja, N. (2004). Emotion-related effects of speech rate and rising vs. falling background music melody during audio news: The moderating influence of personality. *Personality and Individual Differences, 37,* 275–288. doi:10.1016/j.paid.2003.09.002

Kaltz, J., Wolfgang, J., Ziegler, S., & Lohmann, L. (2005). Context-aware Web Engineering: Modeling and Applications. *RIA - Revue d'Intelligence Artificielle . Special Issue on Applying Context-Management, 19*(3), 439–458.

Kalyanpur, A., Parsia, B., & Hendler, J. (2005). A Tool for Working with Web Ontologies. In . *Proceedings of the International Journal on Semantic Web and Information Systems, 1*(1).

Kalyanpur, A., Parsia, B., Sirin, E., & Cuenca-Grau, B., James Hendler. (2005). Swoop: A 'Web' Ontology Editing Browser. *Journal of Web Semantics, 4*(2).

Kamali, N., & Loker, S. (2002). Mass customization: Online consumer involvement in product design. *Journal of Computer-Mediated Communication, 7*(4).

Kano, N., Seraku, N., Takahashi, F., & Tsuji, S. (1984). Attractive quality and must-be quality, Hinshitsu. *The Japan Society for Quality Control, 14*(2), 39–48.

Kaplan, A. M., Schoder, D., & Haenlein, M. (2007). Factors influencing the adoption of mass customization: The impact of base category consumption frequency and need satisfaction. *Journal of Product Innovation Management, 24*(2), 101–116. doi:10.1111/j.1540-5885.2007.00237.x

Karat, J., Karat, C.-M., & Broedie, C. (2003). Personalizing Interaction. In C.-M. Karat, J. O. Blom, & J. Karat, (Eds.) *Designing Personalized User Experiences in eCommerce* (pp. 7 – 14). Dordrecht: Kluwer Academic Publishers.

Karlsson, B., Aronsson, N., & Svensson, K. (2003). Using semantic environment description as a tool to evaluate car interiors. *Ergonomics, 46*(13/14), 1408–1422. doi:10.1080/00140130310001624905

Kaul, A., & Rao, V. R. (1995). Research for product positioning and design decisions: an integrative review. *International Journal of Research in Marketing, 12,* 293–320. doi:10.1016/0167-8116(94)00018-2

Kautz, H., Selman, B., & Shah, M. (1997). Referral web: Combining social networks and collaborative filtering. *Communications of the ACM, 40*(3), 6365. doi:10.1145/245108.245123

Kay, J. (2000). User Modelling for Adaptation. In C. Stephanidis, (Ed.), *User Interfaces for All: Human Factors Series,* (pp. 271-294). Mahwah, NJ: Lawrence Erlbaum.

Kay, J., Kummerfeld, B., & Lauder, P. (2003). *Managing private user models and shared personas.* Workshop on User Modelling for Ubiquitous Computing in conjunction with User modelling.

Kay, M. J. (1993). Making mass customization happen: Lessons for implementation. *Strategy & Leadership, 21*(4), 14-18.

Kelly, K. (1994). *Out of control: The new biology of machines, social systems and the economic world.* Reading, MA: Addison Wesley.

Kettinger, W. J., & Lee, C. C. (1997). Pragmatic perspectives on the measurement of information systems service quality. *MIS Quarterly,* 223-240.

Kettinger, W. J., & Lee, C. C. (1999). Replication of measures of information systems research: The case of IS SERVQUAL. *Decision Sciences, 30*(3), 893-899.

Khalid, H. M. (2001). Towards affective collaborative design. In M. J.Smith, G. Salvendy, D. Harris, & R. J. Koubek, *Usability Evaluation and Interface Design, Proceedings of HCI International 2001* (Vol. 1). Mahwah, NJ: Lawrence Erlbaum.

Khalifa, M., & Liu, V. (2003). Determinants of satisfaction at different adoption stages of Internet-based services. *Journal of the Association for Information Systems, 4*(5), 206-232.

Kiesler, T., & Kiesler, S. (2005). My pet rock and me: An experimental exploration of the self extension concept. In G. Menon & A. Rao (Eds.), *Advances in Consumer Research* (Vol. 32, pp. 365-370). Provo, UT: Association for Consumer Research.

Kihlström, J. F., Barnhardt, T. M., & Tataryn, D. J. (1992). Implicit perception. In R. F. Bornstein & T.S. Pittmann (eds.) *Perception without awareness. Cognitive, clinical and social perspectives*, (pp. 17-54). New York: Guilford.

Kim, W. (2002). Personalization: Definition, Status, and Challenges Ahead. *JOT, 1*(1).

King, W. R., & Epstein, B. J. (1983). Assessing information system value. *Decision Sciences, 14*(1), 34-45.

Knostan, J., Miller, B., Maltz, D., Herlocker, J., Gordon, L., & Riedl, J. (1997). Grouplens: Applying collaborative filtering to Usenet news. *Communications of the ACM, 40*(3), 7787.

Kobsa, A. (2001). Generic User Modeling Systems. *User Modeling and User-Adapted Interaction, 11*(1-2), 49–63. doi:10.1023/A:1011187500863

Kobsa, A., Koenemann, J., & Pohl, W. (2001). Personalized Hypermedia Presentation Techniaues for Improving Customer Relationships. *The Knowledge Engineering Review.*

Kodzi, E. T. Jr, Lihra, T., & Gazo, R. (2007). Process Transformation Mandates for Manufacturing Customized Furniture. *Journal of Forest Products Business Research, 4*(8).

Kodzi, E. T., Jr. (2006). *Mass Customization as a Framework for Manufacturing Transformations in the US Furniture Industry.* West Lafayette, IN: Purdue University, Department of Forestry and Natural Resources.

Kogut, B., & Zander, U. (1992). Knowledge of the Firm, Combinative Capabilities, and the Replication of Technology. *Organization Science, 3*(3), 383–397. doi:10.1287/orsc.3.3.383

Kolb, A.Y., & Kolb, D.A. (2005). The Kolb Learning Style Inventory. *Technical Specifications, Experience Based Learning Systems, Inc.*, Version 3.1.

Kota, S., Sethuraman, K., & Miller, R. (2000). A metric for evaluating design commonality in product families. *ASME Journal of Mechanical Design, 122*(4), 403–410. doi:10.1115/1.1320820

Kotha, S. (1995). Mass customization: Implementing the emerging paradigm for competitive advantage. *Strategic Management Journal, 16*, 21-42.

Kotler, P., & Armstrong, G. (2006). *Principles of Marketing*, (11th Ed.). Upper Saddle River, NJ: Pearson.

Kramer, J., Noronha, S., & Vergo, J. (2000). A user-centered design approach to personalization. *Communications of the ACM, 43*(8), 44–48. doi:10.1145/345124.345139

Krosnick, J. A., Betz, A. L., Jussim, J. L., & Lynn, A. R. (1992). Subliminal conditioning of attitudes. *Personality and Social Psychology Bulletin, 18*, 152–162. doi:10.1177/0146167292182006

Kubiak, J. (1993). A Joint Venture in Mass Customization. *Planning Review, 21*(4), 25.

Kuikkaniemi, K., Laitinen, T., & Kosunen, I. (2008). *Designing emotionally adaptive gaming.* Proceedings of EHTI08: The First Finnish Symposium on Emotions and Human-Technology Interaction (pp. 13 – 17), University of Tampere, Tampere, Finland

Kvale, S. (1997). *InterView.* Copenhagen: Hans Reitzels Forlag.

Laarni, J. (2003). Effects of color, font type and font style on user preferences. In C. Stephanidis (Ed.) *Adjunct Proceedings of HCI International 2003* (pp. 31-32). Heraklion, Greece: Crete University Press.

Laarni, J., & Kojo, I. (2001). Reading financial news from PDA and laptop displays. In M. J. Smith & G. Salvendy (Ed.) *Proceedings of HCI International, Systems, Social and Internationalization Design Aspects of Human-Computer Interaction* (Vol. 2, pp. 109 – 113). Hillsdale, NJ: Lawrence Erlbaum.

Laarni, J., Ravaja, N., & Saari, T. (2005). Aesthetic and emotional evaluations of computer interfaces. In C. Stephanidis

(Ed.) *Proceedings of HCI International 2005.* Mahwah, NJ: Lawrence Erlbaum Associates

Laarni, J., Ravaja, N., Saari, T., & Liukkonen, S. (2004). Effects of color and texture on emotional evaluations. In J. P.Frois, P. Andrade & J. F. Marques (Eds.) *Art and Science: Proceedings IAEA 2004 XVIII Congress.* Lisbon:IAEA.

Ladeby, K. R., Edwards, K., & Haug, A. (2007). *Typology of Product Configuration Systems.* In T. Blecker, K. Edwards, G. Friedrich, L. Hvam, & F. Salvadore (Eds.), *IMCM'07 & PETO'07* (pp. 175-184), GITO.

Lampel, J. & Mintzberg, H. (1996). Customizing Customization. *Sloan Management Review, 38*(1), 21-30.

Lang, A. (1990). Involuntary attention and physiological arousal evoked by structural features and mild emotion in TV commercials. *Communication Research, 17*(3), 275–299. doi:10.1177/009365090017003001

Lang, A., Dhillon, P., & Dong, Q. (1995). Arousal, emotion and memory for television messages. *Journal of Broadcasting & Electronic Media, 38,* 1–15.

Lang, A., Newhagen, J., & Reeves, B. (1996). Negative video as structure: Emotion, attention, capacity and memory. *Journal of Broadcasting & Electronic Media, 40,* 460–477.

Lang, K. (1995). Newsweeder: Learning to filter Netnews. In *12th International Conference on Machine Learning.*

Lang, P. J. (1995). The emotion probe. Studies of motivation and attention. *The American Psychologist, 50,* 372–385. doi:10.1037/0003-066X.50.5.372

Lankoski, P. (2003). *Vallan jäljet. Lähtökohtia pelin ja draamallisen tv-sarjan yhdistämiseen.* Hypermedialaboratorion verkkojulkaisuja 4, Tampere. Retrieved from http://tampub.uta.fi/tup/951-44-5705-6.pdf

Larsen, R. J., & Diener, E. (1992). Promises and problems with the circumplex model of emotion. In M. Clark (Ed.), *Review of personality and social psychology* (Vol. 13, pp.25-59). Newbury Park, CA: Sage.

Lazarus, R. S. (1991). *Emotion and Adaptation.* New York: Oxford University Press.

Lee, Y. H., Kumara, S. R. T., & Chatterjee, K. (2003). Multiagent based dynamic resource scheduling for dis-

tributed multiple projects using a market mechanism. *Journal of Intelligent Manufacturing, 14*(5), 471–484. doi:10.1023/A:1025753309346

Lekakos, G., & Chorianopoulos, K. Spinellis, D. (2001) Information Systems in the Living Room: A Case Study of Personalized Interactive TV Design. In *Proceedings of the 9th European Conference on Information Systems* (pp. 319-329), Bled, Slovenia.

Lekkas, Z., Tsianos, N., Germanakos, P., Mourlas, C., & Samaras, G. (2008). The Role of Emotions in the Design of Personalized Educational Systems. In *Proceedings of the 8th IEEE International Conference on Advanced Learning Technologies (ICALT 2008).*

Liang, W. Y., & Huang, C. C. (2002). The agent-based collaboration information system of product development. *International Journal of Information Management, 22*(3), 211–224. doi:10.1016/S0268-4012(02)00006-3

Liberman, H. (1995). Letzia: An agent that assists in web browsing. In *Proceedings of International Joint Conference on Artificial Intelligence,* Montreal, Canada.

Liechty, J., Ramaswamy, V., & Cohen, S. H. (2001). Choice menus for mass customization: An experimental approach for analyzing customer demand with an application to a web-based information service. *Journal of Marketing Research, (38),* 183-196.

Liker, J. (2004). *The Toyota way.* McGraw Hill.

Liu, Y., & Connelly, K. (2006). Towards Wide Area Context-Aware Environments, In *the 4th IEEE International Conference on Pervasive Computer and Communications,* Pisa, Italy.

Loffredo, D. (1998). *Efficient database implementation of EXPRESS information models.* PhD thesis, Rensselaer Polytechnic Institute, Troy, NY.

Loiacono, E., Chen, D., & Goodhue, D. (2002). *WebQual™ revisited: Predicting the intent to reuse a Web site.* Americas Conference on Information Systems (AMCIS), Dallas, Texas, August.

López de Ipiña, D., Ignacio Vázquez, J., & Abaitua, J. (2007). *A Web 2.0 Platform to Enable Context-Aware Mobile Mash-Ups,* (pp. 266-286).

Lovelock, C. H. (1983). Classifying services to gain strategic marketing insights. *Journal of Marketing, 47*(3), 9–20. doi:10.2307/1251193

Lovelock, C., & Wirtz, J. (2004). *Services Marketing. People, Technology, Strategy,* (5th Ed.). Upper Saddle River, NJ: Pearson.

Lucas, H. C. (1978). Empirical model for a descriptive model of implementation. *MIS Quarterly, 2*(2), 27-41.

MacCarthy, B., & Brabazon, P. (2003). In the business of mass customisation. *IEE Manufacturing Engineer, 82*(4), 30-33.

Macpherson, A., Jones, O., & Zhang, M. (2004). Evolution or revolution? Dynamic capabilities in a knowledge-dependent firm. *R & D Management, 34*(2), 161–177. doi:10.1111/j.1467-9310.2004.00331.x

Madhusudan, T. (2005). An agent-based approach for coordinating product design workflows. *Computers in Industry, 56*(3), 235–259. doi:10.1016/j.compind.2004.12.003

Magrath, A. J. (1986). When Marketing Services, 4 Ps Are Not Enough. *Business Horizons, 29*(3), 44–50. doi:10.1016/0007-6813(86)90007-8

Mahmood, M. A. (1987). Systems development methods—A comparative investigation. *MIS Quarterly, 11*(3), 293-311.

Mandler, J. M. (1984). *Stories, scripts and scenes: Aspects of schema theory.* Mahwah, NJ: Lawrence Erlbaum.

Mandryk, R. L., Atkins, M. S., & Inkpen, K. M. (2006). A continuous and objective evaluation of emotional experience with interactive play environments. In *Proceedings of the SIGCHI Conference on Human Factors in Computing Systems.*

Manhart, P. (2005). Reconfiguration – A problem in search of solutions. In D. Jannach & A. Felfernig (Eds.), *Configuration – Papers from the Configuration Workshop at IJCAI'05* (pp. 68-71).

Männistö, T., Soininen, T., Tiihonen, J., & Sulonen, R. (1999). Framework and conceptual model for reconfiguration. *Configuration Papers from the AAAI Workshop* (AAAI Technical Report WS-99-05) (pp. 59-64). AAAI Press.

Manovich, L. (2001). *The language of new media.* Cambridge, MA: The MIT Press.

Mao, J., Vredenburg, K., Smith, P. W., & Carey, T. (2005). The state of user-centered design practice. *Communications of the ACM, 48*(3), 105–109. doi:10.1145/1047671.1047677

Markillie, P. (2004). A perfect market. *The Economist,* May 13.

Marsden, G., & Jones, M. (2006). *Mobile Interaction Design.* London: Wiley.

Mason, M. S., & Hacker, L. K. (2003). Applying Communication Theory to Digital Divide Research. *IT & Society, 1*(5), 40–55.

Mason, R. O. (1978). Measuring information output: A communication systems approach. *Information and Management, 1*(5), 219-234.

Mathews, J. A. (2003). Competitive dynamics and economic learning: an extended resource-based view. *Industrial and Corporate Change, 12*(1), 115–145. doi:10.1093/icc/12.1.115

Matsubara, Y., & Nagamachi, M. (1997). Hybrid Kansei engineering system and design support. *International Journal of Industrial Ergonomics, 19*(2), 81–92. doi:10.1016/S0169-8141(96)00005-4

McAdams, D. A., Stone, R. B., & Wood, K. L. (1999). Functional interdependence and product similarity based on customer needs. *Research in Engineering Design, 11*(1), 1–19. doi:10.1007/s001630050001

McGuinness, D. L., & Wright, J. R. (1998). An industrial-strength description logic-based configurator platform. *IEEE Intelligent Systems, 13*(4), 69-77.

McLoughlin, C. (1999). The implications of the research literature on learning styles for the design of instructional material. *Australian Journal of Educational Technology, 15*(3), 222–241.

MDA (2003). *Model Driven Architecture, MDA Guide Version 1.0.1, June 2003.* Retrieved March 23, 2006, from http://www.omg.org/mda

Meier, A., & Werro, N. (2007). A Fuzzy classification model for on-line customers. *Informatica.*

Meier, A., Werro, N., Albrecht, M., & Sarakinos, M. (2005). Using a Fuzzy Classification Query Language for Customer Relationship Management. *Proceedings 31st International Conference on Very Large Data Bases (VLDB)*, Trondheim, Norway, (pp. 1089-1096).

Mellor, S., & Balcer, M. (2002). *Executable UML - A foundation for model-driven architecture*. Addison-Wesley.

Meyer, K. (1995). Dramatic narrative in virtual reality. In F. Biocca & M. Levy (Ed.) *Communication in the age of virtual reality*. Hillsdale, NJ: Lawrence Erlbaum.

Meyer, M. H. (1997). Revitalize your product lines through continuous platform renewal. *Research Technology Management, 40*(2), 17–28.

Meyer, M. H., & Lehnerd, A. P. (1997). *The Power of Product Platforms: Building Value and Cost Leadership*. New York: The Free Press.

Miller, J., & Doyle, B. A. (1987). Measuring effectiveness of computer based information systems in the financial services sector. *MIS Quarterly, 11*(1), 107- 124.

Miller, J., & Mukerji, J. (2001). *Model driven architecture white paper*. Retrieved March 23, 2006, from http://www.omg.org/cgi-bin/doc?ormsc/2001-07-01

Mills, P. K., & Morris, J. H. (1986). Clients as "Partial" Employees of Service Organizations: Role, Development in Client Participation. *Academy of Management Review, 11*(4), 726–735. doi:10.2307/258392

Mladenic, D. (1996). *Personal WebWatcher: design and implementation*. Technical report, Department for Intelligent Systems, J. Stefan Institute, Ljubljana, Slovenia.

Mobasher, B. (2005). Web usage mining and Personalization. In M. P. Singh (ed.), *Practical Handbook of Internet Computing*. Boca Raton, FL: CRC Press.

Mok, C., Stutts, A. T., & Wong, L. (2000). Mass Customization in the Hospitality Industry: Concepts and Applications. In *Proceedings of the Fourth International Conference, Tourism in Southeast Asia & Indo-China: Development marketing and sustainability* (pp. 123-139), Singapore.

Monsotori, L., Vancza, J., & Kumara, S. R. T. (2006). Agent Based Manufacturing Systems. *Annals of CIRP, 55*(2), 667–696. doi:10.1016/j.cirp.2006.10.003

Monticino, M., Acevedo, M., Callicott, B., Cogdill, T., & Lindquist, C. (2007). Coupled human and natural systems: A multi-agent-based approach. *Environmental Modelling & Software, 22*(5), 656–663. doi:10.1016/j.envsoft.2005.12.017

Moon, A., Hyoungsun, K., Hyun, K., & Soowoo, L. (2007, April). Context-Aware Active Services. *Ubiquitous Computing Environments ETRI Journal, 29*(2), 169–178.

Moon, S. K., Park, J., Simpson, T. W., & Kumara, S. R. T. (2008). A Dynamic Multi-Agent System Based on a Negotiation Mechanism for Product Family Design. *IEEE Transactions on Automation Science and Engineering, 5*(2), 234–244. doi:10.1109/TASE.2007.896902

Moore, W. L., Louviere, J. J., & Verma, R. (1999). Using conjoint analysis to help design product platforms. *Journal of Product Innovation Management, 16*(1), 27–39. doi:10.1016/S0737-6782(98)00034-4

Motta, E. (1999). *Reusable components for knowledge modelling*. Amsterdam, The Netherlands: IOS Press.

Moukas, A. (1996). Amalthaea: Information discovery and filtering using a multi-agent evolving ecosystem. In *Proc. 1st Intl. Conf. on the Practical Application of Intelligent Agents and Multi Agent Technology*, London.

Mowen, J. (1995). *Consumer behavior* (4th ed.). Englewoods Cliffs, NJ: Prentice Hall.

Mugge, R., & Schoormans, J. P. L. (2005). Product personalisatie. Kan de consument zijn eigen product ontwerpen? (Product personalization. Can a consumer design his own product?). *Product, November*, 9-11.

Mugge, R., Brunel, F. F., & Schoormans, J. P. L. (2007). Psychological and behavioral consumer responses to the mass customization of product aesthetics. In W. Mitchell, F. T. Piller, M. M. Tseng, R. Chin & B. L. McClanahan (Eds.), *2007 World Conference on Mass Customization and Personalization*. Cambridge: MIT.

Mugge, R., Schoormans, J. P. L., & Schifferstein, H. N. J. (2009). Emotional bonding with personalized products. *Journal of Engineering Design, 20*(5), 467–476. doi:10.1080/09544820802698550

Mugge, R., Schoormans, J. P. L., & Schifferstein, H. N. J. (2009). Incorporating consumers in the design of their own products: The dimensions of product personalisation . *CoDesign*, *5*(2), 79–97. doi:10.1080/15710880802666416

Nadia, B.-B. (2001). Kansei mining: Identifying visual impressions as patterns in images. In *Proceedings of International Conference IFSA/NAFIPS*, Vancouver.

Nagamachi, M. (1989). *Kansei engineering*. Tokyo: Kaibundo Publisher.

Nagamachi, M. (1996). *Introduction of Kansei engineering*. Tokyo: Japan Standard Association.

Nagi, L. (1997). Design and implementation of a virtual information system for agile manufacturing. *IIE Transactions on Design and Manufacturing, Special issue on Agile Manufacturing, 29*, 839-857.

Nair, S. K., Thakur, L. S., & Wen, K. (1995). Near optimal solutions for product line design and selection: beam search heuristics. *Management Science*, *41*, 767–785. doi:10.1287/mnsc.41.5.767

NDS. (2005). Retrieved from www.nds.com

Nelson, T. M., & Carlson, D. R. (1985). Determining factors in choice of arcade games and their consequences upon young male players. *Journal of Applied Social Psychology*, *15*, 124–139. doi:10.1111/j.1559-1816.1985.tb02339.x

Nichols, D. (1997). Implicit Rating and filtering. In *Proceedings of the 5th DELOS Workshop on Filtering and Collaborative Filtering* (pp. 31 – 35).

Nielsen, J., & Mack, R. L. (Eds.). (1994). *Usability inspection methods*. New York, NY: John Wiley & Sons.

Nielsen, L. B. (2004). Post Disney experience paradigm? Some implications for the development of content to mobile tourist services. In *Proceedings of ICEC'04, Sixth International Conference on Electronic Commerce*, Delft, The Netherlands.

Nonaka, I., & Takeuchi, H. (1995). *The Knowledge-Creating Company: How Japanese Companies Create the Dynamics of Innovation*. New York: Oxford University Press.

Noy, N., Sintek, M., Decker, S., Crubézy, M., Fergerson, R., & Musen, M. (2001). *Creating Semantic Web Contents with Protégé-2000*. Paolo Alto, CA: Stanford University.

O'Grady, P. (1999). *The age of modularity*. Iowa City, IA: Adams and Steele Publishers.

Oard, D. (1997). The state of the art in text filtering. *User Modeling and User-Adapted Interaction*, 7.

Obrist, M., Bernhaupt, R., & Tscheligi, M. (2008). Interactive TV for the Home: An ethnographic study on users' requirements and experiences. *International Journal of Human-Computer Interaction*, *24*(2), 174–196. doi:10.1080/10447310701821541

Oh, Y., Yoon, S., & Hawley, J. (2004). What Virtual Reality can offer to the Furniture Industry. *Journal of Textile and Apparel Technology and Management*, *4*(1).

Orsvärn, K. (2005). Tacton configurator - Research directions. *Workshop on Configuration, International Conference on Artificial Intelligence (IJCAI 2005), Edinburgh, Scotland.*

Padovan, B., Sackmann, S., Eymann, T., & Pippow, I. (2002). A Prototype for an Agent-Based Secure Electronic Marketplace Including Reputation-Tracking Mechanisms. *International Journal of Electronic Commerce*, *6*(4), 93–113.

Paloheimo, K. -S., Miettinen, I., & Brax, S. (2004). *Customer-oriented industrial services*. Espoo, Finland: Report Series –Helsinki University of Technology BIT Research Centre.

Pargamin, B. (2002). Vehicle sales configuration: The cluster tree approach. *ECAI 2002 Workshop on Configuration* (pp. 35-40).

Pazzani, M., & Billsus, D. (1997). Learning and revising user profiles: The identification of interesting web sites. *Machine Learning*, *27*, 313–331. doi:10.1023/A:1007369909943

Peck, J., & Childers, T. L. (2003). Individual differences in haptic information processing: The "need for touch" scale. *The Journal of Consumer Research*, *30*(December), 430–442. doi:10.1086/378619

Pedersen, J. L., & Edwards, K. (2004). Product configuration systems and productivity. In *Proceedings of International Conference on Economic, Technical and Organisational Aspects of Product Configuration Systems (PETO) 2004*.

Peppers, D., & Rogers, M. (1993). *The One to One Future: Building Relationships One Customer at a Time*. New York: Currency Doubleday.

Peppers, D., & Rogers, M. (1997). *Enterprise One to One: Tools for Competing in the Interactive Age*. New York: Currency Doubleday.

Pignotti, E., & Edwards, P. (2004). *Context-Aware Personalised Service Delivery*. ECAI.

Piller, F. (2003). Turning products into Sustainable Service Businesses. In A.Tukker, M. Charter, (Eds.), *Proceedings of the Conference "Sustainable Product-Service Systems: State of the Art,"* (p. 51-60), Amsterdam.

Piller, F. (2004). Mass Customization: Reflections on the State of the Concept. *International Journal of Flexible Manufacturing Systems, 16*, 313–334. doi:10.1007/s10696-005-5170-x

Piller, F. T., & Stotko, C. (2002). Four approaches to deliver customized products and services with mass production efficiency. In T. S. Durrani, (Ed.), *Proceedings of the IEEE International Engineering Management Conference. Managing Technology for the New Economy*, Cambridge University, Cambridge, UK, (p. 773-778).

Piller, F. T., Moeslein, K., & Stotko, C. M. (2004). Does mass customization pay? An economic approach to evaluate customer integration. *Production Planning & Control, 15*(4), 435-444.

Piller, F., & Müller, M. (2004). A new marketing approach to mass customisation. *International Journal of Computer Integrated Manufacturing, 17*(7), 583–593. doi:10.1080/0951192042000273140

Piller, F., Koch, M., Möslein, K., & Schubert, P. (2003). *Managing high variety: How to overcome the mass confusion phenomenon of customer co-design*. Paper presented at the EURAM 2003 Conference, Milan, Italy.

Piller, F., Meier, R., & Reichwald, R. (2002). eService Customization. In M. Bruhn, & B. Stauss, (Hrsg.), *Handbuch Dienstleistungsmanagement*, (pp. 225-242). Wiesbaden, Germany: Gabler.

Piller, F., Schubert, P., Koch, M., & Möslein, K. (2005). Overcoming mass confusion: Collaborative customer co-design in online communities. *Journal of Computer-Mediated Communication, 10*(4). http://jcmc.indiana.edu/vol10/issue14/piller.html.

Pine II, B. J. (1993). *Mass customization: The new frontier in business competition*. Boston: Harvard Business School Press.

Pine, B. J. II (1993). Mass customizing products and services. *Strategy & Leadership, 21*(4), 6-13, 55.

Pine, B. J. II, Peppers, D., & Rogers, M. (1995). Do you want to keep your customers forever? *Harvard Business Review, 73*(2), 103-114.

Pine, B. J. II, Victor, B., & Boynton, A. C. (1993). Making mass customization work. *Harvard Business Review, 71*(5), 108-119.

Pithers, R., T. (2002). Cognitive Learning Style: a review of the field dependent- field independent approach. *Journal of Vocational Education and Training, 54*(1), 117–118. doi:10.1080/13636820200200191

Pitt, L. F., Watson, R. T., & Kavan, C. B. (1995). Service quality: A measure of information systems effectiveness. *MIS Quarterly*, 173-185.

Pitt, L. F., Watson, R. T., & Kavan, C. B. (1997). Measuring information systems service quality: Concerns for a complete canvas. *MIS Quarterly*, 209-221.

PLib (2000). ISO 13584 Parts Library, ISO TC184/SC4, Part 102, View Exchange Protocol: View Exchange Protocol by ISO10303 conforming specification. *International Organization for Standardization*.

Poole, S. (2000). *Trigger happy: The inner life of video games*. London: Fourth Estate.

Pope, A. T., Bogart, E. H., & Bartolome, D. S. (1995). Biocybernetic system evaluates indices of operator engagement in automated task. *Biological Psychology, 40*, 187–195. doi:10.1016/0301-0511(95)05116-3

Prahalad, C. K., & Ramaswamy, V. (2004). *The future of competition: Co-creating unique value with customers*. Boston: Harvard Business School Press.

Premiere (2008). Retrieved from www.premiere.de ruwido (2008). vocomedia. Retrieved online April 3, 2008 from http://www.ruwido.com/products/voco-media/1/

Przybilski, M., Nurmi, P., & Floréen, P. (2005). A Framework for Context Reasoning Systems. In *Proc. IASTED International Conference on Software Engineering*.

Pugh, S. (1997). *Total design: Integrated methods for successful product engineering*. Wokingham: Addison-Wesley.

Radder, L., & Louw, L. (1999). Research and concepts: Mass customization and mass production. *The TQM Magazine, 11*(1), 35-40.

Rai, A., Lang, S. S., & Welker, R. B. (2002). Assessing the validity of IS success models: An emperical test and theoretical analysis. *Information Systems Research, 13*(1), 50-69.

Randall, T., Terwiesch, C., & Ulrich, K. (2007). User design of customized products. *Marketing Science, 26*(2), 268–280. doi:10.1287/mksc.1050.0116

Rangone, A. (1999). A Resource-Based Approach to Strategy Analysis in Small-Medium Sized Enterprises. *Small Business Economics, 12*(3), 233–248. doi:10.1023/A:1008046917465

Rational (2006). Retrieved March 22, 2006, from http://www.rational.com/uml

Ravaja, N. (2004). Effects of a small talking facial image on autonomic activity: The moderating influence of dispositional BIS and BAS sensitivities and emotions. *Biological Psychology, 65*, 163–183. doi:10.1016/S0301-0511(03)00078-4

Ravaja, N. (2004). Contributions of psychophysiology to media research: Review and recommendations. *Media Psychology, 6*, 193–235. doi:10.1207/s1532785xmep0602_4

Ravaja, N., & Kallinen, K. (2004). Emotional effects of startling background music during reading news reports: The moderating influence of dispositional BIS and BAS sensitivities. *Scandinavian Journal of Psychology, 45*, 231–238. doi:10.1111/j.1467-9450.2004.00399.x

Ravaja, N., Kallinen, K., Saari, T., & Keltikangas-Järvinen, L. (2004). Suboptimal exposure to facial expressions when viewing video messages from a small screen: Effects on emotion, attention, and memory. *Journal of Experimental Psychology. Applied, 10*, 120–131. doi:10.1037/1076-898X.10.2.120

Ravaja, N., Laarni, J., Saari, T., Kallinen, K., & Salminen, M. (2005). Phasic Psychophysiological Responses to Video Game Events: New Criterion Variables for Game Design. In C. Stephanidis (Ed.*) Proceedings of HCI International 2005*. Mahwah, NJ: Lawrence Erlbaum Associates

Ravichandran, T., & Rai, A. (1999). Total quality management in information systems development: Key constructs and relationships. *Journal of Management Information Systems, 16*(3), 124-155.

Reed, W., M., Ayersman, D., J. & Liu, M. (1996). The effects of students' computer-based prior experiences and instructional exposures on the application of hypermedia-related mental models. *Journal of Educational Computing Research, 14*(2), 175–187.

Reichheld, F. F., & Sasser, W. E. (1990). Zero Defections: Quality Comes to Services. *Harvard Business Review*, (September/October): 105–111.

Reichwald, R., Piller, F., & Mueller, M. (2004). A multichannel interaction platform for mass customization – Concept and empirical investigation. *Workshop on Information Systems for Mass Customization (ISMC 2004), Fourth International ICSC Symposium on Engineering of Intelligent Systems (EIS 2004)*.

Reinartz, W. J., & Kumar, V. (2000). On the Profitability of Long-Life Customers in a Noncontractual Setting: An Empirical Investigation and Implications for Marketing. *Journal of Marketing, 64*(4), 17–35. doi:10.1509/jmkg.64.4.17.18077

Resnick, P., & Varian, H. (1997). Recommender systems. *Communications of the ACM, 40*(3), 5658. doi:10.1145/245108.245121

Rheingold, J. (2002). *Smart Mobs: The Next Social Revolution*. New York: Perseus Publishing.

Riding, R. (2001). *Cognitive Style Analysis – Research Administration*. Birmingham, UK: Learning and Training Technology.

Riding, R. J., & Rayner, S. (1998). *Cognitive styles and learning strategies. Understanding style differences in learning and behavior*. London: David Fulton Publishers.

Riemer, K., & Totz, Ch. (2001). The many faces of personalization - an integrative economic overview of mass customization and personalization. In Tseng, M. & Piller, F. (Ed.), *Proceedings of the 2001 World conference on mass customization and personalization*, Hong Kong, October 1-2.

Riis, J. (2003). *Fremgangsmåde for Opbygning, implementering og vedligeholdelse af produktmodeller.* Ph.D. Department of Manufacturing Engineering and Management, Technical University of Denmark.

Robertson, D., & Ulrich, K. (1998). Planning product platforms. *Sloan Management Review, 39*(4).

Ross, A. (1996). Selling uniqueness. *IEE Manufacturing Engineer, 75*(6), 260-263.

Rumbaugh, J. (1998). *UML - The unified modeling language.* Addison-Wesley.

ruwido (2007). Vexo. Retrieved online April 3, 2008 from http://vexo.ruwido.com

Ryan, N., Pascoe, J., & Morse, D. (1997). Enhanced reality fieldwork: the context-aware archaeological assistant. In V. Gaffney, V. Leusen & S. Exxon (Eds.), *Computer Applications in Archaeology.*

Saari, T. (2001). *Mind-Based Media and Communications Technologies. How the Form of Information Influences Felt Meaning.* Acta Universitatis Tamperensis 834. Tampere, Finland: Tampere University Press.

Saari, T. (2003). Designing for Psychological Effects. Towards Mind-Based Media and Communications Technologies. In Harris, D., Duffy, V., Smith, M. & Stephanidis, C. (eds.) *Human-Centred Computing: Cognitive, Social and Ergonomic Aspects. Volume 3 of the Proceedings of HCI International 2003*, (pp. 557-561). Heraklion, Greece: Crete University Press.

Saari, T. (2003). Mind-Based Media and Communications Technologies. A Framework for producing personalized psychological effects. In *Proceedings of the Human Factors and Ergonomics Society 47th Annual Meeting.*

Saari, T., & Turpeinen, M. (2004). Towards Psychological Customization of Information for Individuals and Social Groups. In J. Karat, J. Blom & M.-C. Karat (Ed.), *Person-alization of User Experiences for eCommerce.* New York: Kluwer.

Saari, T., Ravaja, N., Turpeinen, M., & Kallinen, K. (2005). Emotional Regulation System for Emotionally Adapted Games. In *Proceedings of FuturePlay 2005 conference*, 13.-15.10. Michigan State University, Lansing, MI.

Saari, T., Turpeinen, M., Laarni, J., Ravaja, N., & Kallinen, K. (2004). Psychologically targeted persuasive advertising and product information presentation in eCommerce. In *Proceedings of ICEC 2004, 3rd international conference for entertainment computing.* 1.-3.9. 2004, Eindhoven, The Netherlands (LNCS Vol. 3166, 476-486). Berlin: Springer.

Sabin, D., & Weigel, R. (1998). Product configuration frameworks – A survey. *IEEE Intelligent Systems & Their Applications, 13*(4), 42-49.

Salkham, A., Cunningham, R., Senart, A., & Cahill, V. (2006). A Taxonomy of Collaborative Context-Aware Systems. In *Proceedings of the Workshop on Ubiquitous Mobile Information and Collaboration Systems (UMICS'06)*, CAiSE'06, (pp. 899-911), Luxembourg.

Salvador, F., & Forza, C. (2004). Configuring products to address the customization-responsiveness squeeze: A survey of management issues and opportunities. *International Journal of Production Economics, 91*(3), 273-291.

Sanders, G. L. (1984). MIS/DSS success measure. *Systems, Objectives, Solutions,* (4), 29-34.

Sanders, G. L., & Courtney, J. F. (1985). A field study of organizational factors affecting DSS success. *MIS Quarterly, 9*(9), 77-89.

Sanderson, S. W. (1991). Cost models for evaluating virtual design strategies in multicycle product families. *Journal of Engineering and Technology Management, 8*(3-4), 339–358. doi:10.1016/0923-4748(91)90017-L

Santader (2008). Cantabria, Spain, July 1-5, 2008, (pp. 886-890). Washington, DC: IEEE Computer Society Press.

Schafer, J., Konstan, J., & Riedl, J. (1999). Recommender Systems in E-commerce. *ACM Conference on Electronic Commerce.*

Scherer, K. R. (1993). Neuroscience projections to current debates in emotion psychology. *Cognition and Emotion, 7,* 1–41. doi:10.1080/02699939308409174

Schilit, B., & Theimer, M. (1994). Disseminating active map information to mobile hosts. *IEEE Network*, 8.

Schooler, S. B. (2005). Toward a multi-agent information management infrastucture for product family planning and mass customization. *International Journal of Mass Customization, 1*(1).

Schoormans, J. P. L., Morel, K. P. N., & Zheng, Y. (2006). Consumer chatting during online shopping: An exploratory study. In G. J. Avlonitis, N. Papavassiliou & P. Papastathopoulou (Eds.), *Proceedings of the 35th EMAC conference.* Athens: EMAC.

Schreier, M. (2006). The value increment of mass-customized products: An empirical assessment and conceptual analysis of its explanation. *Journal of Consumer Behaviour, 5*(July-August), 317–327. doi:10.1002/cb.183

Schultz, S. E., Kleine, R. E., & Kernan, J. B. (1989). 'These are a few of my favorite things.' Toward an explication of attachment as a consumer behavior construct. In T. Scrull (Ed.), *Advances in Consumer Research* (Vol. 16, pp. 359-366). Provo: UT: Association for Consumer Research.

Seddon, P. B., & Kiew, M.-Y (1994). A partial test and development of DeLone and McLean model of IS Success. In J. I. DeGross, S. L. Huff, & M. C. Munro (Eds.), *Proceedings of the International Conference on Information Systems* (pp. 99-110). Atlanta, GA: Association of Information Systems.

Seddon, P.B. (1997). A Re-specification and extension of the DeLone and McLean model of IS success. *Information Systems Research, 8*(3), 240-253.

Seddon, P.B., Staples, D.S., Patnayakuni, R., & Bowtell, M. (1999) Dimensions of IS success. *Communications of the AIS, 20*(2).

Sedgwick, J., Henson, B., & Barnes, C. (2003). Designing pleasurable products and interfaces, In *Proceedings of the 2003 International conference on designing pleasurable products and interfaces*, Pittsburgh, 2003.

Shannon, C. E., & Weaver, W. (1949). *The mathematical theory of communication.* Urbana, IL: University of Illinois Press.

Shehzad, A., Hung, Q., Ngo, K., & Sungyoung L. (2004). Formal Modeling in Context Aware Systems, *KI-Workshop Modeling and Retrieval of Context (MRC2004)*, Germany, (pp.13-24), September 23-27.

Shen, W., Norrie, D. H., & Barthès, J. A. (2001). *Multi-agent Systems for Concurrent Intelligent Design and Manufacturing.* New York: Taylor & Francis.

Shim, J. P., & Shin, Y. B. (2002). Retailer Web site influence on customer shopping: An exploratory study on key factors of customer satisfaction. *Journal of the Association for Information Systems, 3*, 53-76.

Shin, B. (2003). An exploratory investigation of system success factors in data warehousing. *Journal of the Association for Information Systems, 4*, 141-170.

Shocker, A. D., Srivastava, R. K., & Ruekert, R. W. (1994). Challenges and Opportunities Facing Brand Management: An Introduction to the Special Issue. *JMR, Journal of Marketing Research, 31*(2), 149–158. doi:10.2307/3152190

Shooter, S. B., Simpson, T. W., Kumara, S. R. T., Stone, R. B., & Terpenny, J. P. (2005). Toward an Information Management Infrastructure for Product Family Planning and Platform Customization. *International Journal of Mass Customization, 1*(1), 134–155. doi:10.1504/IJMASSC.2005.007354

Siddique, Z. (2000). Common platform development: design for product variety, Ph.D. Dissertation, Georgia Institute of Technology, Atlanta, GA.

Siems, F., & Walcher, D. (2008). Modularity as base for efficient life event cycle management. In F. Piller (Ed.), *Proceedings of The World Conference on Mass Customization & Personalization (MCPC 2007).* Boston: Massachusetts Institute of Technology (MIT).

Silveria, G. D., Borenstein, D., & Fogliatto, F. S. (2001). Mass Customization: Literature review and research directions. *International Journal of Production Economics, 72*(1), 1–13. doi:10.1016/S0925-5273(00)00079-7

Simon, H. A. (1955). A behavioral model of rational choice. *Quarterly Journal of Economics*, (69), 99-118.

Simpson, T. W. (2005). Product platform design and customization: Status and promise. *Special Issue on Platform*

Product Development for Mass Customization, AIEDAM, 18(1).

Simpson, T. W., Maier, J. R. A., & Mistree, F. (2001). Product platform design: method and application. *Research in Engineering Design, 13*(1), 2–22. doi:10.1007/s001630100002

Simpson, T. W., Siddique, Z., & Jiao, J. (2005). *Product Platform and Product Family Design: Methods and Applications.* New York: Springer.

Slywotzky, A. J. (2000). The age of the choiceboard. *Harvard Business Review, 78*(1), 40-41.

SOA (2006). *The Service-Oriented Architecture.* Retrieved March 23, 2006, from http://msdn.microsoft.com/architecture/soa/default.aspx

Spender, J.C., (1996). Making Knowledge the Basis of a Dynamic Theory of the Firm. *Strategic Management Journal,* (17), Special Issues, 45-62.

Spielberger, C. D. (1983). *Manual for the State-Trait Anxiety Inventory (STAI).* Palo Alto, CA: Consulting Psychologists Press.

Spring, M., & Dalrymple, J. F. (2000) Product customisation and manufacturing strategy. *International Journal of Operations & Production Management, 20*(4), 441-467.

Squire, B., Cousins, P. D., & Brown, S. (2006). Collaborating for customization: an extended resource-based view of the firm. *Int. J. Productivity and Quality Management, 1*(1/2), 8–25.

Srinivasan, A. (1985). Alternative measures of system effectiveness: Associations and implications. *MIS Quarterly, 9*(3), 243- 253.

Stanton, N. (1998). *Human factors in consumer products.* London: Routledge.

Staub, G. (1998). ISO TC184/SC4QC N068, *Interpretation of PLib Services-Guideline for the common interpretation of the "services" provided by PLib using the STEP IR.*

Stauffer, L., & Morris, L. (1992). *A new program to enhance the development of product requirements.* Presented at NSF Design and Manufacturing Systems Conference, Atlanta, Georgia.

Stonebraker, M., & Çetintemel, U. (2008). *"One Size Fits All": An Idea Whose Time Has Come and Gone.*

Svensson, C., & Barfod, A. (2002). Limits and opportunities in mass customization for "build to order" SMEs. *Computers in Industry, 49,* 77-89.

Sviokla, J.J. (1990). An examination of the impact of expert systems on the firm: The case of XCON. *MIS Quarterly, 14*(2), 127-140.

Swanson, E. B. (1985). A note of informatics. *Journal of Management Information Systems, 2*(3), 86-91.

Symenonidis, A. L., Kehagias, D. D., & Mitkas, P. A. (2003). Intelligent Policy Recommendations on Enterprise Resource Planning by the Use of Agent Technology and Data Mining Techniques. *Expert Systems with Applications, 25*(4), 589–602. doi:10.1016/S0957-4174(03)00099-X

Syre, S. (2004). A revolution grows up. *The Boston Globe,* November 30.

Taguchi, G. (1986). *Introduction to quality engineering: designing quality into products and processes.* Tokyo: Asian Productivity Organization.

Tan, G. W., Hayes, C. C., & Shaw, M. (1996). An Intelligent-Agent Framework for Concurrent Product Design and Planning. *IEEE Transactions on Engineering Management, 43*(3), 297–306. doi:10.1109/17.511840

Te'eni, D., & Feldman, R. (2001). Performance and satisfaction in adaptive Websites: An experiment on searches within task adapted Websites. *Journal of the Association for Information Systems, 2*(3), 1-30.

Tellegen, A. (1985). Structure of mood and personality and their relevance to assessing anxiety, with an emphasis on self-report. In A. H. Tuma & J. D. Maser (Ed.), *Anxiety and the Anxiety Disorders* (pp. 681-706). Hillsdale, NJ: Lawrence Erlbaum.

Tepper Tian, K., Bearden, W. O., & Hunter, G. L. (2001). Consumers' need for uniqueness: Scale development and validation. *The Journal of Consumer Research, 28*(June), 50–66. doi:10.1086/321947

Terveen, L., Hill, W., Amento, B., McDonald, D., & Creter, J. (1997). Phoaks: A system for sharing recommendations. *Communications of the ACM, 40*(3), 5962. doi:10.1145/245108.245122

Thomas, H., Pettigrew, A. M., & Whittington, R. (2002). *Handbook of Strategy and Management*. London: Sage Publications.

Thomke, S., & Von Hippel, E. (2002). Customers as innovators. A new way to create value. *Harvard Business Review, 80*(4), 74–81.

Tiihonen, J., & Soininen, T. (1997). *Product configurators – Information system support for configurable products* (Tech. Rep. TKO-B137). Helsinki University of Technology, Laboratory of Information Processing Science. Also published in Richardson, T. (Ed.). (1997), *Using information technology during the sales visit*. Cambridge, UK: Hewson Group.

Tiihonen, J., Soininen, T., Männistö, T. & Sulonen, R. (1996). State-of-the-practice in product configuration—A survey of 10 cases in the Finnish industry. In T. Tomiyama, M. Mäntylä, & S. Finger (Eds.), *Knowledge Intensive CAD. Vol. 1* (pp. 95-114). Chapman & Hall.

Tiihonen, J., Soininen, T., Männistö, T. & Sulonen, R. (1998). Configurable products - Lessons learned from the Finnish industry. In *Proceedings of 2nd International Conference on Engineering Design and Automation (ED&A '98)*. Integrated Technology Systems, Inc.

Tiwana, A. (2001). *The essential guide to knowledge management: e-business and CRM applications*. Upper Saddle River, NJ: Prentice Hall.

Toffler, A. (1980). *The third wave*. New York: Bantam Books.

Topolsky, J. (2007). *Gesture-based remote control developed*. Retrieved online May 5, 2008 from http://www.engadget.com/2007/07/15/gesture-based-television-control-developed/

Tran, T., & Cohen, R. (2002). A Reputation-Oriented Reinforcement Learning Strategy for Agents in Electronic Marketplaces. *Computational Intelligence, 18*(4), 550–565. doi:10.1111/1467-8640.t01-1-00203

Treleven, M., & Wacker, J. G. (1987). The sources, measurements, and managerial implications of process commonality. *Journal of Operations Management, 7*, 11–25. doi:10.1016/0272-6963(87)90003-9

Trireme International (2006). Retrieved March 23, 2006, from http://www.trireme.u-net.com/catalysis

Tseng, M. M., & Du, X. H. (1998). Design by customers for mass customization products. *Annals of the CIRP, 47*(1), 103–106. doi:10.1016/S0007-8506(07)62795-4

Tseng, M. M., & Jiao, J. (1996). Design for mass customization. *Annals of the CIRP, 45*(1), 153–156. doi:10.1016/S0007-8506(07)63036-4

Tseng, M. M., & Jiao, J. (1998). Computer-aided requirement management for product definition: A methodology and implementation. *Concurrent Engineering: Research and Application, 6*(2), 145–160. doi:10.1177/1063293X9800600205

Tseng, M. M., & Jiao, J. (2001). Mass Customization. In *Handbook of Industrial Engineering, Technology and Operation Management* (3rd Ed.)

Tseng, M., & Jiao, J. (2001). Mass Customization. In G. Salvendy (Ed.), *Handbook of Industrial Engineering* (3rd ed., pp. 684-709). New York: Wiley.

Tseng, M., & Piller, F. T. (2003). *The Customer Centric Enterprise: Advances in Mass Customization and Personalization*. New York: Springer.

Tsianos, N., Germanakos, P., Lekkas, Z., Mourlas, C., & Samaras, G. (2008b). Incorporating Human Factors in the Development of Context-Aware Personalized Applications: The Next Generation of Intelligent User Interfaces. In D. Stojanovic (Ed.), *Context-Aware Mobile and Ubiquitous Computing for Enhanced Usability: Adaptive Technologies and Applications*. Hershey, PA: IGI Global.

Tsianos, N., Lekkas, Z., Germanakos, P., Mourlas, C., & Samaras, G. (2008a). User-centered Profiling on the basis of Cognitive and Emotional Characteristics: An Empirical Study. In *Proceedings of the 5th International Conference on Adaptive Hypermedia and Adaptive Web-based Systems (AH 2008)*, Hannover, Germany, July 28 - August 1, (LNCS Vol. 5149, pp. 214-223). Berlin: Springer-Verlag.

Turksen, I. B., & Willson, I. A. (1992). Customer preferences models: fuzzy theory approach. In *Proceedings of the SPIE - International Society for Optical Engineering*, (pp. 203-211), Boston, MA.

Turpeinen, M., & Saari, T. (2004) System Architecture for Psychological Customization of Information. *37th Hawaii International International Conference on Systems Science (HICSS-37 2004), Proceedings*, 5-8 January 2004, Waikoloa, Big Island, HI. Washington. DC: IEEE Computer Society.

Umar (1999). A framework for analyzing virtual enterprise infrastructure. In *Proceedings of the 9ᵗʰ International Workshop on Research Issues in Data Engineering - IT for Virtual Enterprises, RIDE-VE'99* (pp. 4-11). IEEE Computer Society.

Urban, G. L., & Hauser, J. R. (1993). *Design and marketing of new products*. Englewood Cliffs, NJ: Prentice-Hall.

van Barneveld, J., & van Stetten, M. (2004). Desiging Usable Interfaces for TV Recommender Systems. In L. Ardissono, (Ed.) *Personalized Digital Television* (pp. 259 – 285). London: Springer.

Van der Heijden. (2004). Hedonic information systems. *MIS Quarterly, 28*(4), 695-704.

Van Dyke, T. P., Kappelman, L. A., & Prybutok, V. R. (1997). Measuring information systems service quality: Concerns on the use of the SERVQUAL questionnaire. *MIS Quarterly*, 195-207.

Van Dyke, T. P., Prybutok, V. R., & Kappelman, L. A. (1999). Cautions on the use of the SERVQUAL measure to assess the quality of information systems services. *Decision Sciences, 30*(3), 877-891.

Vanwelkenheysen, J. (1998). The tender support system. *Knowledge-Based Systems, 11,* 363-372.

Varki, S., Cooil, B., & Rust, R. T. (2000). Modeling Fuzzy Data in Qualitative Marketing Research. *JMR, Journal of Marketing Research, 37*(November), 480–489. doi:10.1509/jmkr.37.4.480.18785

Vecchi, T., Phillips, L. H., & Cornoldi, C. (2001). Individual differences in visuo-spatial working memory. In M. Denis, R. H. Logie, C. Cornoldi, M. de Vega, & J. Engelkamp (Ed.), *Imagery, language, and visuo-spatial thinking*. Hove, UK: Psychology Press.

Venkatesh, A. (1996). Computers and other interactive technologies for the home. *Communications of the ACM, 39*(12), 47–54. doi:10.1145/240483.240491

Venkatesh, A., Kruse, E., & Chuan-Fong Shih, E. (2003). The networked home: an analysis of current developments and future trends. *Cognition Technology and Work Journal, 5*(1), 23–32.

Venkatraman, N. (1989). Strategic orientation of business enterprises: The construct, dimensionality, and measurement. *Management Science, 35*(8), 942-962.

Vessey, I. (1994). The effect of information presentation on decision making: A cost-benefit analysis. *Information and Management,* (27), 103-119.

Vink, N. Y. (2003). *Customization Choices*. Delft: Delft University of Technology.

Vlosky, R. P. (1998). Partnerships versus typical relationships between wood products distributors and their manufacturer suppliers. *Forest Products Journal, 48*(3), 27-35.

von Hippel, E. (2005). *Democratizing innovation*. Cambridge: The MIT Press.

Vorderer, P. (2000). Interactive Entertainment and Beyond. In D. Zillmann, & P. Vorderer, (Ed.), *Media Entertainment. The Psychology of its Appeal* (pp. 21-36). Mahwah, NJ: Erlbaum.

Vorderer, P., Hartmann, T., & Klimmt, C. (2003). Explaining the enjoyment of playing video games: The role of competition. In D. Marinelli (Ed.), *Proceedings of the 2nd International Conference on Entertainment Computing (ICEC 2003)*, Pittsburgh (pp. 1-8). New York: ACM.

W3C (2006). *World Wide Web Consortium*. Retrieved March 23, 2006, from http://www.w3c.org

Wacker, J. G., & Treleven, M. (1986). Component part standardization: an analysis of commonality sources and indices. *Journal of Operations Management, 6,* 219–244. doi:10.1016/0272-6963(86)90026-4

Wang, J., & Lin, J. (2002). Are personalization systems really personal? – Effects of conformity in reducing information overload. In *Proceedings of the 36th Hawaii International Conference on Systems Sciences (HICSS'03)*. Washington, DC: IEEE.

Want, R., Hopper, A., Falcao, V., & Gibbons, J. (1992). The active badge location system. *ACM Transactions on Information Systems, 10*(1), 91–102. doi:10.1145/128756.128759

Watson, D., & Tellegen, A. (1985). Toward a consensual structure of mood. *Psychological Bulletin, 98*, 219–235. doi:10.1037/0033-2909.98.2.219

Watson, D., Wiese, D., Vaidya, J., & Tellegen, A. (1999). The two general activation systems of affect: Structural findings, evolutionary considerations, and psychobiological evidence. *Journal of Personality and Social Psychology, 76*, 820–838. doi:10.1037/0022-3514.76.5.820

Watson, R. T., Pitt, L. F., & Kavan, C. B. (1998). Measuring information systems service quality: Lessons from two longitudinal case studies. *MIS Quarterly, 22*(1), 61-79.

Wedel, M., & Steenkamp, H.-B. E. M. (1991). A Clusterwise Regression Method for Simultaneous Fuzzy Market Structuring and Benefit Segmentation. *JMR, Journal of Marketing Research, 28*(November), 385–396. doi:10.2307/3172779

Weibelzahl, S. (2003). Evaluation of Adaptive Systems, PhD Thesis, University of Trier, Germany.

Weightman, D., & McDonagh, D. (2003). People are doing it for themselves. In B. Hanington & J. Forlizzi (Eds.), *International Conference on Designing Pleasurable Products and Interfaces (DPPI'03)* (pp. 34-39). Pittsburgh, PA.

Weiser, M. (1991). Computers for the 21st Century. In *Scientific American*, (pp. 94-100).

Welke, R. J., & Konsynski, B. R. (1980). An examination of the interaction between technology, methodology and information systems: A tripartite view. In *Proceedings of the First International Conference of Information Systems* (pp. 32-48).

Wharton, C., Rieman, J., Lewis, C., & Polson, P. (1994). The cognitive walkthrough method: a practitioner's guide. In Nielsen, J. & Mack, R. L. *Usability inspection Methods*, (pp. 105-140). New York: John Wiley & Sons.

Wiener, N. (1948). *Cybernetics: Control and communication in the animal and the machine*. 2nd edition. Cambridge, MA, MIT Press.

Wind, J., & Rangaswamy, A. (2001). Customerization: The next revolution in mass customization. *Journal of Interactive Marketing, 15*(1), 13-32.

Winter, R. (2001). Mass Customization and Beyond - Evolution of Customer Centricity in Financial Services. In C.

Rautenstrauch, R. Seelmann-Eggebert & K. Turowski (Eds.), *Moving into Mass Customization: Information Systems and Management Principals*. Berlin: Springer.

Witkin, H., Moore, C., Gooddenough, D., & Cox, P. (1977). Field- dependent and field- independent cognitive styles and their educational implications. *Review of Educational Research, 47*, 1–64.

Wooldridge, M. (2002). *An Introduction to Mulitagent Systems*. Chichester, UK: John Wiley & Sons Inc.

Wright, J. R., Weixelbaum, E. S., Vesonder, G. T., Brown, K. E., Palmer, S. R., Berman, J. I., & Moore, H. H. (1993). A knowledge-based configurator that supports sales, engineering, and manufacturing at AT&T network systems. *AI Magazine, 14*(3), 69-80.

WS-I (2006). Web services interoperability organization. *WS-I*. Retrieved March 23, 2006, from http://www.ws-i.org

XMI, XML Meta-data Interchange (2006). Retrieved March 23, 2006, from http://www.omg.org/technology/xml/index.htm

Yan, W., Chen, C.-H., & Khoo, L. P. (2002). An integrated approach to the elicitation of customer requirements for engineering design using picture sorts and fuzzy evaluation. *AIEDAM, 16*(2), 59–71. doi:10.1017/S0890060402020061

Yoo, S., & Jin, J. (2004). Evaluation of the home pages of the top 100 university web sites. *Academy of Information Management, 8*(2), 57-69.

Yoosoo, O., Schmidt, A., & Woontack, W. (2007, April). *Designing, Developing, and Evaluating Context-Aware Systems Multimedia and Ubiquitous Engineering, International Conference*, (pp. 1158 – 1163).

Yu, B., & Singh, M. P. (2000). A Social Mechanism for Reputation Management in Electronic Communities. In *The 4th International Workshop on Cooperative Information*, (pp. 154-165). Berlin: Springer-Verlag.

Yu, B., & Skovgaard, H. J. (1998). A configuration tool to increase product competitiveness. *IEEE Intelligent Systems, 13*(4), 34-41.

Yuliang, L., & Dean, G. (1999). Cognitive Styles and Distance Education. *Online Journal of Distance Learning Administration, 2*(3).

Zacharia, G., Evgeniou, T., Moukas, A., Boufounos, P., & Maes, P. (2001). Economics of Dynamic Pricing in a Reputation Brokered Agent Mediated Marketplace. *Electronic Commerce Research, 1*(2), 85–100. doi:10.1023/A:1011523612549

Zarikas, V., Papatzanis, G., & Stephanidis, C. (2001). *An architecture for a Self-Adapting Information System for Tourists Workshop on multiple user interface over the internet: Engineering and application trends in conjunction with HCI IMH.*

Zaslow, J. (2002). If TiVo Thinks You Are Gay, Here's How To Set It Straight -- Amazon.com Knows You, Too, Based on What You Buy; Why All the Cartoons? *The Wall Street Journal*, November 26, A, p. 1

Zeithaml, V. A. (1988). Consumer perceptions of price, quality, and value: a means-end model and synthesis of evidence. *Journal of Marketing, 52*, 2–22. doi:10.2307/1251446

Zeithaml, V. A., Bitner, M. J., & Gremler, D. D. (2006). *Services Marketing. Integrating the Customer Focus Across the Firm*, (4th Ed.). Boston: McGraw Hill.

Zipkin, P. (2001). The limits of mass customization. *MIT Sloan Management Review, 42*(3), 81-87.

Zmud, R., Blocher, E., & Moffie, R. P. (1983). The impact of color graphic report formats on decision performance and learning. In *Proceedings of the Fourth International Conference on Information Systems* (pp. 179-193).

About the Contributors

Constantinos Mourlas is Assistant Professor in the National and Kapodistrian University of Athens (Greece), Department of Communication and Media Studies since 2002. He obtained his PhD from the Department of Informatics, University of Athens in 1995 and graduated from the University of Crete in 1988 with a Diploma in Computer Science. In 1998 was an ERCIM fellow for post-doctoral studies through research in STFC, UK. He was employed as Lecturer at the Univeristy of Cyprus, Department of Computer Science from 1999 till 2002. His previous research work focused on distributed multimedia systems with adaptive behaviour, Quality of Service issues, streaming media and the Internet. His current main research interest is in the design and the development of intelligent environments that provide adaptive and personalized context to the users according to their preferences, cognitive characteristics and emotional state. He has several publications including edited books, chapters, articles in journals and conference contributions. Dr. C. Mourlas has taught various undergraduate as well as postgraduate courses in the Dept. of Computer Science of the University of Cyprus and the Dept. of Communication and Media Studies of the University of Athens. Furthermore, he has coordinated and actively participated in numerous national and EU funded projects.

Panagiotis Germanakos, PhD, is a Research Scientist, in the Laboratory of New Technologies, Faculty of Communication & Media Studies, National & Kapodistrian University of Athens and of the Department of Computer Science, University of Cyprus. He obtained his PhD from the University of Athens in 2008 and his MSc in International Marketing Management from the Leeds University Business School in 1999. His B.Sc. was in Computer Science and also holds a HND Diploma of Technician Engineer in the field of Computer Studies. His research interest is in Web Adaptation and Personalization Environments and Systems based on user profiling/filters encompassing amongst others visual, mental and affective processes, implemented on desktop and mobile / wireless platforms. He has several publications, including co-edited books, chapters, articles in journals, and conference contributions. Furthermore, he actively participates in numerous national and EU funded projects that mainly focus on the analysis, design and development of open interoperable integrated wireless/mobile and personalized technological infrastructures and systems in the ICT research areas of e-Government, e-Health and e-Learning and has an extensive experience in the provision of consultancy of large-scaled IT solutions and implementations in the business sector.

* * *

Mario Belk is currently a Post-Graduate student and a Research Assistant of the Department of Computer Science at the University of Cyprus. He obtained his B.Sc. in Computer Science from the same department. His research interests are in Web Adaptation and Personalization Environments and Systems, Database Systems, Ontologies, Internet Technologies and the Semantic Web. He actively participates in numerous National and EU funded research projects. His bachelor thesis contributed for the publication of several research articles in journals, book chapters and major International conferences in which he was co-author in seven of them. Furthermore, he worked as a teaching assistant of his Professor and the University's Vice-Rector and taught to 4th year senior students at the Department of Computer Science. In the past years he participated in several business projects as a senior software developer collaborating with Microsoft, IBM, Marfin Laiki Bank Ltd. and many more. His future plans after graduation are to continue his research obtaining a Ph.D. enabling him to become an Academic Research Scientist.

Regina Bernhaupt is currently on a sabbatical leave at the university of Toulouse III, IRIT-LIIHS to accomplish her so called habilitation. Since 2002 she is working as an assistant professor at the University of Salzburg on usability and user experience evaluation in non-traditional environments. Some of her recent publications include the usage of usability evaluation and user experience evaluation methods for new forms of personalized and individualized interactive TV. Regina Bernhaupt was involved in several (industrial) projects focusing especially on usability evaluation and user experience evaluation in such un-traditional environments like the home, public places, games or even human-robot interaction in industrial settings. She is co-organizer of the EuroiTV 2008 conference (to be held in Salzburg) and Co-Programme Chair for Euroitv 2008 – short papers.

Kasper Edwards is an Associate Professor at the Technical University of Denmark, department of Management Engineering. He holds a PhD in the economics of open source software development. His research is multi- disciplinary by nature and driven by a passion for understanding human factors in the production and implementation of new technology. His research has been focused on mass customization and the organizational effects of implementing configuration systems. He organized the first interdisciplinary conference on product configuration systems: PETO 2004. The PETO conference later joined forces with the International Mass Customization Meeting (IMCM) to become the annual IMCM + PETO conference, where he continues to be involved. He is currently involved in two research projects: 1) the relationship between organizational performance and psychosocial work environment and 2) the effects on work-related stress from implementing lean production. He co-supervises two PhD projects where medical doctors research diagnostic processes and treatment of chronic patients.

Rado Gazo is a Professor of Wood Processing and Industrial Engineering at Purdue University. He teaches several courses including Properties of Wood, Secondary Wood Products Manufacturing, and Furniture Design for CNC manufacturing. When not in a classroom, he conducts research and technology transfer in value-added wood products manufacturing and industrial engineering areas. He often works as a consultant to furniture companies. His research interests include competitiveness of furniture manufacturers and application of industrial engineering techniques to forest products manufacturing. Dr. Gazo has worked with over 100 companies, published over 150 publications, and given more than 100 professional presentations on the subject of secondary wood products manufacturing. Dr. Gazo is an active member and served on boards of Society of Wood Science and Technology, Forest Products Society and Consortium for Research on Renewable Industrial Materials.

Roger J. Jiao is an Associate Professor of Computer-Aided Engineering and Design in the Woodruff School of Mechanical Engineering, Georgia Institute of Technology, USA. Prior to joining Georgia Tech, he was an Associate Professor of Systems and Engineering Management in the School of Mechanical and Aerospace Engineering at Nanyang Technological University, Singapore. He received his Ph.D. from Department of Industrial Engineering and Engineering Management, Hong Kong University of Science & Technology. He holds a Bachelor degree in Mechanical Engineering from Tianjin University of Science & Technology in China, and a Master degree in Manufacturing Engineering from Tianjin University in China. He has worked as a lecturer in Department of Management at Tianjin University. His research interests include design theory and methodology, reconfigurable manufacturing systems, operations management, and engineering logistics.

Emmanuel Kodzi Jr. is an Assistant Professor of Operations Management at Ashesi University, Ghana. He has maintained a career focus on, and research interests in, sustaining competitiveness at the business-level. His doctoral research at Purdue University examined Mass Customization as a driver of competitiveness for US furniture manufacturers; he later explored levers of manufacturing performance at the Krannert School of Management. He currently teaches New Product Development, Operations Management and Supply Chain Management - all with direct application for successful decision-making in manufacturing and service organizations. Dr. Kodzi's professional background in entrepreneurship, design and manufacturing practice, market development, and cross-cultural collaboration allows him to pursue academic interests with a realistic industry perspective. He has worked in business process development in the US, and consulted for the World Bank.

Soundar Kumara is the Allen, E., and Allen, M., Pearce Chaired Professor of Industrial Engineering at The Pennsylvania State University. He holds a joint appointment with the department of Computer Science and Engineering, and an affiliate appointment with the College of Information Sciences and Technology. He serves also as an Adjunct Professor of C R Rao Advanced Institute of Mathematics, Statistics and Computer Science (AIMSCS), University of Hyderabad. His research interests are in intelligent systems design, complex networks and sensor networks. He has won several awards including the Penn State Engineering Society Premiere Research Award, and the Penn State Faculty Scholar Medal-the highest research award at Penn state. He is also the recipient of PSU Graduate Faculty Teaching award. He is an elected Fellow of the Institute of Industrial Engineers and the International Academy of Production Engineering (CIRP).

Zacharias Lekkas is currently a PhD candidate and research associate in the Laboratory of New Technologies at the Department of Communication and Media Studies of the National & Kapodistrian University of Athens. He holds a BA in Philosophy and Psychology from the University of Athens and a PGDip in Psychology and Msc in Occupational Psychology from the University of Nottingham. His main research interests lie in the area of individual differences and personalization techniques in knowledge management. Moreover, he focuses on emotions, personality theories and decision making approaches using advanced statistical analysis and quantitative methods.

Thomas Mirlacher is currently working as a project assistant within the ICT@HOME project at the HCI Unit of the ICT&S-Center at the University of Salzburg. He holds a bachelor and master degree in Applied Computer Sciences from the University of Salzburg. He was involved in several national and international projects, covering the range from satellite communication, robotics, embedded systems to multimedia processing in both University and Industry. The center of his research interests are human-computer interfaces, in particular in combination with Ambient Intelligence, personalization, embedded and ubiquitous technologies.

Seung Ki Moon is currently a Postdoctoral Research Associate of Mechanical Engineering at Texas A&M University. He received his Ph.D. in Industrial Engineering from the Pennsylvania State University, University Park in 2008, and the B.S. and M.S. degrees in Industrial Engineering from Hanyang University, South Korea, in 1992 and 1995, respectively. He was a Senior Research Engineer at the Hyundai Motor Company, South Korea. His research interests focus on family and platform design for products and services; universal design; strategic and multidiscipline design optimization; agent-based decision-making; engineering knowledge engineering; and intelligent information system and management.

Ruth Mugge is an Assistant Professor of Consumer Research at the faculty of Industrial Design Engineering of Delft University of Technology. After obtaining her PhD on understanding the emotional bonds that people may experience with their products, she now studies consumer responses towards product design and towards mass customization in particular. She published her research in several academic journals, like Design Studies, the Design Journal, and the Advances in Consumer Research, as well as in several peer-reviewed books.

Niklas Ravaja is Director of Research at the Center for Knowledge and Innovation Research in the Helsinki School of Economics (HSE), Finland. He received his Ph.D. in psychology from the University of Helsinki in 1996 and has been an Adjunct Professor of Applied Psychology since 1999. His areas of research interest and expertise include the psychophysiology of attention, emotion, and temperament; media psychology, including psychophysiological responses to media messages and digital games; sense of presence; and time-series analysis. He has authored over 90 scientific papers, including 50 peer-reviewed articles in major international journals, such as Journal of Experimental Psychology: Applied, Biological Psychology, Psychophysiology, Media Psychology, and Health Psychology. He is Associate Editor of Journal of Media Psychology and the Coordinator of the EU-funded international New and Emerging Science and Technology (NEST) project "The fun of gaming: Measuring the human experience of media enjoyment" (FUGA).

Timo Saari is Associate Professor at Temple University, USA. He is also Affiliate Principal Scientist at the Center for Knowledge and Innovation Research (CKIR) in Helsinki School of Economics, is Affiliate Senior Research Scientist in Helsinki Institute for Information Technology (HIIT) in Digital Content Communities Research Group and Associate Director of M.I.N.D. Lab in Michigan State University, USA & Finland. He received his doctorate degree in Journalism and Mass Communication Research from University of Tampere, Finland, in 2001. His research interests and expertise include the psychology of media processing (emotion/mood, cognition and well-being), customized media and games, and mobile and ubiquitous computing technologies. Dr. Saari has authored and co-authored over 70 peer-reviewed journal articles, book chapters and conference proceedings. He has created and coordinated several large-scale international research projects. Dr. Saari has held various visiting professor and researcher positions in Stanford University, University of California at Berkeley, Michigan State University and University of Cologne, Germany. In 1995-2002 he worked in various executive positions at Alma Media Corporation, a Finnish media company.

George Samaras is a Professor of Computer Science, University of Cyprus. He received a PhD in computer science from Rensselaer Polytechnic Institute, USA, in 1989. He was previously at IBM Research Triangle Park, USA and taught at the University of North Carolina at Chapel Hill (adjunct Assistant Professor, 1990-93). He served as the lead architect of IBM's distributed commit architecture (1990-94) and co-authored the final publication of the architecture (IBM Book, SC31-8134-00, September 1994). He was member of IBM's wireless division and participated in the design/architecture of IBM's WebExpress, a wireless Web browsing system. He co-authored a book on data management for mobile computing (Kluwer A.P). He has a number of patents relating to transaction processing technology and numerous (over 100) technical conference and journal publications. His work on utilizing mobile agents for Web database access has received the best paper award of the 1999 IEEE International Conference on Data Engineering (ICDE'99). He also participates in EC and locally funded projects (e.g. HealtheService24, DBGlobe, SeLeNe, MEMO, SEACORN, MB-NET, INTELCITIES, PRISMA, BEEP, e-MINDER, eNLARGE, DITIS, MATHWN). He is a voting member of the ACM and IEEE Computer Society.

Jan P.L. Schoormans is Full Professor of Consumer Research at the faculty of Industrial Design Engineering of Delft University of Technology. His research focuses on understanding consumer responses toward products. He has published three books on the role of consumer behavior in New Product Development. In addition, his work has been reported in several academic journals, like Design Studies, Journal of Product Innovation Management, European Journal of Product Innovation Management, and International Journal of Research in Marketing.

Florian U. Siems, Ass. Professor, studied Economics and Business Administration at the University of Regensburg in Germany. He earned his doctoral degree in 2003 at the University of Basel in Switzerland (chair of Prof. Dr. Manfred Bruhn) and worked as management consultant. In the years 2005-2008 he was Professor for Marketing at the University of Applied Sciences in Salzburg, Austria. Currently, he is Assistant-Professor for Business-to-Business-Marketing Management at the RWTH Aachen University in Germany. He is also a visiting lecturer at several Swiss universities and still working as consultant. His research focus is in the field of Relationship Marketing, Customer Satisfaction and Pricing Management.

Timothy W. Simpson is a Professor of Mechanical and Industrial Engineering at the Pennsylvania State University with affiliate appointments in Engineering Design and the College of Information Sciences and Technology. He is also the Director of The Learning Factory and the Product Realization Minor. His research interests include engineering design and optimization, product family and platform design, trade space exploration, and multidimensional data visualization. He has co-authored more than 200 peer-reviewed journal and conference papers, and he has received more than $10 million in external research support, including three multi-university initiatives funded by the National Science Foundation (NSF). He is the recipient of a NSF Career Award, the 2007 Penn State University President's Award for Excellence in Academic Integration, the 2006 Outstanding Service Award for the AIAA Multidisciplinary Design Optimization (MDO) Technical Committee, the 2005 SAE Ralph R. Teetor Educational Award, and several research and teaching awards at Penn State. He is active nationally in ASME, AIAA, and ASEE, and he currently chairs the AIAA MDO Technical Committee and is Past Chair of the ASME Design Automation Executive Committee. He received his Ph.D. and M.S. degrees in Mechanical Engineering from Georgia Tech, and his B.S. in Mechanical Engineering from Cornell University.

Nikos Tsianos is a PhD candidate at the Faculty of Communication and Mass Media of the University of Athens, and research assistant of the New Technologies Laboratory, located at the aforementioned Department. He has a bachelor degree in Communication and Mass Media and Msc in Political Communication and New Technologies. His main research area is the personalization of Educational Adaptive Web Hypermedia on the basis of psychological individual differences, such as cognitive and emotional parameters. He has participated in the design and development of Web-applications and corresponding psychometric tools, as well as in assessment procedures. His research interests also include the social impact of locative media and mobile appliances, both in terms of psychological research and HCI design.

Marko Turpeinen holds a chair in Media Technology at The Royal Institute of Technology (KTH), Sweden, where he leads the Social Media research group. He is also the Principal Scientist of the Network Society research programme and the leader of the Digital Content Communities research group at Helsinki Institute for Information Technology (HIIT), Finland. He has a Ph.D. Degree in Computer Science from Helsinki University of Technology (TKK) and a M.Sc. Degree in Media Arts and Sciences from Massachusetts Institute of Technology (MIT). His academic research addresses issues in customized media content, active computer-mediated communities, ageing society, and the role of media in promoting sustainable development. He has also extensive industrial
experience from the media industry, as between 1996 and 2005 he worked in various executive positions at Alma Media Corporation, a Finnish media company.

Gulden Uchyigit has a PhD in Artificial intelligence and data mining from Department of Computing, Imperial College, University of London. At present she is a senior lecturer at the department of Computer Science and Mathematics, University of Brighton. She has authored over 30 papers in refereed books, journals and conferences. She serves on the programme committees of several international conferences and has organised and chaired several workshops in the area of data mining and personalization systems.

Dominik Walcher, Professor, after completing the studies of architecture at the University of Stuttgart Dominik Walcher studied Business Administration at the Technical University Munich as well as at the University of California at Berkeley. He received his doctor's degree from the Technical University Munich (chair of Prof. Ralf Reichwald). Since January 2007 Dominik Walcher is Professor for Marketing and Innovation Management at the Salzburg University of Applied Sciences. His research focus is in the field of Mass Customization, Open Innovation and Brand Management. Results from his empirical research are numerously published and part of his academic teachings as well as practical consultancy. Dominik Walcher is founder of the Institute for Market- and Innovation Research and visiting lecturer at universities in Munich, Stuttgart, St. Gallen, Wels and Helsinki.

David Wilfinger is responsible for the information design at ruwido research and is a research fellow at the HCI Unit of the ICT&S Center. He is currently working on his PhD thesis in the area of user experience prototyping. He holds a masters degree in Information Design (2007) from the University of Applied Science (FH Joanneum) in Graz. Since he joined the ICT&S Center in Summer 2006 he is focusing his research on Interaction Design and User Experience Design. Currently he is engaged in several company related projects like itv4All. Besides that he is doing research on emotional interfaces and the development of interaction techniques, related to different contexts.

Qianli Xu is currently a research fellow in the Nanyang Technological University. He obtained his Ph.D. from the Department of Mechanical Engineering, National University of Singapore, 2007. His major areas of interest include: affective engineering and human factors design, intelligent products and manufacturing systems, and mass customization and personalization. Dr. Xu is a member of ASME, IEEE Technology Management Council, and IIE.

Index

A

abstract data type (ADT) 55
adaptive e-learning 109
adaptive hypermedia systems (AHS) 137, 138
aesthetic preferences 11
affective customers 162, 163, 164, 165, 166, 169, 170, 173, 178
affective design 162, 163, 164, 166, 167, 168, 169, 173, 175, 177, 178, 180
affective needs 162, 163, 166, 167, 168, 169, 170, 173, 174, 175, 176, 177, 178
agents 36, 37, 39, 40, 42, 43
agents, customer (CA) 39, 40, 42, 43, 44, 45
agents, manager (MA) 39, 40, 42
agents, seller (SA) 39, 40, 41, 42, 43, 44
agility 23
ambient intelligence 162, 168, 169, 176, 177, 178, 179
application protocols (APs) 54
association rule mining 168, 170, 178, 180
augmented reality (AR) 169

B

bill-of-material (BOM) 82, 165
business objects (BOs) 54

C

centrality of visual product aesthetics (CVPA) 14
choiceboards 244
cognitive processing efficiency 109
cognitive style, holistic-analytic 112
cognitive styles 109, 112, 113, 114, 115, 121, 123, 128, 132

cognitive style, sensory preference 112
communities, online 18, 19
company reputation 24, 32
computing everywhere paradigm 133
configurable products (CP) 76
conjoint analysis 162, 165, 168, 171, 172, 174, 179, 180
context-aware systems 133, 140, 141, 143, 144, 145
cultural probing 234, 236, 237, 238, 239
customer-direct model 23, 24, 25
customer relationship networks 24, 32
customer relationships 1, 2, 3, 5, 7
customer retention 3
customization 182, 183, 185, 187, 188, 189, 191, 193, 196, 210, 211, 216, 217, 218, 230
customization, adaptive 183
customization, adjustable 183
customization, cosmetic 182
customization, psychological 182, 183, 185, 186, 187, 188, 189, 191, 192, 193, 194, 195, 196, 197, 199, 201, 202, 203, 205, 207, 208, 209, 210, 213, 214
customization, transparent 182
Cute Editor Web authoring tool 118

D

data-implications correlation diagram 124
data mining 133, 134, 138
Davis, Tim 1, 2, 8
degree of commonality index (DCI) 165
Dell computers 11
design freedom 15, 16, 18